Regeneration

Journey Through the Mid-Life Crisis

Regeneration

Journey Through the Mid-Life Crisis

Jane Polden

continuum
LONDON • NEW YORK

Continuum

The Tower Building, 11 York Road, London SE1 7NX
370 Lexington Avenue, New York, NY 10017-6503
www.continuumbooks.com

First published 2002

British Library Cataloguing-in-Publication Data
A catalogue record for this book is available from the British
Library.

ISBN 0-8264-5374-0

Typeset by YHT Ltd, London
Printed by MPG Books Ltd, Bodmin, Cornwall

Keep Ithaka always in your mind.
Arriving there is what you're destined for.
But don't hurry the journey at all ...

Ithaka gave you the marvellous journey.
Without her you wouldn't have set out.
She has nothing left to give you now.
And if you find her poor, Ithaka won't have fooled you.
Wise as you will have become, so full of experience,
You'll have understood by then what all these Ithakas mean.

From 'Ithaka' by C. P. Cavafy

The best way out is through.

Ralph Waldo Emerson

For Katie and Alex

Contents

List of Illustrations

A Note on Confidentiality

The issue of confidentiality raises some thorny questions for the psychotherapist who also writes. On the one hand, psychoanalytic ideas must – if they are to evolve – continually be tested out within real encounters, and psychotherapists who are not willing to substantiate their thinking cannot expect to have it taken very seriously in the world beyond the consulting room. On the other hand, the obligation upon psychotherapists to preserve the privacy and safety of the analytic relationship and to keep confidential the personal information with which we have been entrusted is – in my opinion – absolute.

To some extent, I have been able to resolve this conflict by drawing on material already in the public domain – including, most centrally, the *Odyssey*. In terms of relevant material and observations from my own work, my focus has been to illustrate the repetition of universal dynamics within individual lives. With this in mind I have imagined, selected and combined circumstantial details to illustrate what I wish to say as appropriately as I can. While none of the cases I describe will, I believe, be identifiable as the case histories of actual clients, any of them could have been.

This is a risky enterprise for – as psychotherapists have more reason to know than most – the devil is in the details. The reader will judge for him or herself to what extent I have succeeded.

Acknowledgements

I would like to offer my appreciation and thanks to the following: to Mike W. and Mike R. for making me think about the *Odyssey* as a metaphor for mid-life crisis; to Jean Clark, Miriam Barnett and Nagasri for their support and helpful comments on different chapters in the process of writing; to my agent Andrew Lownie for believing in the book and helping me to shape it initially; to David Hayden at Continuum for his constructive and helpful editing, and Martin Barr for his thorough and diligent copy-editing; to Dr Nicola Blandford who supervised my clinical work and helped me formulate my psychoanalytic thinking over the period of writing; and to all my clients, patients and supervisees who have taught and continue to teach me. I would also like to thank Alex and Katie for their forbearance, and Arthur, who went with me to Ithaca.

Thanks also to Faber and Faber for permission to quote from T. S. Eliot, Sylvia Plath and W. H. Auden; Harcourt for permission to quote from T. S. Eliot; David Higham Associates for permission to quote from Louis MacNeice and Dylan Thomas; The Estate of Cavafy c/o Rogers, Coleridge and White for permission to quote from C. P. Cavafy. Copyright Kyveli A. Singopoulo, 1963 and 1968; Penguin Press for permission to quote from Jorge Luis Borges (translation copyright W. S. Merwin 1999).

I would like to acknowledge my indebtedness to E. V. Rieu's prose translation of the *Odyssey* (Penguin 1946) which I have relied upon, and which is quoted in italics at different points throughout the book.

Every effort has been made to locate holders of copyright material; however, the author and publishers would be interested to hear from any copyright holders not here acknowledged so that full acknowledgement may be made in future editions.

Preface

James, a married forty-two-year-old executive with a four-year-old son, has been secretly having an affair for some time. His girlfriend is putting pressure on him to leave his wife, who has just told him that she is pregnant again. He is having increasingly vivid fantasies about walking out on everything. Last week, while overtaking at speed, he narrowly avoided a head-on collision with a lorry coming in the other direction, and this has frightened him.

Angie's parents have both died within the last three years. She thinks this should have freed her from the past, but finds instead she is feeling haunted by memories, and she is having flashbacks relating to their bitter divorce when she was still a child. At 37, she regrets her own lack of children and although she is a reasonably successful journalist she feels aggrieved by what she sees as her failure to achieve as much as she could have done in her career. Her partner is keen to move in with her and is wondering out loud about children. But Angie is keeping him at a distance. She is wondering whether, after all, she can become the writer she has always wanted to be – and if so, what it will cost her.

Steve, a forty-year-old architect, is on his third marriage. He says the last thing he needs is another divorce, but his marriage is shaky. He was the one to leave both his earlier marriages but now his current wife, an academic, has been offered a new contract which would take her to Europe for part of each year. He is feeling more anxious than he can understand, and has started having dreams about murdering his wife and burying her at the bottom of the garden.

If you are aged between your mid-thirties and forties, insert your own life circumstances here.

The dramas of mid life are dramas of abandonment and freedom, of highly charged sexual engagements in real time or in fantasy, and sudden encounters with mortality and loss. The details are as varied as people's lives are diverse, but similar themes reappear with unerring regularity over and over in the decade of mid life. It is a time when everything – from the most fundamental questions of identity and meaning, to the daily experience of our own bodies and our sexuality – is thrown into upheaval, making the mid-life transition for many people the most disturbing period of life since the onset of adolescence.

And like adolescence, the mid-life crisis can evoke feelings of anguish, despair and insecurity, alongside deepening awareness of a momentous and irrevocable change percolating through the self. Like adolescence too, the advent of mid-life transition and the changes it brings in its wake tend to elicit an uncomprehending exasperation from others which leads in its turn to deepening feelings of isolation and loneliness. But what begins to happen at mid life is also quite new – by now there is so much more to lose and perhaps also to gain, alongside a growing awareness that there is, no longer, all the time in the world. If not now, when?

While at adolescence the route through to adulthood is clearly enough marked and signposted, the path at mid life can seem to peter out – ending up as it did for Dante Alighieri, at the age of 42, within a dark wood:

> In the middle of the journey of our life, I came to myself within a dark wood where the straight way was lost. Ah, how hard it is to tell of that wood, savage and harsh and dense, the thought of which renews my fear. So bitter is it that death is hardly more . . .[1]

We fail to see the woods of mid life, for all the trees; we get lost in them, going round and round in circles until overcome by exhaustion or despair. Yet for the exiled and homeless Dante, the dark wood in which he so unhappily found himself wandering turned out in the end to be the starting point for the unfolding of his *Divine Comedy*, one of Western literature's great works of spiritual renewal. In retrospect, the directions we take and the choices we make at this time may prove to be of momentous significance for the rest of our lives.

---

[1] Dante Alighieri, *The Divine Comedy, 1: Inferno*, tr. John D. Sinclair, Oxford University Press by arrangement with The Bodley Head (1961).

Many of us begin to feel, sometimes very much to our own surprise, that we have lost our way at mid life. We begin to think about ourselves differently and to look, tentatively, for some source of illumination. We try to understand and to get to grips with the discontent and doubt that have disrupted our previously well-ordered lives. In doing so we are recognising the crucial, even decisive, nature of the transition that is upon us, but it is confusing and often a source of intense inner turmoil to find oneself being drawn from the well-signposted road of first adulthood and into the uncharted territory of the second half of life. This transition is too often negatively dismissed by our youth-obsessed society, leaving those in its grip feeling profoundly isolated and disempowered.

Yet underneath its surface confusions, the mid-life crisis has a dynamic significance. It is essentially a journey, a process which will resolve itself finally one way or another – for better or for worse. This book is an exploration and an investigation of this journey, interweaving contemporary narratives with Homer's story of the Greek hero Odysseus' journey back from the fall of Troy, and of the trials of his wife Penelope in his absence. At the beginning of his journey home – which he confidently expects will be a short one – the victorious Odysseus is already a seasoned warrior. But nothing goes as expected, and by the time he finally gets back to Ithaca ten years later, everything has changed in ways he could not have imagined. The mid-life crisis in modern life has its own parallel narrative logic which defies conscious control, a momentum which unfolds stage by stage as it moves towards its own resolution.

Mid-life transition can be a very lonely time. Everyone's mid-life crisis is different, but the practice of psychotherapy suggests that its underlying themes are far more universal than we realize. As a phenomenon it is both individual and general. Mid-life crisis, when it looms, cannot be avoided – or can only be avoided by the sort of defensive behaviour which leads ineluctably to a stagnant, embattled or embittered middle age. But if we respond to it by developing forms of insight and understanding which are able to penetrate beneath its surface, and fresh resolve to face its challenges, then the crisis can lead through to renewal, regeneration and, ultimately, fulfilment.

This process does not happen overnight: the changes of mid life are likely to take several years to work their way through the system. It takes three miles to turn an ocean-going liner, longer to turn a life. Though deep-seated changes are often painful, there are no gains without pain – and there are great gains to be made at mid life. By becoming more self-aware and more able to understand the underlying significance of the problems that preoccupy our attention at this time, and the choices that demand to be made, we can begin to lead lives more truly informed by the values that will serve us best in the second halves of our lives.

Part One

REACHING MID LIFE

1

The Most Famous Mid-Life Crisis in History

Three images:

Lashed tightly to the mast on the lower of the two decks, he braces himself. The breeze has dropped, the waves are lulled and a calm has set in. The sails have been drawn in and stowed in the hold, and the men are rowing methodically, their blades slicing the surging grey water. Their eyes – averted from the figure at the mast who sweats and moans under the brutal midday sun – are fixed straight ahead, and their ears are blocked with the beeswax he had softened with his own fingers. They do not turn their heads as they approach the island, and only the man tied to the mast sees what passes to their left so close now, within hailing distance. Only he can hear the sounds which float across the water. . . *The lovely voices came to me across the water.* When they untie him a while later he falls huddled, motionless at their feet.

Night falls. Lying still and straight in her solitary bed she waits until there have been no more sounds for some time. Silently she pulls back the covers and creeps into the hallway, the stone flags cold under her bare feet. Feeling her way over the cracks, she almost trips over the splayed body of a drunken man lying snoring on his back. An empty wine jug falls from his outstretched hand and rolls in an arc across the floor. He stirs in his sleep and she freezes. He settles and she moves on to the window where her work lies waiting. There by the uncertain flickering of a single candle she recommences her task of destruction, her small blade swooping and stabbing as she swiftly cuts and unravels the threads. A faint smile curls her lip. On the window ledge a black cat stares down gravely and unblinkingly, the end of its tail twitching slightly in the moonlight.

He leaves the house of his mistress, brushing aside the heavy vine growing round the doorway, walking upwards through the thickly planted woods of alder and dark cypress surrounding the house, up through the meadows of parsley and irises to where the narrow cliff path begins, pulling himself up between the boulders, slipping on the scree, bruising the knots of dusty thyme which catch at his feet. Reaching the headland he sits down, and stares out towards the empty horizon. So much space, so much water for a man to drown in. *Life with its sweetness was ebbing away in the tears he shed for his lost home ... At nights, it is true, he had to sleep with her ... But the days found him sitting on the rocks or sands, torturing himself with tears and groans and heartache, and looking out with streaming eyes across the watery wilderness.*

These images of Odysseus' encounter with the Sirens, Penelope's nightly destruction of her daily weaving and Odysseus' unhappy entanglement with the nymph Calypso are all scenes from the epic poem the *Odyssey*. The *Odyssey* is believed to have been written around 700 BC in the unimaginably different world of the late Bronze Age, although its actual date – along with virtually everything else about its composition and its author Homer – remains obscure. What meaning can this story have for us as we reach mid life today, at the dawning of the computer age, almost three millennia later?

'And he began to read *The Odyssey*' says Arthur C. Clarke of his lonely astronaut in *2001: A Space Odyssey*, 'which of all books spoke to him most vividly across the gulfs of time ...'.[1] The *Odyssey* is the story of the Greek hero Odysseus' journey back from the fall of Troy to his homeland Ithaca, and of what happens in Ithaca before and after his return. It is divided into three sections. The first, four chapters long, opens upon a council of the Olympian gods who decide that Odysseus (who has been adrift on the seas for ten years after incurring the wrath of the sea god Poseidon and is now stranded helplessly on the remote island of the nymph Calypso) has suffered long enough. We are then introduced to life on Ithaca during Odysseus'

---

[1] Clarke, Arthur C., *2001: A Space Odyssey*, Orbit (2000).

4

absence, where his wife Penelope is keeping at bay a gang of unruly suitors who have violated all the conventions of hospitality. Prompted by the gods, Odysseus' son Telemachus realizes that a decisive moment has arrived, and he sets out from Ithaca to discover whether his father is alive or dead.

In the middle section of eight chapters we meet Odysseus, who has been left moping for seven years on Calypso's island. Released from his spell by the gods, Odysseus now bestirs himself and builds a boat in which to return home. But setting sail towards Ithaca, he runs into a great storm and is washed up shipwrecked and naked on the island of Scherie. He is discovered by the lovely Nausicaa, daughter of King Alcinous of the Phaeacians, who takes him to her father's palace. Here, Odysseus tells Alcinous and his people the story of his earlier wanderings: his visit to the island of the Lotus-eaters, his escape from the Cyclops' cave, and his sexual encounter with the goddess Circe, who turned his men into pigs. Odysseus goes on to tell them of his ordeal in the Land of the Dead, of the narrow passage between the rocks of Scylla and the whirlpool of Charybdis, of his journey past the island of the Sirens, whose song lures impulsive sailors to ugly deaths, and of his final arrival upon Calypso's island, where he languished for seven years and from whence he has now set sail, only to be shipwrecked and washed up upon this new island.

Having told his story, Odysseus falls into an exhausted sleep, and as he sleeps the Phaeacians finally and somewhat mysteriously deliver him back to Ithaca, where they leave him on the beach, still sleeping. Odysseus wakes up alone and confused, and initially does not recognize the island he had left twenty years before. The final twelve chapters of the *Odyssey* take place upon Ithaca, where Odysseus, disguised as a beggar, stealthily goes about the task of taking revenge and ousting the suitors, reclaiming his home and becoming reconciled with his son, wife and father.

At the core of the *Odyssey* is the story of Odysseus' disorientated and windswept wanderings around the islands of the Aegean and Ionian seas as he tries to return from the sacking of Troy to his homeland. His defiance of the Cyclops incurs the enmity of Poseidon, the god of the sea, and dooms him to circle the seas helplessly for years – he discovers as he does so that nice girls really do like sailors, that sexual desire can turn men into pigs and that a casual encounter can become an entanglement as long and sad as any failed marriage. Escaping with a shudder from the sinisterly calm land of the drug-addicted Lotus-eaters, he faces a nightmarish monster, while trapped within in a bloody cave from which he escapes only with the loss of his own identity, comes close to being dashed to death on the Sirens' rocks and has to look his own dead mother in the face. Interwoven with the story of Odysseus' adventures is the more enigmatic and oblique tale of his wife Penelope left struggling for her survival and freedom back on Ithaca, and then finally of their somewhat ambiguous *rapprochement* upon Odysseus' unexpected return home.

At one level, the *Odyssey* is a tightly plotted tale of sexual buccaneering, romantic faith in the teeth of death, and the hero's return. But in the great ten-year sweep of its narrative it also evokes experiences of despair and of fragile hope, of loneliness, insignificance and vastness: it traverses great wastes of the soul's internal landscape, and focuses on those intimate moments of connection and recognition which have the potential to change lives forever. As a story, the *Odyssey* reminds us of the potential for chaos lurking beneath our best-laid plans and most well-ordered existences, suggesting that the forces that really guide our lives may be greater, and stranger, than we realize.

The *Odyssey*, epic in form and in intention, is explicitly not an account of the adventures of youth. Odysseus was already a husband, a father and the established King of Ithaca before he ever set sail to rescue Helen, and spent a further ten long years at the siege of Troy before the adventures of the *Odyssey* even began. The fall of Troy seemed itself the event of a lifetime – having engineered and weathered it, Odysseus had embarked on what he had every reason to anticipate would be a speedy and uncomplicated journey home towards a conqueror's welcome. Odysseus, as we encounter him, is no hot-headed young hero but a battle-hardened and weary father and warrior, already somewhere in his mid-to-late thirties. This puts him well into his forties a decade later, when he eventually wakes up to find himself alone and bereft upon the beach of Ithaca – an Ithaca which has itself become almost unrecognizable through the passage of time. The span of the *Odyssey* covers the span of Odysseus' middle years – as it also covers the middle years of his wife Penelope, left to her own devices, alone yet besieged upon Ithaca. Homer's epic is, in effect, the story of the most famous mid-life crisis in history.

As for Penelope, we can see her as a blank screen for the projection of men's fantasies about what women do in their absence, a woman who crumples and collapses and waits to be rescued – or, alternatively, as a proto-feminist icon of the resourceful single parent who negotiates her own integrity and preserves her own domain within a hostile world. The drama of the *Odyssey* unfolds within the tension between the destinies of Odysseus and Penelope, and what Seamus Heaney has called the eerie flow of intimacy between them.[2] They are complementary in their energies, the one turbulent, restless, sexually adventurous, forever pushing into new territories, and the other mysterious, withdrawn from action, suspended in a silence that is perhaps despairing, perhaps contemplative, maturing and letting go, moving through disappointment and depression towards doubtful hope and final fulfilment, while pondering and clarifying in the process what is still worth believing in. Odysseus and Penelope are two lonely, beleaguered yet compelling figures. Purposeful and yet baffled, they move through their perilous worlds with cunning, assumed confidence, courage and grace – given the ways in which the mid-life crisis continually destroys, changes and re-invents relationships, the flux between them seems as promising a place to begin exploring its dynamics as any other.

'The most beautiful, the most all-embracing theme is that of *The Odyssey*' enthused James Joyce – himself a wanderer far from home – to one of his pupils in Zurich. 'It is greater, more human, than that of *Hamlet, Don Quixote*, Dante, *Faust*.'[3] It's

---

2   Introduction to *The Odyssey*, tr. Fitzgerald, R., Everyman Library, Random House (1992).

3   Quoted in Rubens, B. and Taplin, O., *An Odyssey Round Odysseus*, BBC Books (1989).

also surprisingly accessible and readable, and its vivid character-
ization, direct and lucid style and skilful chapter structure led
Robert Graves to describe it as the first Greek novel.[4] I was
myself drawn back to the story by the half-remembered
resonance of particular images, such as the ones with which this
chapter began. Then the process gained its own logic and
momentum. The poem's images and stories began to illustrate
and amplify in my mind different aspects and stages of the mid-
life process, and eventually began to crystallize as a metaphor for
the entire mid-life transition. Establishing itself symbolically in
my mind, the *Odyssey* has remained there as an imaginative
resource, structuring and illuminating my efforts to make sense
of mid-life crisis as a significant rite of passage, both personally
and through my practice as a psychotherapist in working with
that substantial proportion of people who first present themselves for psychotherapy at this time in their lives, seeking
illumination and direction.

Myths, wrote Freud, partly describe the structure of the
human mind.[5] The need to find new and more promising ways
of accounting for oneself – which is at the centre of mid-life crisis
– has been met through human history by the development of
myths, both religious and secular. By virtue of their universality
and their transmission from one generation to the next, myths
such as the story of Odysseus and Penelope reveal the archetypal
or universal elements of the human condition and its drive
towards the fulfilment of personal destiny. Through our
identifications with its protagonists, the myth – like successful
psychotherapy – enables us to explore more deeply what it is to
be human, to retrieve and organize value and meaning from the
arbitrary inconsequentialities of ordinary life, and to generate
theatres for the facilitation of our individual potentials for self-
actualization. Writing of the impoverishment of narrative in
modern America, Joseph Campbell suggests that only in myth or
ritual can be found a powerful enough countervalence to our
unconscious fixation to the unexorcized images of our infancy,

---

4 Graves, R., *The Greek Myths*, Penguin (1992).
5 Freud, S., 'Totem and Taboo' (1913), in *Penguin Freud Library* 13.

which render us disinclined to negotiate the necessary passages of our adulthood. 'It has always', he says, 'been the prime function of mythology and rite to supply the symbols that carry the human spirit forward, in counteraction to those other constant human fantasies that tend to tie it back.'[6]

For the seasick weaving of Odysseus' boat from island to island seems – like so much of the mid-life journey – exhausting, disaster-prone and disconcertingly random in both its triumphs and its shipwrecks. Yet the wanderings of the sailor fallen from grace with the sea generate their own purpose, revealing themselves as the conflicts of a self at war with its own unconscious. As the dynamics of the mid-life crisis unfold, such conflicts express both our capacity for confusion and destruction and also, ultimately, the ability of the psyche to attract to itself those encounters and experiences it needs to sponsor its own growth towards maturity, which is at the heart of the successful ultimate resolution of the mid-life crisis. But what are these dynamics, these conflicts? In which direction does ultimate resolution lie? And what, really, is the mid-life crisis all about?

---

[6] Campbell, J., *The Hero with a Thousand Faces*, Fontana (1993).

2

So What Is the Mid-Life Crisis?

Jeremy is a software designer in his early forties who arranges an assessment for psychotherapy. When we make the initial appointment on the phone
he says, slightly awkwardly, that he has been having some relationship difficulties and has been under a lot of stress recently, but does not elaborate
further. Jeremy arrives for the assessment a few minutes late. A tall, lanky
man with fair hair greying slightly at the temples, his initial manner is enga-
gingly boyish, although a little furtive. He sits forward in the chair with his eye-
lids slightly lowered, scanning the room. I'm aware of him rapidly checking
over the contents of the bookcases, the pictures on the wall, the objects on
my desk, and me – I think of a combatant edging through guerrilla country
who knows that any rustle or snap of a twig might signal the positioning of an
enemy, and that any wrong move might detonate a landmine that could blow
him to bits.

Jeremy tells me that he married in his mid-twenties and has three children
with his wife, Judy. Judy initially stayed at home to look after the children, taking a part-time job as a library assistant as they got older, while Jeremy was
successful in his own career, eventually starting his own consultancy. Then,
about three years ago, Jeremy fell in love with Adele, the director of a company for whom he had done some programming – a very different woman,
he says, from Judy. They began an affair which they kept secret at first, but at
the beginning of last year Adele became pregnant. After much anguish and
soul-searching, Jeremy left his wife and moved in with Adele. He had to tell his
elderly widowed mother that he was leaving his wife and children, which he

found extremely difficult. His mother had not taken it well and the following month she had a stroke, from which she died a few weeks later.

A week after the death of Jeremy's mother, and in the same hospital, Adele gave birth several weeks prematurely to a son, Joe. Joe had some initial difficulties but is now doing well. However, Jeremy and Adele's sex life, previously vibrant and exciting, has died away. Jeremy is haunted by the thought that he was responsible for his mother's death. He misses his three older children very much – when he sees them they are guarded and sullen towards him, and hostile to Adele. He also finds coping with the demands of a new baby much harder and more exhausting than he had remembered first time around, and he is having difficulty summoning up the energy and inspiration which he needs if he is to keep his business afloat. And Adele, he says, has changed.

After outlining the turbulent events of the past three years, Jeremy falls silent. His face pale, he sits examining his shoelaces, apparently lost for words. 'I've lost the plot' he says eventually. 'That's it. I've lost the plot.'

Reaching the decade of life between the mid-thirties and the mid-forties, many of us find that our well-ordered and apparently unassailable lives begin to change in ways we could not have anticipated, while previously cherished plans and commitments go into free-fall. Like Jeremy, we may feel lost for words to make sense of it all, while others – as if to name a thing were to explain it – tell us that we are having a mid-life crisis. Meaning what?

The mid-life crisis is a turbulent and often dramatic time likely to unfurl in fits and starts, over a period of several years. Its advent may announce itself through the appearance of nagging doubts and self-questionings, or apparently irrational or uncharacteristic actions. Sometimes a coincidence of unexpected or bizarre events seem to foretell – at least with hindsight – that great change may be on the way. Slipping into daydreams or erotic fantasies which are disturbing in their vivid intensity, we become haunted by strange obsessions and struggle with creeping dependencies, while at the same time the need to cut free of everyone and everything becomes sometimes overwhelming. It is a time when we may suffer unmanageable encounters with death and loss and become subject to intense but changing moods: disorientating confusion, self-doubt, depression, fierce joy or sudden tearing rage, moody free-floating angst and questioning: *is this all?*

The external signs of the mid-life crisis are familiar enough: the marriage in trouble, the passionately erupting love affair, the ambitions of a lifetime suddenly called into question, the life run out of steam. It's easy to get caught up in an impulsive reaction – fearful, excited or disapproving, depending upon our personal standpoint and the nature of our vested interests – to these dramas of love and hate, desire and loss, life and death. But however momentous and life-changing such external events may be, they are at the same time indications of yet deeper internal changes starting to unfold – if permitted to do so – within an individual reaching the midway point in life. For the mid-life crisis represents a central turning point, a profound shift in values, a watershed in the life of an individual which is likely to have a profoundly determining effect upon the way the second half of life subsequently pans out – for better or for worse.

The mid-life crisis has today become a familiar enough concept – a 1992 Gallup Poll, for example, revealed that two-thirds of middle-aged men believed in the mid-life crisis, and over half thought that they had had or were having one. Yet it has been largely ignored by classical theories of psychology and psychoanalysis with their predominately infant-centred orientation. This is a bias which may not reflect back to us the truths of our own experience, that the whole of life – not just the first bit – is a developmental process, in which each stage has its own particular pressures, preoccupations, conflicts and potentials for growth and change. In human life seen as a trajectory, the transitional periods of life – toddlerhood, adolescence and the transition between the stages of early and mature adulthood which is the mid-life crisis – volatile as they are, have a particular determining importance of their own. This is not to diminish the importance of early experiences and ways of relating which become imprinted and embedded at a structural level within the unconscious. Aroused by the particular demands and stresses of the mid-life period, they are likely to resurface and demand reworking with a peculiar urgency at this time: the mid-life crisis returns us to the unfinished business of the past at the same time as it moves us on towards an unknown future.

The crisis of the mid-life transition blows apart the cherished fantasy that adulthood would be an orderly, competent progression between the half-forgotten dramas of adolescence and an as yet only dimly conceived senility. We tend to invest a great deal in our adult identities – but the upheavals of mid-life crisis may lead us to examine the values upon which we have structured our lives and to re-evaluate, in a big way, what adulthood is really all about. Like a boil being lanced, mid-life crisis sometimes reveals the suppressed madnesses dwelling beneath the well-tended surfaces of our sanity, for mid-life crisis asserts the primacy of the inner life and warns us that we ignore it at our peril. Mid life, no less than the earlier transitions of life, can be the harbinger of deep-seated change, accompanied by disturbing and profound identity crises.

As we progress through the developmental dramas of our childhoods we lack the capacity for systematic reflection upon their significance. But maturity bestows upon us new resources, and by the time mid life is reached these resources can enable us to reflect upon our experiences as we live them and respond to them creatively and constructively. In comparison with the relative dearth of clinical material, there is a wealth of literary and biographical accounts of the mid-life crisis: tales of epic journeys such as the *Odyssey* and *The Divine Comedy* offer themselves as rich metaphors for the struggle through mid-life transition, while contemporary treatments in the novel, biography and film deal with it more explicitly and knowingly.

Such an account is Jung's description in his autobiography of how his own mid-life crisis took him to the edge of psychosis and then back again, ultimately releasing a surge of confident, mature creativity.[1] Jung saw mid life as a crucial time of transition, believing that if – through fear of letting go, fear of the unknown, fear of suffering – we dodge or deny what it has to teach us, we will end up shrinking back upon ourselves. To some extent this moving forward, shrinking back and moving forward again is an inevitable part of the process of transition, but if fear ultimately wins the day, then the attempt to live the second half

---

[1] Jung, C. G., *Memories, Dreams, Reflections*, Chapter VI, Fontana (1983).

of life according to the values of the first half will, he believed, become a cycle of ever-diminishing returns with the mind becoming ever narrower, more cramped and rigid. On the other hand, the successful negotiation of the challenges of mid life may open the door to an expansive, creative and fulfilling second half of life.[2]

It seems that many people share, at a more or less private or intuitive level, this sense of mid life as a potentially momentous time of life. Many of us may have at this time a sense of drifting and pitching upon seas no less perilous, uncharted and unpredictable than those which scuppered Odysseus' romantic fantasies and left Penelope a widow and a single parent in all but name, and in this predicament find ourselves floating with little help and less understanding. As more and more of us live longer and longer lives, from which we expect more and more, the mid-life crisis gains an increasingly pivotal place in our lives – yet as a phenomenon it is under-researched and little understood, spoken of more often cynically or dismissively than with real interest or curiosity. Why should this be?

THE MID-LIFE CRISIS AND THE WORLD WE LIVE IN

Social groupings are generally suspicious and hostile towards individuals going through turbulent inner change, who in their turn tend to repay the compliment by threatening and challenging established social values – people going through a mid-life crisis are likely to find themselves being given (like toddlers and teenagers, those other self-indulgent and unstable pariahs of society) a wide berth by others.

Superficially, Western society at the turn of the millennium seems diverse, fragmented, tolerant – superficially, we have liberated ourselves from that hierarchical, paternalistic morality of obedience which structured our individual expectations and aspirations (or the lack of them) until relatively recently. Nevertheless, our ranks tend to close quickly against the truly

---

[2] Jung, C. G., 'The stages of life' (1930–1) in *Modern Man in Search of a Soul*, Routledge (1984).

(as opposed to the meretriciously) subversive, against the genuinely suffering and against whatever effectively calls into question the values of consumerism: *I work, I shop, I keep the economy going, therefore I am.* It's risky to ask of life different sorts of questions from the ones to which Microsoft, Sony and Hollywood have already provided the answers, but consumerism does not make the mistake of dignifying its enemies by taking them seriously. It just paralyses them within the passivity and cynicism which it so pervasively promotes.

The mid-life crisis challenges the validity of the materialistic solution, but although its advent often heralds a dawning dissatisfaction with the limitations of earning, spending and sex as the only antidotes to the problems of life, the trouble is that it does not necessarily point towards anything with which to replace them. Yet if in the long run it is not able to do so, all the anguish which it has generated will be to no avail, and the crisis is likely to peter out into the mood of sulky resentment which can steal up upon the second half of life and end up holding it to permanent ransom.

A fundamental human need, especially at moments of existential crisis, is to be able to locate ourselves within a framework of values and meaning capable of providing an answer to the question of what it is to be human, and of what we can and should expect from life. Such a framework has, for the most part of human history, been found in religion, which mediates the intensity of individual crisis by placing it within a more expansive context – for example, through the beliefs and rituals which provide hope and consolation at times of loss and bereavement. Mid-life passage is one of the significant transitions between the stages of life which sponsor change and growth but at the same time call pre-existing values into question and often leave the individual in transition feeling isolated and bereft. But times of transition – the *bardos* of Tibetan Buddhism – are also known as junctures in which the possibility of liberation or enlightenment is heightened.[3] As such, mid life is a time when

---

[3] See *The Tibetan Book of the Dead*, tr. Fremantle, F. and Chogyam Trungpa, Shambhala (1989).

the religiously inclined are most likely to turn towards their spiritual beliefs for solace and guidance, and to re-evaluate them. Those without beliefs may grieve the lack of them for the first time, while others become newly interested in exploring spiritual questions.

When the materialistic mood which tends to permeate early adulthood no longer seems to have all the answers, spiritual beliefs may offer a new and more interesting perspective upon life. Hinduism, for example, teaches that life is made up of four stages, or *ashramas*, each with its own duties and responsibilities: *brahmacharya*, or studenthood; *grihastha*, the stage when one must assume worldly responsibilities, become a householder, marry and have children; *vanaprastha*, or retirement; and *sannyas*, the time of renunciation of the world and devotion to the spiritual life. The fourth stage is optional, yet while it is true that relatively few Hindus will renounce the world entirely, the values of *sannyas* will nevertheless begin to permeate their lives as they grow older, and to influence the ways in which others see them.

Hindus who no longer feel compellingly engaged with material responsibilities and who are in a position to wind their obligations down, accordingly have the option of passing on their wealth to their appreciative children and becoming *sanyassins*, wanderers who are dedicated to reflection, contemplation and the development of wisdom and who, as such, are supported, valued and revered by the whole community. In a sense, Hinduism seems to provide an elegant solution to the problems of mid-life crisis – albeit one which, in terms of our own individualistic values, may seem over-programmatic and predetermined. Yet in comparison, do not Western mid-life rites of passage – the facelifts, the sports coupés, the Prozac and Viagra prescriptions, the furtive and anxious sexual liaisons, the panicked denial of ageing and the fears about the loss of usefulness and respect which ageing will entail – convey a relative lack of dignity?

It may be that our brains are hardwired for religious belief in its widest sense – we need a model with which to make sense of the world, a scale of aspirational values by which to live. Lacking as we do, in today's diverse, fragmented and individualistic society, any overarching ethical or transcendent values, we run the risk of turning materialism itself into a new and strangely perverse form of religion in which religious superstition is replaced by commercial gullibility, and authoritarianism by the dogmatic demands of fashion and the cajolings of the advertising industry. A character in one of J. G. Ballard's novels muses that maybe the human race discovered religion too soon[4] – having exhausted its use and worn out its moral authority, it is failing us now, just when we needed it most. The collapse of spiritual values leaves a vacuum in which consideration of the meaning of a life in terms of its transience and individual smallness, and reflection upon the passing of time, death and even ageing itself – aspects of life which traditional religions made bearable – become terrifyingly taboo. Yet as we face mid life, these are the thoughts which begin to haunt us.

Instead of taking seriously where we are and where we might be going, we stumble gracelessly backwards with eyes only for what we're leaving – a regressive progression described by Campbell as the pathos of inverted emphasis, in which the hopeless goal is not to grow old, but to remain young.[5] Our need to avoid acceptance of our own mortality leads us to overrate youth: in our flight from our fears about ageing we have fetishised it, and the values of youth culture – of instant gratification, impulsivity, unquestioning materialism, aggressive competitiveness and clamorous self-centredness – become so structured into the very bones of the world in which we live that we have nowhere to go when their glamour begins to fade in the cold and revealing light of the following day.

It isn't easy, after all, to think about ourselves as we are: easier to think about those who are younger, smoother, emptier than ourselves. Perhaps the nagging sense of disquiet which begins to beset us somewhere around our forties is just too much: too confusing, too embarrassing, too jarring to our images of what being grown-up is supposed to be about, to make a big deal of it, to take it seriously. Yet what if we do take it – and ourselves – seriously? For Jeremy, the answer was far from clear. But

---

[4] Ballard, J. G., *Cocaine Nights*, Flamingo (1997).
[5] Campbell, J., *The Hero with a Thousand Faces*, Fontana (1993).

running through the turbulent events of his life as he reached mid life, we can begin to trace the threads of the four interrelating and interdependent dynamics which structure the mid-life crisis and give it its unique nature: sex and death, letting go and gathering up.

THE FIRST THEME: LETTING GO
THE LONGING TO SHED EXCESS BAGGAGE

At the moment when Adele came into Jeremy's life, he had already been feeling increasingly restless and dissatisfied for some time. On the surface he had everything he should have wanted and exactly what he had planned: a successful (but stressful) career, a secure (but dull) marriage, three healthy (but self-centred) children and a new car every two years, which he drove fast and impatiently. Yet he had been bored to death and too guilty to admit it. Carrying on as ever, but motivated more by will-power than by any genuine pleasure in achievement, Jeremy had, for the last few years, been walking around like a zombie. His eyes had glazed over, his smile become more fixed, his laugh more forced and his interest in sex sporadic, at best. He could scarcely believe that no-one had noticed, or seemed to care. But no-one did.

We may not notice – or care about – the harnesses we're strapped into until they start to chafe and to blister the softer skin beneath. Then, slowly but inexorably, life's glittering prizes start to lose their lustre, bringing the most fundamental issues of personal identity (*but who am I, really?*) into doubt. What was security becomes a prison; what was an anchor becomes a burden. But how to separate the wheat from the chaff, to distinguish what has genuinely been outgrown from what still matters? At this point in time – whether we stick our heads in the sand or throw caution to the winds in one wild impetuous leap to freedom – it may in truth be impossible to make sound long-term choices (we are involved, too scared). Afraid of getting it wrong – afraid especially of ending up the loser in a nightmare game of musical chairs, getting older alone, rejected and unwanted – we cling anxiously to the job, the relationship, the situation that seems bereft of point or value. What we may need most is a temporary period of time for reflection and consideration, at a protected distance from the routines of ordinary life. But in the pace of modern life this is easier said than found.

The failure of our environment to help us formulate and make sense of our inchoate urges may lead us to try to deny them, deadening them by retreating into numb depression, becoming obsessed with work or starting to drink too much. Lacking a preordained frame of reference through which our changing values, needs and preoccupations may be mediated and placed in perspective, we make our own changes – sometimes creatively, sometimes destructively, turning to dreams and fantasies or towards new intense relationships with those who do seem to understand.

In fantasy or reality (in our emotional absences, at least) we leave our homes and families, sometimes – like Jeremy – because we have fallen in love, sometimes just following some indistinct urging which we seem only dimly to understand. For Dante the experience was like being lost in a dark wood where the straight way was lost, savage, harsh and dense. For the writer Martin Amis, the advent of mid-life crisis in his early forties was similarly disorientating. In the glare of exposing and unwelcome publicity, Amis left his wife and two young sons for another woman and also broke away from his former agent and her husband, one of his best friends, over the bargaining for a massive book deal. Amis described it as feeling like something had died: 'You wake up in another country, where you don't know the language or how to get around on the subways. You have no idea how to be, or what's expected of you. It's only being there that you begin to figure it out.'[6]

The desire to cut loose brings us up against our own vulnerability as well as our own rage, and our own need for security as well as that of our children, if we have them, who will themselves be – as we may uneasily realize – affected by the choices we make at this time. But the demands for change, for

---

[6] Quoted in Sheehy, G., *New Passages*, HarperCollins (1997).

growth – to find something, at least, to do about it all – will not be easily outfaced. Our future, as well as our past, seems to demand our loyalty.

THE SECOND THEME: SEX
THE UPSURGE OF EROTIC ENERGY

For Jeremy, Adele provided the catalyst for change. Something in Adele – her careless freedom, or perhaps her own hunger and need – spoke to Jeremy. He said that he had been a drowning man: he had not realized quite how dead he was until he started to come alive with her. The intensity and overwhelming nature of his new-found sexual passion generated hope for Jeremy that it might provide a conclusive solution to the problems and questions which were arising for him as he reached mid life – or at least a refuge from them. At the same time, though, his own life experiences played a warning counterpoint to the melody of romance, making him question just how enduring a solution sexual love could really be.

The intoxications of desire make a lover more attentive, more tender to the vulnerabilities of the other. Lovers, as they connect, express the yearning to know and to be deeply known, to penetrate and dissolve, to relax into total acceptance. Within the feeling of coming home which is falling in love, there is a dissolution which seems to promise the possibility of a new and truer reconstitution of the self. Falling in love at mid life may touch a deep and hidden vulnerability within, particularly when we have never previously allowed ourselves to question our own inherited constructs about how life was supposed to be lived – constructs which for Jeremy were represented most powerfully in the unconscious need which had gripped him all his life up until that point, to live up to his mother's expectations of him.

The mating rituals of first adulthood tend to reinforce social and familial expectations, but the mid-life love affair is more likely to undermine them, to fly insolently and carelessly in their face. At mid-life transition, the yearning for the romantic solution re-emerges intensified, partly as a response to the anxieties induced by the maturation process: the partially realized, partially denied awareness of ageing may bring about a great upsurge of sexual desire and the astonishment of falling in love with an intensity buried since adolescence. Sexual relationships embarked upon at mid life may fluctuate as a reprise of the heedless desire of first love, while underneath a darker theme – more desperate but, in its own way, more heroic – plays out. This theme is the determination to hold on to something – perhaps the battered ideal of love itself – in the face of one's own disillusionment. Jeremy shakes his head ruefully over the hot passion he describes first feeling for Adele: he was like a teenager, he said, he should have known better. But that did not make the let-down – as their relationship slid inexorably into domesticity and parenthood – any less poignant.

Long-standing relationships inevitably come under pressure and threat at mid life. Sometimes irreconcilable differences prompt the initiation of an extramarital affair which then, in its turn, provides the impetus to leave an existing relationship that has become stagnant and hopeless. But other long-term relationships prove themselves strong and flexible enough to take the changes on board and become revitalized – though often not without suffering and soul-searching on both sides. And sometimes the yearnings which surface at mid life, erotic in their nature and intensity, don't actually connect very convincingly, or very enduringly, with a new lover at all – or not a flesh and blood one, anyway. They may take the form of a longing to discover a different way of connecting with one's existing partner, a passionate engagement with a new cause, the discovery of a vocation or the realization of a dream. Sometimes they may be more nebulous and unfocused still, recognized only as a yearning for what is, as yet, not.

THE THIRD THEME: DEATH
ENCOUNTERING MORTALITY

For Jeremy, the intensity with which he connected with Adele was in part determined by his anxieties about getting older and the need for reaffirmation of his identity as a potent and attractive man. Loss comes at mid life most obviously in the

21

form of loss of youth, but by mid life most of us have begun to experience other losses too, most particularly the deaths of some of those we have loved. Further loss had come to Jeremy through the collapse of his idealized notions about marriage and the family which for so long had held his own marriage in place, through the rift with his wife and children, through the subsequent collapse of the romantic ideal he sought with Adele, and through his mother's death. The death of his mother and the problems with his new baby came in a dramatic form, underlining the guilt he was already feeling about the damage his departure had done to those he loved. For these events, he was blaming himself very much. Later on, he said that his mind sometimes felt like a graveyard, a place full of dead things. And despite his awareness that he had in reality a great deal to live for, sometimes he could not help feeling that there seemed little point.

The death of Jeremy's mother brought into focus already underlying anxieties. The decline and death of elderly parents is often a central precipitating factor of mid-life crisis. However prepared one may feel and however peripheral they may have become in adult life, the death of a parent can make a great, and astonishing, clutch at the heart. The contrast between the vigorous healthy parent of childhood and the frail elderly being now loosening his or her hold upon life, announces – perhaps more eloquently than anything else could – the inexorable marching on of time. The death of one's parents represents not only the death of an elderly mother or father as they are now, but the awareness that now there is only oneself to maintain the connection running through them to the past, to their parents and to one's ancestors going back through history. There is also the loss of the experience of being held in the mind of another who has watched us growing from babyhood through to adulthood: as they witness this, our parents seem somehow to preserve the continuity of our being. With the death of parents, we have no-one left to carry these memories but ourselves, just as there is no-one left any more to stand unshakeably between ourselves and the fears of childhood, the fears of death itself.

It is one thing, armoured by the confident immortality of youth, to know that death is inevitable at a theoretical level, but quite another to really begin to feel it. At mid life, the awareness of impermanence as a psychic fact – gentle, subtle, persuasive as a fifth columnist – begins to undermine all the solidly reinforced certainties and achievements the ego has painstakingly built up through the first half of life. At mid life we reach the mid point, the brow of the hill, and glimpse, for the first time, the other side. It is a glimpse that we must either accommodate or fearfully deny.

Depending upon how fixed, how attached to our youthful belief in our personal invulnerability and immortality, the words *this too, will pass* may be experienced as a threat or as a promise. Coming to terms with transience is one of the major tasks of mid life: allowing life to flow through us instead of grasping tightly on to everything, we become able to live in a way that is less defensive and full of striving, and more relaxed, flexible and harmonious, able to enjoy life more through trying to control it less. Those who have touched death already, through near-fatal accidents or through learning to live with terminal illness, sometimes report that they have become more intensely alive than ever, more in touch with the beauty and preciousness of all lived experience. 'He hath borne me on his back a thousand times ... Here hung those lips that I have kissed I know not how oft. Where be your gibes now?' says Hamlet, perhaps incredulously, perhaps tenderly, as he holds in his hands the skull of Yorick – the man who was more a father to him, we might guess, than his own ever was.[7] At the same time Hamlet is also anticipating the mystery of his own impending death: at such a moment the encounter with death may bring forth a new awareness of the preciousness of life, love and the bonds of human relationship.

---

[7] *Hamlet*, Act V, Scene 1.

THE FOURTH THEME: GATHERING UP
FINDING A NEW WAY TO ACCOUNT FOR ONESELF

We pay for the choices we make, and the price we pay is the life we lead. In the second half of life this becomes more and more irrefutably obvious. In the same way, with the same patterns and ways of relating and the same sorts of successes and failures coming predictably around again and again, our own responsibility for shaping our destiny, which is beyond praise or blame, becomes increasingly self-evident. Sherry Lansing, an executive producer in Hollywood through the 1980s and 1990s, described it as follows: 'At fifty you have to say "*What am I missing...*" By that time you can't blame it on circumstances or other people. Whatever is incomplete, it's you who have left it out.'[8] And at the same time the dawning realization that our lifespan is not, after all, infinite and therefore infinitely expendable, raises with a new urgency the question: *if not me, who? And if not now, when?*

At times of crisis we wander round the same old endless mental perambulations, designed with unconscious skill to avoid looking at ourselves and to put pressure on others to do what we want them to do (*Why won't he change? Shall I leave my wife? If I won the lottery...*). Trapped within the compulsive search for external sources of pleasure, satisfaction and solace and the inevitable resentment when life, as is its wont, fails to deliver, we chase our tails round and round. Only when we finally take responsibility for our own well-being do we truly become adult; and it is a paradox that by doing so we become more able to love, and also more lovable.

Part of the pain which steals up on us at mid life comes from the sense that what was previously sufficient is sufficient no longer. Yet, for a while at least, nothing seems to replace it. If only we knew what was happening (and if a safe landing and a happy ending were guaranteed), we might dare to go forward into this unknown. But *we just don't know*; and it seems a characteristic of the mid-life transition that this dissolution of

---

[8] Quoted in Sheehy, G., *New Passages*, HarperCollins (1997).

meaning is both deeply feared and devoutly desired. The American author Gail Sheehy, in her survey of predictable crises in the lives of over a hundred American adults, describes this lost and fearful feeling: 'People whose biographies I have taken can say at 44 or 45, "I really went through hell for a few years, and I'm just coming out of it" but their capacity to describe what "it" felt like is often limited. People right in the middle of midlife passage may be so panicky that the only descriptions they can summon are of "living in a state of suspended animation"or "I sometimes wonder in the morning if life is worth getting up for." To be any more introspective seems dangerous.'[9]

'*I've lost the plot*' says Jeremy. Jeremy had believed for most of his life that if he performed as well as he could and satisfied others' expectations of him, he would be rewarded with the world's approval and with personal fulfilment. But the internal dissatisfactions and self-questionings which had begun to nag at him as he neared his forties had been steadily undermining these beliefs, and the losses that he had suffered over the last three years – partly self-inflicted, partly not – had exploded all his previous expectations of life. Loss may come abruptly as bereavement or severance from what is familiar and loved, or in more teasing and subtle forms as the loss of youth and fracture of youth's idealism. Whether it is borne unwillingly or deliberately inflicted upon oneself and others, loss entails disorientation and the destabilization of personal identity. Like a black hole, major experience of loss seems to collapse all value and meaning into its gravitational pull, leaving – as it had done for Jeremy – a devastated and bankrupt internal world.

At times of change, the loss of the working model which we have used to make sense of the world – to explain the past, predict the future and modify our responses accordingly – is likely to create an alarming internal vacuum. When this happens our minds may struggle desperately to restore lost meaning, and finding any way of making sense of something – even an impoverished, punitive or self-destructive sort of sense – can sometimes seem better than living with the fear that there may

---

[9]   Sheehy, G., *Passages: Predictable Crises of Adult Life*, Bantam (1977).

25

be no sense at all. Jeremy was unconsciously searching for a way of making sense of things that would enable him to move on. But because he was, as yet, unable to free himself from the old ways of thinking that had dominated the first half of his life, this search was leading him helplessly to the conclusion that the losses and disappointments of the last three years (in particular the death of his mother, the days after Joe's birth when his son's life had hung in the balance, and the deadness he was now feeling in his relationship with Adele) must be a punishment for his attempt to take his life into his own hands. Jeremy had hurt others, most particularly his wife and his three older children, but his thinking was dominated not by concern for them but by anxieties about retaliation and retribution. His unconscious belief that his current unhappiness was a punishment for his own wrongdoing, and especially for his forbidden defiance of parental expectations, was weighing him down, and beginning to draw him down a slope of depression and despair.

Punctuated as it is by loss, the mid-life crisis demands a shift from one framework of meaning, underpinned by one set of values, to another. As authority figures start to lose the power that has been invested in them and the youthful urge to prove oneself as an adult by impressing others and competing with them decreases in urgency, other values begin to struggle to the fore and to make a claim for primacy. They embody the need for a shift from external to internal referents in which the need for personal integrity, peace of mind and internal harmony can begin to take priority over ego-centredness and the need to achieve and prove oneself, and in which the basis for relating to others can begin to shift from one of compliance or exploitation to one of concern and kindness.

Jung describes it as the movement from ego-orientation towards a more expansive self-orientation and towards individuation, the process whereby people become more fully and more profoundly themselves.[10] Erik Erikson, in his writing upon the stages of life, outlines a movement through adulthood in

---

[10] Jung, C. G., 'The stages of life' (1930–1) in *Modern Man in Search of a Soul*, Routledge (1984).

26

three parts. In young adulthood, he says, we define ourselves in terms of connectedness to others (intimacy as opposed to isolation). Then, as we move into middle adulthood, the need to develop the internal capacity to create and to give (generativity as opposed to stagnation) comes to the fore. Finally, in fully mature adulthood our concern will be with the self's internal relationships and existential state of balance (integrity as opposed to despair).[11] As we move through mid-life crisis, the need to recreate or rediscover personal meaning becomes incrementally more agonizing and more vital. In the hope of the discovery of a new sort of plot (which may require us to find a new way of talking and of being heard) there is the hope of discovering a structure within which the messy fragments of lives, of memories, dreams, fantasies, anxieties and yearnings, can be gathered and held together until new meanings and themes start mysteriously yet organically to emerge.

When my own younger daughter was about six, she went through a period of intense anger towards her older sister, marked by increasingly explosive and violent incidents. Attempts to make use of quieter moments to talk about what was happening proved fruitless – whenever the problem was tentatively broached she would be off, hands over ears, feet stamping: 'I HATE HER NO NO NO GO AWAY BE QUIET.' But the problem was clearly not resolving itself. One summer morning, as I was hanging out the washing and pushing her on the garden swing, inspiration came to me: 'Once upon a time' I said, 'there was a guinea pig called Waffle who had a big sister she didn't always like very much.' My daughter's gaze slowly softened from a suspicious scowl to grudging curiosity, and drifted over thoughtfully towards the run at the other end of the garden where her own two pet guinea pigs were grazing obliviously in the long grass. There was a moment's pause. 'Why not?' she said. I began to develop a story, trying to weave what I was guessing her own concerns might be, as well as the perspectives of others, into the story. After a while, my daughter began to join in, enjoying herself and correcting me on details, especially

---

[11] Erikson, E. H., *The Life Cycle Completed*, W. W. Norton (1997).

concerning the ways in which Waffle had felt herself wronged and misunderstood. The story became a collaboration with her prompting. '*What happened next, mummy?*' whenever I paused.

What happened next? It's the question we all want to know the answer to, the one that keeps us hanging on in there. It seemed that as the story developed my daughter had become able to think about herself in relation to something (her angry jealousy) that had felt too upsetting and overwhelming to think about when confronted with it directly. Locating herself in the narrative, she could place herself in time, and from there (in the middle) we could begin together to trace causes and understanding of what had happened (beginnings) and to play with possible outcomes (ends).

Jeremy, similarly, came to psychotherapy because the story he had told himself about his life was no longer proving fruitful. If psychotherapy does anything, it begins to make conscious and to explore the old unconscious narratives that the self tells to the self. As these begin to dissolve in the light of consciousness, they will over time – if the work goes well – begin to be replaced with new narratives which are more encompassing in perspective, more emotionally resonant, more interesting and more empowering.

Such newly emerging narratives sponsor internal growth and open up new possibilities for living. (In unsuccessful psychotherapy, narratives will also be created or reinforced, but if these narratives are rigid, self-indulgent, or collusively denying, the work will become stuck and founder.) It is in this sense that psychotherapy itself is a process of contemporary, collaborative myth-making. Its narratives may replace the stories of the past or they may rediscover them and reinvest them with meaning – as Freud rediscovered the myths of Oedipus and Narcissus, and in so doing turned the notions of the oedipal complex and the narcissistic personality into part of the common currency which we use to understand ourselves and others. So also, the myth of Odysseus and Penelope becomes available as a narrative to illuminate the journey of mid-life crisis.

Maturation is a process rather than a goal, not a static state but a discovery of meaning that is always in the process of becoming. As we move through life we become more aware of the finite and therefore precious nature of time itself. Means begin to matter more than ends and the quality of moment-to-moment experience more than the quantity of achievement. Our self-awareness may at times intensify our suffering and disillusionment, but it also gives us the power to transform them through the development of a new narrative which – at best – may be able redeem the past, transform the present and create new futures which will be worth investing in. Thinking of the mid-life crisis in this way, as a process, enables us to begin to give it a shape, out of which discrete stages begin to emerge.

THE MID-LIFE CRISIS AS PROCESS

Aristotle's theory of drama famously maintained that every drama has a beginning, a middle and an end. In the beginning, there is an establishment of the various threads that make up the plot. Then in the middle, there comes a point of no return – the protagonist reaches a point at which he discovers something about himself. After reaching that point, he can no longer go

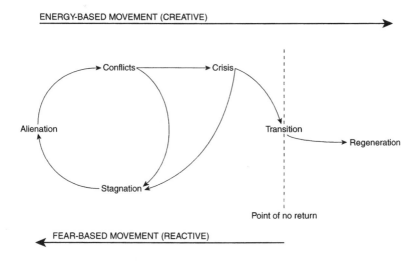

Figure 1   The mid-life cycle: from alienation to stagnation (fear-based movement) or onwards to regeneration (energy-based movement)

back, no longer be what he was. Then inevitably there comes the denouement, the unravelling, the time of reckoning. And so it is with the journey through mid-life crisis.

The most frequent experience at the beginning of mid-life crisis is a sense of *alienation*, the feeling of being trapped, to a greater or lesser extent, in a life become increasingly meaningless. Wedged between the despair that things will continue exactly as they are and the terror that they will change for ever, the desire to protect what we most love from threat, and the dawning awareness that the longing for change as well as the dread of it is located deep within our own psyches, we squirm unhappily.

The attempt to suppress these first treacherous stirrings of discontent may lead towards *stagnation*, in which the self identifies with the feelings of alienation and becomes defended against change, using whatever means are at its disposal to preserve and to reinforce the status quo. But if we take the stirrings of discontent seriously we may begin to become more aware of the existence of major *conflicts* in central areas of our lives, particularly related to work, sexuality and the family – the threads, in Aristotle's terms, that make up the plot. As such conflicts become more obvious and harder to avoid, we may begin to have a sense of becoming engaged in a quarrel with life which seems as monumental as it is incomprehensible, a quarrel that seems unwinnable, and sometimes pointless. This cycle of irritation, arousal, awareness and suppression may be repeated many times with increasing insistence and urgency. Upon each repetition, the figure in the carpet emerges with greater clarity from its background, as former strategies for defusing problems are resorted to with increasing desperation and decreasing efficiency.

Yet even as they are dreaded, conflicts go on being sought, even engineered. Betrayal, loss or failure in the external world – and who by their mid-thirties is not familiar with these? – may be the catalyst. Or, as if urged onwards by some evilly inspired genius, the impetus towards upheaval and mayhem may come entirely from within ourselves. Most often of all, a sinisterly escalating conspiracy between internal and external destructive forces seems to be at work. Sometimes (more often than we care to admit) we may covertly foster the very conflict and crisis in our lives which we ostensibly deplore, for – according to the same principle that makes admissions to mental hospitals drop sharply when a war is declared – catastrophe in the outside world can provide a sort of relief, a timely rescue from the more pervasive and nagging aches of inauthentic living, from the denial, avoidance, self-betrayal, emptiness and futile expenditure of energy required to keep stagnation in place and conflict at bay.

Conflicts prematurely resolved lead back to stagnation and to alienation, but if they are followed through and allowed to come to a head, the *crisis* itself is reached. In crisis there may be a sense of release, of letting go, of no longer trying to defend the indefensible, yet at the same time the self may begin to feel flooded with unwelcome and previously denied self-experiences. This is the point at which we begin to learn new things about ourselves, and from which there can be no going back.

A crisis, crippling at the time, may in retrospect be seen as necessary and ultimately benign, for it is often the collapse of hope in external solutions which forces us to turn inwards to examine the state of our own psyches. So, the initial conflicts and dramas of the mid-life crisis feed into a longer and more difficult period, less superficially dramatic but marked by uncertainties and sometimes by suffering and depression in which it becomes difficult to engage with the external world as before. Being caught up in the process, in the anxiety generated from not knowing what to do any more (so much of our adult identity, after all, has been invested in this sense of being the one who knows), in the grief-stricken contemplation of loss, in the guilty confrontation with our own potential for destruction, may be an intense and deeply unwelcome experience. It is exacerbated by the unwillingness within our own culture to acknowledge, let alone to permit or support, the periods of withdrawal from the world and the struggle with internal demons that may be demanded at such times – instead we tend to pathologize or just deny them. This tendency to see pain as personal failure or sickness, rather than as an inevitable facet of life which may potentially herald the birth struggles of a new experience of the self, is something we experience in wider social attitudes to suffering and also, often, in our own responses to our personal pain.

31

In the face of inner confusion and lack of understanding or support from the outside world, the desire to retreat to the haven of past security may become overwhelming. It's one thing to wander off whimsically, experimentally or under the dizzying spell of sexual desire from the well-trodden and signposted route onto the rougher, wilder and more treacherous terrain upon which paths seem to start and then peter out into nothingness. But it's something else to keep faith with this impulse when night falls, fear clutches the heart and we find ourselves going round and round in circles, seemingly going nowhere but further into the heart of darkness itself.

And yet if we do – by accident, design or force of circumstance – manage to keep faith with this inner struggle, we may find that the darkest hour heralds the dawn, and discover that we are moving into a period of *transition*. At this time, a capacity for inner space will begin to become inalienably established – a place in which the maturing psyche can feel at home and less at the mercy of the whims of time and fate, and the misunderstandings and disappointments inherent in relationship. This space established, we discover ourselves becoming less driven, less anxious, less judging; we become kinder, more creative and more playful. Things start to fall into place differently. Insoluble, intransigent problems start to resolve themselves, blocks start to dissolve, energy returns and hope for the future revives. A new feeling of relaxation and acceptance of what was formerly experienced as unbearable may begin to arise as we start to realize just how much we have learnt over the last few difficult years, and how much we are changed. When these gains have been worked through enough to become irreversibly integrated within the self, the conditions are created for the movement into *regeneration* as the basis for the second half of life.

Of course, it is never so clear-cut. The mid-life transition tends to be a very stop-start affair, full of premature resolutions and unexpected restartings, spread out over years; yet the bare bones of the movement described above and in Figure 1 may nevertheless hold true as an approximate working paradigm for the process of the mid-life crisis. In the remaining sections of this book we will explore how it is all likely to pan out, and begin to follow the crisis through towards its ultimate resolution.

Part Two

ALIENATION

3

Stagnation: the End of First Adulthood

Is it like this
In death's other kingdom
Waking alone
At the hour when we are
Trembling with tenderness
Lips that would kiss
Form prayers to broken stone. . .

This is the way the world ends
Not with a bang but a whimper

From 'The Hollow Men' by T. S. Eliot

Jeremy, whose story was described in the previous chapter, had reached the point at which he had achieved the aims of first adulthood. His marriage was stable, his children were growing up and doing well, and he was financially secure and successful in his work. And this – as he had become painfully aware – was the problem. He had been feeling flat, stale, bored, angry without knowing why. He was ready for trouble. But it was not a problem in respect of which – as he was also aware – he could expect much sympathy.

DIFFERENT TIMES, DIFFERENT NEEDS

In a sense, the mid-life crisis is a symptom of success. It is a disease of affluence and, as such, is unlikely to present itself as much of a problem to those millions in the world whose lives are so marginalized and deprived that they may count themselves unexpectedly fortunate if they reach forty at all: people whose entire lives are a crisis do not have mid-life crises. But if having a mid-life crisis advertises a success story of sorts, it may also reveal to us the cost at which our success has been bought.

The mid-life crisis tends to erupt most strikingly in the lives of those who – like Jeremy – are well-educated and lead affluent, stable and successful lives. What does this reveal about it, and about us? To some, this fact will confirm what they believed already – that the so-called crisis is a self-indulgent irrelevance which doesn't deserve to be taken seriously. Yet if we condemn the kind of emotional turbulence which the mid-life crisis embodies, we may reveal ourselves as too defended to see the self-indulgence at the heart of mainstream society which the eruption of the mid-life crisis – however cack-handedly – challenges. Our indignation about the very idea of the mid-life crisis may, in other words, be fired less by concern for the genuinely gross inequalities of the world than by discomfiture with the very notion that material success alone can't provide all the answers.

Freedom from need is a necessary basis for contentment. But the hunger generated by a way of life based entirely on material values – fuelled by disappointment in the inevitable failure of consumer products to ever really satisfy us – keeps on escalating. And the pursuit of material success and status to the detriment of all else has its own cost, to which we may be peculiarly blind – until it becomes too great to ignore at a personal level. We have, as the American psychologist Abraham Maslow observed, different levels of need, which call to be answered in different ways.[1] Maslow believed that human needs subsist within categories, which he ordered within a hierarchy. In general, one level of need must be satisfied before we are able to move

---

[1] Maslow, A. H., 'A theory of human motivation' (1943), *Psychological Review* 50.

on, at which point another level of need can emerge and be identified. So, people whose houses are on fire don't sit around pondering ultimate values – yet in more congenial circumstances, to do so may be a useful activity.

Maslow represents this hierarchy of need as a pyramid (see Figure 2), the base of which is formed by our most fundamental and non-negotiable need for physical survival, including a reliable supply of food and water. The next most essential need is to be able to rest secure from the fear of attack. If these needs are satisfied in a consistent and reliable way, they will form the basis, in a healthy life, for new levels of need to emerge and to be entertained – conversely, if at a later point the base needs fail to be met, the pyramid will start to collapse and we will need to redirect our attention back towards them. The next levels refer to our emotional and social needs – the need to love and to be loved, and then after that to have a sense of belonging to a

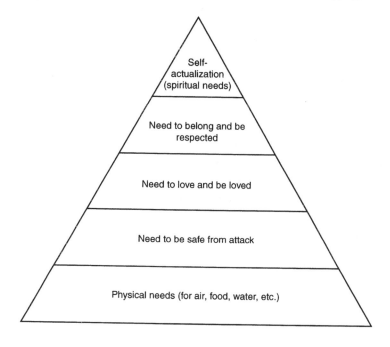

Figure 2   Maslow's hierarchy of needs (adapted from Maslow A. H., 'A theory of human motivation', 1943, *Psychological Review* 50)

community, and to be respected by our peers. Once we have confidence that these needs, too, will continue to be reliably met, we move up towards what Maslow calls meta-needs – the need to make sense of ourselves and of the world we inhabit, the need for aesthetic satisfaction, and so on. Maslow places self-actualization itself at the apex of this pyramid, the ultimate need which cannot be addressed until our lower needs for physical survival, emotional security, a degree of self-awareness, and so on, have been met.

The advent of the mid-life crisis may – in its muddled way – represent the emergence of the desire to move towards self-actualization, with all that this entails, in a fundamental restructuring of internal values. If all goes well in the process of this restructuring, the goal-orientated, approval-seeking strivings which have shaped the first half of our adult lives begin to be transformed over time into the more expansive, relaxed and mature sense of self which sponsors, in Maslow's terms, self-actualization. Yet paradoxically, we cannot turn our backs on the need to succeed until we have succeeded – that is, until we have first managed to establish ourselves in the world according to our own prior measures of success. Only by doing so will we be released from the biological and emotional exigencies of dependence, reproduction, material security and the need for approval. And only having done so – with a life perhaps not yet half lived, at the peak of our resources and with energy that is undiminished and even increased with the diminution of external demands – are we in a position to ask: what next?

The opportunity presented through the mixed blessing of the advent of mid-life crisis is to create new ways of living built on greater self-awareness, less dependent upon external forms of validation and more congruent with our emergent inner sense of self. The advent of the mid-life crisis advertises firstly, at a cultural level, our participation in a society wealthy and secure enough to facilitate the exploration of higher (non-survival) needs and secondly, at an individual level, the successful negotiation of first adulthood.

FROM THE TWENTIES TO THE MID-THIRTIES: FIRST ADULTHOOD AND THE *ILIAD*

The priorities of first adulthood tend to be orientated towards the establishment of the adult self within society. Early adulthood is a time when social patterns of co-operation and competition must be negotiated – Erikson's core conflict of intimacy versus self-absorption.[2] For most of us, first adulthood is a constructive and busy time during which, having left behind the constraints of the parental home and the turmoil and fluidity of adolescence, we establish a solid adult identity in the world. This sense of adulthood generally starts to solidify in the twenties, through the choices we make in our sexual and social lives, the careers we train in and begin to pursue and the particular world views and ideologies which we develop at this time. The thirties are typically a time when the shape of a working life consolidates, offering greater opportunities and responsibilities which demand to be taken up, if we are not to fall behind.

In our thirties, we build up a sense of our personal power and potency – as professionals, as parents, as protagonists and movers in our own lives. Through the career, financial and family-orientated achievements of first adulthood, we establish our capacity to make independent choices, to carry them through and to maintain a life organized consistently in accordance with chosen values and priorities. First adulthood is to do with the shouldering of real responsibilities, but also a time in which success is calculated to a great extent in terms exterior to the self, in which the gaining of respect and self-respect from the fulfilment of socially condoned goals tends to be a primary motivating factor.

Reading Homer shows us that – allowing for the ways in which the scenery and the props have changed over the last three thousand years – there is little new in the struggle for self-awareness which emerges, often unexpectedly, from the achievements and ultimate dissatisfactions of the active life of

---

[2] Erikson, E. H., 'Growth and crises of the healthy personality' in *Identity and the Life Cycle*, W. W. Norton (1994).

first adulthood. If the *Odyssey* is a mid-life epic, its precursor the *Iliad* is a story of first adulthood removed to a simpler, idealized landscape. And in the movement between them, it is as if we see the halting beginnings of the capacity for self-reflection of the human mind – in this sense, it is not the antiquity but the modernity of the two epics which is so startling. Odysseus in particular, who we meet in the *Iliad* as only one of many, but who emerges as the eponymous hero and chief protagonist of the *Odyssey*, comes to embody this sense of self-aware humanity emerging from the more primitive world of gods, primeval forces and small helpless humans which is the world of our civilization's infancy, as well as the world of our own young lives.

The *Iliad* covers a short, intense episode of the Trojan War. It is a story of first adulthood in mood and theme, for its main protagonists are young warriors – though getting older all the time, as they themselves are becoming painfully aware. It explores the glories of the self-promoting heroic ideal and, increasingly, its limitations and self-defeating nature – and the ensuing feelings of disillusionment consequent upon it. The story of the *Iliad* opens upon the Greek warriors, including Odysseus, who had originally banded together and sailed to Troy to rescue Helen, who had previously been seduced away from her Greek husband Menelaus by Paris, one of the princes of Troy. By now, many long years have passed since that day, but our heroes are still clustered – increasingly grumpily – beneath the walls of the resolutely unfallen Troy. A quarrel over a girl between Achilles, the greatest of the Greek warriors, and his commander Agamemnon, escalates into a feud. Achilles refuses to fight any more, and withdraws to his tent for a prolonged sulk. He resists all entreaties from his comrades until his lover Patroclus replaces him as leader of his force and is killed beneath the walls of Troy by Hector, leader of the Trojans. Achilles, in rage and grief, is then reconciled with his fellow Greeks, hurls himself back into the fray and kills Hector. Shortly thereafter Achilles himself dies, killed by an arrow aimed at his famous heel: his death is foreshadowed but not covered by the *Iliad*, which ends with the funeral of Hector and an uneasy truce between Trojans and Greeks.

The belligerent momentum of the *Iliad* is the momentum of

the heroic quest.[3] Heroic epics like the *Iliad* – or *The Magnificent Seven* or *Star Wars* – tend to map out an idealized version of the territory of first adulthood. In these stories, would-be heroes are usually required to set out alone from their childhood homes upon a mysterious quest to a foreign land, in which new abilities and skills must be learnt the hard way, unknown dangers confronted and personal values reappraised. There is often some sort of sexual initiation. Eventually the wicked are outwitted at their own game and good is restored to the world: the hero returns and is recognized and rewarded by an appreciative society. The universality of these myths articulates the universal craving of the young adult to develop a recognized and admired identity in the world by carrying his or her own projects through to successful fruition. And this craving is realized nowhere more brilliantly – or more ambiguously – than in the *Iliad*'s jostlings for position and victory, its confrontations, its horse tradings, and its blood-stained obsession with fame and reputation.

THE FAILURE OF THE HEROIC SOLUTION

Yet on the Trojan plain, the initial heroic quest to rescue the girl and sack the city fizzles out into ten years of increasingly weary siege and stalemate. There is, in the end, no villain and, despite the violent partisanship of the protagonists, no clear right and wrong, for Homer has as much sympathy with the Trojans as with the Greeks. The *Iliad* concludes not with a triumphal victory march but to the sound of a funeral and the desolate wailing of Hector's bereaved parents and his widow Andromache. At the same time, the petulant, narcissistic and self-obsessed antics of Achilles have brought the whole idea of

---

[3]   Campbell, J., *The Hero with a Thousand Faces*, Fontana (1993).

honour into question. A subtext of the *Iliad* suggests that the struggle for honour, fame and status within the peer group or tribe is not necessarily compatible with the establishment of personal integrity and moral responsibility – however much we would like to convince ourselves of the contrary. As the hot-headed young warriors turn imperceptibly but relentlessly into battle-hardened cynics, it becomes increasingly clear that if they go on thinking in the same way, caught in an endless cycle of reaction and retaliation, they will just go on getting the same unsatisfactory results. The siege may just go on for ever. And if things don't change, they will only stay the same.

As forty approaches and as the glow of achievement turns imperceptibly into the burden of responsibility, life can indeed begin to seem like an intractable siege. Career challenges no longer exert the same adrenaline-charged thrill, and feelings of powerlessness in the face of work's inherent insecurities, irritations or limitations become more pronounced. Much of the modern world of work is inherently concerned with the achievement of goals predetermined by others, and as we become older and more independently minded, this can begin to prompt uneasy questions about our own personal values. Work is no more a universal panacea than sex, and throwing oneself into it ever more intensively (whether from panic or necessity or both) may create more problems than it resolves.

As far as sex itself is concerned, the approaching watershed of forty may prompt much self-questioning among those until now contentedly, or at least resignedly, single. For single women, there may be a realization that parenthood cannot be indefinitely postponed into an ideal but hazy future once career goals are achieved and the perfect mate secured – fertility declines sharply in the late thirties and for some this realization may come, to their sorrow, too late. For those with families, the close couple bonding of the early years of child-rearing may begin to break down, exacerbated by the exhausting drain on resources made by growing children. And as children begin to move outwards from the family into the world, the focus for parents begins, sometimes with relief but sometimes uncomfortably, to shift. As we start to think about ourselves once more as people in our own right and to reclaim the territory of our own needs and longings, insecurities to do with ageing and the feared loss of sexual desirability and potency begin to emerge. With a shudder, we catch ourselves inadvertently coming out with the same turn of phrase, tone of voice or gesture we remember from our own parents when we were young, and find ourselves locked into the same stultifying family dynamics.

We begin to live our days not to the soundtrack of the victory march we expected to have deserved by now, but to a cacophony of the voices of exacting employers, disappointed lovers, demanding spouses, shrieking children, disapproving parents and – loudest of all – our own critical internal voices. This unpleasing and unremitting blend of sound permits little peace of mind. Underneath all the worries which begin to pile up, to snag and to snare, an epic disillusionment may be building up, a painful loss of faith in the perfect solution – the ideal of marriage, the corporate ethos, or the uncomplicated trust of children that if we are good, work hard, stay clean and tidy, keep our noses down, aim to please and don't ask too many awkward questions, everyone will be happy ever after. It doesn't seem to be working out that way. On the other hand, however, nor does change itself – the movement out of the orbit of first adulthood – come easily. And the fear of change itself may create feelings of internal stagnation, deadness and alienation which are not easily to be shifted.

Fear of change binds us to the past, but our attempts to repeat the dramas and triumphs of first adulthood may founder in increasing desperation and futility – the law of diminishing returns is at work and, deprived of a sense of real purpose to wrestle with, we may unconsciously begin to resign ourselves to a long and passive wait for death. If the opportunity for transition is shirked, the likely outcome is a sense of increasing banality, rigidity and futility in the second half of life. As Jung said, those who avoid the first death (meaning the painful identity dissolutions of mid life) are haunted by the second. Is the second half of life to be no more than a drearily unconvincing reprise of the first? 'We cannot live the afternoon of life according to the programme of life's morning; for what was great in the morning will be little at evening and what in the morning was true will at evening have become a lie. I have given psychological treatment to too many people ... not to be moved by this fundamental truth.'[4]

BREAKING THE SIEGE

Like the siege of Troy, the years of early adulthood begin to teach us that while we keep on solving problems in the same old way, the same old problems keep coming back. The more force is used, the more resistance arises. For the Greeks, their ten years of conflict have produced not glory but stalemate, a growing pile of corpses and an escalation of unedifying bickering among the erstwhile comrades. The relentless passage of time changes the siege of Troy from a life-defining adventure into a dreary stalemate that must be broken.

And it is broken – by Odysseus, who, famously, emerges from the ranks of the assembled princes with an entirely new idea. He persuades the Greeks to pack up camp and set sail, apparently heading for home in defeat but actually to wait around the headland. They leave a large wooden horse behind them on the shore, apparently as a propitiation to the gods. The triumphant and now careless Trojans drag the horse inside their walls, disarm themselves and start feasting, whereupon the Greek troops hidden within the body of the horse emerge to raze the undefended city to the ground.

The stalemate could be broken because Odysseus becomes able to take a problem which everyone had been seeing as a military question (whose strength is greatest, whose courage fiercest?) and to reframe it in a completely different way, as a psychological question (what will make the Trojans open their gates?). In doing so, Odysseus is discovering a new way of solving problems, as well as a new way of making jokes (Troy, *Ilium* in Greek, means 'city of horses'). The apparent withdrawal of the Greeks from the beaches of Troy represents both a literal and a metaphoric stepping back – *reculer pour mieux sauter*. So we may find ourselves solving previously intransigent problems

---

[4] Jung, C. G., 'The stages of life', (1930–1) in *Modern Man in Search of a Soul*, Routledge (1984).

when, by stepping back and thinking, we shift our awareness out of its existing context into a more expansive one – when we start, in other words, to ask different questions of life from the ones we asked before. Around every circle, a larger circle can be drawn.

The story of the wooden horse is the end of one story and the beginning of another. Like the first resolution that things must change, the first doubtful step in a new direction, and the first unconfident assertion of a new voice, the tale of the wooden horse is the overture to the mid-life crisis, the introduction to the themes that will play out hereafter. At the same time it is also an interlude between the concrete, violent battles of the *Iliad* and the more psychologically complex and uncertain world of the *Odyssey* itself.

As the sun-baked, arid and self-limiting landscape of the Trojan plain begins to dissolve into the mysterious seascapes of the *Odyssey*, Odysseus is cast upon the seas not through his failure but through his success – through having achieved, by his own ingenuity and daring, the ultimate triumph of the defeat of Troy. This was the success towards which the previous ten years had been single-mindedly geared. Our own personal Troys may be the parents we have sought to please, the partners we have tried to make love us in the way we always wanted to be loved, the financial security or the ambitions we have courted and hunted through years of persistence – only to find, at last, that these projects no longer exert the same fascination upon our minds which they once did. Troy, like all transient and tender objects of desire, falls. Our own disillusionments may be somewhat less spectacular and abrupt, yet it is from such collapses of belief or faith that we find ourselves setting sail upon the wide and treacherous seas of the beginning of the second half of life.

4

Denial: Eating the Lotus

> ... a land
> In which it seemed always afternoon,
> All round the coast the languid air did swoon
> Breathing like one that hath a weary dream
> ... A land where all things always seem'd the same.

From 'The Lotos-Eaters' by Tennyson

Monica refers herself for psychotherapy. She hopes her problem can be re-solved quickly – she has tried, she says, everything. 'Relaxation exercises, hypnotherapy, cognitive behavioural therapy, you name it ...' Monica is friendly and co-operative, and answers my questions easily and thoughtfully. A petite and elegant 38-year-old woman who works in the pharmaceutical industry, she is immaculately turned out, from her sleek blonde bob to her high-heeled ankle boots, and her demeanour is brisk and businesslike. Yet there is something fixed about her smile, something vacant about her eyes, a tightness in the muscles around them.

Monica's problem is her fear of flying. She says that she has never liked it very much but in the past she could grit her teeth and do it. Recently, however, her anxieties have begun to obsess her. With a horrified fascination, she finds herself compulsively reading accounts of plane crashes and watching films about them. When she lies down at night and closes her eyes, these images flash before her in terrifying detail and she imagines herself plummeting down into inky darkness. Monica realizes that she is inventing scenes with which to terrify herself, but she cannot seem to stop.

Monica's boss is encouraging her to apply for a new position, representing a considerable promotion, which she believes is within her reach. It is a dream job, she says, the job which for years she has been longing and secretly planning for. The problem is that it will require her to make several long-haul flights each year to the factories of subcontractors in Sri Lanka and Malaysia, to oversee production. Monica has not been able to tell anyone in the company about her fear – which has now made her, she says, absolutely unable to step on a plane. But if she does not go for the promotion, she feels that there is nowhere else for her to go. And how could she live with herself?

The possibility of change may create a powerful reaction against it – a case of one step forward and two steps back. Why had Monica's fear of flying, previously controlled within manageable limits, suddenly become all-consuming and obsessive – just at the moment when the heights of success were within her grasp? Change can be more disturbing than we like to admit, even when it comes, as it did for Monica, as the realization of a long-term dream. Our sense of selfhood may be more fragile than we know, and deliberately or unconsciously we may employ powerful forces to keep change at bay. Like Monica, our minds may become obsessed with inventing worst-case scenarios – like the monsters with which children torment themselves at bedtime – as if to bully ourselves back into fearful submission. At other times, however difficult things may be in the present we just deny the need for change, refusing to go with life's flow. We act as if change were optional, not compulsory, failing to notice that in a constantly changing world, the inevitability of change is virtually the only thing that we can really rely upon. Our unconscious fear of change may have a blank and paralysed feel to it, a playing safe that is also a copping out.

Monica raises her eyebrows slightly when she is asked about her own past, but answers accommodatingly enough. Over the next few sessions a sense of her background begins to emerge. Monica's mother had had to marry her father, a factory worker, when she became pregnant with Monica at the age of 23. There were no more children, although Monica thinks her mother may have had a miscarriage a few years later. When Monica was young, her mother worked part-time as an assistant in a chemist's shop. By the time that she retired, her mother had become the manager of the shop, yet she always told Monica that she could have achieved far more had she not fallen pregnant with Monica and had to marry Monica's father. Monica describes her mother as energetic to the point of being driven – her easy-going father's lack of aspiration was an increasing source of bitterness and acrimony, and her father had withdrawn emotionally from the marriage.

In this atmosphere Monica grew up, the sole object of all her mother's frustrated ambitions and yearnings for a better life. Monica says she loved her father (and her eyes momentarily fill with tears), but always felt she was her mother's daughter, and eventually she too came to despise him. She begins to say something else, then hesitates. After a moment, she says that when she was younger – she thinks around twelve or thirteen – she would often wake up in a panic, with a sensation of falling from a great height.

After college, Monica got a job working as a PA in industry. Always ambitious, she soaked up everything she could about the business, seized opportunities when she saw them, and within a few years was doing her former boss's job. Monica has been contentedly married for several years to a man who works in the same company. The new promotion will, if she takes it, make her several levels senior to her husband, as well as increasing the long hours she already works. I ask Monica whether children are an issue, and there is a silence. She says softly that she had never really thought about it until a year or two ago, because she was so engrossed in her work. She admits that she feels daunted by the idea, and does not think she would make a good mother. Yet it is hard to close the door on the idea entirely, partly because she does not know for sure what her husband really wants. She knows there is not much time left, but I get the impression that Monica believes taking the demanding new job will be a way of resolving the question of children, without needing to address it directly.

It becomes clear that the question of whether to take the job or not raises many difficult questions for Monica. She fears that her own accelerating career may damage or destroy her marriage. Her mother had been proud of her, but her own unrealized ambitions also made her resentful and envious of what Monica had achieved in comparison to herself, and their relationship has deteriorated as Monica has become more successful. Secretly, Monica is afraid that her relationship with her husband will go the same way if she begins to outshine him. She loves her husband – she speaks of him as her anchor – yet she also loves her work and cannot bear to think of falling by the wayside. And she feels very ambivalent about having children. To what extent has she taken on board the message she had picked up from her mother, that children were a burden who stopped you fulfilling your promise in life? Monica begins to get in touch with anger towards her own mother who was so driven, who never relaxed and played with her, who had always made her feel that love was dependent upon high achievement but then seemed to begrudge Monica her successes.

On the wall of my consulting room is a small print, which Monica remarks upon. It is a print of Matisse's *Icarus*, a black figure with a red hole in its chest, silhouetted against a midnight-blue background punctuated by yellow star-bursts. Does Monica secretly fear that if, like Icarus, she defies her warning voices and flies too high, her wings will burn and melt and she will plummet to her death? She tells me that she used to believe that women like her were not supposed to achieve the heights she feels herself capable of reaching.

Monica is tending to see things in black and white. Her choices seem agonizing, and agonizingly impossible. The dramatic images of exploding and disintegrating planes which fill her mind seem to serve as a sort of protection from the other thoughts she cannot let herself have, which seem to demand she find some internal reconciliation between her mother's and her father's values.

Monica's fear of flying seems richly symbolic, but it is a symbolic meaning she is very ambivalent about unravelling. A part of her realizes how much is at stake for her now, in terms of the choices she makes at this time of transition. As we begin to explore some of the underlying questions, Monica begins to feel more anxious and upset – although she also reports that she is obsessing less about plane crashes. But another part of her feels that there is no point in confronting these conflicts. As a child, she had felt impossibly pulled between her mother's and her father's values: there was no shared ground between them, no meeting point, no ability to compromise and negotiate between different perspectives.

In a dreamy voice, Monica describes lying in bed and listening to her mother shouting at her father and the sound of slamming doors. Then she abruptly exclaims that the sound of doors slamming was just like the sound of the planes slamming into the ground which plague her waking nights now. After saying this, Monica is withdrawn for the rest of the session, and does not appear the following week. Instead, she sends me a polite short note with a cheque enclosed, saying work pressures mean that unfortunately she has had to terminate.

When we can neither retreat authentically into a lost past nor move into the future with any real confidence, we deny the conflicts that face us, and become blocked. The feeling of self-alienation which then develops has a reactive and fearful quality to it, a sense of 'stuckness' and paralysis. Lot's wife, looking backwards instead of forwards, turns into a pillar of salt. If the possibility of growth and change can be opened up to, lost energy will return to the self. Yet resistance to change can be powerful and may last for months, years, or a lifetime. While it holds sway, relationships become compliant and emotionally dead – nothing can be gained, for nothing can be risked. There is too much to lose. A sense of fixedness and rigidity in role and repertoire gains a grip; unwittingly, we have reached the dreadful closed-mindedness of defensive middle age. An underlying sense of grudge and resentment gains a purchase, and a vague feeling – located somewhere between disappointment and cynicism – that somehow, a promise has not been kept. Energy blocked in this frozen state turns into fear and starts to express itself – as it did for Monica – in ways that are more or less harmful to the self, like the retreat into obsessional behaviours and dependencies, and the onset of stress-related illnesses.

IN THE LAND OF THE LOTUS-EATERS

After the fall of Troy, Odysseus and his men set sail, hoping for a swift return to Ithaca. But a storm blows them off course for ten days, eventually landing them upon the shores of an unknown island. They disembark to draw water and after a brief meal Odysseus sends three of his men inland to explore. They discover that upon this island time seems to stand still and all things slumber in a heavy haze: it's a prehistoric suburbia, a junkies' paradise, inhabited by the mild-eyed, melancholy Lotus-eaters who greet the intruders with a curiously disengaged friendliness and ply them with the honeyed fruit upon which they themselves live.

But to eat the lotus fruit is to destroy memory and desire, and as they share the fruit the exploring party is seduced into apathy and forgetfulness. Their previously fierce yearning for their homes and families dwindless rapidly into nostalgic dreaminess. Sinking into a lethargic contentment, their willingness to brave the perils of the turbulent seas dissipates in the perfumed, intoxicated air. Odysseus himself, disturbed and sickened, has to bring the drugged sailors back on board by force. He drags them under the benches in chains to sweat the lotus out of their systems and commands the remaining crew to set sail with all speed, aware of how easily they could all succumb and end up staying on the island forever.

RETREATING FROM CONFLICT:
DRINKING AND DRUGS

'Are you familiar with the stoical aspects of hard drinking, of heavy drinking?' enquires John Self, the central character and narrator of Martin Amis' *Money*. 'Oh it's heavy. Oh it's hard. It isn't easy. Jesus, I never meant me any harm. All I wanted was a good time.'[1] John Self is a promising British film director in his mid-thirties whose new project is taken up by American backers. Winging back and forth over the Atlantic, Self mixes with the serious players, the big money. But he also has a self-destruct button which sends him in a downward spiral of heavy drinking and drug-taking and sexual debauchery, until his world finally shatters around him.

Separations and major life changes, whether brought about through our own actions or forced upon us, are likely to evoke fears of abandonment and failure, and to induce high levels of stress and anxiety within us as we move through them. Odysseus' sailors encounter the lotus-eaters at the beginning of a long sea journey which threatens hardship, loss and danger as well as great uncertainty as to its eventual outcome. At times like these, the state of conflict-free ease and warm, serene confidence which drinking and drug-taking seem to offer can exert a powerful regressive pull. Like the Lotus-eaters' island, such a state can seem like a haven at times of stress or insecurity when it is all too much and nothing else can be relied upon – all the more so if the fundamental anxieties and conflicts which underpin the threatened changes are not being articulated or even brought into consciousness.

While some drugs (such as cocaine, amphetamines and caffeine) are stimulants, many others have a soothing or

---

[1]   Amis, M., *Money*, Penguin (2000).

numbing effect which may follow upon the heels of an initial euphoria (alcohol, for example, operates by killing brain cells and stripping neural transmitters). In the short term, a friendly, soothing respite from potentially intolerable feelings becomes available, upon which it is easy to begin to rely. But one of the problems with becoming reliant on drugs is that such reliance may itself be feeding our belief that there are parts of our psyches and areas of our emotional lives which are just too bad, useless or shameful to deserve attention, and that our underlying needs can never be really understood, let alone met. They can only be displaced, or bought off.

In the supermarket, we see an enraged or embarrassed parent trying to silence a screaming toddler by sticking a bottle in her mouth or a bag of sweets in her hand. Sometimes parents respond like this not just in the heat of the moment but habitually, unthinkingly – perhaps they are too preoccupied, too harassed, too unaware or too uncomfortable within themselves to be able to engage more thoughtfully with the child, or they may just be repeating the patterns of their own upbringing. As children, we exist within a matrix of relationships – we are programmed to mature through watching and imitating those around us. We internalize within ourselves our parents' patterns of care, learning to care for ourselves as they cared for us. An adult who responds empathically and thoughtfully to a child's anger or pain becomes internalized over time as a figure within the child's own psyche, a resource for coping constructively with the difficulties of later life. But we can also internalize our parents' unawareness and impatience, their anxious denial, their judgemental disapproval or their need to buy us off and distract us, making it our own response to our own distress as well. We learn to stick the sweets – or the bottle – in our own mouths, to silence ourselves.

Critical or denying responses to emotional need or pain harden over time into an attitude of emotional self-neglect, underpinned by the conviction that our more awkward or unhappy feelings must indeed be negligible, contemptible or unfathomable. People who come to depend upon drinking or drugs often have a surprisingly harsh and condemnatory attitude towards all needs of their own which are not directly connected with their habit. As we get older, our needs may become more insistent, yet at the same time (in terms of the adult selves we have learnt to construct) more unacceptable – while the substances available for soothing and stifling our needs become more seductively powerful. We end up ignoring our pain as it was ignored, drugging it into silence with drink and tranquil-lizers.

Such methods of managing and controlling inner needs, and the states of distress that develop when they are not met, become entrenched. They prove themselves fertile soil for drink and drug dependency and other compulsive forms of thinking and behaving to take root in when crisis looms. In *Money*, John Self explains that his mother died when he was still a child and we see him, for all his hard-boiled sassy cynicism, blundering through the novel like a huge, deranged baby. Collapsing into increasingly infantile states of rage and despair, he hovers upon the edge of a void which he tries to fill by stuffing something – anything! – into his mouth, and grabbing hold of any warm and available body that wanders by.

No-one sets out to become dependent, but dependence can creep up by stealth for, in addition to the physically addictive nature of many drugs, there is also a psychologically addictive aspect, due to the short-term nature of the symptom relief provided. As the initial effect wears off, the underlying problem returns, worsened through having been silenced again, as well as by the damage accumulated in the meantime to health, relationships or self-esteem. Responses become blurred and confidence begins to plummet – and the drink or the drug may seem all that there is left to rely on. The dose must then be upped to silence the pain again, setting up an addictive spiral which can end up becoming structured into the psyche in a more permanent way. The cycle of despair (*my problems are hopeless and no-one cares*) is fed, diverting energy away from engaging with the distress or anxiety in any sort of constructive way. A collapse into apathy and self-pity tends to follow, from which it is notoriously difficult to emerge.

Nevertheless, it is easy to see how the relationship with the bottle or the pill which is always there for you and reliably under control can – especially after loss, disappointment or a challenge too fearful to countenance – become preferred to relationships with people. Relationships which dangle before them the offer of yearned-for love and understanding, only to disappoint when followed through, may evoke unbearable anxieties about intimacy or the loss of selfhood that will follow merging with an uncaring other. By comparison, the temporary loss of self offered by drinking, for example, may be preferable because it offers the (illusory) comfort of control and non-dependence without emotional risk. When they eat the lotus, the sailors' feelings of responsibility to the wives and families waiting for them at home fade away, along with their unspoken anxieties about the voyage and homecoming which lie ahead. Everything dissolves in a pleasant haze.

Prozac Nation. Even gangsters rely on the little pills to get them through the day, like Joey Soprano, the mafia boss played by James Gandolfini in the TV series *The Sopranos*, who gets Prozac prescribed to him to soften the edges of his unusually bloody mid-life crisis: '*how many people have to die*', asks Joey's incredulous shrink, '*for the sake of your personal growth?*' Joey starts to get panic attacks, and his surges of violent rage alternate with fits of incoherent depression. Lacking Joey's opportunities for acting out, we are more likely to turn our latent rage inwards in attacks against the self, where it can calcify and deaden our inner worlds, killing off all spontaneous pleasure, all hope. Anti-depressant medications may, over the short term, have a useful role to play in the treatment of depression, but we should not overlook the correlation between today's spiralling rates of alcoholism and drug dependency (both prescription and recreational) and the descent into an ever harsher, more judgemental and more unremittingly competitive work ethos in all sectors of society.

The worse it gets, the more we need a drink or two when we get home, or the pills, just to keep going. Within the modern world, drug use is so widespread, so tolerated and normalized that the distinctions between recreational or therapeutic use and full-scale dependency have become blurred. Alcohol and cigarette consumption, the use of recreational drugs from marijuana to heroin, and of prescription drugs such as tranquillizers, sleeping pills and anti-depressants, not to mention disturbed or compulsive patterns of eating, sexual activity, shopping or gambling – it is probably almost impossible to overestimate how these habits subsidize the way we live. Imagining a world in which all these crutches suddenly vanished without warning, it is almost impossible to conceive how unsustainable much of modern life might immediately become, and how desperate.

The temporary soothing and blurring induced by habitual drug or alcohol use offers an attractive regression from a hard, cold, competitive and fundamentally disappointing world back to a warm, comforting and undemanding womb in which all the problems, responsibilities, disappointments and growing pains of life dissolve. The comfort and confidence bestowed by drinking, smoking, sniffing and popping may have a fatal attraction for those parts of us which are fearful and pessimistic about conflict, and which long for a retreat into an easy life. *Let us alone* sing Tennyson's Lotus-eaters. Given the anxieties, stress and lonelinesses which sometimes beset us as we reach mid life, and the previously latent vulnerabilities which they may trigger, these desert sands can start to look like a good place to stick a weary or pain-filled head into, at least for a while.

RETREATING FROM CONFLICT: STRESS-RELATED ILLNESSES

Lost nights cradling the whisky bottle, and the sort of obsessive anxieties to which Monica had become prey, are signs that the mid-life crisis is knocking at the door – but still being denied – and so are stress-related illnesses. As we approach mid life we may become inexplicably vulnerable to a plague of stress-related illnesses and discomforts ranging from the trivial to the immobilizing – stress may be a contributory factor in back and shoulder pain, irritable bowel syndrome and digestive problems, migraine, skin irritations such as psoriasis and eczema, cystitis and other genito-urinary problems, asthma and chronic fatigue, to name only some.

Bodily ageing, which itself diminishes our ability to cope with both environmental stress and physical ailments, is a reality as we move into our forties. We are confronted on a daily basis with the ineluctable realities of living within a body which neither looks, performs nor feels as it used to, but how we respond to this reality is another matter. It is ironic that anxieties about change, especially the inevitable changes connected with ageing, may themselves induce stress-related illnesses and problems which can make things seem much worse than they would otherwise. As well as the physical debilitation they cause, stress-related illnesses can sap energy and confidence, locking the sufferer into spiralling feelings of despair and powerlessness, not to mention time-consuming and ultimately futile searches for external remedies and solutions.

The problem of TATT (tired all the time) is the second commonest presenting symptom reported by GPs. At mid life it may signify the unacknowledged presence of simultaneous boredom and exhaustion, and the pernicious cocktail of resentment and anxiety which fuels it. For men, anxieties about both illness and death seem particularly prevalent as they get older, perhaps reflecting men's relatively greater need to demonstrate capability, potency and non-dependence. Men are also notoriously far more likely to suffer, if not in silence, at least without actively seeking help. The man who is gripped by secret terror that every twinge of indigestion signifies a heart attack or every unexplained lump the advent of cancer, often would rather walk through fire than go to his GP for a check-up. Behind such dramatized anxieties may lurk a creeping but inadmissible awareness of the reality of how the body is beginning to age and to slow down. Anxieties about loss of sexual potency may be mentally associated with more general fears about dysfunction and death, and these can become magnified and more difficult to disentangle when men are reluctant or inarticulate about expressing vulnerabilities verbally. 'Suddenly he knew that denial was great' writes Martin Amis in another novel. 'Denial was so great. Denial was the best thing. Denial was even better than *smoking*.'[2]

Some women may have underlying anxieties about not being needed in the same way by their families any longer. Others, like

---

[2] Amis, M., *The Information*, Flamingo (1996).

Monica, may have to negotiate a final coming to terms with childlessness. Women may also fear the loss of sexual desirability and fertility, and the early symptoms of the menopause may be a further complicating factor (see Appendix). Women of Monica's generation live in a world in which the opportunities open to them are unimaginably different from those open to their mothers. Yet even though women over forty are by no means socially, culturally and economically invisible in the way they used to be, this contrast can in itself create a sense of dislocated identity and anxieties about entitlement, while fears about ageing in general can be unsettling in a way which can sometimes lead to physical illness – and the mixed blessing of opting out which illness entails.

Kate, the heroine of Doris Lessing's *The Summer Before the Dark*,[3] is a forty-year-old housewife who has spent most of her adult life holding a home together for her frequently absent doctor husband and her four children, who have now grown up. Due to a chance encounter with a friend of her husband's, and much to her own astonishment, she is suddenly transported to a temporary job as an official translator on the glamorous, moneyed international conference circuit. After the contract ends Kate is left feeling entirely uprooted. Realizing that all the ties which had previously held her are slipping away and that no-one is expecting her back at home, she wanders south for a holiday in the sun with a younger lover. But then a mysterious illness strikes. Kate flies back to London, checks into an anonymous hotel and succumbs to fever. When she emerges weeks later, emaciated and drawn, it is to find she has apparently become invisible to everyone, and she herself begins to see the world differently. Walking down the street, she looks into the faces of other forty-year-old women: 'Twenty years was the difference, that was all it needed to set these brave faces into caution and suspicion ... the faces and movements of most middle-aged women are those of prisoners or slaves.'

The curious state of limbo Kate spends lying in her London hotel looks, at one level, like the collapse of a woman who has

---

[3]   Penguin (1981).

bitten off more freedom than she can chew. But it is also a hiatus, a place of transition between the shedding of the identity of the old family-centred Kate who lived to please others, and the development of a newly regenerated sense of self. Kate emerges from her illness determined that her future after the summer will not be a continuation of her previous life. 'No, the future would continue from where she had left off as a child. For it was seeming to her more and more ... as if she were just coming round from a spell of madness that had lasted all the years since that point in early adolescence when her nature had demanded she must get herself a man ... all those years were now seeming like a betrayal of what she really was.'

Kate's illness gives her a period out of the world during which she disengages and finally begins to reorientate herself in a new way, following through a process initiated by the events of the summer. Illness, especially when it strikes without warning, can be frightening as well as debilitating. But stress-related illness also indicates that a serious reappraisal of lifestyle and values may be overdue. Particularly for working parents, and anyone whose work binds them to relentless schedules, such an illness may provide a crucial time out of ordinary life to reflect and take stock.

In stress-related illnesses, our bodies attempt to communicate with our minds in ways to which our minds may or may not be willing to listen. The membrane between the psyche (mind or soul) and soma (body) is a fluid and permeable one, which may become particularly weakened at mid life when changes at the physiological level, to do with altering hormonal balances and the processes of ageing, influence and interact with the struggles of the psyche to come to terms with a changing body and a changing role in life. Much of the activity of our minds is unconscious and this is nowhere more so than at the deepest interface between the psyche and the soma. When mid life looms, serious conflicts and anxieties which are bubbling under the surface but not yet being addressed can erupt as physical symptoms, such as lethargy, tiredness and paralysis, as well as the various manifestations of panic or anxiety attacks – dizziness, breathing problems, claustrophobia and hot flushes. Sometimes these may have organic or hormonal causes (hot flushes, for example, may indicate the onset of menopause), but they may also represent the denied distress of the mind written on the body.

The ways we use to describe ourselves – we have cold feet, someone is a pain in the neck, we are sick to the back teeth of something, our hearts are aching or breaking, or leaping for joy – demonstrate how naturally body experiences present themselves not just as metaphors of emotional experience, but as actual concrete counterparts of them. A woman whose husband has just died says: *I never realized before that your heart really could ache.* Emotional states do manifest through the body, a truth that no-one who has ever shed tears of distress or trembled with anger is in a position to deny.

When we succumb to stress-related and psychosomatic illness, our bodies become the theatres in which our unconscious conflicts are acted out according to scripts which go as far back as early childhood.[4] Sometimes, once the process of uncovering and working through the conflicts which underlie them gets under way, the symptoms may start to dissolve of their own accord. Yet the distress which becomes somatized in physical symptoms often does so precisely because of the mind's refusal to entertain it – perhaps because this distress signals the presence of something within us that may give the lie to some of our most fundamental fixed beliefs about ourselves. For this reason, and despite their prevalence in the modern world, the exploration of the underlying significance of physical symptoms of distress is a process which we may be disinclined to pursue to any depth.[5]

For – despite all the evidence – we still often dislike having to admit that something as fluid and amorphous as our emotional states can concretely and measurably affect our physical states; still less that unintegrated emotional experiences may sometimes make their presence felt as disturbances or dysfunctions in body processes. Perhaps our reluctance is due to the archaic, superstitious linking of illness to notions of punishment and wickedness which still exerts a residual but forceful power over our minds[6] and makes it hard for us to accept possible causal

---

[4] McDougall, J., *Theatres of the Body*, Free Association Books (1989).
[5] Showalter, E., *Hystories*, Picador (1997).
[6] Sontag, S., *Illness as a Metaphor*, Penguin (1983).

connections between the two levels, harder for us to read the urgent signalling of our own bodies.

The presence of pain within the body is not a moral judgement or a punishment. It is, however, functional. Whether it comes as a sudden searing pain caused by inadvertently lifting a red-hot poker from the fire or as the nagging chest cramps of the overworked executive, the presence of pain is an efficient survival mechanism, a warning that demands our attention and response. Pain and illness cannot be argued away or contradicted, but sometimes stress-related illnesses and symptoms may dissolve as mysteriously as they came into being once they have, so to speak, done their work, and have succeeded in focusing the sufferer's mind in a constructive way on the underlying problems whose existence they have been so assiduously and determinedly advertising.

In many families, children's physical aches and pains will elicit far more concerned responses from their parents than their mental distress or anxiety. Mental distress, while just as debilitating, may be ignored through lack of understanding or through the unwillingness to recognize it, in case it reflects badly on the home environment or parenting, or leads to unwelcome interference. In the adult world too, we see that physical injury and ill health, especially emergencies, are usually responded to with rapid, devoted and specialized help from skilled professionals. This is not the case in mental health care, where a lethal combination of personal shame, lethargy, stoicism and mistrust – as well as underfunding and the failure of resources in both private and public sectors – ensures that for many people a medical response (take this pill until the symptoms clear up) is the only show in town.

The message is a simple one: your physical problems will be responded to attentively and sympathetically, but your mental pains will be ignored – unless you frighten the horses. It is over a century since Freud first had the revolutionary idea of simply trying to listen to what the hysterically paralysed women who came to his consulting room for treatment for their nerves were telling him about their lives, their frustrations and their unhappinesses, but we can be as keen as ever to attribute the psychological distress of ourselves and others to moral weakness,

60

failure or malingering. In such a climate, the conversion of psychological turmoil to stress-related physical symptoms is likely to continue – however much our well-being, relationships and careers continue to suffer as a result of it.

The boundaries between mind and body may never be quite as firm as we like to imagine, but it is at times of great stress when the problems looming over us overwhelm our adult coping skills, that they are most likely to weaken or dissolve, and it is then that stress-related illnesses are most likely to appear. Sometimes our illnesses may be our techniques for psychological survival, the ropes to which we cling, the only means at our disposal with which we dare express ourselves and demand attention. For this reason they can be difficult to let go of, especially when the sufferer has no confidence in being taken seriously at other levels, or fears all change may be for the worse. In such circumstances, chronic illness may, like alcohol or drug dependency, provide an indefinitely prolonged refuge for the sufferer. But why the struggle? What are the sort of forces which can make change, even when it is most longed for, so difficult to countenance?

TRUE AND FALSE SELVES

The English psychoanalyst Donald Winnicott likened the gaze of a baby studying the face of his depressed or preoccupied mother to the way in which we look into the skies to study the weather and decide upon our plans for the day. Winnicott is reminding us that a mother initially *is* her baby's environment. Maternal withdrawal, tears or storms will be experienced by the dependent child as far more disastrous than any damage that the natural world has power to unleash on him.[7] Shakespeare makes a similar point when he reproaches his lover for having promised him such a beauteous day so as to fool him into travelling forth without his cloak, only to let her base clouds overtake him. The

---

[7]   Winnicott, D. W., 'Mirror role of mother and family in child development' (1967) in *Playing and Reality*, Penguin (1988).

loss suffered, the damage done, he goes on to say, is not easily dried off by the return of a sunny smile.[8]

Through our lives we learn to read the signs and to dress accordingly. Right from the beginning, our nascent selves are scanning first our mother's face and then the wider environment for clues as to who we are and who we can safely be allowed to be, without bringing the storm clouds down on our heads. Looking at a baby for the first time, the focused intensity with which the baby's eyes lock your own and scan your face can be astonishing. Even in the first week of life, babies show preference towards looking at a human face, focusing best at 8–10 inches (the distance of the adult's face when holding or feeding the baby). Similar preferences for the human voice are also apparent.[9]

The tendency to study the facial and verbal cues of others to provide an orientation in an uncertain world is universal and lifelong, revived most strongly at moments of intense love – or danger. It has its roots in the comparatively long period of helplessness and dependence of the human infant. The length of this period makes our survival as humans contingent upon our ability to make sure the mothers who give birth to us do not amble off and forget all about us as soon as we are weaned, as most non-human mothers do. We require our mothers, and fathers, to remain attentive for far longer, tied by that emotional attachment and investment which we will in due course learn to call love.[10]

To become loved, to be accepted into human society and endowed with status – in other words, to make it – is our first strategy. We long to be loved unconditionally, but on the whole we may find that our ability to bind others to us may depend upon how well we can learn to produce images of ourselves that they will find lovable or impressive. So all through our lives we organize our information and develop beliefs about the sort of people we will have to be to elicit acceptance and approval, and we modify our behaviour accordingly.

---

[8] Sonnet 34.
[9] Wright, K., *Vision and Separation*, Free Association Books (1991).
[10] Bowlby, J., *Attachment and Loss* Vol. 1, Hogarth Press (1969).

A mother whose face lights up with delight when her baby son stretches out a tiny grasping hand towards her is signalling to the child that she sees him as a significant and lovable being in his own right. The experience of being recognized in this way, if sufficiently reaffirmed through the coming years, will enable her son to develop a secure experience of himself and a trust in his environment and in his capacity to interrelate with it in a satisfying and authentic way. This in turn will form the basis of a capacity for creative enjoyment as well as the ability to form fulfilling relationships and to experience, in his own turn, love and empathic concern for others.

But the legend of Medusa, the enchantress whose terrifying gaze turned all who looked upon her to stone, tells the other side of the story. The image of being turned to stone is an apt one for the feeling of panicked paralysis (which can fossilize into a feeling of depressed deadness) that may overwhelm a child being stared at angrily or in an unresponsive, depressed manner by the parent who is the centre of the child's world. It is also an apt image of the way in which, as we grow, our capacity for spontaneity and creativity will atrophy within an alienated or hostile environment. This leads us to the notion of the false or caretaker self which develops to protect us when we are exposed to an environment in which there is a significant failure of empathic response.

Perhaps a parent, depressed or preoccupied like the mother Winnicott describes above, may stare blankly back when her baby gurgles at her, or she may turn her face away in irritation from the baby's exploratory grasping hand. She may not easily be able to respond to her child's spontaneous initiatives or needs and may substitute her own, demanding compliance with them as the price of retaining love. The false self develops in response to such demands, based on the need for compliance and the fear that disobedience will be catastrophically punished by the withdrawal of love: the real self carries on existing – as it must to some extent for all of us – as an isolate. Buried within, it is protected from the impingements of the external world which are managed or fended off by the caretaker (false) self. We may come to identify with the false selves we have so constructed, even learning to enjoy being impinged upon and coming to rely on the stimulation such impingements give – our constructed identity may become codeterminous with our ability to respond competently to them. They fill time, and in the end can structure a life.[11]

Living within false self structures, we may demonstrate ourselves to be highly competent and able, especially in work or relationships which require a high degree of adaptability rather than intuitive or creative thinking. False self ways of structuring and managing experience are essentially unconscious; yet central to the experience of false self living is a feeling of deadness and a tendency to see the possibility of spontaneous change as very threatening. There may also be dread of being left alone, as if to rest unstimulated and unshaped by others' demands might be a form of dying, and a sense sometimes of physical dislocation, as if one were watching oneself from a distance.

FRANCESCA: STRUTTING AND FRETTING UPON A STAGE

Francesca enters psychotherapy at the age of 36, having discovered she is pregnant for the first time. An attractive, exuberant yet somehow fragile-looking woman from a wealthy Southern European background, she talks rapidly and without pauses between her sentences. Francesca remembers a highly structured and supervised childhood. She looks slightly startled when she is asked whether she remembers daydreaming as a child. No, nor does she ever remember making a mess: she was always busy, she thinks, always being watched.

Francesca was born a year after the cot-death of her elder sister at the age of nine months. Was the way her mother structured her time for her a way of unconsciously trying to keep Francesca stimulated and thus alive? Might a child who was sometimes reflective or introspective have looked to an anxious mother too much like a child in danger of slipping away into death?

It seemed as if Francesca always had to be kept alive by other people's efforts, and by her own restless, butterfly energy. In her turn, Francesca developed an

[11] Winnicott, D. W., 'Ego distortion in terms of true and false self' (1960) in *The Maturational Processes and the Facilitating Environment*, Karnac (1990).

ability to make herself the centre of attention, apparently by transforming herself into whatever others wanted her to be and thereby ensuring their continuing devoted attention. Yet having initially felt charmed by Francesca and also rather protective towards her, I start to feel exhausted and somehow trapped by her. I notice that as she talks, my own breathing becomes shallower, and that I sometimes get the beginnings of a headache.

Francesca says that she did not really apply herself to anything very consistently at school, and shrugs – it had not seemed important. She dropped out of college and became a model, with some initial success. Since then she has dabbled at photography and various artistic projects, eventually marrying a successful photographer a number of years older than herself. Francesca seems at a loss to describe how she now spends her time, but she says that she is always busy, she and her husband have many friends. Francesca's friends are important to her, for she does not like to be alone. She says she has never felt unhappy but – frowning slightly – adds that sometimes she feels empty, and not very real. Is this not normal? She has vivid dreams, of which the following is typical:

> I discover I am an actor's understudy. I find I have to go on stage to perform in the central role. The whole production depends on me getting it right but the play is in a foreign language which I do not speak and no-one is there to help me.

Despite the fact that she has been married for some years and has been taking no precautions, she has nevertheless been astonished to find herself pregnant. Despite her lovely face, Francesca has literally almost no sense of herself as someone with an inside as well as an outside, let alone an inside capable of conceiving, sustaining and bearing such a complex creation as a baby. Francesca decides to keep the child – if she doesn't have a miscarriage, which she half-convinces herself that she will. But as she contemplates motherhood she feels uncomfortable and edgy. As the birth approaches she becomes absorbed with a flurry of activity in the externals of coming motherhood, decorating the baby's room and buying baby clothes. It is difficult for her to imagine her baby as a living being, difficult to trust the spontaneous unfolding of a relationship between herself and her child. When her baby is born, to what extent will Francesca be able to recover in this new relationship some of her own locked-away capacity for reflectiveness and also for genuine playfulness? To what extent will she replicate with her own baby the anxiously over-stimulating way of relating that she herself experienced as a child?

THE FALSE SELF AT MID LIFE:
COMPROMISE OR SELL OUT?

A woman unexpectedly catching the eye of an attractive, flirtatious stranger acts differently from how she behaves when she is tobogganing with her ten-year-old son, or visiting her grandmother in hospital. Which is her true self? It's a meaningless question; the richness of having a repertoire of different roles for different situations and classes of relationship is not at all the rigidity and deadness of false self organization. Adjustment or compromise is one thing, compliance another. Yet it is also true that we all accept a certain degree of inauthenticity in our relationships with others as part of the arrangement of civilized living, and we may find ourselves accepting more and more inauthenticity as we get older, for the sake of a quiet life – or so we tell ourselves.

Winnicott suggests that the test is whether we still go on doing so *when the issues at stake become crucial*. When this becomes the case, are the needs of the true self able to override the false or compliant self, or not?[12] When the demands of living through external achievement, through keeping up appearances or through compliance with the demands of others start to feel hollow, are we able to find ways of breaking out of our false self structures, or do we wilt listlessly and passively within them? Our anxiety or lack of faith in plausible alternatives may create a self-perpetuating cycle in which genuine impulses and experiences of self become more and more buried and ways of structuring living and relating ever more inauthentic and deadened. Then, truly, we are back where we started – in the land of the lotus-eaters.

The psychoanalyst Christopher Bollas has suggested that there may be some, perhaps many, people in society suffering from what he describes as normotic illness – an illness which by its very nature is unlikely to be diagnosed.[13] In the ordinary course of events, we all suffer conflicts between internal reality (or subjective desires and feelings) and external reality (in the form

---

[12] *Ibid.*

[13] Bollas, C., 'Normotic illness' in *The Shadow of the Object: Psychoanalysis of the Unthought Known*, Free Association Books (1987).

of the demands of the outside world). In psychotic illness such conflicts cannot be contained within the self – internal reality becomes overwhelming and external reality has to be obliterated and transformed into a delusional version of itself. In normotic illness, suggests Bollas, the opposite may happen. The need to comply with the demands of external reality may become for some people such a powerful and non-negotiable force that it will override and eventually annihilate a person's sense of their own subjectivity 'in favour of a self that is conceived as a material object among other man-made products in the object world'. This drive to be normal, as Bollas describes it, is reinforced by prevailing economic and social conditions which encourage us to see ourselves first and foremost, or exclusively, as worker – producers and consumers. The normotic personality will live consistently in this way to the exclusion of all other possibilities, Bollas suggests, in a world of clichéd and prepackaged experience.

We become normotic when we give up, finally, on our own subjectivity. When our sense of survival depends to a lesser or greater degree upon false self structures, the possibility of the sort of change which happens from within may be impossible or alarming to conceive of. We may not locate this fear of ours within ourselves, but instead connect it to imagined reprisals from the actual external world. Other people may be experienced as quite brutally punitive and prescriptive in their determination to keep the status quo in place. Today's lands of the Lotus-eaters may be the executive housing estates, the corporate headquarters, the clipped and pesticided landscapes and the suburban shopping malls of middle America or England, peopled by the fierce corporate wives and the mild-eyed, melancholy corporate husbands of modern suburbia, lulled by gin, Prozac and shopping – the lands where all things always seem the same. *The Stepford Wives* and two more recent films *Pleasantville* and *The Truman Show*, are films set in these lands. Each in its own way satirically exposes their shadow side: a ruthless intent that will not stop at murder to keep the pleasant surfaces of suburbia undisturbed.

The Stepford Wives is Bryan Forbes' 1975 film adaptation of a John Updike novella. A couple arrive in a picturesque New

England town, but the extent of the conformity they encounter there begins to drive them apart. The husband is drawn into the local community while the wife becomes suspicious. She eventually finds out that the men of Stepford have murdered all their wives and replaced their insides with smiling complaisant robots. Eventually the wife, too, succumbs to the same fate, doomed to patrolling Stepford's supermarkets, endlessly murmuring '*have a nice day ... you must give me that recipe ...*'

The camera sees Stepford as a land where the values of conformity and materialism reign undisturbed, and where any stirrings towards rebellion, emotionality or imagination will be smoothly and efficiently suppressed in the service of profitability and unruffled peace of mind; and what the camera sees is the reassurance which our own eyes, too, so often want to see. We are all, the film suggests, complicit. In Gary Ross' 1998 film *Pleasantville*, we initially see the black, white and greyness of the town (*no coloureds allowed*!) through the TV screen as a gently reassuring 1950s sitcom. But the pleasantness of Pleasantville is protected by a cohort of middle-aged men who, once their values are threatened, will stop at nothing to maintain the status quo – when colour and complexity begin to seep into the town, before our eyes they become transformed into a bunch of fascist thugs, mobilizing in a *Kristallnacht* of burning books and breaking glass.

Our own implied complicity in structures which promote false self living is even more powerfully suggested in Peter Weir's film, also of 1998, *The Truman Show*. The life of Truman Burbank (played by Jim Carrey) has apparently unfolded within a pleasantly middle-class, if somewhat self-referential, small American community. But in fact and unknown to Truman, it is all taking place in a giant TV studio under a huge artificial sky-like dome. The family and friends Truman has known since childhood are all in fact paid actors, directed through invisible headsets from a central monitor and control centre. Truman's entire life is a TV show (*The Truman Show*) beamed out 24 hours a day to America and the world.

Francesca felt a sort of inchoate unease from time to time, and dreamt of being an actor in a play in which everyone knows the script but her. Truman, too, feels something is wrong, and he can't place it either. Everyone in town, actors all, smilingly shakes their head in denial at his increasingly urgent interrogations. Truman Burbank, like Odysseus in the land of the Lotus-eaters, is ultimately repelled by this world of artifice and self-infantilization in which he lives, sickened by its easy comforts and its facile pseudo-intimacies. Like Odysseus he finally turns his back on it, throwing himself upon the cold and uncertain mercies of the sea. On the journey which lies ahead of them there may be more obviously frightening confrontations, but perhaps none so temptingly corrupt.

Part Three

CONFLICTS

5

Work

No-one was cheered and nothing was discussed;
Column by column in a cloud of dust
They marched away enduring a belief
Whose logic brought them, somewhere else, to grief.

From 'The Shield of Achilles' by W. H. Auden

In Philip Kaufman's 1983 film *The Right Stuff* there is a scene in which the test pilot Chuck Yeager (played by Sam Shepard) drives to the base where he works, strolls into the hangar where a newly delivered state-of-the-art jet plane sits waiting, and without authorization climbs up into the cockpit and taxies the plane out along the runway. The laconic gum-chewing Yeager – a war hero who does not have the right paper qualifications nor, it seems, the right attitude – has been passed over by NASA in their search for the men who will be trained as America's first astronauts.

Ignoring ground control's increasingly disconcerted radio interrogations, Yeager takes off and flies the plane right up through the clouds. Then he lifts its nose into an almost vertical trajectory, flicks the switches and drives the powerful engine up towards the outer reaches of the atmosphere, coaxing it, urging it softly ... The needles on the dials start to revolve wildly, the plane lurches and jolts and then suddenly he's out in dark space, floating, enclosed by a canopy of stars. The camera closes in on Yeager's face, bathed in sweat and wonder, then tensing. As he wrestles with the controls, the plane starts to fall backwards, staggers, swoops and veers out of control in a wild corkscrew spin. Yeager loses consciousness, then revives enough to eject in flames from the plane as it somersaults towards the ground. The camera cuts to the rescue vehicle moving out through the desert haze towards the smouldering, silent ruin of the plane. Then one of the men points to something moving in the wreckage, and a blackened figure walks slowly out to meet them.

Yeager walks from the wreckage of his plane, but the real-life Chuck Yeager (*The Right Stuff* is a dramatized account of an essentially true story, from Tom Wolfe's book of the same name) never got to fly in space again. His uncompromising courage and initiative were not the right stuff at all as far as NASA were concerned: Yeager did not have the right profile to become one of the new astronauts being created for its new space programme, on the back of a bandwagon of showbiz razzamatazz. To capture America's imagination and keep public opinion – and funding – on NASA's side, the astronauts had to be presented as heroes, yet were required to do little but sit in a pod, flick switches and smile to order. (At one stage chimpanzees were assessed as being equally dexterous and more obedient than the men, and trained alongside them, but their smiles proved less winning and they were dropped.) One of the things the film suggests is that to have what it takes – the right stuff – to reach for the stars in the modern corporate world may be to fail as a man and as a human being. It also suggests something that may start to become apparent for the first time at mid life: that the relationship between career success on the one hand and personal worth and achievement on the other may be more tenuous and accidental than we might previously have imagined.

CORPORATE VALUES

To an extent never known before in history, the work we're paid to do for others has come to define our sense of identity. Our relationship to it is likely to have a central place in our negotiation of mid-life changes: it's common for people reaching mid life to discover that they are at a watershed in their careers. By the time the late thirties and forties are reached, some have already spent decades working long hours in the same high-pressure career and are beginning to feel that their work has been allowed to over-define their identity at an unacceptably high cost in stress and exhaustion. Others are struggling to come to terms with disillusionment or bitterness occasioned by redundancy or failing to get an expected promotion, while others still – thinking about changing horses in mid stream, or returning to work after raising a family and wanting to pursue previously unfulfilled ambitions before it is too late – are weighing up their options accordingly.

Whatever our personal circumstances as we reach mid life, the situation is complicated by the rapidly changing nature of work itself. The changes in working conditions over the last thirty years have been massive, and are still accelerating. The pace of innovation means that new technologies and programmes are constantly being introduced only to become obsolete and superseded within a year or two, along with the expertise that sustained them. With the deregulation of markets, organizations in both private and public sectors are endlessly restructured and rationalized, while pressures on their workforces to meet deadlines and targets become ever more punitive, and working hours lengthen as insecurities increase. These changes affect the entire workforce, but they may affect people in the mid-life period – traditionally, the time of greatest investment in the working life – hardest.

Neither charged up by the adrenaline-fired ambition of early adulthood nor consoled by the prospect of imminent retirement, people reaching mid life tend to work the longest hours and bear the heaviest burdens, frequently in managerial or professional positions which carry great responsibilities for others. Modern working conditions can be bewildering, even toxic, and yet the changing structures of how we work are also full of possibilities. Work matters, not just for the material security it provides but because of the sense of identity, continuity and meaning it endows us with, and the opportunities it provides for effective and significant self-expression. It is a fundamental human need to engage in goal-directed activity that is both meaningful to ourselves and valued by others: work that is well-channelled and congruent with our deepest sense of identity – and whose demands are kept in proportion to other areas of life – does not lead to burn-out, apathy or cynicism. At its best, work has the potential to enrich our lives, and our relationships with others and with the larger community. The mid-life period is when our capacity for meaningful work comes into its full maturity and potential for fulfilment – sometimes precipitated by unexpected changes and developments.

Throughout history up until the present moment, most people's lives had to be fitted around the edges of their work, if they were to survive. Today – for the first time ever – we have the expertise and resources to tailor work to suit our lives instead. Some of us are already doing so; probably, many more could. The problems that we face in turning round our attitudes to work at mid life are multifaceted, but there are three central ones which appear over and over in our working lives, and these must be faced if the foundations for fulfilment in the second half of a working career are to be secured. The first is to find creative ways of handling the competitiveness endemic in modern work culture, which is youth-biased and so militates against developing work values more orientated towards maturing needs and values. The second is to address over-investment in work – both in terms of the time we put into work and the expectations we consequently have of it; and the third is to rediscover work as personally meaningful.

Competing to Survive

The Greek poet Hesiod argued that there are two forms of strife. Bad strife, he said, leads to war and destruction, but good strife leads to competition and drives up standards. In modern deregulated markets, the aggression which once sent men to their deaths in pitched battle is now channelled more profitably into the competitiveness which is the driving force both between and within companies. Employee is nevertheless still pitted against employee, and for the modern corporate warlord as much as his predecessor, winning the battle counts for more than the amount of incidental human wastage along the way. Restless and ceaseless restructuring, downsizing and rationalization make organizations – from the perspective of the boardroom – fitter, leaner and meaner. But these changes also mean that the market uncertainties which used to be mediated within companies themselves are now passed down to be absorbed by the individuals who work for them.

A deputy head teacher working in an inner-city school struggling in the lower reaches of the league tables spends more and more time compiling forms and reports, and this eats into the time previously available for building up personal relationships with the deprived and disturbed children in his class. His head teacher collapsed under the pressure of an upcoming Ofsted inspection and is off sick, and he has to take up the slack. The teacher feels nobody values the work he does and the results he achieves against all odds. Unsupported and unmanaged, he gets noticed only when something goes wrong.

A solicitor has to complete a daily charging sheet in which every ten-minute segment of her day must be charged to a client. She is expected to stay in the office until at least seven o'clock every evening, and knows that her partnership prospects depend upon the amount of new client work she brings in, from contacts she is expected to make during after-hours socializing. She has lost all the idealism which drew her into law. Her clients are no longer individuals with problems whom she wants to help, just economic units to be processed so she can meet her targets.

A site foreman has been put in charge of a prestigious new building contract. To win the contract by undercutting the opposition, his company had to put in a bid that his managers knew will be virtually impossible to bring in on time and under cost, even given the fourteen-hour days he and his men are already working. But if they fail to do so, the company will face a severe financial penalty and may go bust.

Downsizing (the economic doctrine of our age which affects the conditions most of us work in either directly or indirectly) is the management strategy of reducing fixed costs by paring employees down to a core of essential managers who are paid more to deliver more, farming out extra work as and when needed to contract workers and thereby increasing output while reducing costs.[1] The idea is that downsized companies, freed from having to maintain unwieldy and costly infrastructures, end up with more resources and greater flexibility for delivering their services. Paring down increases competitiveness and, in theory at least, sponsors efficiency. And for those who can stand the heat – the relentless, single-minded pace and the demand for constant availability and unflagging achievement, often at the cost of family and private life – the financial rewards for succeeding in a competitive downsized environment are immense.

But many – like the deputy head, the solicitor and the site foreman described above – do not find this sort of pressure conducive to giving their best. Work pressures that are exhilarating in the twenties and satisfying but exhausting by the thirties, become simply exhausting by the forties. A weary cynicism takes hold, as expressed by this manager in his forties: 'Employers ... expect more from less. The bottom line is that you are expected to find ways of absorbing greater demands, satisfying ever moving targets and to be grateful for your employment ... whilst your employer will ditch you if it feels under threat, or if the numbers demand it.' Another manager, also in his forties, echoes this view: 'Despite publicity ... about people being an organisation's most valuable asset – I believe that employees at all levels are treated as disposable commodities and not as human beings ...'[2]

Sooner or later, the crunch may come. The single-minded high-energy devotion that modern organizations demand of their key employees suits younger workers better than mature ones, and the average age at which senior managers are made redundant has decreased in the last few years from 48 to 46. Many who become unexpectedly jobless in their 40s – at whatever level – may remain so; the number of over-50s in work has dropped by 25 per cent since 1979,[3] and around a third of men over the age of 55 today have been made redundant, or have taken early retirement. A quarter of all supervisory positions

---

[1] Handy, C., *The Empty Raincoat*, Hutchinson (1994).
[2] Quoted in *Time to Choose*, a *Management Today*/Ceridian Survey, (2000).
[3] Report by management consultancy Sanders & Sanders, quoted in the *Independent* (24 March 2000).

in UK industry have been axed since 1987,[4] creating a bottleneck through which fewer will pass as they become more senior. Phil, a former bank manager interviewed on Anthony Clare's *Men in Crisis* radio series described an industry in turmoil, with constant restructuring and a workforce functioning under conditions of ever-accelerating demands for performance in an insecure and sometimes hostile environment. For Phil, redundancy was 'something I saw coming. You were just glad to survive each year ... Eventually it did catch up with me. At the time, it almost came as a relief ...'[5]

This relentless competitiveness is a system of values based on the supreme priority of the product and the need to deliver the most results for the lowest costs. But the needs of those who work and invest so much of their personal resources in their organizations' achievements are not so clear-cut. The human factors which are ignored in the service of enhanced competitiveness are likewise repressed by individuals who want to succeed in this environment – only to return as the familiar litany of stress symptoms: irritability, inability to concentrate, broken sleep and loss of appetite, addiction, depression and psychosomatic illness. Ironically, these costs may in the long run have to be borne by companies anyway. The 1988 HMSO report *Mental Health at Work* claimed that up to 40 per cent of employee absenteeism can be attributed to mental or emotional problems either originating in, or exacerbated by, conditions of work. Stress is now recognized as the second greatest cause of occupational ill health (after muscular and skeletal problems), and according to the International Stress Management Association some 80 million working days are lost through stress each year in the UK, at a total yearly cost to our economy of £11 billion. But unlike companies, an individual cannot write off a stress breakdown as a business expense.

We have not – yet – reached the situation in the United States, where murder is the second most frequent cause of work-related

---

4   *Cannon and Taylor Working Party Reports*, Institute of Management (1994) and *Long Term Employment Strategies*, Institute of Management (1995).
5   BBC Radio 4 (2000).

deaths, but the accumulation of anxiety, mistrust, misery and rage in the modern workplace suggests that we may be heading that way. The unquestioned mantra of our age is that greater prosperity brings greater contentment. But the great consensus of both statistical and anecdotal evidence suggests that this is only true until a certain degree of material wealth is reached. As income rises, a diminishing utility of returns sets in – after a certain point, increasing productivity seems to increase general well-being scarcely at all, while its side effects of stress, insecurity, pollution and the disintegration of family life are damaging to all of us.[6] Competitive environments create their own sense of urgency, purpose and achievement which can be addictive, but they also generate much essentially meaningless work – the report or tender which someone has stayed up all night to produce may be tossed into a bin by someone else the next day with barely a second glance. Much competitive activity turns out in the end to be informed less by the drive towards substantial achievement than by the need to gain or consolidate a precarious place in the hierarchy by impressing others.

And great enterprise, even when real achievements are at stake, has hidden costs. In *The Right Stuff*, the breathtaking beauty of the occasional moments in the skies when the pilots' planes tunnel the clouds at the speed of sound is placed in counterpoint to the dealings and manipulations in the smoke-filled rooms where the real power resides. Competition takes place at ever more rarefied levels, between the test pilots to break the sound barrier, between the astronauts to become the first American in orbit, and between the USSR and the USA to colonize space. But it is revealed as a deadly form of motivation: the wives who wait on the ground know that the test pilots have a one in four chance of not coming back from each mission, yet their husbands blind themselves to the risk so they can keep flying. Today, at the earth-bound levels of competition-orientated professional and managerial work, issues to do with quality of life and health must be weighed in balance by those

---

[6] See James, O., *Britain on the Couch*, Arrow (1998), or Etzioni, A., *The Spirit of Community*, HarperCollins (1995) for an American perspective.

who are passing beyond the imperviousness of youth towards an awareness of the finite nature of life, and of their own mortality.

In 1959 American medical researchers identified the Type A personality as 'a characteristic action–emotion complex which is exhibited by [those] who are engaged in a relatively chronic struggle to obtain an unlimited number of poorly defined things from their environment in the shortest period of time, and if necessary, against the opposing effects of other[s] in the same environment'.[7] The capacity to cope at pressure with unlimited demands is at a premium in modern business life – developing a Type A personality may make you destined for success in the higher echelons of corporate management, but Friedman and Rosenman's research suggested it may also put you on the fast track to coronary disease. In 1975, the American Heart Association further discovered that Type A personalities were five times more likely to suffer a second heart attack than others,[8] while the *Guardian* recently cited a report which found that the majority of all heart attacks happen between eight and nine o'clock on Monday mornings. The constant stimulation of adrenaline in the fight–flight hormonal system elicited by the pressures of an ambitious working life suits a younger body better than one that is starting to feel its age. We are facing an epidemic of work-induced cardiovascular disease, migraine and irritable bowel problems, the effects of which are only temporarily anaesthetized and kept under control by the alcohol, painkillers, anti-depressants and tranquillizers upon which a sizeable sector of our workforce relies to get through each day.

One of the reasons that companies favour hiring younger workers may be due to a subliminal awareness on everyone's part that after around the age of forty, older workers – having begun to work out for themselves that there may be more to life than wearing yourself out achieving someone else's goals – become

---

7   Friedman, M. and Rosenman, R., 'Association of specific behavior pattern with blood and cardiovascular findings' (1959), *Journal of the American Medical Association*.

8   Rosenman R., *et al.*, 'Coronary heart disease: final follow-up experience of eight and one-half years' (1975) quoted in McDougall, J., *Theatres of the Body*, Free Association Books (1989).

less amenable to the extreme demands of the modern workplace; younger workers, more pliable and eager to prove themselves, are less likely to think this way. A competitive world is a specialized, single-minded world. Single-mindedness in pursuit of objectives – without ever pausing to reflect from a wider perspective on the nature of those objectives – can become self-defeating. Over-specialization may make us successful as individual achievers but is not necessarily in our wider interest as human beings living within an ecology of complex interdependent relationships, with an emotional and spiritual dimension to our lives as well as a materialistic goal-orientated one. As we get older, this existential or spiritual dimension to living begins to make a more determined claim to be included within our frame of values and the way we live our lives. It is under the shadow of our developing, though sometimes unconscious, awareness of the finite nature of individual existence that a life based solely on materialistic competitive striving can begin to seem futile.

Women and competition

Attitudes to competitiveness may change with age; they also tend to vary according to gender. Some women are fiercely competitive and some men are indifferent to status, and each of these traits commingles in each of us, yet there is some evidence from studies of gender differences that single-minded specialization is a more masculine bias.[9] Women, for example, are generally more willing than men to accept lower earnings or status at work in return for other benefits such as fewer or more flexible hours, a supportive work culture or the chance to do interesting work orientated towards their personal development. Men more consistently prioritize earning more – even when they already have more than they can realistically spend or more than they have time to enjoy, suggesting the motivation is less

---

[9] See Moir, A. and B., *Why Men Don't Iron: The New Reality of Gender Differences*, HarperCollins (1999), and Tannen, D., *You Just Don't Understand*, Virago (1992).

acquisitiveness than the enhanced status that a higher salary confers.[10] Some of the crushingly competitive conditions of today's corporate world may be tailored as much to meet the psychological need to compete of younger men (or of men who are determined to go on thinking of themselves as young), as they are necessary to sponsor optimum economic growth.

Women today may work on a level playing field with men, but still have to play by the rules which were in place before they arrived. For women who are now reaching mid life and either reassessing their long-term careers or planning to return to more demanding work after bringing up a family, this may mean that success in a chosen field is conditional upon the acceptance of entrenched macho values, aggressive point-scoring and endlessly protracted working hours, conditions which may not in fact suit most women – or indeed, many men – that well. 'The notion of equality takes the male status quo as the condition to which women aspire. Men live and work in a frighteningly unfree and tyrannical society', writes Germaine Greer in *The Whole Woman*,[11] 'constructed upon the oppression of junior males by senior ones, on grooming of favoured males' succession at the expense of others, on confederacies and conspiracies, on initiation and blooding rituals, on shared antisocial behaviour, on ostracisms and punishments, practical jokes, clannishness and discrimination ... As these masculine realms have been constructed to withstand outsiders and have grown stronger and more effective in doing so over many generations, they are virtually incapable of transformation. Aspirants to rank in such groups have to learn the ropes and then bounce their rivals on to them.' Women who want to have an impact and rise in their chosen field may have to bite the bullet and join in.

Elizabeth Perle McKenna was such a woman, who took on the corporate world on its own terms and succeeded. A high-flying American publishing executive who followed a one-track path for twenty years, her career was 'sacred ground and synonymous with

---

[10] See Franks, S., *Having None of It*, Granta (1999). Franks amasses evidence to show how gender approaches to work differ and how current conditions play to women's disadvantage.

[11] Transworld (1999).

who I was ... throughout my twenties I concentrated on work. I worked at work, flirted at work. Occasionally, I dated at work. I loved work ...' But then in her thirties McKenna began to suffer from what she described as indigestion in the soul. 'My self esteem was in the toilet from trying to be everything to everyone and I ending up being nothing to myself.' By her late thirties, faced with (as she saw it then) a choice between an all or nothing work life, she had reached a point where she had to walk out.

Out of her experiences came a book *When Work Doesn't Work Anymore*,[12] in which McKenna lists and analyses the rules she sees governing the modern working world. They include: that work always comes first, above family; that long hours are a requirement and if you're not seen to be putting them in, you'll be replaced; that there is only one career, one path, one aim – to get as close to the top as you can. McKenna considers the dangers for women – and also, by implication, for many men – of allowing themselves to become over-defined by their work identity and their earning potential, a way of life which may bring external success at the cost of silent internal misery or emptiness. She also criticizes feminism itself for having been too willing to take as its own aims those of the dominant class – of male overachievers with low self-esteem who use work primarily to exercise their fixation about who'll be top dog of the pack. More than half of the successful women she interviewed for her book felt dissatisfied with their work, though more than two-thirds of these were doing nothing about it: because they did not know what else to do, because they said they could not afford to change, or because they felt they had invested too much in their careers to question them.

Like immigrants arriving in a foreign country, the current generation of women has worked hard to learn the language and customs of the working world and to gain acceptance by its (male) natives. McKenna suggests that this may not last. 'There is a clear generational reason why women are beginning to take a more jaundiced view of conventional success: America's pioneer fast-track businesswomen are hitting midlife and their own

---

[12] Simon and Schuster (1997).

version of the famed mid life crisis ... meaningful work and a balanced home life are deep rooted and genuine human needs. Like any needs they can be ignored or repressed for years at a time, but sooner or later, they're going to assert themselves.' It takes maturity and self-confidence to stand back and critically assess a system that you have relied on to develop your confidence in the first place and to demand something different.

Even women reaching mid life who have been high-achievers may not find it easy to turn the system around, to learn to work it for their own benefit rather than being worked over by it. Women who have more limited track records – because they are returning to work at mid life after raising families, or for whatever other reason – are likely to feel even more disadvantaged. But more new businesses are being started today than ever before and a majority of the ones that thrive are started by women, often offering more flexible and sympathetic working conditions than traditional male-dominated companies. Women generally have had less of their identities invested in the current status quo than men, and this may make them more willing to break free, to ask different questions and to innovate – and in a changing world such willingness can be valuable.

Innovative information-based industries also tend to value collaborative skills alongside competitive ones, and to value qualities such as empathy, emotional intelligence, the ability to think laterally and the capacity for creative teamwork as much as traditionally masculine skills in manufacturing and construction, aggressive risk-taking and a preference for hierarchical ways of relating. The unemployment rate for women in their fifties is strikingly lower than it is for men – although at the other end of the power scale, it is still, of course, older men who hold the reins and create the working conditions under which most of us live. It remains to be seen whether this will start to change over the next generation.

Men and competition

The fast, competitive pace of modern working life may suit younger men better than older ones, but older men are more likely to continue working – and suffering – stoically in it, for several reasons. Men who have been working in the same career for all their adult lives may see no meaningful or dignified alternative to doing so. They may be afraid of acknowledging even to themselves that their values and needs are changing as they get older, in a culture which seems to value only youth. Men may also fear the loss of respect of other men who (however much they themselves are secretly suffering) may only be able to see questioning or dropping out of the system as failing, and consequently find the thought of breaking ranks to articulate their dissatisfactions very difficult.

At the root of many of these difficulties lies the issue of the fragility of male identity itself and its need for the external reinforcement which a high work status provides. This is a need which starts to declare itself from the earliest age. Both boys and girls start life connected physically and emotionally to their mothers, a female identification which is available for girls to build upon as they mature. The growing boy, however, begins to discover his masculinity as something *other* – something which (unlike female identity) cannot be taken for granted and must be constructed through personal effort. To reinforce it he must turn decisively away from the world of his mother's body and from the archaic world of comfort and emotional security which it represents, which is also the foundation of his own being and his earliest experiences. This turning away may ultimately extend to the repudiation of the whole of the emotional dimension and interconnectedness of life.

Nobody minds much if little girls want to wear jeans and play with toy cars. But a little boy who wants to wear a pretty dress or to copy his mother's caregiving by playing with a doll will arouse anxious consternation among adults and suffer rejection and hostility from his own peers. Once, however, he conforms to what is required of him and puts away girlish things, he is likely to find himself well rewarded. When boys assume their ordained masculine identity, most cultures – as if by way of a bribe or a compensation for what has been so difficult and painful, and in some ways so contrary to nature to relinquish – distinguish male difference with an automatic entitlement to enhanced status, power, privilege and deference. The anthropologist Margaret

Mead described how, worldwide, men's identity is defined and exalted primarily through the status of their work. The exact nature of the work does not matter – in some societies, fetching water or obstetrics will be the job of men, in others, the job of women – but the point is that whatever men do is recognized by society as more prestigious and important.[13] The prevalence of this pomp and circumstance which surrounds the efforts of men suggests a certain over-compensation and an anxiety about the fragility of masculine identity. It also explains why a man who loses his work may feel so disorientated and anchorless, and why an unemployed man is far more likely to be at risk (of alcoholism, depression or suicide) than a woman in the same situation.

This identification between a man and his work – based upon the assertion and separation of the individual and the denial of interconnectedness, and reinforced as it is by assumed privilege – is a powerful one. But as they begin to get older, many men begin, at least unconsciously, to question the totality of the identification required, and to become aware of how much the notions of masculinity to which they have subscribed and which they enact through their work are in fact based on the repudiation and alienation of parts of their own selves. By the time men are in their forties, the proving of masculinity is likely (for all but the most insecure) to cease to be such an urgent issue; it begins to be superseded by broader questions concerning the meaning of life, the finite and transitory nature of most endeavour, and mortality itself. As men's bodies start to slow down and their values change, the real costs of permanent competitiveness may start to seem unattractive and questionable; a man's realization of the cost of his alienation from the potential emotional, sensual, aesthetic and spiritual dimensions of his own life becomes a more urgent issue. For the mid-life executive living a life from which such considerations are banned, the pain of this alienation may only be able to find its expression somatically,

---

[13] *Male and Female: A Study of the Sexes in a Changing World*, Gollancz (1949).

through the coronary, respiratory, digestive and sleep disorders which, apparently inexplicably, start to dog his life.

Living in a competitive society

In the final count, both men and women may find that by mid life the once exhilarating struggle to get to the top has become exhausting and dispiriting. Competition encourages us to be restless and dissatisfied: the fear of failure keeps us motivated but also ensures we can never feel at ease with ourselves or truly content. The range of supposedly infinite opportunity which we are today led to believe is our birthright goads us in the cold light of mid-life self-assessment as we constantly measure ourselves against others' achievements – finding, like Gore Vidal, that every time we hear of the success of a friend, a little something inside us dies.

For if we have not visibly outshone our contemporaries, reached the pinnacle of a chosen profession or become media stars or dot com millionaires by our mid-thirties, who is there to blame but ourselves? The tendency to make comparisons upwards leads us to devalue our personal achievements and to become obsessed with relative failures, a tendency described by psychotherapist Peter Hildebrand as the Failed Nobel Prize Syndrome.[14] In fact, the nature of competition within hierarchies means that only a very few, by definition, can ever reach the top; the rest of us live, numbed by dissatisfaction and secret self-criticism, vexed by envy, in the gap between our imagined sense of entitlement and our actual lack of opportunity.

If competitiveness affects our attitudes to work, it also affects the closely related subjects of what we earn, and how we spend. The choices available to us in work are, inevitably, closely tied to the economics of our lives, and to our financial priorities. Much of what is earned in a consumer society goes to pay not for needs or even genuine wants to be fulfilled, but for those so-called positional goods and privileges which keep us ahead of our

---

[14] Hildebrand, P., *Beyond Mid-Life Crisis*, Sheldon Press (1995).

neighbours – as if to relieve the sense of inner numbness or depletion induced by work which itself has no aim other than that of beating others. It is a no-win situation, the most vicious of circles. Our restless, unfulfilled aspirations propel us not towards satisfaction but towards more work, more consumption, more comparisons. This needy, dissatisfied state of mind is most skilfully encouraged and exploited by a mass media which is itself almost entirely dependent for its own existence upon the advertising industry's ability to shift goods. The mission of business, as Galbraith observed, is now to create the wants it seeks to satisfy.[15]

Working is itself expensive too, full of hidden costs like commuting and child care, and longer hours mean everyone needs to pay more, for more conveniences and more services. Getting more stressed, we demand more elaborate recreations – from recreational shopping (*Because I'm worth it!*) to health club subscriptions, weekend breaks and long-haul holidays – just to help us unwind. And internal insecurities are exacerbated by our winner-takes-all economic structures. Overwhelmingly, the increases in wealth over the last 30 years have gone to the top 30 per cent of society, with the result that Britain is now more unequal than at any time since before World War II.[16] In the race to earn more and more, comparisons and competition keep raising the marker of how an acceptable living standard is defined, pushing up prices and making the need to succeed more urgent than ever – another version of the vicious circle which keeps the mid-life worker's nose firmly to the salary grindstone.

At the same time, the fragmentation of families (partly due to the strain put on relationships by long working hours) and the stealthy dismantling of the welfare state deprive us of the safety net we may all need one day. We become anxious about crime, about pollution, about the fragility of our personal relationships, increasingly aware of our own vulnerabilities as our bodies start to age. And we end up feeling that, in the increasingly dangerous

---

[15] Galbraith, J. K., *The Affluent Society*, Houghton Mifflin (1984).
[16] *Households Below Average Income* (1994), a government report which also revealed that by the mid-1990s, 25 per cent of people were living on less than half the average income, compared to 9 per cent in 1979.

and insecure world in which we live, we can rely on nothing but our own efforts – and the money we manage to accumulate in the bank through our own efforts – to support us in sickness, disability and old age. Some of our anxieties, we may be aware, have more to do with fears of loneliness, isolation or ageing than with real financial need, but these factors seem more and more to be outside our control. On the other hand, we can always work harder. Money can understudy everything, however falteringly, and by mid life it may above all be these anxieties which are now binding us, more insidiously but also more joylessly, into forcing ourselves onwards to achieve more and more.

How has this state of affairs come about? Why – having already reached a plateau of widespread material well-being unequalled in history – are we allowing work to take up more and more of our time, and letting divisive competitiveness become ever more the primary defining – and distorting – dynamic in our relationships? There is a notion that this is inevitable – competitiveness is not just efficient but natural, *ergo* to be encouraged.[17] But such an assertion should be treated with caution, particularly given how well it supports the powerful vested interests of free-market capitalist economics.

The study of evolutionary psychiatry suggests that while external conditions have changed beyond all recognition in the last 300,000 years, the human mind has evolved very little. Today we are approaching information-age problems with a neolithic mindset, and to this lack of congruence many of our internal problems – and the social problems which beset modern society – can be traced.[18] But this does not mean that rampant competitiveness is the natural human state. The dawn of human society came as individuals began to recognize their mutual interests and interdependencies with others and to come together in relationships which contained and gave limited sanction to competitive and aggressive urges. Early group structures enshrined these interdependencies through reinfor-

---

[17] See Dawkins, R., *The Selfish Gene*, Oxford University Press (1976).
[18] See Stevens, A. and Price, J., *Evolutionary Psychiatry*, Routledge (1996).

cing and promoting relationships of attachment – between parents and children but also between couples and, more widely, between members of the tribe or community. As the survival of the group came to guarantee the well-being of its members, it became a priority to protect its cohesion both from external threat and from rifts due to aggressive competition between its members. Attachment relationships were prioritized and protected by behaviour codes, which over time began to develop into recognizable systems of morality and ethics, backed up by religious or spiritual authority – the very authority which today, throughout the Western world, is being tested and found lacking.

It is young males who, in the majority of societies, exhibit the most aggressive competitive urges, and it consequently tends to be a priority of the larger tribe or community to ensure that these are properly controlled and directed for the good of the community as a whole. Otherwise this aggressive energy, unmonitored and uncontained by an ethical consensus, is likely to run riot and end up threatening the cohesion and security of the group, and the physical and mental health of the individuals who depend upon it. This delicate balance – between competitiveness (promoting aggression and initiative) on the one hand, and attachment (promoting connection with others and concern for them) on the other – is today under threat in our affluent but often lonely society, through which competitive values rampage.

Prioritizing our emotional needs alongside our material ones draws us towards work which offers flexibility, family values and friendlier conditions, and there is today some evidence that skill shortages in areas of full employment are nudging innovative companies in this direction. Yet on the whole – in a society in which members of the New Labour cabinet were told to take their football strips away to a working weekend – the world of work is still being run largely in accordance with the values of the young male. The workforce, winnowed down by redundancy and early retirement, is getting younger and younger, at the same time as the population itself is getting older.

The enormity of top executives' salaries is often justified in terms of market forces. What this may mean in practice is that it is extremely difficult to find senior people who have the steady maturity and judgement required to steer a large company, yet who have not grown out of the status-orientated scheme of values that makes people willing to commit to the single-minded, rigid discipline and back-breaking, coronary-inducing hours that are required to stay top of the pile. As Gerry Robinson, former chief executive of the Granada group, put it: 'Very well-balanced, very well-rounded people rarely make it to the top ... in my experience [those who do] are trying to make up for something.'[19]

If it is internal insecurities which distort our lives – demanding the relentless and exhausting expenditure of energy, the accumulation of more and more income to compensate for an impoverished sense of self, and the fortification of an insecure gender identity by having to stay 'one of the boys' into one's forties and fifties – then it is through confronting and overcoming these insecurities that we create the conditions for a new source of internal energy to begin to arise. This energy may first come to awareness in an unfocused way as anxiety or frustration. But taken seriously and followed through, it can lead towards the creative integration of competitive dynamics within more humane, mature values. 'My attitude to work/home has changed quite dramatically on reaching age 50' says one manager. 'Things which were very important work wise are now not so, and conversely I now work to enjoy my family and holidays – that is, work is now a means to an end and not an end in itself.[20]

What takes courage – and skill – is to find a way to negotiate this reorientation positively, becoming able to leave behind destructive or outgrown aspects of a career while developing working structures which will be congruent with the ways in which one is changing within oneself. This brings us face to face with another related aspect of modern work: the degree to which working hours today encroach upon personal time – our time poverty in the midst of plenty.

---

[19] *In the Psychiatrist's Chair*, BBC Radio 4, 6 October 2000.
[20] *Management Today* /Ceridian Survey, *op. cit.*

Personal Over-Investment in Work

As Suzanne Franks remarks in *Having None of It*,[21] the old Marx brothers joke – that if work is so great why don't the rich do it – isn't very funny any more. Today, the more successful you are the longer hours you will probably be expected to work, and the seniority gained by reaching mid life tends to increase work demands inexorably. One of the most spectacularly mistaken prophecies of a few decades ago was that advances in labour-saving technology would by the third millennium be giving us far more leisure time, which we would use to become healthier, better educated and more relaxed. The technologies have delivered, but work itself just keeps on expanding to fit the time available.

Today's creeping culture of presenteeism requires long hours to be put in, and to be seen to be put in, as the price of being taken seriously at work, in a world where no job can be taken for granted any more; Britons today reportedly carry out around £23 billion worth of unpaid overtime for their employers each year.[22] Unnecessary rounds of meetings at which attendance is compulsory, unspoken competitions to be the last to leave the office, and the denial of any personal claims on one's life, are all part of this trend, in which increasing maturity is bound to lead us to participate less enthusiastically. Long hours spent peering at PC screens should imply productivity, but may just mean that the same tired thoughts are being robotically shuffled round and round the same tired minds. The ideology of presenteeism demands the kind of unquestioning, fervent devotion that used to be reserved for religion, but is fuelled by a culture of control, mistrust and suspicion.

---

[21] Granta (1999).

[22] September 2000 TUC employment poll, quoted in the *Independent on Sunday*, 17 September 2000.

Workforce surveys regularly report debilitating levels of stress and exhaustion at all levels of employment.[23] Pressure and overwork cause incivility, harassment and outbreaks of rage, which are damaging to the work environment, but also spill over to contaminate personal relationships and the fabric of society itself. Punishing work regimes encourage people to prioritize work above the needs of their families, their peace of mind, their health and even their need for sleep.[24] The engineer responsible for the faulty wiring which caused the 1988 Clapham rail crash, in which 39 people died, was revealed at the inquest to have been working a 60-hour week, without a day off in the previous 13 weeks. He was the father of a young child. The *National Child Development Study* reported in 1997 that fathers of children under 11 work on average 48 hours a week and 1 in 10 – like the Clapham engineer – work over 60 hours a week.

The 40 or 50-hour week has its roots in the mid-twentieth-century family structure comprising a wage or salary-earning dad and a housewife mum. But today's workers in their thirties and forties are far more likely to live alone (though perhaps with dependent children) or with a partner who works equally long hours, and rarely enjoy the luxury of such a domestic infrastructure to support their efforts. Housekeeping must be organized, elderly parents monitored and growing children provided for and looked after – a generational squeeze on both sides – on top of the rigours of a full working week. The importance of active parenthood is emphasized more than ever before – but always second to the demands of work, which are understood to be absolute. Families unravelling through neglect cease to be the havens of support which breadwinners expected as their right and reward a generation or two ago. And because staying late at the office may feel a lot less soul-destroying than

---

[23] *Taking the Strain*, an Institute of Management survey (2000) in which 81 per cent of managers admitted they experienced excessive tiredness and 71 per cent loss of temper, both stress-related. A September 2000 TUC poll revealed that 12 million employers believed their job made them more irritable and bad-tempered, and 4 million had suffered damage to their personal relationships (*Independent on Sunday*, 17 September 2000).

[24] *Management Today*/Ceridian Survey, *op. cit.*

going home alone to an empty bedsit or to a house of resentful semi-strangers and a sink of dirty dishes, it is easy to end up reinforcing the system, putting less and less into personal relationships and more and more into work.

In America – where two weeks' annual holiday is the norm and many demur at taking even that – the situation is even more extreme. In *The Overworked American*,[25] Juliet Schor describes how the average American today is working the equivalent of an extra month a year more than his or her equivalent fifty years ago and estimates that, on current trends, the average American will within twenty years be working a sixty-hour week. She suggests we need to re-examine the culture we have created which equates longer and longer working hours with success and in which making money always wins out over having time and a quality of life that money can't buy. In fact, it is not difficult to create a different sort of equation, to find a new way of making work work better for us. Schor calculates that advances in productivity and labour-saving devices mean that, were we to be satisfied with the prosperity and living standards of 1950s America (a standard of living still unimaginably high to most of the world today), none of us would have to work more than twenty hours per week, thereby echoing a proposal of Bertrand Russell seventy years ago: 'There should not be eight hours per day for some and zero for others, but four hours per day for all.'[26] Other calculations suggest that most of us could cut our income by twenty per cent (equivalent to one day's work a week), with little evident change in lifestyle.[27]

The implications of working a four-hour day or a three-day week – or working for six months each year and having six months off – are radical: 'Automation threatens to render possible the reversal of the relation between free time and working time: the possibility of working time becoming marginal and free time becoming full time' wrote Herbert Marcuse in *Eros and Civilisation*. 'The result would be a radical

---

[25] Basic Books (1991).
[26] Russell, B., *In Praise of Idleness and Other Essays*, Allen and Unwin (1935).
[27] McKenna, E. P., *When Work Doesn't Work Anymore*, Simon and Schuster (1997).

transvaluation of values and a mode of existence incompatible with the traditional culture. Advanced industrial society is in permanent mobilisation against this possibility.'[28] In *The End of Work*,[29] American economist Jeremy Rifkin describes how modern technology means that globally, far fewer jobs are now being created than those lost, and this process is continually accelerating. Labour, suggests Rifkin, has today only a limited commodity value – yet our political institutions, social conventions and economic relations are based on it. Today we have the chance to challenge and change this outdated ethos, distributing productivity gains more widely through the community and prioritizing the social market over the economic one. The choice, argues Rifkin, is stark: if we fail to implement such changes, we will end up in an unstable situation of global unemployment, in which the wealthy elite who control information retreat away from their social responsibilities into their rich ghettos, leaving a world ravaged by crime, depression and social breakdown for the rest of us to inhabit. But if we do begin to make the shift, it will take us towards a new liberty to pursue the sort of leisure and volunteer activities which lead to personal enrichment and social enhancement. Life beyond the marketplace is based on inclusiveness rather than fear, a social exchange founded in a personal sense of indebtedness and generosity towards others and an awareness of the interconnectedness of all life.

The benefits of reworking the time/money equation are obvious and tangible, and doing so may at a stroke do away with much of the stress, tension and exhaustion which blights the unnaturally extended working week. People working around twenty-five paid hours a week are consistently shown to have higher levels of personal well-being than either those who work over forty hours or those who do no paid work at all. This suggests that such hours may approach an optimum personal balance – despite the fact that we still rather disapprovingly call such arrangements *part*-time, as if they inevitably represent a

---

[28] Marcuse, H., *Eros and Civilisation*, Abacus (1972).
[29] Rifkin, J., *The End of Work*, Putnam (1995).

falling-short of an ideally ordained whole. On the whole, we get most out of what we put most into. A work-obsessed culture inevitably leads us to neglect our families and personal relationships, as well as our own health, personal development and other interests. The work environment greedily and gracelessly absorbs too many of our personal resources – our capacity for perceptiveness, foresight and intelligent reflection, our ability to relate to others productively, our skill at finding creative solutions and the energy and resolve to carry them through. Having given all we have to sorting out others' problems at work, we let our own build up at home because we are too tired to care and because our best has already been had, leaving only weariness and resentment.

Working long hours reinforces self-limiting identifications with working roles. Ignored and uncultivated, other aspects of the self begin to atrophy and we begin to lose faith in them – it's not surprising if society is dumbing down, when most of us are too exhausted to do much more when we get back from work than slump down in front of a game show and drink ourselves to sleep. Grimly, the two chief leisure activities of Wall Street bankers are today said to be jogging and masturbation.[30] Rebalancing the work–life ratio, on the other hand, releases the energy for the sort of creative and cultural involvements which take us down new paths and into new sorts of relationship and engagement with the world. The need to do this – which cannot be indefinitely postponed – becomes more urgent as we begin to grow older. The career ladder does not lead on endlessly to new sources of fulfilment, and absorption in paid work alone will not provide us with the resources we need to develop to face the challenges of the second half of life successfully.

Our reluctance – both individually and as a society – to make these sorts of changes is partly due to the major financial commitments which accumulate by mid life: high mortgages, school and university fees, child maintenance, car loans, health plans, pension contributions, and so on. But it is also partly due

---

[30] Study presented to the American Psychological Society, reported in the *Independent on Sunday*, 24 September 2000.

to the firmness with which we tend to be wedded to values of the past which may in fact have outgrown their usefulness. Closer examination sometimes reveals the plea of financial necessity to be more about keeping ahead in an aspirational society than real need, and also about conformity. Work can infantilize us. Under our adult competence may lurk an unconscious but nevertheless powerful fear of the consequences of challenging the work ethic and the social norms and parental values that inform it, and it is this fear which conspires to keep us trapped within systems which chew up the best of us and spit the rest out. The need for approval, security and social recognition (far more than the desire for money itself) is often the glue that holds acquiescence to the crippling demands of work in place.

It is not easy to buck the trend; many who might like to cut down their working hours keep silent because they feel it would be career suicide to do so[31] – tantamount to an admission that you're just not up to it in a world where single-minded commitment is valued more than ability itself. When, many years ago, I worked as a solicitor, I became involved during my free time in setting up a new company offering (ironically enough) career development workshops. As this interest began to take up more of my time, I asked if I could reduce my working week from five to four days. The senior partners at my law firm were not taken with the idea, but eventually agreed to it for a trial period. In fact it worked well. For my part, I had the stability of an existing career which I enjoyed, but also the freedom to develop my new company, which flourished (eventually leading me to leave the law firm, but that is another story). I found that by reorganizing my schedule, cutting down on social time in the office and working more efficiently and for slightly longer hours, I could get almost as much done in four days as I had previously in five. Because I was doing what I wanted to do, my motivation and energy were high, and I did not suffer from end-of-week burn-out and staleness. Nobody suffered. From my employers' point of view, they ended up getting virtually as much work from me as before, while reducing the cost of employing me by a fifth.

---

[31] Franks, S., *Having None of It*, Granta (1999).

One of the reasons the law firm had not been keen to consider my proposal was that they felt it might send out the wrong signals. By this they meant that if I were unavailable to one client because I was doing work for another, there would be no problem – no values would be threatened. But if I were unavailable because I were doing something else entirely (different work in my case, but it could as easily have been looking after young children – or snorkelling, for that matter), this was not acceptable – when clients phoned on my day off, my secretary was always instructed to say I was 'in a meeting'. My absence did not endanger efficient functioning, but it did – blasphemously – threaten the ideology which said: *thou shalt have no other god but thy employment*. Besides, they said, what if the scheme worked and everyone wanted to do it? Then where would they be?

At mid life we find ourselves changing in a changing world, a world in which some of us are suffering from work exhaustion while others lose all sense of self-worth through having no work at all. Yet to question whether we could do better than to go on managing our work patterns in terms of a traditional forty-hours-plus working week – in which we troop dutifully off at the same time, to spend the day sitting in small cubicles tapping machines or talking on the phone, and then troop dutifully home again nine or ten hours later – nevertheless still draws defensive or disapproving responses. This conflict, between vested interests and the quiet but increasingly tenacious voice which questions them, is a conflict to be worked out within the workplace but also within our own minds.

'I've given this company the best years of my life. And where has it left me now?' Martin was a forty-five-year-old executive with an international oil corporation.

Married with three children aged between six and fifteen, Martin usually worked a fifty or sixty-hour week, and would often be sent on business trips abroad at short notice. His substantial earnings paid for a rambling and beautiful house in the Sussex countryside which Martin rarely saw in daylight during the winter months, and for expensive private schooling for his children – of whose daily lives, preoccupations and interests he knew almost nothing.

Martin had always been a company man, engrossed in his work. The

99

youngest of five brothers, as a child he had had to work hard to get his parents' attention. His father was a vicar and family life was managed by Martin's mother entirely around the demands of the parish. In this large, impoverished family, competition raged between the brothers for what fragments of attention they could get from their mother and father. The family were highly visible in the rural community where they lived, and from early childhood Martin had absorbed the belief that parental love was conditional upon being a credit to his parents and never letting them down. He had contrived to become his overworked and underappreciated mother's favourite. Intuitive and sensitive to her moods and her silences, he learnt how to support her and how to cheer her up when she was feeling down.

When Martin was ten, a family tragedy occurred. One of his elder brothers, who had become involved with drugs at university and had drifted aimlessly after failing his degree, died of a heroin overdose. Martin's mother collapsed with grief and shame, and it was Martin to whom she turned for comfort and consolation and for reassurance that her mothering was not to blame for what had happened, while Martin's father retreated behind a wall of silence.

Then after a few months, his mother 'pulled herself together', as his father had admonished her to do, and the episode was rarely referred to again. It had, however, a powerful effect upon Martin, who concluded then that he must never let his parents down – or the worst might happen. When the time came, Martin decided not to go to university. Instead, he gained a technical qualification in engineering and was recruited straight into the oil corporation for which he was still working twenty-five years later. Martin was good at his job and very diligent. He was also willing to put the company first, and made sure he was seen doing so. Along the path of his steady progression he married, had children and did all that was expected of him. He did well, although not that well – by his mid-forties there were signs that he might not be destined for the very highest positions. Then the news came. Martin's company was being taken over. There was to be a massive restructuring and everyone from the highest executive level downwards was being put through a series of assessments and interviews. Successful applicants in Martin's department would be offered positions in the restructured company and substantial resettlement packages, before being relocated to the Middle East. Though Martin began the selection procedures, he did so very reluctantly. Many of his co-workers were angry about the cavalier way in which the takeover was pushed through and Martin's immediate boss, who was in his early fifties, decided to take early retirement. Despite the exhortations of the company's senior executives that company morale must be positively kept up during the period of reorganization (and the unspoken threat that failing to do so would damage employees' future prospects), a number did crack under the pressure and went off work suffering from stress – including, for the first time in his life, Martin.

Under the strain of the selection procedures Martin had become depressed and anxious, could no longer concentrate and had begun to have panic attacks. What is more, his wife had put her foot down. Fed up with years of taking second place, sick of operating for most of the time as if she were a single parent, tired of having family holidays and anniversaries cancelled or spoilt by Martin's absences, she flatly refused to even think about uprooting the children and herself at the company's behest.

Martin's GP put him on medication and referred him for psychotherapy which, after some hesitation, he began. As Martin began to talk about himself, it started to become clear how much his role within the company was a repeat of his role within his own family – an attitude which the company itself had paternalistically fostered. Far more of Martin's unconscious emotional life than he had realized had been invested in his job, in acting out the rivalries he had once had with his brothers with his co-workers, and in endlessly vying for the approval of his superiors. From Martin's perspective the deal was as follows: put the company first, give it all your energy, all your loyalty and all your commitment, and it will look after you. It was a deal based on an identification of interests: I want what the company wants, because what the company wants is best for me and the company will always look after me because I'm an important part of the team.

But now this implicit deal had been broken. A cold, appraising eye was being run over Martin and his colleagues. He had managed to convince himself that he was a favoured son: now he realized that the company itself was completely indifferent to his personal concerns and family life, and the fragility and unreality of the pact in his own mind was revealed. His disillusionment was severe. One of the worst aspects was that no-one seemed accountable for this collapse of trust: all Martin's immediate bosses were in the same predicament as him. Martin wryly noted the similarity to his own family, for his parents too had never taken personal responsibility for the disappointments and deprivations he had suffered as a child – everything had always been because God demanded it, or the Bishop, or duty. To question the necessity of permanent sacrifice was wrong, sinful even – the system could never be questioned, never brought to account by those who served it. And now it was the same, except that market forces had superseded the Will of God.

It was extremely difficult for Martin to start unravelling how much – despite his successful career and his family – he had never really felt that he had grown up. The very qualities which had facilitated his success – his compulsive need for approval, his willingness to accommodate and to find solutions for other people's problems while ignoring his own feelings – had all been trans-ferred directly from his relationship with his parents to his relationship with the company. Martin also had to face up to how much the choices he had made in his life had been influenced by his parents' shame and anxiety about what had happened to his brother. He had been seeing things in black and white, in a way that left no room for a middle ground. Either you complied, obeyed and let the company (in his case the oil company, in his father's, the Church of England) guide your life – or dropped out and took the path that led to failure, destitution and damnation.

Martin became despondent and then angry as the long-term consequences of his single-minded commitment to work began to be acknowledged: the damage to his relationship with his wife and children, the neglect of earlier in-terests and pleasures which had left him feeling a grey-suited, grey-minded nothing outside his immediate work environment, and the physical cost of the permanent pressure he had been under at work which had been silently endured by his body. Martin had for many years suffered from migraines and also digestive problems which his doctor said were brought on by overwork, but which he had treated with painkillers and doggedly ignored as much as he could.

For the first time in his life, Martin decided to say no to the company and to the new post he expected them to offer him. But what then?

Martin's life to this point had been underpinned by two unconscious but powerful beliefs. The first of these was the belief that his own well-being was identical with that of the company for which he worked and that to further the latter would automatically enhance the former. The second was that the closer he got to the top and the more recognition and income he was rewarded with, the happier and more secure he would feel. But in fact, for some time both these beliefs had been looking increasingly dubious. Martin's headaches and gut problems, his remoteness from his children, his wife's resent-ment, his disturbed dreams, his feelings of deadness and irritability and his need to rely on will-power rather than enthusiasm to get him through each long day – all these warning signs had actually been accumulating for years before the merger, but Martin had wilfully ignored them. He had invested too much in believing that the pattern of his working life was in his own best interest, to reconsider. In common with many other people reaching mid life, the immediate upheaval he faced

102

at work was determined by economic forces beyond his control. But as a result of it he had to ask himself some hard and searching questions about what work meant – and could mean – to him.

Making Work Meaningful

Before leaving on a journey, a rich man distributes coins known as talents among three of his servants. Two of them trade theirs and acquire more, and they are praised and rewarded when they present their gains on the master's return. But the third servant digs a hole in the ground and buries his talent in it. When the master returns and asks him what he has done with it, he digs it up and holds it out, grubby and intact. 'Lord,' he says, 'I knew thee that thou art a hard man ... And I was afraid, and went and hid thy talent in the earth: lo, there thou hast that is thine.' His master replies angrily that the talent should have been used and invested so there was something to show for it, not buried in the ground. He takes the talent away from the servant and gives it to the others who had prospered: 'For unto every one that hath shall be given, and he shall have abundance: but from him that hath not shall be taken away even that which he hath'.[32]

I gave thee so many talents, what hast thou done with them? A question to make us toss and turn through the small hours, while the rest of the world sleeps peacefully. Fastened to a single work identity, buckling down to an endless sequence of tasks in hand, we blind ourselves to the wider perspective, form too limited and fixed views of ourselves and value ourselves too exclusively in terms of the specific skills for which our employment rewards us. Industriously and conscientiously, we dig holes and bury our talents in them. There is more to us – we may need reminding – than our ability to negotite car park leases or to sell shampoo.

And even when work is something to which we have been deeply committed emotionally or morally, we may find

---

[32] Gospel According to St Matthew, 25:14–29.

ourselves, as we reach forty or so, feeling trapped on a plateau of overfamiliarity, boredom and frustration. Once the lifelong ambition – the directorship, the headship or the hospital consultancy – has been achieved, where is there to go? Twenty more years of doing the same thing, with fewer and fewer challenges, becoming superseded by younger people with newer ideas and more energy? Or promotions into more and more remote realms of management, with the threat of redundancy always hanging over? The other question now likely to emerge is this: *if not now, when?* At mid life several decades of a working life, and much energy to potentially devote to it, still remain. Yet there comes an awareness that time is not unlimited. New opportunities arise and if they are not taken – or created – now, the chance to fulfil old ambitions or to pursue new paths may recede in time into a regretful *if only.*

In the middle of the nineteenth century, John Ruskin published *The Stones of Venice*, a study of the architecture of that city, which had as its subtext a critique of the materialist economy of his age. Ruskin suggested that while increasing specialization developed the expertise which enabled men to build great cathedrals, it also began a process by which workers became more and more alienated from the end products of their own labour. The products themselves became more refined and more impressive, but at the same time less informed by the emotional or spiritual values which had once infused them – and so, less meaningful to those who had laboured to produce them. Or, as another writer put it at around the same time: 'the more the worker exerts himself in his work, the more powerful the alien, objective world becomes which he brings into being over against himself, the poorer he and his inner world become, and the less they belong to him.'[33] The more money we have, said Marx, the greater is our alienated, estranged life, the life we could have lived but didn't because we were too busy making money. Marx also observed how we wilfully blind ourselves to the fact that – as Martin painfully discovered – our interests and those of our employer are not identical and may indeed be in

---

[33] Marx, K., *Economic and Philosophical Manuscripts* (1844).

opposition. Sometimes the interests of worker and employer may coincide, for example when a worker is motivated by a personal sense of vocation. Quite often, they do not.

If we are not careful, Marx also suggested, we are liable to end up inverting subject and object – living to serve our products instead of using them to serve our lives.[34] A tyrannical work ethic ends up distorting not just our lifestyles but our personalities themselves. Ambition can lead us to developing within ourselves the qualities demanded by modern socio-economic conditions, described by Erich Fromm as the market-ing character:[35] cheerful, reliable, well-presented, adaptable, ready to subsume self to the company's aims and to eliminate as necessary the possibility of any internal life or personal ethical values which might conflict with this intention. But as commitment to the work ethic peaks and begins to decline in our forties and fifties, the onset of the mid-life crisis warns us that different qualities are called for if we are to weather it successfully: humour, a sense of proportion, kindness, generosity, imagination, independent thinking, aesthetic appreciation, and spiritual awareness. The challenge is to find new patterns and ways of working that reflect these changing values.

Martin, with much trepidation, refused his company's offer of relocation and handed in his notice. To his surprise, the company invited him in to negotiate; they did not want to lose Martin's highly specialized skills, especially to a rival. It transpired that they were most keen to retain Martin for the innovative, creative part of his work which was the part he himself particularly enjoyed and which could (it transpired) be done just as easily on a contractual basis from his home in the UK once the company relocated abroad. The company were keen to slimline their permanent staff and reduce overheads anyway, and this arrangement suited them very well. Eventually a generous package was arranged by which Martin traded in his job for a flexible consultancy contract extending over a number of years. Martin and his wife used the severance money to pay off their remaining mortgage, and to convert an outbuilding into office space for Martin.

Martin also bought a sailing boat. When young he had loved sailing, but for many years he had not had time for it, although the family home was only ten

---

[34] Marx, K., *Capital* Vol. 1, Oxford University Press (1995).
[35] Fromm, E., *To Have or To Be*, Sphere (1987).

miles from the sea. However, his new freedom to take on or refuse individual projects as he wished, together with a great reduction in hours previously spent travelling and immersed in departmental meetings and politics, meant that far more of his time became his own again. When he was younger, Martin had had a dreamy and reflective side to his nature, which he started to rediscover while out sailing. He also began to take his younger son out with him in the boat, and the two became much closer. As he started to relax, so did his body, and his migraine attacks and digestive problems grew less frequent and finally vanished altogether.

Initially the plan had been to take on more contracts so he could maintain his work and income at its previous level. But as Martin approached fifty and became further removed from the office environment his enthusiasm for this began to wane, although he kept on his original contract and took on a few other smaller ones which interested him. Martin's more frequent presence at home had enabled his wife to return full-time to her work as a speech therapist and this, together with paying off the mortgage, had greatly decreased the pressure on Martin to earn. Although not as well off as previously, the family was financially secure. As he spent more time out sailing, Martin had also become interested in the technicalities of boat-building. He underwent specialist training and started up as a sideline a small yacht-making business, for which his original training as an engineer, together with his business experience and contacts, stood him in good stead.

Over time, Martin succeeded in freeing himself from the unconscious attitudes he had previously invested in his job, in which his employers had been authority figures to be exhaustingly propitiated and appeased by his own hard work. This new freedom gave him the space to reconsider what he really wanted from his work at this new stage of his life, and over time he was able to make a new balance between three areas of life. Firstly, he kept on parts of his former work that he enjoyed (the renegotiated contract with the company). Secondly, he started to gain new skills and to develop his working life in a new area (the boat-building business) which enabled him to express previously unarticulated enthusiasms and abilities. Thirdly, and no less importantly, these changes enabled him to give a new priority to other previously neglected areas of his life (such as spending time with his children and sailing) which were extremely important to his own well-being. The reduction in income and the loss of the executive status and perks, initially dreaded, seemed in retrospect a small price to pay.

The economic factors which had caused the apparently disastrous upheaval in Martin's life eventually worked out in his favour. Today, even core jobs at the heart of organizations do not last as long as they used to, and in any event they may not be best suited to the constitutions or the skills of mature workers. Burn-out is, in a sense, built into the system and is likely to affect increasing numbers of those reaching mid life, who still have many years of productive life ahead. Unwavering single-mindedness may still be required to succeed in many careers, but in these times of unstable economic and personal conditions, rigid adherence to a single fixed work identity may start to look like more of a liability than an asset. Flexibility and diversification is the name of the new game.

In *The Age of Unreason*, management consultant Charles Handy suggests we may need to start seeing a high-energy corporate career having a natural end date somewhere in the forties – just as we are already accustomed to think of the careers of gymnasts or chess-players as naturally self-limiting. The loss of an existing work structure in these circumstances may feel like a betrayal or a bereavement; yet for those able to embrace change, several decades of working life remain to be put to good use. New attitudes to working create new pressures and insecurities but they also create interesting new freedoms and possibilities.

More and more of us are likely to be faced – voluntarily or involuntarily – with the sort of options open to Martin. Downsizing and deregulation have made more work available for those outside the central employment core than ever before, and for those with relevant skills much of it is well paid and flexible, in terms of both when and where it is done. As Martin's story shows, rewarding work is by no means synonymous with a full-time job, and changes in working patterns may actually suit people reaching or passing mid life well. For increasing numbers of us, after the full-time job ends the age of the portfolio worker begins.[36]

---

[36] Handy, C., *The Age of Unreason*, Century (1993).

The point of portfolio work is that it varies as much as individuals do. Typically it includes some paid work on a salaried or self-employed basis, or both, some of which is likely to be carried out from home; some study or further training, either with a view to further work prospects, or undertaken for its own benefit; perhaps some community work such as serving as a school governor, setting up arts projects or volunteer work with children or the elderly; and some non-income-producing work on personal projects in the home or allotment, taking up a new sport or periods spent travelling abroad. Portfolio work may sound like something designed for the high-flying entrepreneur, but in reality it bears a much closer relationship to the patterns of work of ordinary people over centuries before the industrial revolution, which can still be seen today in many rural economies. Portfolio work, in its infinite individual combinations, provides less money and less status than full-time employment, but more time, more flexibility, more control and generally higher levels of satisfaction and fulfilment.

Many factors around mid life combine to show that a new stage in life is being reached on the economic plane as much as anywhere else, and many of these factors – such as mortgages being paid off, children starting to leave home or the inheritance of capital from deceased parents – create new freedoms. Couples in stable relationships become freed to make changes, perhaps involving one returning to full-time work while the erstwhile breadwinner returns to further education, gains new qualifications or builds up a new business. Teleworking (literally, distance working) facilitates moving from expensive built-up commuter areas to a life of rural ease, freeing up more capital in the process. Downshifting is the trading-in of lengthy hours at high-stress, high-status jobs in return for reduced earnings, a less materialistic lifestyle and more time to use for one's own benefit.[37]

Concepts like portfolio working and downshifting may purport to identify new trends but in a sense they are just describing natural and timely ways of responding to the changes

---

[37] Ghazi, P., *Downshifting*, Coronet (1997).

of mid life, for those who have freed themselves from the tyranny of conformity to a crushing work ethic. If we expect our lives to carry on fitting around work – to continue in the same career with the same structure throughout life until we are finally cast off unwanted – the advent of retirement will be a traumatic shock. But taking seriously the dissatisfactions of the mid-life crisis as they relate to the working life makes it possible to break this pattern and become more proactive in developing new patterns of work which better reflect the reaching of a new stage of life.

ACHILLES OR ODYSSEUS: NEW OPTIONS

Achilles is the star of the *Iliad*, the hero who is invulnerable (save for his famous heel) yet marked to die. Homer's story of pitched battles on the plains of Troy seems a long way from the market economics and the hours at the screen or on the phone which measure out our own working lives, yet the competitive aggression which forged the young civilization of the Bronze Age continues, in more sophisticated forms, to shape the world in which we live today. Achilles is a creature of this world: he is skilful at battle and courageous, yet his thinking is rigid and his honour – his *raison d'être* – is brittle and reactive. It is not informed by overarching moral values but is all about his status in the eyes of his fellow warriors, and it is ultimately reinforced only by escalating systems of threat and attack.

When Achilles withdraws sulking into his tent because his status has been threatened, he sets off a chain of events which ultimately leads to a disastrous assertion of himself, and to his own death. Today, the Achillean type – aggressively extrovert, strategically adroit, company-minded – is likely to rise quickly in the employment hierarchies of his world. But his inflexible thinking, his tendency to respond to everything as a threat, his lack of concern for others and his compulsive, relentless need for achievement and praise mark him out as a prime candidate for a mid-life heart attack or stress collapse – if the long knives of his enemies don't get him first. Ready to face external conflicts with the utmost energy and courage, the Achillean personality is too extroverted, intransigent and brittle to cope with internal conflicts or threats to his identity. Lacking a repertoire of internal resources, Achilles will not find it easy to transcend the challenges of his own ageing and to transform himself at mid life. Instead, he will keep doing more and more of the same – less and less successfully – until he snaps.

Achilles dies at Troy, but his comrade Odysseus both masterminds and survives the fall of the city. For him, the best and most interesting years of his life are yet to come. In the *Iliad*, Odysseus as a young soldier is essentially undifferentiated from Achilles and the others, motivated like them by the desire for fame and status and the respect of the group. But after Troy falls, Odysseus reinvents himself and separates out from his peers. Because he depends no longer on group values to give him meaning and identity, Odysseus can shed them and move on while others fall by the wayside. As flexible, pragmatic, wily and easy-going as Achilles is rigid and impulsive, Odysseus is also self-contained and reflective, a natural survivor. Achilles lives in a public, hierarchical world of orders and deference, in which nothing is truly private; Odysseus by contrast survives and thrives outside the arena of war, and the new relationships and bonds he makes with others as an individual after the fall of Troy, save his life and help him on his way. In the *Odyssey* he is sustained by his sense of individual purpose – to return to Ithaca.

Mid life sees us entering a new landscape in our working lives, which may be as different from what has gone before as the watery expansiveness, erotic transitions and mysterious encounters with mortality of the *Odyssey* are different from the focused clarity of action and the landlocked narrowness of the *Iliad*. Odysseus, once a soldier but now a sailor, is able to surf these changes. Constantly reassessing his situation, he cuts his cloth to fit his sail, as needed. At a deeper level, he can make radical self-transcending changes when they are called for: the journey of Odysseus suggests the possibility of change and evolution through internal process.

As far as work is concerned, as one door closes another opens. The changing conditions that can seem so threatening also create new opportunities for those who are ready to change themselves. Portfolio working, flexitime, self-employment, downshifting and continuous learning are all part of the

110

kaleidoscope of possibilities at mid life, options for more people than may realize it. The mid-life transition forces us to look honestly at the state of our working lives, and to engage more actively with our personal priorities. The result may be the creation of a working life that is more satisfying, more flexible and more congruent with our own internal values.

6

Sex

Twice or thrice had I loved thee,
Before I knew thy face or name;
So in a voice, so in a shapeless flame,
Angels affect us oft and worshipped be;
Still when, to where thou wert, I came,
Some lovely glorious nothing I did see.

From 'Air and Angels' by John Donne

SEXUAL CONFLICTS I: SHIPWRECKS AND SEDUCTIONS

The Mid-Life Love Affair

Lost at sea, Odysseus coasts over the surface of a vast, lonely ocean on a few planks lashed together, the last battered splinters of the ship in which he had once confidently set sail from Troy. He drifts, blue sky dissolving into blue sea, days blurring into weeks, months, years ... empty sea, empty sky, empty horizon. Hopelessly trapped, infinitely exposed, he floats on passively through the waste of time. Hopes and schemes, ambition and purpose, all evaporate in the haze, returning as phantoms or deliriums to mock the sailor without sails or compass. Rebuked by memory, plagued by desire, he scans the horizon for signs of life, for an orientation, a direction. As he looks, an island comes into his gaze and then another. The islands are peopled by nymphs, sirens, ghosts, witches: Nausicaa, Circe, Calypso, the lost souls of Hades. They call to be explored. And Odysseus continues drifting, from island to island, from lover to lover.

The apotheosis of the mid-life crisis is the mid-life affair – what else presents itself so enticingly and malleably redolent with potential to redeem the feared emptiness of the middle years of life? Like Odysseus' islands on the horizon, such possibilities manifest as points on the thin blue line between fantasy and reality, the interstice where unconscious desire reaches out to meet the coincidences of fate.

David's wife had a miscarriage three years ago when pregnant with their third child, and had to have an emergency hysterectomy. Since then she seems to have lost all interest in sex, and the relationship has deteriorated. David has started an affair with a colleague at work. The sex is furtive and thrilling, but he is terrified his wife, whom he says he still loves, will find out and leave him. He has already ended the affair once when his wife became suspicious, but now he somehow seems to have slipped back into it again. His fear of discovery is, in fact, something of an aphrodisiac.

Jean and Matt moved in next door to Suzanne and Nigel and the two couples became close friends. When Jean left Matt for someone else, Matt collapsed with shock and grief, and Suzanne has spent many evenings listening to him and comforting him over bottles of wine at the kitchen table while Nigel was working late. Suzanne has discovered that Matt brings out a different side of her from Nigel, and she has begun to feel irritated when Nigel arrives home and joins in on their increasingly intimate conversations. She says that she and Matt are just close friends, but she flushes when Matt's hand brushes hers, and their hugs last longer than they used to.

Jess has been married for many years to Gavin, an actor and theatre director. She supported him while he was at drama school, followed him round the country when he toured in rep as a young actor, and brought their children up while he was away on tour and performing in the West End as his career prospered. Jess has often suspected Gavin of having affairs, but none of them came to anything. Then last year, at the age of 46, Gavin announced that he had fallen in love with one of his leading ladies. He said that he needed some space to try and find himself and moved out to live with her, but the relationship did not work out. Within a year he was back, begging Jess's forgiveness for his folly. In the meantime, however, Jess had met Howard, who was everything Gavin wasn't – supportive, a good listener, considerate of her needs. She cannot believe how different it feels to be in a relationship with a man who seems to take her seriously, to whom she is not expected to be just a constant foil and admiring reflection. But will it last? And – now Gavin has returned, repentant and determined to make their marriage work – is Howard really worth throwing away her thirty-year-old relationship with Gavin for?

Stories of restless dissatisfactions and imaginings, fantasies, experimentations and betrayals. Like the voices of the Sirens which troubled Odysseus – seeming to offer so much but putting so much at risk – the unanticipated upsurge of sexual desire at mid life inevitably calls into question much that has long been taken for granted. This questioning, equally inevitably, reaches into the most intimate areas of our relation-ships, and marriages and the conduct of our erotic lives.

We begin life monogamously, attached to our mothers at first physically and then, for a number of years, by emotional ties no less binding. This fiercest of loyalties seems at the time as if it will last for ever, but in due course it is frayed and then broken by the troubling, exciting development of adolescence. Lifting anchor, we find ourselves lured out towards the open seas of sexual flux, pitching and tossing far from any port. In due course, these turbulences wear themselves out. Drifting towards a new harbour, we begin to experience once again the lull of domestic quiescence, within the security of a settled relationship. This state – in its turn – seems to offer permanence until, when least expected, the call of the sea lures us once more from the fixed certainties of our settled lives and returns us to our own unfaithful desires.

At the same time, of course, mid-life sexual turmoil is very different from the disruptions of adolescence. Now it is no longer our parents' complacencies but our own which get called to account, our own families which come under threat – and our own children who may end up being hurt. And while the successful negotiation of the storms of adolescence leads into the

114

more settled state of first adulthood, mid-life erotic disturbance raises some much bigger questions than it can answer on its own terms. Some relationships will in the long term prove themselves flexible, resilient – and loving – enough to weather the storms and to come through them proved and made stronger. Others will not.

Our erotic longings pull us backwards into states of infantile need or adolescent rebellion and self-pity, sometimes prompting acts of self-centred destructiveness we may live to regret. But our longings are progressive as well as regressive, and they also lead us forwards, into experiences of deeper and more tender intimacy, towards self-transcending transformations. Why (at a time when it seems our body energies should be slowing and stabilizing) should it be disturbance in the sexual arena which becomes so frequently, and so intensely, the catalyst of mid-life crisis?

The Roots of Mid-Life Sexual Disturbance

There is a time, characteristically around forty or so, at the symbolic mid-point of life, when couples who have spent years together in settled relationships begin to become increasingly aware of the inexorable passage of time and the changes it is visiting upon their partners and themselves as they begin to age. Anxieties about ageing and about death itself, postponed in the hectic period of first adulthood, now begin to close in as the other changes of mid-life – the death of parents, the departure of children, the anticipation of retirement – unfold around. A strong relationship is a bastion against such anxieties, a place in which they can be mediated and negotiated, but even in loving relationships couples begin to mirror each other's anxieties – avoiding and often reinforcing them, as they avoid their own. The dawning of the awareness of mortality can be quietly traumatic, a trauma that a materialistic, secular culture offers little help in negotiating. And it is sexual relationships – for many the only available means for the expression of the emotional and existential dimension of life – which inevitably end up taking most of the strain.

Within the context of anxieties about ageing, a long-term partner may become the reflection and daily reminder of everything in ourselves we would most like to forget or deny as we move into mid life – the fixed daily habits (somehow less endearing in their idiosyncrasies than before), the predictable ways of thinking and the unspoken insecurities which inform them, the changing contours of the softening, spreading body, the failure to find anything new or interesting to say. From these irritations and anxieties and the quiet unconscious despair which they engender, erotic fantasy offers a retreat and a haven. Flight into fantasy enables us to consign the dread of ageing to the silenced and abandoned other. And the fantasy of escape may prepare the ground for the reality of escape, through a relationship – should the opportunity arise – with a new lover.

The joke about trying to recapture a lost youth neatly defines the cliché of the mid-life love affair – the desire to deny the feared loss of one's own sexual desirability through discovering a youthful self mirrored back in the gaze of an adoring (but, as the joke suggests, possibly inattentive) younger lover. Desire based upon fearful denial becomes sterile and self-defeating, trapped in the compulsive repetition of short-lived affairs with relays (in fantasy at least) of younger lovers – yet mid-life love affairs don't always fit this stereotype. They may be painfully, excruciatingly profound; they may be the driving force through which aspects of the self are rediscovered, or revealed for the first time.

For if the arousal of sexual desire can be a form of denial, it can also be a form of affirmation and an expression of hope. Arrival at mid life and the awareness that time is not unlimited itself becomes a catalyst for change. To begin to take ourselves seriously once more we may need to be taken seriously by someone else, to be seen through new eyes. The faltering impulse towards personal evolution, grown stagnant within an unresponsive or denigrating relationship, begins to seek out more encouraging and generous forms of relationship. The hidden plea within the claim that *my wife (or husband) doesn't understand me* is not necessarily cynical or manipulative.

In the moment of catching a stranger's eye, a flirtatious exchange or an unexpected word of kindness or understanding, we find ourselves discomposed or blushing – such moments have the power to destabilize our complacencies. They become the germ not just of what might have been but of what could be. The need for recognition and articulation of something – an intangible yet compelling something stirring within the self – may never be greater. It is the erotic urgency and intensity of this need which determines the tendency of new relationships entered into under its pull to end up as sexual ones, even when we had intended otherwise.

At the beginning of the twenty-first century, sex presents itself everywhere both as a conduit for internal disturbance and as a reward for achievement. Click on and select sex from a menu – click again for more choices. Sex, flatteringly and glamorously free from the trappings of emotional vulnerability and social constraint, sells everything and especially itself. The sexual options so assiduously stimulated and promoted by the flaunting of young, unclothed bodies throughout the media inevitably provoke a sense of entitlement which interacts disturbingly at mid life with the sense of years passing, of missing out. Small wonder if couples plodding along side by side in the harness of long-term relationship begin to raise their heads as their load lessens, and to sniff the breeze; and as a belligerent spring enters their step, they may toss their tails, flare their nostrils and start to pull in different directions.

But is there another reason why we arrange our problems so compulsively in terms of romantic affairs, couch them so intently in the language of sexual desire? Perhaps our sexual relationships end up bearing the brunt of our mid-life reinventions of ourselves because of the dearth of any compelling or interesting alternatives. Freud observed that for a thought to become conscious, it must be capable of being expressed in language.[1] Our shared language and terms of reference, and the cultural values which they embody, both form and limit how we express ourselves, the stories we tell about ourselves to others and to ourselves, and even the nature of the thoughts which we allow ourselves to have. We live in a highly materialistic society, that is

---

[1]   Freud, S., 'The Unconscious' (1915), in *Penguin Freud Library* 11.

at the same time a highly sexualized one. As our identities become ever more entirely and exclusively those of producer–consumers, sexual love has a uniquely privileged position as the matrix in which the primacy – and privacy – of internal emotional life holds sway. Romantic or sexual thoughts, and the language of erotic desire in which they express themselves, may today have become the only thoughts available to us for the articulation of our existential crises, our yearning for transcendental meaning.

Upon the hope of sexual love is targeted the urgency of our need for it to be encompassing, enduring – and ecstatic – enough to articulate and meet our frustrated human yearning for self-transcendence. This tendency to convert struggles that may at their core be spiritual or existential (in the sense of being concerned with fundamental issues of life, death and the search for connection and meaning) into sexual struggles is not new. But never before has it been so all-encompassing; never before has it existed in cultural conditions that provide so few alternative opportunities for articulating conflicts that may not essentially be sexual at all.

Steve is a forty-two-year-old athletics coach. He is married with two children aged sixteen and eighteen and refers himself for short-term psychotherapy under his employment scheme. He says he has been having panic attacks, and initially presents his problems very much in terms of current pressures at work. Then at the end of the first session he abruptly says he thinks he is about to start having an affair with Emma, a nineteen-year-old member of the team he is coaching.

One summer evening a couple of months previously, Steve had been locking up at the track after a training session, when he found Emma crying in a corner of the women's locker room. Emma still lived at home with her parents, who had just told her that they were divorcing and that her father was leaving home. Steve comforted Emma, and had offered to drive her home, as she had missed her last bus. Over the next few weeks, driving her home became a habit and as Emma poured out her distress, Steve began to tell her about dissatisfactions in his own marriage. What Steve only hinted at very obliquely to Emma was that he had been impotent with his wife for about eighteen months. He has been unable to talk to anyone about this, and had become very angry and walked out of the room when his wife had broached the subject. Since then he had become increasingly short-tempered, and the marriage has deteriorated further. But now the desire he is feeling for Emma is convincing him that the problem lies with his wife, and that if he begins an affair with Emma he will regain his potency.

Steve's mother is still living, but his father died abruptly of a heart attack at the age of 45, when Steve was 20. Steve was close to his father, who was himself an amateur athlete, but their relationship was at the same time very competitive. Steve remembers going out cycling with his father when he was about 15 and winning a race to the top of a local hill. Steve had felt thrilled but also disconcerted that − for the first time − he had beaten his father. He said his father had made a joke of it, but he thought he had also been quite shaken.

At this point Steve becomes visibly upset and has to pause for several minutes to collect himself. He then says that the week his father died, he had come home from college for the weekend and had gone out cycling again with his father. He thought perhaps his father had pushed himself harder than he should to keep up with him − but then, no-one knew that he had a weak heart. On the following Tuesday, Steve received a phone call from his mother to say that his father had been rushed to hospital with a suspected heart attack. He died before Steve got there. Steve said he realized − as everyone had kept telling him − that the heart attack would probably have happened anyway, but ever since then he has secretly blamed himself for causing his father's death. Now he himself has a teenage son, and is approaching the age at which his father died; the panic attacks and sexual problems had started soon after his own fortieth birthday. Steve's involvement with Emma had been allowing him to become young again in his own mind, and to escape from his unconscious fear that nemesis would catch up with him − that he would die early like his father, in retribution for causing his father's death.

Steve had grown up with a sense of masculine identity modelled on his father's, that required him to be strong, capable, jocular − and infinitely reticent about his own feelings. The relationship with Emma had been tremendously exciting for him, because in it he was able to express some of the vulnerabilities he had never felt able to share with his wife, while at the same time Emma's own neediness and admiration evoked his protectiveness and made him feel − he said − like a man again. In the past, sex had been very important to Steve, allowing him to contact and release a more openly emotional side than he permitted himself in the rest of his life. He had been experiencing his impotence as a form of death.

Now Emma was making him feel alive again. The depression and anxiety which had been circling his mind had been banished by his erotic preoccupation with Emma; it was difficult to consider the possibility that these same morbid thoughts might lurk behind his desire for her. But the panic attacks had not stopped. They had in fact become worse, and he was also, for the first time, plagued by a great many groundless fears about his own health. Steve was also well aware of how much he had to lose. To have an affair with a girl he was coaching could wreck his marriage and perhaps his career. Would there be an element in this of his unconscious sense of guilt contriving a way of punishing himself? The focus of the psychotherapy shifted from his relationship with Emma to his relationship with his father, to the way in which the meaning he had given to the circumstances of his father's death had affected how he felt about himself, and to how much his expectations of himself as a man and the urgency of his need to preserve his own youth had kept him imprisoned behind a wall of fear and self-blame within his marriage.

As Odysseus first fled his wife Penelope and his baby son Telemachus to rescue Helen at Troy, Steve fled into the relationship to rescue Emma – fearful of ageing and change, fearful of no longer being the object of desire, fearful of being usurped by the next generation and especially by his own son. In such a flight resides the hope that youth will be magically restored. The self fantasizes, and sometimes contrives, its own re-creation as hero in the eyes of a new lover. In Steve's case, the catalyst was drawing near the age his father was when he died, and at that point meeting Emma, whose unconscious desire for a powerful father – rescuer – lover mirrored his own desire to be one. Unhappy people gravitate to each other, drawn by the desire to rescue each other and, by doing so, themselves. The role of rescuer encourages us to believe in our own potency and steadfastness and our ability to restore goodness and meaning in the face of deep fears about impermanence and mortality. At the same time it enables us to deny these fears (and the deep need to be securely held which they engender) by projecting them into the other who demands rescuing, thereby flattering our desire to preserve our sense of ourselves as mature and protective adults.

Love in a Time of Hostility

As time passes, unfolding its usual sequence of losses and the occasional disaster, we see more wear, more vulnerability, more damage around us and in those we have loved – some have already died or become old and frail, while others have been injured or scarred by life's vicissitudes. We live within domestic proximities which we feel obliged to protect. As the recklessness of youth softens into the caution of the middle years, the fear of rocking the boat or of causing harm to partners, children or parents can lead to denial of resentment, anger, and hostility. And yet as mid life looms, we may discover that we have a lot to be angry about. Love and hate, desire and fear, entwine within the unconscious: it's only in conscious life that we have to come down on one side of the fence: love *or* hate, protect or attack, stay or go. Fear of damaging those from whom we derive our security makes us play safe, holding back, withdrawing emotionally from those to whom, notionally, we are closest.

Like Steve, we may defend ourselves from the pain of loss and suffering (and from the awareness that most of it is, in fact, entirely beyond our own control) by constructing, however irrationally, unconscious beliefs which omnipotently attribute the damage we see or imagine around us to our own aggressive impulses. Such beliefs create intense feelings of guilt and self-blame (which often manifest as depression). Yet at the same time they provide an unconscious reassurance: if it's all our own fault, it must be – despite all evidence to the contrary – within our control. If the bad things that have happened to us are a punishment brought upon us by our own wrongdoings, then we risk making them happen again unless we keep a firm grip on ourselves. Superstitious beliefs such as these tend to be buried deep in our unconsciousness, making it difficult to bring them into the rational awareness that would start to dissolve them.

The protectiveness which Emma evoked in Steve enabled him to re-create himself (*she makes me feel like a man again*) and to deny his fearful expectation of punishment for his father's death. This fear had made him withdraw from his wife and his family, but his panic attacks and his unfounded fears about his own health showed how his aggression had become turned against himself. Withdrawal from others in such circumstances is itself a form of hostility, serving both to deny angry, aggressive feelings and to express them, changing a once loving and alive relationship into a sham in which fear of real involvement masquerades as tolerance and love degenerates into sentimentality.

Winnicott describes how love which is sentimental is of no use to anyone because it contains a denial of hate: an atmosphere which denies hate will eventually paralyse love.[2] Desire – starved of both the energy of aggression and the hope that all aspects of the personality can be reconciled and accepted in the other's love – will deaden and atrophy once partners end up playing caring parents and needy children to each other, avoiding the erotic, playful and aggressive engagement of lovers. Desire itself sometimes hungers – in its ruthless way – for hostility, for things to matter so much that they *do* hurt. The *Kama Sutra* instructs lovers in techniques for drawing blood from each other's flesh.

David, as we saw at the beginning of the chapter, starts an affair after his wife's miscarriage and hysterectomy. Her withdrawal from him has triggered buried anxieties about his own sexual aggression, for unconsciously he feels his sexual demands have been responsible for the suffering she has gone through. Suzanne likes to think of herself as a kind and stable friend to Matt but she is uneasily half-aware that her genuine sympathy is adulterated by excitement, triggered by the rawness and openness of Matt's anguish; she is disturbed by unspoken comparisons with the complacencies of her own marriage. Jess is secretly sick to death of playing the adoring wife, both scenery and audience to Gavin's performances. Whatever happens in the end between her and Howard, a part of her is secretly enjoying seeing Gavin, for once, being the one to sweat. David, Suzanne and Jess have all suppressed and denied parts of themselves, apparently in the service of keeping their marriages on track; but their long-term accumulations of unspoken hostility, resentment and anxiety are the cold draughts which fan the flames of desire starting up elsewhere.

Withdrawal to protect ourselves or others from the effects of aggression makes a relationship stagnate, while the aggression

---

[2] Winnicott, D. W., 'Hate in the countertransference' (1947) in *Through Paediatrics to Psychoanalysis*, Hogarth (1987).

itself will probably return anyway, in the form of covert undermining, sarcasm or nagging. Erotic self-expression, by contrast, is as directly aggressive and ruthless in pursuit of its own desire as it is loving. 'New lovers are nervous and eager but smash everything, for the heart is an organ of fire' writes Katharine to Almasy at the start of their adulterous love affair in Anthony Minghella's 1996 film version of Michael Ondaatje's *The English Patient*. The greatest longing of a lover is to be known completely, and completely loved. For love to remain exciting and interesting it must recognize and contain the individual's capacity for passionate aggression, yet this very quality is what is most often lost in the routine of long-term relationship.

The expression of anger enables us to assert our independence and to experience ourselves, with relief, as separate from the other – and also expresses a certain faith in the robustness of our partner. There is nothing so endearing or so reassuring as the capacity of those we love to survive our attacks on them without collapsing or retaliating. When aggression is disallowed within a relationship, so is the energy that fuels it, the desire to hunt and to be hunted which is at the centre of the erotic game. It may return unexpectedly – as it did for Almasy and Katharine – in the urgent, violent, ruthless and devastating upsurge of passion which characterizes the mid-life love affair.

Erotic bonds deepen our capacity for relatedness to others, and blur and breach boundaries in a way that can perilously assail our sense of self. The ultimate danger and excitement at the heart of erotic engagement is its capacity to threaten our prior sense of existence at a most fundamental level, even to upturn the experience of what it means to be male, or to be female.[3] In states of intimacy we allow ourselves to change and be changed by the other. We reveal our most hidden selves, our softest underbellies. Love reminds us how fragile, how dependent, how full of need we can be under the surface of our adult maturity, and for this reason we both yearn for it and fear it. As anyone

---

[3] Stoller, R. J., *Sexual Excitement: Dynamics of Erotic Life*, Karnac (1986).

who has gone through a relationship breakdown knows, the passionate engagement of love can swing into all-consuming hatred with surprising rapidity. The fragility of long-established relationships at mid life suggests how brittle and unstable romantic love may be – and how unwise we may be to make too much of the underpinning of our lives dependent on its endurance. Even at the best of times, within the state we call love and within the intensity of our most powerful desire, there may inhabit more insecurity, jealousy, mistrust and even hate than we like to think. The story of Odysseus' encounter with Circe explores the potential transformations afforded by sexual desire, and how badly these can backfire if the mistrust behind desire cannot also be confronted.

Odysseus and Circe: Lovers and Pigs

Odysseus first takes flight from the binds of domesticity by embarking upon the heroic crusade to rescue Helen, but by the time he meets the equally lovely Circe many years later, he is older and warier. At the start of his long trip back from Troy, Odysseus had been presented by King Aeolus with the gift of all the wind tied up in a bag of ox leather, and to help him further the King summons up the west wind to speed the ships back to Ithaca. Almost in sight of Ithaca, Odysseus' men – not knowing what the bag contains but greedy for gold and jealous of the secret gift – steal and open it. All hell breaks loose, and a great tempest sweeps the boats back to King Aeolus – but this time he gives them short shrift and sends them on their way without further assistance. Gloomily they row away, and after seven exhausting days reach the lands of the savage Laestrygonians, who tear the crews limb from limb. Only Odysseus' own ship escapes the massacre and limps eventually into a haven on the island of Aeaea, home of the witch Circe.

And wolves and mountain lions lay there, mild in her soft spell ... Circe lives in a smooth stone house in an open glade in the forest thickets. Wild beasts fawn around her table, begging like dogs for scraps. There is, evidently, magic in the air but not the kind of which the sailors – who begin to feed greedily on Circe's sweetmeats and wine – might have dreamed, for as they

124

scoff, their noses and mouths begin to lengthen into snouts and their limbs turn to trotters. Bristles sprout from their leathery pink skins and little curly tails from their now capacious rumps as – quivering and squealing with piggy outrage – they are herded by Circe into her pigpen.

Circe has changed the sailors into beasts who look and behave as pigs, but suffer as men. But Odysseus holds back and watches. Forewarned and forearmed, he resists this porcine transformation. He confronts Circe with his sword outstretched, and his demand that she treat him with respect and as a man proves powerful enough to break through her enchantment. *Circe complied and swore that she had no evil intentions. So when she had given me her word with due solemnity, I went with the goddess to her beautiful bed ...* Before becoming Circe's lover, Odysseus extracts from her the promise to restore his men to their full humanity. She does so, and the men emerge from the transformation younger, handsomer and taller than before – the story is not suggesting that sexual pleasure is to be avoided, only that it should not be stumbled into ignorantly and impulsively.

The scheming, castrating witch who is tamed and made docile by a devastating combination of superior male cunning and a mighty unsheathed weapon is, of course, a familiar staple of male fantasy. But the dark underside of the story expresses the terror of the loss of ego-control in sexual desire, and it is this fear that lurks under the sailors' swaggering sexual bravado as they first enter Circe's domain. It is to her table that the sailors – who have failed to learn anything from the theft of the bag of the winds and the ensuing tempest and slaughter – are greedily drawn. The regressive, instinctive aspect of sexual desire and its link to the most primitive oral appetite is emphasized: poetic justice turns the men into pigs. Circe is a dazzlingly seductive image of desire and revulsion, and the men's response to her illustrates the strange tricks that desire can play on the mind, the self-deceptions which ensue and the blind alleys down which impulsivity leads.

In his poem 'Circe', Louis MacNeice expresses how the desire for sexual solutions may trap us into a world of sensual surfaces which finally becomes deadening:

This despair of crystal brilliance.
Narcissus' error
Enfolds and kills us –
Dazed with gazing on that unfertile beauty
Which is our own heart's thought . . .

Obsession with sensual beauty ('Which is our own heart's thought') is unfertile, and leads us into the same error which destroyed Narcissus – gazing into glassy, sterile, ungiving surfaces for a reflection of our own desirability. Our complaints about others' preoccupation with appearances only serve to advertise our own dependence upon such views. When we are obsessed with appearances, we are paradoxically at our most vulnerable, and never more so than when we begin to age. Women have always known this and now men – no longer protected by the privileges of patriarchy and the deference of women – know it too. Both are today judged physically by the pneumatic, airbrushed standards of the fashion and pornography industries, liable to be found lacking with neither consideration nor kindness, looked at in lust, judged without love. To this pitiless gaze we are invited to surrender and betray our maturing bodies by cutting, starving, stretching, peeling and injecting them, all in the unwinnable battle against ageing.

Only partially protected by a hollow, sardonic humour, we assess our own selves and others as the consumer objects we have made ourselves into – objects with limited shelf-lives, soon past our sell-by dates. No matter how undignified, painful or ultimately fruitless this self-appraisal, the centrality of sex as a semi-consumer relationship within the world in which we live makes it difficult to avoid. And when we use others to satisfy our own narcissistic need for a youthful reflection of ourselves, we open ourselves to them to use, abuse and discard us for their own reasons. The rebellious infidelity of the mid-life love affair turns us into outlaws from the moral community of interest and concern which protects the defenceless. In the jungle of adultery, it is every lover for him – or her – self.

Circe and Odysseus do eventually manage to negotiate a relationship built on respect and, finally, trust. Initially, however, Circe represents for the sailors the possibility of fulfilment of desire without strings – a possibility set up in the story only to be exquisitely demolished. Real intimacy poses a threat to the autonomy of the self, and casual sex appeals most when this fear is strongest. Love renders us undefended and vulnerable and love can make fools of us. The older we get the more we have to lose (and as the poet Edward Young remarked, a fool at forty is a fool indeed). The fear of *falling* in love – falling like toddlers or drunks who have forgotten how to walk, vainly trying to renegotiate a relationship to gravity – is common to all of us. Casual sexual encounters seem to offer a solution to the dilemma which pitches the intensity of desire for erotic connection against fear and mistrust of where desire may lead, but the encounter with Circe suggests that such strategies may in the end dehumanize us. And when we become no more than animals, we will suffer as helplessly and dumbly as animals, as Odysseus' captured soldiers suffer until they are set free.

The pig, the cock and the snake are the three animals at the centre of the Tibetan wheel of life, representing respectively ignorance, sensual desire and hatred. According to Buddhist doctrine, it is these three tendencies which keep us tied to the wheel of life as it goes monotonously round and round, bound to the karma that they create for us, and to the suffering to which it leads. Only insight into the true nature of reality enables us to find happiness as – through beginning to transcend our reactive attachments – we move on from the revolving wheel to the spiral path which leads towards enlightenment. The story of Odysseus and Circe likewise suggests that desire chains us to our basest instincts, as pigs to the trough, and from the pull of this doubtful enchantment there is no salvation except self-awareness. In the story, Odysseus alone is able to break through the force of instinctive behaviour and to challenge Circe as a thoughtful man, instead of reacting to her sensual beauty as an animal.

When he confronts Circe, Odysseus refuses to deal with her on any ethical terms but his own – at which point a loving relationship becomes possible between them. And Circe proves as good as her word. She provides Odysseus and his men with a safe haven for a year and when they finally leave, she warns them of the perils that lie ahead in the Land of the Dead and explains how they can pass through safely; love, it seems, can conquer death after all. Later still, Odysseus will pass by the island of the Sirens, whose melody lures men to their death on the rocks. He will be able to enjoy their song and escape with his life – not through magic, but through the precaution of tying himself to his own mast, in full awareness of his own limitations as a man. Only the entirely non-magical capacity of non-deluding self-awareness is strong enough to triumph over the magic, regressive powers of sexual desire and survive intact.

Intimacy, *Going Round Again and the Law of Diminishing Returns*

'After a certain age sex can never be casual' muses Jay, the narrator of Hanif Kureishi's *Intimacy*.[4] The novel takes the form of Jay's interior monologue as it unfolds through the night which will end with him walking out on his wife and two young sons: 'It is the saddest night, for I am leaving and not coming back.' Jay has resolved to take flight from his family – and, as becomes clear, from aspects of himself and his own past – into a new relationship which pulsates with sexual promise. The intimacy of the title is the ironic intimacy of hurting someone, of hating and being hated: Jay asks 'like a child' for his friend Victor to tell him once again the story of why Victor's own abandoned wife hates him so. He feels he must do something to stop his own wife being so angry all the time but does not know what: 'if only she knew how I stammer within'. His own hatred, and the anxieties and self-hatred that inform it, cannot be expressed in words but only acted out in abandonment. Jay retreats into an aloof, self-regarding silence.

For Jay has a lover – the most recent of several – a young woman who desires him and in whose desire he experiences himself coming alive. A modern narcissus, he watches himself in a mirror, buoyed up by the sight of himself lounging naked on a bed as the object of his new lover's desire. But then later he

---

4   Faber and Faber (1998).

disorientatingly catches sight of himself in another mirror while masturbating alone and sees in the glass a crazed and desperate animal. Jay's flight is from his unhappy, angry wife but also from the depressed mother of his own childhood whom he could neither cure nor distract, a woman whose mind hurt so much she could only think of herself. 'Where have all the fathers gone?' he wonders ... 'Is it when women become mothers that they flee? What is it about mothers that makes it so essential that they be left?'

Jay himself has always felt scornful of the susceptibility and vulnerability of women or of anyone who loves another: 'how foolish they were to let themselves feel so much'. But he is caught in a painful dilemma, trapped in an identification with his own mother, her failure to engage with others and her lack of enjoyment. It seems that only sexual desire can rescue him from boredom and from the silent, secret litany of his own anger. But, he ponders, that same desire which keeps human endeavour alive, also mocks it. For long enough, surfing the ebb and flow of sexual desire, he has kept love at bay. But now he finds himself embarrassed by his own urgent need to reach out, so much so that he could punch through a window.

What is the point in leaving, wonders Jay, if the failure with one woman reproduces itself with all? Can he really start afresh with each new lover, or will the failure of relationship turn out to be an illness with which he will infect all his lovers? But Jay leaves anyway – as many do. Around 50 per cent of all divorces happen between the ages of 35 and 54,[5] and a divorce rate of 27 per cent was recorded among British women in the 45–54 age group in 1992.[6] Many people hovering on the brink of leaving one relationship and beginning another will find themselves wondering, like Jay, whether they should put trust in a hazardous fidelity to an unknown future over fidelity to the past. But then the same dilemma reoccurs: is the only freedom ultimately worth having the freedom to let go of freedom, in favour of the

[5] Divorce Statistics for 1997, from the Office for National Statistics.
[6] Mori General Household Survey 1992, Table 2.4.

obligations that tie us to life and to others? And will the relationship failure, which is consolidated and finalized by the act of leaving, replicate in a new relationship? Second and subsequent marriages do have a much higher failure rate (around 70 per cent) than first marriages, suggesting that we are not always as good at learning from experience as we would like to imagine.

Under stress, fearful of being blamed or found lacking, we look for external solutions to internal problems – an attentive, stimulating lover to replace a marriage grown inexplicably flat and dull or one reduced to simmering, incomprehensible hostility. It's easy to forget that there is one person whom we always take with us to a new relationship. Resisting looking inside at our own resentment or self-centredness, we set up the conditions for a repetitive cycle of excitement, conflict, stagnation, break-up, new relationship – of which it has been ruefully said that the screwing you get isn't always worth the screwing you get.

Desire – especially sexual desire – generates meaning. Desire urges towards its own fulfilment, seeks to fill its own lack, and yet desire itself can only survive in lack. In fulfilment it collapses, and takes meaning with it. *Post coitem*, every animal is sad. So Freud observes, concluding that there seems to be something in the nature of the sexual instinct itself that is unfavourable to the achievement of full satisfaction. Unrestricted sexual access within marriage does not lead to full satisfaction – but neither, evidently, does unrestricted sexual freedom with multiple partners. And why, asks Freud, should the desire for erotic satisfaction make us want to keep changing sexual partners anyway? Has anyone ever heard of heavy drinkers moving restlessly from one type of drink to another? On the contrary, he says, 'if we listen to what our great alcoholics . . . say about their relation to wine, it sounds like the most perfect harmony, a model of a happy marriage. Why is the relation of the lover to his sexual object so very different?'[7]

Freud, of course, thought that the root of the longing for

---

[7] 'On the Universal Tendency to Debasement in the Sphere of Love' (1912), in *Penguin Freud Library* 7.

sexual variety lay in the fact that many of us unconsciously retain our deepest love-feelings for our parents. Because sexual desire between parent and child is not permitted fulfilment, it becomes split off from love, and targeted at sexual objects outside the family. But once the new sexual object itself becomes loved, familiar and domesticated, the old unconscious anxieties and incest taboos will be triggered again, automatically shutting off sexual desire and launching a search for a new object of desire. The wish to endow sex with meaning struggles against the fear that it may have no meaning, and the determination to keep it free of meaning. Desire must then be kept alive in the never-never land of sexual fantasy, in extra-marital affairs or in rapid serial monogamy, shedding one object as soon as the hunt is won and replacing it with a new one. The inevitable failure of desire can only be denied by constantly replacing lovers until sexual life becomes a parody of the consumerism to which it once seemed to offer an alternative.

Courted for excitement, treasured for their ability to provide erotic experiences beyond the domestic realm, affairs reach a danger point when they begin – as they must – to become over-familiar. Odysseus stays with Circe for only a year, but his adventures after leaving her eventually land him on the island of Calypso, from whose toils he extricates himself by no means so adeptly. He remains stranded there for seven years, paralysed in the spell of the failing relationship; it is on Calypso's island that we first encounter Odysseus in the fifth book of the *Odyssey* – moody, disconsolate, looking out to sea and weeping. Had he once sat – as moody and as lonely – on the headland of his own country Ithaca, looking out to sea for salvation, until the call came to go to Troy? In Mario Camerini's 1954 film *Ulisse* the same actress, Sylvana Magnano, played both Calypso and Penelope, similarly suggesting the repetitive nature of erotic attraction and dissatisfaction. 'Calypso' means 'concealer' – the new lover who promises so much more than the old one may not in the end be all she, or he, seems.

Odysseus' lonely but necessary meditation upon the headland suggests that perhaps only in a time of quietness – when the dramas and upheavals of the breakdown of one relationship and the honeymoon period of another are over – is it possible to experience the grief of loss and the failure of ideals, and to reflect on one's own contribution to them. In the quietness and relative security of settling into a new relationship, the same problems come round again until, finally, our capacity for self-justification and self-deception is exhausted. Such moments can lead to despair or to a final reckoning, a coming to terms and a new beginning.

Second relationships or renewed first relationships based not upon excited idealization but upon consideration, kindness and the willingness to make realistic accommodation are less likely to become overburdened by the unconscious baggage of the past. Divine prompting – in the form of a visit from Hermes – makes Calypso realize she must release Odysseus. Odysseus himself realizes he must stop relying on lovers, living on their terms and in their pretty prisons, pining for a rescue which will itself ultimately lead to further imprisonment. He must move forward by his own exertions, by building his own boat. *When she had shown him the place where the trees were tallest the gracious goddess left for home, and Odysseus began to cut the timber down ... Finally he dragged* [his boat] *down on rollers into the tranquil sea.*

Odysseus' waywardness and disorientation rendered him, like Blanche Dubois in Tennessee Williams' *A Streetcar Named Desire*, temporarily but disastrously dependent on the kindness of strangers. Blanche herself was too fragile and self-dramatizing to change, but if we are fortunate, and determined, the confusions of desire at mid life finally bring in their wake the chance to break though to a new sexual realism. Odysseus' renewed intention to return to Ithaca evokes the vision of a boat. He discovers within himself the determination to build it, gives up moping and finally knuckles down to work. Like the narrator of Robert Frost's poem 'Stopping by Woods on a Snowy Evening', Odysseus still has promises to keep, and miles to go before he sleeps. There is as yet no final resolution – for Odysseus and Calypso, separation looms – but for now he gets on with the task in hand, which will take him home. The world is full of lonely idealists, and married pragmatists. The willingness to work at what is imperfect, the possibility of the language of responsibilities replacing the dictates of rights, and of affection and reconciliation repairing the ravages of desire, may not, for some, be a bad resolution of the sexual conundrums which have tormented them for too long.

SEXUAL CONFLICTS II: THE TANGLED WEB

Autonomy and Intimacy in Mid-Life Relationships

Maggie is a sub-editor in her mid-forties and, following her divorce six years ago, a single parent to three teenage children. A year ago she was asked out on a date by Jon, a publisher whom she knew through her work, and the relationship quickly became intimate. Jon is a widower in his fifties, whose own children are grown up. The to-ing and fro-ing between their houses and all the uncertainties and duplications involved add stress to their already complicated lives, but so far Maggie has resisted Jon's tentative suggestion that they could try living together. She is most tempted at times when financial pressures build up, or when everything in the house breaks down just when a work crisis looms. The pressures on her as a single parent to keep everything ticking over are sometimes overwhelming. But is this a good reason for living together? Recently, memories of the painful disintegration of her marriage have been returning to her in flashbacks, and Maggie tells herself she would be mad to chuck away all her hard-won security and peace of mind by letting Jon move in. But when Jon isn't there her bed feels cold and empty, and her body aches for him. She is deeply in love with Jon and the pleasures of her single life have begun to pale.

Some of Maggie's reasons for deciding to go on living separately for the time being are to do with her teenage children. Together, she and they have managed to negotiate a relatively harmonious, settled and democratic way of living together, which has gone a long way to healing the wounds left by their father's departure. Valuing this, she is wary of introducing an unknown new dynamic into their lives. But it's not just her children towards whom she feels protective. Shaking her head in disbelief, Maggie says that when she was married she changed over the space of twelve years from being a dynamic, confident woman running her own business to a downtrodden, depressed martyr who was afraid to go to parties because she had nothing to say to anyone. She remembers having the strange feeling that she was mutating against her will into her own mother-in-law, a woman who would jump up apologizing when anyone walked into the room, and whose entire life was a doomed and fruitless series of attempts to please her surly husband and indifferent children.

Maggie thinks marriage changed her so much partly because of how her husband behaved after they were married, losing interest in her as a person and acting towards her – apparently obliviously – as his father had to his mother. But she is aware that she got caught up in it too; her husband had not seemed to like the person she had turned into very much either. Maggie is aware of how powerful the pull to dwindle into a wife can be. Her experience of marriage has made her alert to her own tendency to try to please and appease Jon when they are together, making concessions for the sake of a peaceful life which she will secretly resent. 'At least now, I recover my sense of myself when we're apart; and when I'm with him I enjoy it more because we still feel like lovers. So something stays alive. It seems very hard for me otherwise to find a way of being with a man and being true to myself. Maybe it's my generation – despite our educations and careers, it wasn't as easy as we thought it would be to free ourselves from the shadows of our own mothers' lives. I think by this point, I've partially succeeded – but only partially.' Like Odysseus, Maggie has recognized the call of the sirens – in her case towards submission and loss of selfhood within a sexual relationship – and is protecting herself accordingly.

At mid life, relationships are sought and valued as a source of intimacy and comfort as well as to keep loneliness and the fear of ageing alone at bay. Yet as the confidence of maturing judgement leads us to value our independence more, we also become warier of the threat to autonomy which intimacy poses. 'Love one another, but make not a bond of love. Let it rather be a moving sea between the shores of your souls' said the Sufi poet Kahlil Gibran in a much-quoted verse about marriage. 'Give your hearts, but not into each other's keeping ... stand together yet not too near together.'[8] Dorothy Parker, along the same lines, suggested that we shouldn't put all our eggs into one bastard. Sometimes, like Maggie, we try to solve the problem by keeping a lover at bay somewhere beyond the snares of domesticity, sometimes by playing one relationship off against another.

Homer's Penelope is preserved in legend as the model of the devoted wife, living off her wits to preserve her husband's

---

[8] Gibran, K., *The Prophet*, Pan Books (1984).

kingship and her own chastity from the throngs of insolent suitors who invade the palace in Odysseus' absence, pressing themselves upon her while feasting off her resources. But Penelope is also the archetype of the woman with an abandoning or absent partner who has to struggle for the survival of herself and her child in a man's world. This was a lesson learnt early by Penelope, who was rejected at birth and flung into the sea by her father Icarius, who had wanted a son. Her life was saved by a flock of purple-striped ducks who towed her to shore – at which point Icarius, impressed by his infant's ingenuity and tenacity, relented and allowed her to live.[9]

In patriarchal cultures, women were rarely allowed even limited autonomy – the exception being during the frequent absences of their lords and masters on hunting expeditions or in wartime. (As recently as the Second World War, unprecedented new freedoms were granted to women to learn commercial skills, to drive, to fly, to work outside the home and to conduct love affairs – freedoms which were abruptly withdrawn when the boys came home.) In such circumstances, some women will be sorrier to wave their husbands goodbye than others. Penelope's solitude brings her grief and tears, but may not be literal – although Homer's epic stresses Penelope's fidelity, in another version of the myth Penelope becomes the mother of the god Pan as the result of her liaison with Hermes, the messenger.[10] And it guarantees her the sovereignty which, as Chaucer's much-married Wife of Bath observed, a maturing woman values above all else – the double-edged freedom to be obliged to fend for herself as the lonely queen of Ithaca.

The constraints which patriarchal systems imposed upon the sexual and social self-expression of women are fading. But today, men and women both may still labour under internal constraints and prohibitions which are no less harsh and oppressive, and which do not willingly allow us to live except through pleasing

---

[9] Graves, R., *The Greek Myths*, Penguin (1992).
[10] *Ibid.*

others, or as the objects of others' desire. Penelope achieves a precarious freedom by playing her suitors off against each other, keeping them all guessing. Like Maggie, she contrives to remain the loved and valued object of desire – without ever taking the final step of commitment, which would make her once again the dreaded taken-for-granted, unseen object of no-desire: the wife. When Penelope is pressed to make a commitment to one of the suitors, she says she will give her answer when she has finished weaving the shroud she is making against the death of her father-in-law, old Laertes. So she hides her own determination to stay free, teasing and tantalizing the waiting suitors and spinning her web – the centre of attention, the focus of desire. But each night Penelope creeps down alone to untangle the deceptions she has woven in the daytime, and then she goes alone to her bed and weeps for her lost love.

When we deceive, we create a secret internal space, free from the intrusive, controlling or disapproving gazes of others. In an interim sense – through purchasing separation of the self from the forces which conspire to control it – deception may become a matrix for growth. Yet at the same time, successful deceit often makes us uneasy – it gives us too much power to reinvent our lives, too much rope with which to hang ourselves. And the failed or transparent lie may indicate the self's discomfort at having been split between two antagonistic parts (one that seems and one that is), and its desire to become whole again through exposure. Women, as they mature, begin to become more confident in their own sense of identity, less dependent upon male approval and support and more likely to prioritize their own emotional and sexual needs, and this can put great stress on a marriage where the man has previously been the dominant partner; yet women are still far less likely than men to walk out on their homes and families. The creation of a secret internal space, through planning or conducting an affair while preserving conformity on the home front, may come to seem an attractive option.

Repeated studies in America and Britain show that while both men and women in happy marriages have high well-being, it is women who suffer worse in poor marriages, and married women who tend to be in worse health, both physically and emotionally, than single ones.[11] Like Maggie during her marriage, these women's constant efforts to please their husband and children and retain their love may make them end up erasing their own thoughts and desires from their minds, and feeling like automatons. Dalma Heyn's book *The Erotic Silence of the Married Woman*[12] describes the process by which women who have become over-identified with the role of a wife and mother begin to deny their own sexuality, and to repress desire itself. It is this desire – denied at home yet still subsisting within a culture which constantly reiterates the importance of sexual self-expression – which is likely to break out in an extramarital affair. Lovers chosen by married women tend to be younger, often less affluent and less educated than their husbands are, and more willing to please. In other words, a woman who already has stability and financial security may start to choose her sexual partners for the reasons men have always done – for pleasure, and also to enjoy the deceiver's pleasure in secret power, having her cake and eating it too.

Yet however clandestinely they are initiated or conducted, the tensions created by many affairs will – sooner or later – lead to the destruction of the original relationship. It may not be as easy as we had hoped to live split lives built on subterfuge. Sooner or later, we will be faced again with the same problems of how to create intimate relationships in which both partners can be recognized and valued, and in which an appropriate and flexible balance between the needs for freedom and for intimacy can be negotiated. Marriage in traditional cultures solved this problem by devising and maintaining complementary roles for men and women. In social structures still prevalent throughout the East and the Mediterranean today, men and women would generally live, work and pursue their recreations within different worlds, in which contact even between married couples is limited. In a clash the man's will, backed up by law, would usually prevail; yet in practice, the fact that men and women led such different lives and had such different spheres of involvement and influence

---

[11] See Bernard, J., *The Future of Marriage*, Penguin (1976) and Gottman J., *Why Marriages Succeed or Fail*, Simon and Schuster (1994).
[12] Mandarin (1993).

tended to mitigate the frequency of such conflicts and their likelihood of causing real destabilization. This possibility was further reduced by the fact that within the extended family the sexual bond was only one of a network of interrelationships and interdependencies, and often not the primary source of companionship or support for either of the partners anyway. The fact that most people spent far more time in single-sex groups also limited the opportunities for making the kind of unfavourable comparisons of partners that tease and torment us today.

Whatever its limitations, such a system at least may encourage tolerance (or indifference) towards those ordinary human failings of one's partner which are placed in a glaring spotlight by our idealization of sexual relationship. We expect our partners to heal all our wounds and to satisfy all our needs, to want the same things as ourselves, and to think in the same way. Best-sellers like *Men are from Mars, Women are from Venus*[13] indicate that we are at least beginning to think about the problems inherent in attributing our own needs and feelings to our partners across the gender divide – to become aware that men and women may expect very different things from relationships while labouring under the delusion that they are just the same. Nevertheless, gender rancour – fuelled by the bitterness of disappointed ideals – has never been greater than it is today. The modern companionate marriage may promote the ideal of sharing and equality, at the same time as the ideal of freedom; yet in the minds of many of us these ideals are not at all commensurate, and may in fact create a whole new raft of problems.

Belinda brings her husband Anthony to couples therapy; she says she is on the brink of leaving him. Since their daughters have grown up and left home, Belinda has been feeling increasingly lonely and neglected. She says that their marriage has become an empty shell, while Anthony is aware of her un-happiness and feels paralysed and confused by it. Neither of them are in-volved with anyone else. Anthony is a gardening writer and historian and he quite often brings work home in the evenings, disappearing with it up to his

---

[13] Gray, J., Thorsons (1993).

study. He is also becoming an expert in the orchids which he grows in a huddle of sheds and greenhouses at the bottom of their garden, and is often away at weekends exhibiting them. Anthony feels surprised and hurt by the depth of Belinda's bitterness. In his own terms he has been a good husband but by nature he is, he says, quiet and reflective while Belinda is far more extrovert, exuberant and warm – and also more emotionally demanding. For many years he had not really felt his life and energies were his own because he had to work so hard to support the family and to be a good and attentive father to their children. Fair enough, he says – but now he wants some time for himself again.

Belinda acknowledges that Anthony had, indeed, been a loving – though somewhat absent-minded – husband and father. But her own, previously unexamined, expectation of how their lives would be after their children had left home was very different from his. Belinda misses her daughters very much; the house, she says, feels sad and empty without them. She had expected Anthony to step in and bridge this gap and for them to start spending far more time doing things together – because that, she says with considerable exasperation, is what couples do.

Closer investigation reveals that Belinda's expectations are modelled upon her own parents. Her father had been a gentle, mild-mannered man (not unlike Anthony in some ways) whose life revolved around his home and family. Her parents were inseparable until her father died at the age of 63. But Belinda then says that she had come to believe that her father had actually been far more contented in the marriage than her more gregarious mother. In fact, after her father's death her mother, who had been left unexpectedly well off and was still in her mid-fifties, had blossomed. She had started to dress differently, and had begun to go to the theatre and to travel abroad – things she had never done when Belinda's father had been alive. She learnt to drive, got a job as a hotel receptionist, developed a new network of friends and eventually got a new boyfriend, showing a zest for life which according to her daughter still continued as she reached her mid-seventies.

The great change she witnessed in her mother has left Belinda feeling that there must have been far more stifling compromises within her parents' marriage – at least on her mother's side – than she had realized when she was growing up. Her parents had never argued and always seemed happy together – it seemed it had never occurred to her mother to question the way their lives were, until released by her father's death. Now Belinda is seeking her own release before she herself is too old to enjoy it. Unconsciously, she identifies with her mother and thinks her liberation can only be achieved by another death – in this case, the death of her marriage. As her mother seems to have felt, Belinda believes that to seek any sources of enjoyment or fulfil-ment outside her marriage would be disloyal and likely to harm it irreparably – otherwise, why would her mother have limited herself so much? Feeling that change within her marriage is prohibited, she gives herself no option but to leave it. Starting to cry, she keeps shaking her head and saying des-pairingly that there just wasn't any point in being together if they were always doing different things.

It turns out that Belinda is baffled by but also quite envious of the freedom Anthony accords himself to enjoy his own interests. He has never seen this as a problem – his parents also had a long and stable marriage, but his back-ground was very different from Belinda's. His parents were both academics who had seemed contentedly engrossed in their own worlds, in their writings and in their separate college lives. Belinda then acknowledges that she has always felt inferior to Anthony because she never went to university – despite her intelligence, it was something that her parents would never have seen the point of, especially for a girl. Belinda's own lack of confidence in herself after twenty years as a wife and mother has interacted disastrously with her par-ents' limited expectations of her, and with her unconscious belief that her marriage could only be preserved at the cost of her self-suppression and complete immersion in the roles of wife and mother – neither of which, it seems, are now further required.

Rather reluctantly, Anthony concedes that despite his pleasure in his work and his orchids, he has probably retreated into them more than he might have done, mainly to avoid conversations with Belinda in which he feels constantly recriminated without understanding why. He feels exhausted and demora-lized by her; he fears her demands are a bottomless pit and that nothing he ever does will be enough for her. He has given up reaching out to her sexually for fear of further rejection and has, he acknowledges, withdrawn emotionally from the marriage. She says he never listens to her or tries to understand – he says that all she ever does is criticize him and tell him how unhappy she is without showing how it could be better. Anthony says he still loves Belinda, but he cannot rescue her and he cannot bear feeling he is all she has in her life.

The discussion returns to Belinda's feelings of inferiority. When the counsellor remarks that her lack of a university education still seems to be a live issue for her, she becomes anxious, but her anxiety has an edge of excitement to it. Anthony, for his part, begins to brighten up and become more engaged; he says that he has often felt that Belinda had an unjustified lack of intellectual confidence, and that she has underachieved.

But for Belinda, it still seems that – in theory at least – the thought of taking

140

herself seriously enough to apply to do a degree is a lot more frightening than the thought of leaving the marriage. She admits that his curiosity, his intellectual confidence and his passion for ideas are qualities she finds deeply attractive in Anthony – but in her admiration there is also envy and frustration. The counsellor wonders whether Belinda is attracted to these qualities in Anthony because they already exist in a nascent form within herself. What would happen if she tried to develop them?

If Belinda can overcome her anxieties and self-doubt, and the fixity of her self-image, if she can rescue herself by discovering new sources of intellectual and creative stimulation and sharing them with Anthony instead of waiting passively and resentfully for Anthony to rescue her, and if Anthony can learn to take Belinda's feelings seriously – and extend himself emotionally towards her instead of freezing like a rabbit in a car's headlights whenever she gets upset – then perhaps their marriage will have a future.

Belinda and Anthony are, like Maggie and Jon, struggling in their different ways with issues of intimacy and autonomy and the disparate fantasies, beliefs and expectations that these issues evoke in them. Their very different attitudes have only really become apparent since their children left home – the first time they have really been alone together since their early twenties, in a social climate that has changed enormously in the meantime. Belinda has over-idealized marriage, expecting it to give her everything at the cost of the eradication of her individuality. Anthony has gone in the opposite direction, taking it for granted that their marriage would just rumble on, however little of his own resources he puts into it. He is also afraid that he will lose his sense of self if he risks opening more towards Belinda's feelings.

It remains to be seen whether Belinda and Anthony will be able to construct together a middle ground in which they can begin to enjoy encountering each other, and within which their marriage can flourish and endure. This is what Maggie and Jon have found, at least temporarily – their accommodation involves spending part of the week separately and part together while maintaining their separate houses and domestic arrangements. In a different and more unconventional way, it works to guarantee the needs they share for intimacy and mutual support, and for their own freedom and separate space. 'It's not ideal' says Maggie of their arrangement, and yet in many ways it works well enough – certainly better, for the time being, than her marriage did. And the future remains open. Perhaps, despite its real frustrations, its the fact that this relationship isn't ideal that makes it work in practice.

SEXUAL CONFLICTS III: TOWARDS THE TRANSFORMATION OF DESIRE

We idealize love and falling in love, turn our lovers into divinities whom we (temporarily) worship. In return we demand that it – and they – provide us with the meaning of life, our personal reason to believe. To believe what? Through sexual love we hope to work out the project for our own self-discovery and self-fulfilment, to discover wholeness through ecstatic connection. Love has hijacked the religious language of the soul's yearning for reunion with God, a state in which suffering and yearning themselves are eroticized and transformed. As sinners relied on salvation through God's love, we rely on the promise of sexual love to redeem our banality, our emptiness, our loneliness, our sense of personal insufficiency. In its yearning for union or reunion with the beloved, idealized other, love thrives upon absence and frustration. And in the yearning for the unobtainable, in the space between present pain and imagined bliss, meaning is forged.

Sam Mendes' Oscar-winning film *American Beauty* explores this relationship between the idealization of desire and the search for meaning through the mid-life crisis of its fortysome-thing narrator Lester Burnham (played by Kevin Spacey). Lester is trapped within an unhappy marriage and a futile suburban life: 'American Beauty' is the name of the glossy, dark red specimen rose which borders his apron of suburban lawn and which is pruned and sprayed within an inch of its life by his uptight, driven wife Carolyn (Annette Bening), but the rose's crushed petals are also the dark, velvety bed into which the teenage nymphet Angela, the schoolfriend of Lester's daughter, sinks naked and enticing in his most secret fantasies.

Carolyn is an estate agent who harangues herself, slapping and convulsing her own body to psych herself up to drive home another property sale in the wasteland of arid consumerism which is her life. Her husband's desire for Angela is the catalyst which makes Lester the worm not only turn, but rise and challenge the soul-crushing deadness of his suburban wage-slave existence. The surging of Lester's desire opens the floodgates to much bigger changes, and the repressions and evasions of the lives of Lester, his family and his neighbours begin to fall like a row of dominoes.

Lester's epiphany comes towards the end of the film, when Angela finally makes herself sexually available to him. As he starts to lower himself onto her, she tells him it's her first time: Lester suddenly sees behind her precocious sexual sophistication to the frightened insecure child beneath, and his fantasy implodes. The generational difference between them – which his rebellion against his own arrival at mid life had wilfully erased – is differently restored and with it, Lester comes into his own humanity. He relaxes – no longer predatory, he becomes full of humour and tenderness, without desire. Seeing she is hungry, he invites Angela into the kitchen and (in a neat inversion of the Circe story) feeds her, instead of attempting to satisfy his own desire upon her. As the pigs became human again when Circe ceded to Odysseus' demand to be respected, Angela now sees Lester for the first time as a person instead of just her friend's lecherous old father. She asks him, a bit tentatively, how he is. Lester muses that it's the first time anyone's asked him that for years. His face starts to light up, as if a huge burden has dropped from it. He tells her that he feels great.

American Beauty is an ironic celebration of the beauty that can appear even within a culture of deadening materialism, in the most surprising places – like the video which Lester's neighbour's son plays of a white plastic bag blowing in the wind, which he describes as being like God staring back at you, just for a second. It is about the beauty which transforms Lester's life when he stops trying to hold on to his object of desire and, through renouncing it, finds freedom. This view of liberation is a heretical one, both within the film (by its end there are three different sets of characters lining up to kill Lester for his iconoclastic irreverence) and within our wider culture – at least one middle-aged male critic found the film finally implausible on the grounds that nothing would make a middle-aged man like Lester forgo sex with a seventeen-year-old like Angela, if he got the chance.

In *American Beauty* it is sexual desire which has become the vector of meaning and the mediator of existential crisis within individual lives, taking the place vacated by the collapse of religious belief – a process under way in England as long ago as 1867, when in *Dover Beach* the poet Matthew Arnold described the 'melancholy, long withdrawing roar' of the sea of faith which, in its draining away, left his generation

> . . . as on a darkling plain
> Swept with confused alarms of struggle and flight,
> Where ignorant armies clash by night.

In this moment of profound spiritual desertion and anguish, the poet can offer no consolation other than the promise of romantic fidelity – 'Oh love! Let us be true to one another!' – which, depending on your perspective, makes *Dover Beach* either a great love poem or a case of stoically making the best out of a bad job. Today we find fidelity harder and harder, but the idealization or fetishization of sexual love continues unabated. The Austrian psychoanalyst Otto Rank was born seventeen years after *Dover Beach* was first published, and belonged to a generation which had largely lost its faith, however much it still clung to the outer vestiges of religious belief. In his book *The Trauma of Birth*[14] – the publication of which in 1924 precipitated Rank's own traumatic separation from his mentor Freud – he suggests that the ecstasy we experience in sexual love is due to love's capacity to erase the anguished experience of separation and the dread of annihilation which stem from the agony and separation of birth itself.

The idealization of romantic love, said Rank, relieves us of the burden and responsibility of our separate existence while the gratification of desire within sexual union creates an ecstasy of merging. The awareness of mortality which begins to dawn at

---

[14] Dover Publications (1993).

mid life draws us back with renewed urgency towards this erotic solution, while simultaneously rendering us more deeply, more tragically, aware of its limitations. For sex's capacity to relieve us of the burden of separate existence is only transitory: the reason that the loss of love is so agonizing is because it surrenders us back to this primal dread (Rank would have appreciated that the Elizabethan slang for reaching orgasm was 'to die').

Sexuality is the religion of our age, in relation to which it is heresy to wonder how far the sexual revolution, and the opening-up of sexual choice and freedoms unimaginable to previous generations, have made us truly happier. Belinda wonders if she would be happier leaving her marriage, but is not sure, while Maggie, on the other side of the fence, thinks – on balance – she is probably better off divorced, but she also is not sure. Sometimes her life is difficult; sometimes she feels she has too many choices and not enough security; sometimes she wishes she and her first husband could have worked it out and found a way of being together while more emotionally separate. If they had been able to free themselves from the resentment and rage left by the collapse of the romantic ideal and to steer a path that was different from that of their own parents, could they have found a way to live affectionately together, running their house, parenting their children and supporting each other emotionally as well as financially? Now another chance has come round with Jon. If she goes with it, will she be courting further disappointment and failure? Or will she – taming the secret siren desires of her own treacherous heart, which lure her to want far more of Jon than she knows he can offer – be able to develop a more realistic, in some ways more limited but also more genuinely loving, relationship with him? Like Prometheus discovering fire, Eve biting the apple or Pandora opening the box, our espousal of sexual freedom sometimes gives us more – or less – than we had bargained for.

Psychic Androgyny: Towards Sexual Contentment

In the *Symposium* Plato conceives of erotic desire as a yearning for a lost state: love as the desire for wholeness. Eros, he says, is 'the pain wherewith the Demon, who through his own enigmatic guilt was plunged into birth, reclaims the lost paradise of his pure and original Being.'[15] In his famous allegory, he conceives of us as originating from primal, hermaphroditic beings, who became cut in two. The two halves, male and female, remembering their Ideal – their 'pure and original Being' – were destined to search always for reunion with each other. The bliss of intercourse, suggests Plato, derives from the transitory re-experiencing of this state. But Plato does not just see romantic love as a regressive yearning for hermaphroditic wholeness or (as Rank suggests) for the return to the womb. He is aware of the progressive aspects of Eros also, its potential to move us on in life through a hierarchy of growth towards higher, deeper and more intricate forms of relationship. Sexual love can return us into needy or greedy infantile states, but it can also be innovative and creative, ushering in new self-experiences and leading towards states of greater integration and transformation.[16]

This pull between the regressive and progressive aspects of Eros reaches its climax – and also its best chance for creative resolution – in the middle years of life, sponsored by drives which begin to go to work at this time in the body as well as the psyche. 'Men's attention is stimulated by signals no more complicated than what leads the gosling; and for all her adult life, her sexual life, let's say from twelve onwards, she had been conforming, twitching like a puppet to those strings' thinks Doris Lessing's Kate, concluding later in her own odyssey through the mid-life crisis, that 'the light that is the desire to please had gone out. And about time, too.'[17] At mid life, the draconian changes which polarized the sexes at puberty and made them strangers to each other begin to be reversed by further changes that are physiological and biological as well as psychological, precipitated by the draining of reproductive hormones out of our bodies. These changes facilitate the

---

[15] Plato, *Symposium*, tr. Waterfield, R., Oxford University Press (1994).

[16] See Mann, D., 'Erotic narratives in psychoanalytic practice' in *Erotic Transference and Countertransference*, Routledge (1999).

[17] Lessing, D., *The Summer Before the Dark*, Penguin (1981).

reclamation of those parts of the self – the mischievous adventurousness of the little girl, say, or the wide-eyed tremulous concern of the small boy – which were jettisoned under the self-conscious tyrannies and alienations of the reproductive years.

These psycho-physical changes may make women (like Kate in *The Summer Before the Dark* or Chaucer's Wife of Bath) more independent, more able to articulate their own desires directly and honestly, and less willing to live through fulfilling others' needs. At the same time, men (like Lester in *American Beauty*) start to become more moody, more vulnerable and more open to emotions such as tenderness, gentleness and humour which may have been repressed throughout early adulthood by the exigencies of the male need to prove masculinity. Both men and women may begin to open to the possibility of erotic and emotional connection that is more sexually diffuse, more fluid, more androgynous. In the sense that it is connected with the reclamation of parts of the self previously projected onto the opposite sex, this way of relating may feel more complete in itself and more satisfying, and may open the door to less urgent, more relaxed and more playful forms of erotic engagement.

But in the short term, as men start to become more moody and impulsive and women more opinionated and assertive, great strains may be placed on existing relationships. And as Germaine Greer notes in *The Whole Woman,* such changes may also be difficult to come to terms with internally: 'the dependent woman is obliged to believe that only her turmoil of passion, fear, rage, expectancy and disappointment is living and that when she is no longer tormented by desire, insecurity, jealousy and the rest of the paraphernalia of romance she will be dead as a spent match'.[18]

But it need not be so. The movement towards the integrity and calm potency of psychic androgyny can feel like a coming home, a restoration of the potential for enjoyment of self which was lost – we had thought for ever – in the confusions of puberty. Such changes may put already precarious relationships

---

[18] Doubleday (1999).

under great strain. But at best they can lead towards a diminution of the role-stereotyping and the brittle, neurotic neediness and projections which typify the sexual engagements of first adulthood, and enable relationships, whether long established or recently contracted, to become less anguished, and more authentic and companionable. It is paradoxical that developing a stronger sense of self-reliance may make us more able to love and also, probably, more deeply lovable.

'She Became a Living Figure within my Mind': Internalizing the Contrasexual Image

If sexual frenzy can lead us into relationships of use, abuse and over-dependence, its abatement leads us to value and enjoy – perhaps for the first time – sexual friendship. Odysseus' reliance upon the kindness and friendship of women saves his life many times over during the ten-year haul back home from Troy: for Odysseus, the willingness to respect and trust women develops alongside his deepening awareness of his vulnerability and his own drift towards psychic androgyny, as one by one all the trappings of patriarchy loosen or are cut from him – Odysseus, as Homer wouldn't have put it, begins to discover his feminine side.

His changing attitude to women places Odysseus in contrast to his compatriot Agamemnon, offspring of the cursed house of Atreus. Like Odysseus, Agamemnon finally returns to his home after the fall of Troy, but to a less cordial welcome. Before his departure, Agamemnon had stolen his wife Clytemnestra from her first husband, raped her and later sacrificed their daughter to secure victory at Troy. Agamemnon's absence at Troy gives Clytemnestra ample time to brood over these matters and to plan her revenge. When Agamemnon returns, she runs him a bath, and murders him in it – leaving their son Orestes torn agonizingly in two, between love for his mother and his obligation to revenge his father. Contempt for the feminine ensures Agamemnon's downfall; respect for it sponsors Odysseus' survival, and his ultimate reconciliation with his own son Telemachus. Odysseus' relationship to the feminine is also personified in the figure of the goddess Athene, as the split-off feminine intuition and wisdom returning as a divine guide to help Odysseus in his times of need.

Athene presents herself to Odysseus like a muse to an artist at the moment of inspiration. Male artists may unconsciously recognize that their maleness defines, but also limits them. Openness to our repressed contrasexual elements (the feminine within a man and the masculine within a woman) creates the moment of inspiration, leading to higher states of integration which themselves imply an active relationship between male and female parts of the self.

> *My brain I'll prove the female to my soul,*
> [says Shakespeare's imprisoned Richard II]
> *My soul the father, and these two beget*
> *A generation of still-breeding thoughts.*[19]

This mingling of contrasexual elements may be a model for creative self-fulfilment not just in the fine arts but in all areas of life.

Over the Christmas of 1912 and following his break with Freud (an event which had as great repercussions in Jung's unconscious as it had in Rank's) Jung, then aged 37, entered into his own mid-life crisis. He was to struggle with it, through varying states of darkness, fear and disorientation, for the next six years, and later recounted the experience in his autobiography.[20] The onset of the crisis was marked that Christmas by a dream in which a dove appeared to Jung and transformed itself into a little blonde girl who ran off and then returned, placing her arms lovingly round his neck and saying: 'only in the first hours of the night can I transform myself into a human being, while the male dove is busy with the twelve dead'.

Over the next few years, Jung recorded a female figure or muse often appearing to him in a transpersonal form, through dreams or visions or as a disembodied voice. It seems that Jung's breakdown had psychotic elements – of which he himself, as a psychiatrist, was troublingly aware – yet with rash and no uncertain courage, he pursued his promptings. 'I once asked

---

[19] *Richard II*, Act V, Scene 5.
[20] Jung, C. G., *Memories, Dreams, Reflections*, Fontana (1983).

myself "What am I really doing? Certainly this has nothing to do with science. But then what is it?" Whereupon a voice within me said, "It is art." I was astonished … I knew for certain that the voice had come from a woman. I recognised it as the voice of a patient, a talented psychopath who had a strong transference to me. She had become a living figure within my mind …' Later he came to see this inner feminine figure as archetypal, and called it the *anima* or soul.

Creative self-expression is still mediated in our minds through the masculine forms and genres of the past, nowhere more than in the traditional relationship between the male artist and the female muse. Where masculine creativity is the norm, the unconscious (and the muse) will be seen as female, as it was by Jung. This model leaves female creativity with specific problems, which Jung's unsuccessful notion of the woman's *animus* singularly failed to address. Virginia Woolf identified the female stereotype which she warned would destroy female creativity and enterprise as the *angel in the house*. 'If there was chicken, she took the leg; if there was a draught, she sat in it – in short, she was so constituted that she never had a mind of her own, but preferred to sympathise always with the minds, and wishes of others … I turned upon her and caught her by the throat, I did my best to kill her … had I not killed her, she would have killed me. She would have plucked the heart out of my writing.'[21]

Even today, a lack of internal masculine figures to offer encouragement and inspiration may still dispose women struggling with their creativity towards a concrete over-dependence on real men, such as the controlling fathers and Svengaliesque mentors which have defined and limited female creativity in the past. Writing on the relationship between creativity and femininity, and taking Woolf's angel as her central image, Rozsika Parker suggests that women who wish to free themselves from being the object of masculine desire and the source of masculine inspiration, and to reclaim the right to their own creative self-expression, must discover their own masculine muses – internal masculine accomplices to replace the control-

---

[21] Woolf, V., *Killing the Angel in the House: Seven Essays*, Penguin (1995).

ling father-figures of the past.[22] Parker suggests that traditional female roles of receptivity, concern, mirroring, giving and avoidance of conflict must be transcended by the creative woman who must learn to recognize and own her aggression. The capacity for divergent thinking, the ability to make self-transcending changes, the openness to new emotional states and ways of thinking, the passionate involvement and the independence of judgement which she identifies as necessary for a woman to live and work creatively will be never be more required than now, in promoting the fruitful unfolding of the second half of life.

Jung noted how often love seems to be trying to deliver us to the power of a partner compounded of all the qualities we fail to realize in ourselves, like the qualities in Anthony that both attracted and enraged Belinda, and vice versa. Such love objects have a me-and-yet-not-me quality to them; through valuing these contrasexual qualities in others they may, in time, become integrated within ourselves and sexual polarizations transcended. Jung himself learnt, over time, to contain his *anima* figures within him. He learnt also not to be led astray by them but to turn to them when he felt his emotional behaviour was disturbed, signifying that something was constellating in his unconscious. ' "Now what are you up to? What do you see? I should like to know." After some resistance, she regularly produced an image. As soon as the image was there, the unrest or the sense of oppression vanished.' The intensity of renewed erotic energy at mid life which seeks its recognition and consummation in a sexual affair may – if like Odysseus we are able to listen to the music of the Sirens without crashing onto the rocks that surround them – be a symptom of the energy released from the underlying internal shift away from the rigidity of gender stereotyping towards a more complete sense of self, composed of both masculine and feminine elements.

Erotic desire reminds us of our own feelings of lack of completeness. In the West we have come to worship it, but in

---

[22] Parker, R., 'Killing the angel in the house: creativity, femininity and aggression' (1998), *International Journal of Psychoanalysis* 79(4).

Buddhism sexual desire is seen as a source of suffering rather than joy. Unlike the Judaeo-Christian tradition, however, which sees desire as sinful (against which teaching our society, through the compulsive sexualization of all its aspects, is still rebelling), Buddhism sees desire and the suffering to which it leads as being based in ignorance rather than in sin, and consequently to be transcended by insight rather than punished. Sexual dimorphism (the separation into male and female) is seen as only existing on the plane of sensual desire, and is an inevitable cause of suffering to the unenlightened mind. Spiritual life therefore in part consists of a progression towards a state of spiritual androgyny, a state of self-sufficiency, harmony and contentment which transcends gender limitations. In meditation one ceases to be, for the time being, either male or female. This state is traditionally achieved through chastity – but *Brahmacarya*, the Sanskrit word for chastity, literally means not merely abstaining from sexual activity but transcending the sexual dimorphism on which it is based, and so there seems no reason why it cannot be attained within a settled relationship.[23]

In Sufism, the mystic branch of Islam which emphasizes direct experience of God, instead of seeking possession of the desired one, an aspiring lover would take himself off alone into the desert, sometimes for many years, to meditate on the qualities of the beloved with the aim of integrating these qualities into his own soul. The death of a Sufi mystic is not considered an end but a final union with God, the ultimate beloved – its anniversary or *urs*, meaning marriage, is a cause for celebration. When Odysseus himself reaches the Land of the Dead and is most in need of spiritual solace and guidance, it is to Teiresias, the blind Prophet who has been in his lifetime both man and woman, to whom he is directed. And in other traditions, figures of spiritual devotion such as the Buddha or Jesus often have an androgynous appearance – masculine in form yet with open arms, bare breasts and an expression of gentle, encompassing maternal love. Such objects of spiritual aspiration are embodied as higher forms of the self which seeks to transcend sexual division.

---

[23] Sangharakshita, *A Guide to the Buddhist Path*, Windhorse (1995).

'Consciousness must always remain ... an island surrounded by the sea and like the sea itself the unconscious yields an endless self-replenishing supply of living creatures.'[24] For Jung as for Odysseus, the sea – like the psyche – is a vast and enigmatically shifting space teeming with hidden life under its empty broken surfaces, the universal symbol for the power of the unconscious, a great moving matrix which sustains the emergence of self-awareness, a free field for the development and exploration of previously unconscious and unrecognized self-states. Ceaselessly washing up against its beaches, sea bestows upon land the shorelines through which land defines and shapes itself, just as the self's unconscious contents and fantasies define and shape our conscious identity and expectations in a constantly evolving process. At sea, with a sense of purpose that is as yet almost entirely unconscious, often going round in circles, Odysseus progresses – in a sense, he dreams himself – through maturing states of erotic awareness, from the first romantic flight to rescue Helen, through the sexually charged and belligerent confrontation with Circe and the sadder, more introspective years with Calypso, to the bittersweet sublimation of desire in the song of the Sirens, forever heard and forever out of reach, and still onwards towards Ithaca, where Penelope has been struggling within her own webs of desire. Odysseus' progression shows how we are defined and changed by the ways in which we use those we desire and love, and also how our use of our erotic relationships is itself likely to change over time.

After a certain age we realize that genital friction alone won't bring the erotic into being, and mid life also brings a sad realization that the persistent ideal of the happy-ever-after couple may be attainable only partially, at best, within our own lives. Yet at the same time, the draining of concrete sexual and reproductive need and the maturing of our internal resources yield their own rewards. The cultivation of courage, patience, humour and kindness begins to augur better for a more satisfying sexual relationship than we might have expected. And creative aliveness and fulfilment – which once seemed

---

[24] Jung, C. G., *The Psychology of the Transference*, Ark (1983).

within the gift of erotic union alone – may, after all, be within our own gift, more securely realizable within ourselves than we could have known.

7

Leaving Home

Daddy, daddy, you bastard, I'm through.

From 'Daddy' by Sylvia Plath

About 250,000 people will go missing in the United Kingdom this year, as they do every year. Many will be under 18, and most will turn up again within a few days. But of the 20 new cases deemed serious enough to be registered every day by the National Missing Persons Helpline, four or five will involve people at mid life (between 36 and 55 years old). The families they leave are as likely to be comfortably middle-class as they are to be poor and disadvantaged, but disappearing men outnumber disappearing women by more than three to one.[1]

Some of those who go missing return voluntarily weeks or months later, but many others do not. And at least another six people in the same mid-life age group will, today, take the even more drastic exit route of killing themselves (these official figures are generally agreed to be an underestimate, as suicide verdicts are only recorded where suicidal intent can be conclusively proved). It is not easy to kill yourself – the Samaritans estimate

---

[1] National Missing Persons Helpline, *Case for Support* (2000).

that for every successful suicide there are around 100 attempts.[2] Again, men outnumber women by about four to one in cases of completed suicide, though not in attempted suicide. Then there are the thousands who leave their homes and families each year by more conventional means, often burning their bridges behind them. Half of all divorces are granted to people at mid life, an average of 200 divorces per day in England and Wales.[3] These statistics too are the tip of an iceberg, representing only a fraction of all the long-term relationships fracturing and breaking at this time and all the individual stories of shattered hope and numb despair which make them up.

On the other hand, of course, the solution of ditching everything, drawing a line and starting again unencumbered can have an appealing simplicity and straightforwardness about it, at least in comparison with what is left behind. A new life to match – or to sponsor – a new self. A man who has for a long time felt helpless, silenced, hemmed in by the demands and agendas of others may, in leaving, be making his first act of assertion in years. People who walk out of their lives may feel they are taking their destinies back into their own hands. After years of having felt taken for granted, the act of leaving may restore to those who leave a sense of visibility and of mattering – both to themselves and also, paradoxically, to those they leave behind.

Leaving is a solution which, the figures suggest, appeals to men more than women. Men are more likely to feel betrayed by the gender revolution and alarmed or resentful about the transformation of women's expectations, more likely to feel passive, helpless or inarticulate in emotionally turbulent situations, and more likely to feel too ashamed to reveal the depths of their inner uncertainties, dissatisfactions, and feelings of failure. Finding their own emotional lives and needs to be as much of a problem – or a puzzle – as their own fathers did, they may at the same time have lost faith in their fathers' moral certainties, which reiterated belief in the value of sticking it out anyway.

At times all of us – men and women – may find the internal

---

[2] Samaritans Information Resources and Key Fact Sheets (2000).
[3] Figures from the Office for National Statistics, marriage rates for the period 1987–97.

disturbances evoked by relationship problems too difficult or uncomfortable to engage with, sometimes because of the forbidden nature of the feelings of anxiety, anger or guilt which they engender. Difficulties which can neither be confronted nor denied are likely to be projected outwards, and mentally reframed as the problem of the other – the cold, unloving partner, the undermining boss, the impossible teenager. Becoming emotionally passive or paralysed by depression, we come to see our problems as existing outside ourselves and outside our own ability to do anything about them. In such circumstances, cutting and running may seem like the only solution, and the urgency to believe this is the case fires up the resolve to carry it through.

When a man leaves without warning, the woman he leaves behind will often say: 'I knew he'd been down, but he never said much. I had no idea it was that bad. Why didn't he say anything?' The man who leaves because he is having an affair is giving her a sort of answer; but he may know in his heart it is less of an answer than it seems.

A corporate lawyer in his forties walks out on his wife and young children, having begun an affair. Initially he had planned to move in with his eager new lover:

> Yet I just can't get it together. I just keep moving from one hotel room to another. When I was still with my wife, every time I touched her I'd ima-gine my girlfriend's face, her smell, her body, and I'd feel cold and numb inside; now when I'm with my girlfriend, my wife's face as I was leaving keeps flashing in front of me. My girlfriend's been talking about us find-ing somewhere to buy together. I say nothing. Inside I start to feel trapped again, to panic. Am I going through all this, all this pain, for it just to end up the same again? I think I'm still in love – I still burn with desire for her. But after I've had sex with her, sometimes I just start crying for my children. I leave the room so she can't see. I'm scared I'll end up going back to my wife and everything will close in round me again.

> Actually, the only thing that seems to bring me peace at the moment is going for long walks in the dark all by myself, thinking about my girl-friend, seeing her face before me, imagining her body yet not really wanting to touch it. I think of myself as a prowler, a hunter, an outcast; I look in through lighted windows at families sitting watching television or

157

round the meal table, domestic scenes like the one I left . . . I feel a sadness and a wildness inside me. All I want to do is to keep on walking.

Beware the premature solution. Between a third and a half of
divorced people are said to regret their divorces and wish, in
retrospect, that they had tried harder to save their marriages
(these are high figures, given such regrets may be difficult to
confront even privately). Sometimes leaving may prove to be in
the best interests of everyone concerned, but it is still a drastic
remedy and it may take the impulsive, rash courage generated by
falling in love again to carry it through. Moving from a failed
relationship straight into a new one may open up new horizons –
or may be a leap out of the frying pan and into the fire. Even
apart from the suspended and shattered lives that walking out
leaves behind, abandoning the accumulated securities and
achievements of a lifetime is a solution that can only be carried
through at great personal cost, emotional and otherwise. The
degree of loss which leaving entails – loss of emotional stability,
loss of children, loss of family, social networks and support
systems, loss of financial solvency and social status, loss of
identity and even loss of life itself – is a testament to the number
of disturbed and unsettled people walking the streets of Britain
today, and to the quiet desperation which ferments unseen
behind our prosperous urban and suburban façades.

The restless urge to become more separate and less
encumbered is a significant and in some ways propitious aspect
of mid-life transition. But the angry destructiveness and
desperation of many abrupt acts of departure – which sometimes
become final not so much because finality was meant but
because of the degree of damage and loss of trust incurred along
the way – demonstrate our weaknesses, as individuals and as a
society, in understanding and negotiating the conflicts which
lead to crisis. More often we divert or stifle the warning signals,
ignoring them in the hope that they'll go away – until the
pressure becomes intolerable and something explodes. And the
tendency to ignore such difficulties until they do become
overwhelming, and the dilemma of whether – or how – to
continue in a life that has lost meaning, is for no-one more acute
than for the fathers and mothers of dependent children.

COMING ROUND AGAIN: THE MID-LIFE FAMILY AND THE GENERATIONAL RETURN

As parents we see living evidence every day of the intensity of our children's vulnerabilities and the non-negotiable nature of their need for continuity, stability and reliability. We are moved by the openness and directness with which they express these needs, recognizing, however dimly, the stirrings of similar needs in the most private and vulnerable parts of our own psyches. What dependent children demonstrate absolutely is true more relatively for all of us in those intimate relationships where we have risked allowing vulnerable and trusting parts of ourselves to be invested and revealed over time. Yet at the same time, the demands within us to respond to the call of the future – for change, for something new – may be as powerful as our most deeply entrenched loyalties to the past. And while our children demand of us that we stay, and stay the same, it is our children also whose accelerating lives remind us that only change is constant. For they too grow and leave us; they are leaving us all the time.

At the beginning, and for a while, we are the centre of gravity around which our children's lives revolve, a responsibility both paralysing and profoundly focusing. But as our children start to move outwards and into different orbits, themselves torn between the security of the family and their desire to escape its confines, we, their parents, may also begin to feel the stirrings of a wayward drift within ourselves. Mutinous feelings towards authority, parental figures and the demands of family are a common feature of mid-life reorientation, profoundly affecting our lives within the families we have created around ourselves as adults, as partners and as parents. Reassessment of our places as adults within our own families makes us look at our children differently, just as the movement of our children through their young lives may stir forgotten memories within ourselves, returning us in imagination to our own childhoods and adolescence – and in so doing, also reconnecting us with just what it was that we ourselves wanted so urgently to get away from.

As more of us prioritize our careers and postpone parenthood into our mid-thirties or beyond – and as more of us are tending

159

to have children at different times of our lives with different partners – the children and step-children of mid-life parents range from the very young to those who are becoming adults themselves. As parents we make powerful unconscious identifications with our children as we see them negotiating their own transitions through the conflicts of infancy and toddlerhood, and through the agonizing self-consciousness and furtive excitements of adolescence. Our identifications with our children form the basis of empathic parenting – but we should be wary of using them to collapse the generational gap instead of just to bridge it. The newly single mother who borrows her seventeen-year-old daughter's make-up and clothes to go clubbing with her, and the father in the throes of a painful divorce who takes his teenage son and friends to Glastonbury and spends four days getting stoned in the mud with them, may only end up further confusing both their children and the turbulent nature of their own mid-life transitions. Changing relationships with growing children may provide the impetus for our own transitions, and complicate still further our already complicated mid-life crises. They cannot resolve them for us. To unravel the domestic dynamics that are working themselves out as we reach mid life, we may need to take a step back to look at how our families came together in the first place.

Nora Ephron's novel *Heartburn*[4] is a thinly disguised account of the breakdown of Ephron's own marriage to Watergate reporter Carl Bernstein. 'I realized' says the novel's narrator, a seven-months-pregnant cookery writer in her late thirties whose husband begins an affair with a Washington socialite, 'something . . . no-one tells you: that a child is a grenade. When you have a baby you set off an explosion in your marriage and when the dust settles, your marriage is different from what it was . . . all power struggles have a new playing field.' The advent of children within a relationship is a cataclysmic event which can hurl us into a maturity for which we are not really ready and against whose demands we may be propelled to take evasive action, precipitating the desire for flight. However joyfully anticipated – and

---

[4] Heinemann (1983).

however fulfilling it indeed proves to be – parenthood is often a more traumatic shock than we had bargained for. It involves loss as well as gain, and despite bringing couples together in an initial blossoming of love and pride it may also begin to deepen any invisible hairline fissures already present in the relationship between them.

We wander into our marriages heady with romantic expectation, but underpinning the intensity of our feelings there lingers sometimes an unconscious longing for the final consummation of the unfulfilled needs of childhood – for kind, stable and unselfish parental devotion, now (best of all) sexualized, and for undemanding, unconditional support and affirmation. One of the reasons that marriage in the past worked so well for men was that the traditional marriage contract did indeed implicitly require women to shoulder this maternal burden – intended to pass without demur from mother to wife – of managing their husbands' internal lives as well as those of their children, processing their emotional disturbances and soothing their egos as well as ironing their shirts and warming their beds.

Although women are as likely as men unconsciously to desire the restoration of unconditional maternal love and nurturing within marriage, the same implicit contract by no means required men to take responsibility for their wives' emotional well-being or bolster *their* sense of self-esteem. As umpteen studies – and the statistics for divorce petitions, most of which are lodged by women – have shown, marriage may accordingly be a far greater source of disillusionment and disappointment to women. Fetching up with only the uncertain emotional solace of becoming mothers themselves, women in families who are approaching mid life often find they have to do all the nurturing themselves. It may never occur to anyone – including themselves – that it should be otherwise. As they get older, women also start to forgo more of the sexual attention and affirmation from men which may once have offered a satisfactory (or enhanced) alternative to maternal nurturing. Invisible, existing only to serve others' needs, the child hidden within the maturing woman often languishes deprived, hopeless and silent. Women who do not have a good store of maternal love from their own childhoods upon which to draw will be most at risk, and the maternal depression which ensues may extend for many years beyond the post-natal period.

Some couples create relationships of reciprocal love and concern in the years before children arrive, and are able to reclaim each other once their children start to grow up. But there is no doubt that starting a family puts such finely-tuned arrangements under threat. Sometimes our expectations of family life prove too inflexible to adjust to our changing sense of personal entitlement, and then something must give. Today one in five women say they do not want children of their own (the reluctance of men is taken for granted and rarely reported upon), and many others delay parenthood as long as possible. These figures reflect the many other avenues of fulfilment now open to women, but also apprehension about the effect that becoming a mother may have on their careers, their aspirations, their relationships – and their mental well-being.

The unspoken resentment we feel as parents in complying – as initially we must – with our children's relentlessly insistent demands (often with scant support or understanding from the wider community) is mitigated by the varied consolations, richnesses and pleasures of family life and by the mature feelings of love and protectiveness which are stimulated by, and evolve through, our relationships with our children. The sheer exhaustion of life as a working parent of young children also inevitably (a mixed blessing, this) circumscribes time for brooding introspection about one's own unmet needs. But these unmet needs may nevertheless dispose us towards feeling usurped by our own children, resentful of their endless demands, envious of their glowing youth. We may find ourselves jealous too of their confident hold upon the affections and the body of their other parent – a territory over which we ourselves once unthinkingly enjoyed first claim. Sometimes these feelings are denied and split off into unconsciousness, festering unseen or grumbling quietly underneath the surface, to flare up many years later.

Josie and Max were both absorbed in their careers in journalism, rising stars in their own fields. They postponed having children until Josie was 37 and becoming increasingly aware of the ticking of her biological clock. Their son's birth was not difficult, and he proved an easy-going baby. Having organized a nanny, Josie went back to her full-time job on the features desk of a national newspaper for the following two years, until her daughter was born.

This time the pregnancy did not go so well. Josie had complications and her daughter, who was slightly premature, did not immediately thrive. Josie had planned to return to work full-time again after her maternity leave. But she thought, prompted by guilt, that the stress of her work had probably contributed to the complications of her second pregnancy and the difficulty she was now experiencing in bonding with her daughter. She was also finding the broken nights and the demands and needs of two children – a jealous and now fractious toddler as well as the new baby – very much harder to cope with than one. So as Max was now earning enough to support the family comfortably, they decided she would not go back to her job, but stay at home with the children and, over time, build up a more flexible freelance career. Josie duly handed in her notice.

But Josie became listless and depressed. She felt a gulf opening between herself and her circle of former friends, who drank and gossiped at the same bars every night, and found it more difficult than she had expected to summon the motivation to succeed at her freelance career. Moping and dawdling around the house in a dressing gown most days, Josie started to comfort eat and put on weight, and this fed into the cycle of low self-esteem which was gaining an insidious hold over her. She also hid the fact that she had started to drink more.

Objectively, Josie felt that their previous lives as dual-career parents of young children had become a nightmare of exhaustion, and with no-one except a variety of hired help holding things together, the infrastructure of the family had been beginning to fall apart. She did not want to end up like that again. But although it made sense for Josie to be the one to slow-pedal for a while, she was unconsciously feeling deeply envious of Max's thriving career. She felt she had become invisible.

Over the next few years, Josie became more and more emotionally dependent upon Max, but was aware that she had at the same time become colder and more withdrawn and critical towards him. She felt resentful and jealous when he came home from work, often late, and was engulfed immediately by the children whom he adored. She began to wonder if he was having an affair. As they seemed to have less and less in common beyond the children, and as she felt him seeming to withdraw from her, she began to panic.

> There are days when we don't speak until he phones from the office to say he'll be late back, or ask if I mind if he stays out another bloody evening. I try and keep the edge from my voice when I say it's fine. Then I put the phone down, the children start fighting or demanding some-

163

thing and I just start crying. When he finally gets back, something will trigger it and then all this anger and criticism flood out. We end up in another cold silence, and it drives us further apart.

Josie's own parents had divorced acrimoniously, due to her father's absences and infidelities, once Josie left home to go to college. Josie had never been close to her mother: she was always her father's daughter. Her father had been the charismatic editor of a national newspaper, and she describes him as a flirtatious and charming womanizer. She remembers as a child being alone with her mother in their house, which seemed cold and grey during his long, erratic absences: she remembers listening for the sound of her father's car swinging into the drive, the scrunch of gravel, the slam of the door, the booming voice, the smell of his cigars, the sense of life switching back from black and white into colour. She remembers being swung round and round by him until she was dizzy, being tickled until she screamed in delight and agony, waving her legs in the air, begging for mercy. She remembers her mother watching in the shadows, saying nothing.

Josie remembers hanging over the banisters at night, eavesdropping on her parents' raised voices behind closed doors, her ears straining for the sound of her own name. She remembers running out after her father when he left the house in anger, walking out on her mother's recriminations. Later, she remembers time with him alone, or with him and his girlfriend of the moment, time snatched in restaurants, nightclubs and aeroplanes.

For Josie, the intense and possessive love-relationship of her childhood was all between herself and her father, and from this her mother had been excluded. Some of the passion with which Josie turned to her father was made up of her displaced longing for maternal love, frustrated within her unhappy relationship with her mother. Josie's decisive turning towards her father was an act of revenge against her mother, as well as an attempt to make up the deficit. Within the flirtatious and always precarious relationship with her father, these longings for maternal love were partly eroticized, partly buried.

Josie's confidence as a young adult stemmed from her triumph in having won, in her own mind, the battle with her mother for her father's love. In the short to medium term, this confidence served her well enough and enabled her in due course to find her own niche in the self-promoting, thrusting world of journalism, where she revelled without too much reflection in its hothouse atmosphere of backbiting intrigue, ruthless competition and the ever-present urgency of the deadline. In this world, as far as Josie was concerned, the seductive, exciting father reigned – embodied in the succession of older male editors for whom she worked, whose language she spoke and whose desires she knew so well how to stimulate and flatter.

Parenthood draws us towards an identification with our same-sex parent. Those who, like Josie, saw this relationship founder in anger or disappointment, or in the parent's absence or depression, will inevitably have a harder time of it when they become parents themselves. Not until Josie was left alone with her own children (a situation she had herself engineered, motivated by her own guilt and anxiety in relation to her daughter's needs) could she understand how dependent she had been upon men – latterly upon Max – to reflect warmth, light and meaning into her life. Now with the birth of her own daughter, the whirligig of time seemed to be bringing in its revenges. With a heavy though unconscious internal fatalism she felt, rather than saw, the inevitability of Max turning from his dull wife to his adoring young daughter. And Josie waited with paralysed dread to become the silent mother over whom she had once, a generation ago, so casually triumphed.

Like Josie's memory of being swung round, tickled and disorientated by her father, particular memory images (especially early ones) condense and convey a wealth of symbolic meaning. And, like Josie, we remember the past not just through our conscious memories but through our bodies and the relationship structures we create in our adult lives, and through the unconscious fatalism and expectations which shape our choices. Forgotten childhood experiences – especially traumatic ones or those which do not fit in with our conscious ideas of who we are – return in adulthood as otherwise inexplicable illnesses, moods and beliefs about life. Our adult selves may not easily recognize as our own these feelings and impulses, which we have previously made a point of avoiding.[5]

Feelings we have denied return, not in connection to the

---

[5] Freud, S., 'Inhibitions, Symptoms and Anxieties' (1926), Part XI: Addenda, in *Penguin Freud Library* 10.

memories which might explain them, but as free-floating states of anxiety or depression, while the forgotten dynamics of early relationships get transferred to present ones, where they are acted out for better or for worse. Adults, thought Freud, repeat forgotten memories as actions – the impulsion to remember becomes replaced by the compulsion to repeat.[6] It is in this sense that hysterics suffer, he suggested, from remembering – or more accurately from the failure to remember. So, the inexplicable stomach pains and fragmented thought patterns of the woman diagnosed as hysteric or borderline may be a subverted language demanding – incoherently yet insistently – recognition of the abuse she suffered as a child. Women like Josie who become depressed after the birth of a child may be unable to find within themselves a good internal experience of having been nurtured upon which to draw. Instead, they re-enact the despairing relationship between depressed mother and lonely child.

A parent's own individual patterns and idioms of care – that is, the particular way this parent relates to and cares for this child – are learnt and stored within the child's unconscious, sometimes reviving and re-emerging a generation later when powerfully triggered by the birth of a new child.[7] We are taken aback to hear our mothers' and fathers' long-forgotten turns of phrase come unbidden from our own mouths when we become parents, and surprised to discover how familiar our relationships with our new babies seem to us already. In the words of George Santayana, those who cannot remember the past are bound to repeat it.[8] At the edges of our awareness we struggle for mastery of the unconscious habits and patterns of relating which besiege our minds. One way or the other – through understanding and integration or, if that is not possible, through repeating – the circle demands to be completed, the gestalt achieved.

[6] Freud, S., 'Remembering, Repeating and Working Through' (1914) in *Standard Edition* XII.

[7] See Winnicott, D. W., *The Maturational Processes and the Facilitating Environment*, Karnac (1990), and Bollas, C., *Forces of Destiny: Psychoanalysis and Human Idiom*, Free Association Books (1989).

[8] *The Life of Reason* (1905).

The urge to repeat the past – the pull created by the unconscious transmission from one generation to the next of internal psychic reality – is likely to be at its strongest when we become adults and parents ourselves, for the real powers and freedoms of adulthood give us licence to re-enact actively as agents what we could once only suffer helplessly as children. Sometimes what we recreate without realizing is our internalized experience of spontaneous affection and understanding – of being held within a secure and trusting relationship which can be taken for granted. But sometimes the young psyche has to split off and deny difficult or painful experiences because it is too immature to confront them directly without becoming over-whelmed. These most traumatic and painful scenarios of our childhood are liable to become repeated, re-engineered within situations of haunting similarity.

Marriage breakdown 1

As a child, Harry is repeatedly beaten by his father. His father's rage is arbitrary but is most rapidly provoked when some trivial childish misdemeanour of Harry's has 'upset your mother'. For this, the child is thrashed brutally around his head. Cowering silently in a corner, Harry also observes his drunken father returning home and laying about his mother, as well as any of his own brothers and sisters who try to stand up to him.

Thirty years later, Harry is a married man. Shrinking inwardly from his wife Liz's verbal tongue-lashings, smiling absent-mindedly at her as he does so, Harry plots to leave her as once he plotted to leave his childhood home. In the course of fifteen years of marriage (he married as soon as he left his parents' home, seeking from marriage the loving security that had eluded his childhood) he has never really talked openly to Liz or expressed any anger and pain to her, as this might 'upset' her, and that is what he knows he must never do. Obviously, though, walking out on the marriage may upset her. As Harry's secret plans start to crystallize and his anxiety intensifies, he has flashbacks to childhood and his father hitting him around his head and ears. These flashbacks leave him feeling stunned and dizzy. Nevertheless, one winter morning just after Christmas Harry packs a suitcase, leaves a note and his front door key on the kitchen table, and walks out.

He settles down into a rented bedsit, but the dizzy spells and blackouts get worse. The following week his car skids as he is driving too fast along an icy road and crashes into a lamp-post. He is cut from the wreckage and taken to hospital with severe head injuries. When he is discharged, it is back to his family house, for Liz has agreed to take him back. She has realized, she says, that he had not been himself. Harry knows he must be grateful for her forgiveness. The absent-minded smile returns.

Marriage breakdown 2

When Andrew is six, his mother suffers a breakdown into paranoid psychosis which climaxes on the night she flees the family house with him stowed away, terrified, in the back of the car. She is hospitalized, medicated and eventually returned to the family. The episode is never mentioned again and the family seems to make a good recovery: Andrew grows up, qualifies as a vet, marries and has a son. When their son is eleven, Andrew persuades his wife Sarah – on account of the soaring crime rate, poor air quality and dreadful local comprehensives – to uproot from their urban professional lives to the part of rural Scotland where he grew up, and which he still thinks of as home. In the stress consequent upon their move, the marriage deteriorates. Andrew's work helps him to re-forge his local connections and he settles down well, but Sarah feels more and more isolated in their remote village among people with whom she has little in common. Previously an affectionate husband, Andrew starts to seem irritated by her, and withdraws emotionally. He responds to Sarah's increasingly frightened attempts to reach him by saying that he will not speak to her while she is hysterical. First, in subtle ways, then more obviously, he says things to his wife which undermine and confuse her but which he later denies, staring at her in blank incomprehension and shaking his head when she repeats them back to him. Depressed and lonely, with no-one to turn to but her son, and feeling increasingly unstable, Sarah thinks: 'I feel as if he's trying to drive me mad. That's ridiculous. I must be going mad'.

Sarah feels as if she is being helplessly drawn down a dark tunnel by a pull outside herself. Afraid for her own state of mind if she stays and equally afraid that her husband will never agree to a separation from his son, in the dead of night she secretly packs her bags, stows her son away in the back of the car and flees with him back to the city.

Harry and Andrew both sought marriage and children out of their determination to create families different from the ones in which they had grown up, only to discover, in the end, that the pull towards repetition is not so easy to legislate against. But does this imply that we must be bound helplessly to our histories? Fate – or fatalism – binds us at an unconscious level only, and coming into awareness can in itself be transformative. To engage with unconscious forces as they are embodied and

168

enacted in the individual circumstances of our lives takes courage
– it challenges and confronts our constructed sense of identity
and certainty, but at the same time paves the way towards self-
reconciliation and liberation. Sophocles' *Oedipus Rex*[9] tells –
with the same stomach-churning sense of inevitability that
suffuses the stories of Harry and Andrew – the story of people
who bring about what they most dread (in Sophocles' story, the
fulfilment of the curse that Oedipus will kill his father and marry
his mother), and do so entirely as a result of the efforts which
they stumblingly and self-deludingly make to avoid it. In his self-
hatred and shame, Oedipus blinds himself when his own part in
bringing about the fulfilment of the curse – which he has himself
insisted upon discovering – is revealed to him. But this is by no
means the end of the story. In *Oedipus at Colonus*, the final part
of the trilogy, the blind Oedipus discovers an ability to look
inwards unflinchingly, with clarity and compassion, and to take
responsibility for his own destiny. In doing so, he finally attains
peace of mind.

The path which leads – should we choose to follow it –
towards the acceptance of personal responsibility for our own
perspective, and the way in which it has shaped and informed the
world we once inherited, takes us through difficult and
confronting territory. It is not surprising that many of us will,
at times, take refuge from it – from our subjectivity, our
complexity and our essential aloneness – in a domestic life which
reproduces the helpless certainties of childhood. Writing on the
pertinence of Sophocles' myth to the world which we inhabit
today, Bollas suggests that for many, a retreat from the
sometimes unbearable responsibility of possessing one's own
mind may be necessary for survival:

> This retreat has been so essential to human life that it has become an
> unanalysed convention, part of the religion of everyday life. We call this
> regression 'marriage' or 'partnership' in which the person becomes
> part of a mutually interdependent couple that evokes and sustains the
> bodies of the mother and father, the warmth of the pre-Oedipal vision of
> life, before the solitary recognition of subjectivity grips the child. Ego

---

[9] *The Three Theban Plays*, tr. Fagles, R., Penguin (1984).

development is thus a transformative regression: back to being in the family, this time through the vicarious rememberings generated through raising a family, absorbing oneself in cultivating a garden, and putting out of one's mind as best one can quite what one has seen when leaving the garden in the first place.[10]

Bollas benignly conceives of this place of pseudo-security – the family life in which refuge from the terror of essential aloneness is sought – as a garden which we can (like Candide) learn to cultivate. But when these families which we have created become unhappy or oppressive, or when the longing for a new experience of selfhood begins to reassert itself and to shatter domestic complacencies, this garden may start to feel more like a dungeon or a cave, policed by those internal parental figures who coerce us into self-sacrifice and obedience as the price of retaining their approval and protection. In such circumstances, a violent crisis – powerful enough to shatter all our fortified and over-rehearsed reasoning about how it has to be this way – may become as hopefully anticipated as it is feared.

ENCOUNTERING THE TYRANT: INSIDE THE CYCLOPS' CAVE

After leaving the land of the Lotus-eaters, where time stood still in a narcoleptic haze, Odysseus sails on to the land of the Cyclops, a luxuriant island of mountains, forests, rich soil and lush water meadows – the lyrically evoked landscape suggests a baby's-eye view of the hills, hollows and free-flowing streams which form the geography of a mother's body. But this fertile land is, unfortunately, in the possession of a violently uncivilized race of giants, the one-eyed Cyclops. Arriving at the mouth of a great cave overhung by a growth of laurel bushes – the parallel with the entrance to the womb could not be more graphic – Odysseus and twelve of his men penetrate into a space full of delicious cheeses, baby lambs and goats, and vessels swimming in whey. Revelling in the apparent security which the cave offers,

---

[10] Bollas, C., 'Why Oedipus?' in *Being a Character*, Routledge (1993).

they help themselves to cheese and kill and roast one of the beasts. In the circumstances, the appearance of the towering one-eyed giant at the mouth of the cave, angrily returned to reclaim his rights, does not bode well for the small and greedy interlopers.

Odysseus watches in helpless horror as the Cyclops, whose name is Polyphemus, replies to his greeting and request for hospitality by seizing two of his men, dashing their brains out and eating them up, and then falls asleep on the floor of the cave in a drunken, sated stupor. Odysseus' first instinct is to kill the giant, but he realizes that this would mean his own death, as he and his remaining men would never be able to roll aside the great boulder Polyphemus has placed at the mouth of the cave to trap them, intending to feast on the fresh bodies of the remaining men at his leisure. So Odysseus bides his time. Eventually, having drugged Polyphemus with wine – and having told the Cyclops his name is Nobody – he plunges a heated stave into the giant's sole eye, blinding him. The other Cyclops come running in response to their neighbour's anguished screams; but upon being told that Nobody has harmed him, they trudge off grumpily and dimly back to bed, wondering what all the fuss was about. The next day, as the blinded Polyphemus sits by the mouth of the cave feeling the fleece of his flock and counting them out to pasture, Odysseus and his surviving men make their escape by clinging on to the underbellies of the sheep.

Among the peaceful Lotus-eaters, food was freely available, but at the cost of stagnation and denial of the self. Arrival in the land of the Cyclops depicts a progression of sorts, from dependence and compliance towards self-assertion and confrontation with the parental figure in its most primitive and oppressive manifestation – the cave was initially entered hopefully, as a place of potential refuge, but it soon becomes a place of nightmare constriction and escalating deadly conflict. Desire can no longer be indulged at will, in an orgy of milky guzzling; everything now must be paid for, and more. Conflict – and the possibility that aggression will cause real and irreparable damage – becomes terrifyingly real. Against this tyrant, such civilized social overtures as Odysseus essays, bringing the giant wine as an offering and calling on him for hospitality in the name of Zeus, are pointless – the benign daytime Zeus-father is by no means the same figure as this nightmare parent poised to crush and destroy the greedy, sensual child.

Stories like *Jack and the Beanstalk* and *Snow White* evoke, at a safe remove, the power of the huge, violent fathers and murderously envious mothers who haunt the fringes of our imaginations. Such figures may bear little resemblance to our own parents, especially from the perspective of our adulthoods. Yet as children we sometimes experience our parents as self-centred, undermining or controlling towards us. Sometimes our perspectives are magnified and distorted by our own childish rage or jealous and rivalrous feelings of inadequacy, while some parents can be genuinely unpredictable, abusive or violent – like the father of Harry, the man whose headlong flight ended in a car crash on an icy road. In our infancy, our parents are all-powerful, and throughout our formative years their perspectives construct and construe the world for us. Nearly always, and come what may, we carry on loving them throughout our childhoods with devotion of an intensity that we will never surpass, blinding ourselves to their shortcomings and striving endlessly for their approval. But at the same time our unconscious rage and jealousy towards them may create split-off tyrant figures within our own minds that return to haunt our dreams and our lives.

Enveloped in the psychic atmosphere that our parents have created for us, our choices and ability to express ourselves are directed and censored by our need for their approval and love. The rage and jealousy which they also evoke – our images of them as monsters – may be pushed deep down into the recesses of the unconscious or the dreaming mind. Like the Cyclops, these unconscious images slumber uneasily when they are propitiated and appeased by our sacrifices, but spring to life with a terrifying roar when they are confronted. So, popular anti-heroes such as the suave Hannibal Lecter in Thomas Harris' *Silence of the Lambs*,[11] who tears off a man's face with his bare hands and sautés another's liver with fava beans, reflect back the primitive violence and greed within our own hearts, allowing us to identify with them – at a safe distance.

---

[11] Mandarin (1991).

Our world is more violent than ever, but much of this violence takes place behind closed doors, kept carefully within the family. There is uproar on the rare occasions when a woman is killed by a stranger after breaking down on a motorway, or a child is abducted while walking home from school or lost in a shopping mall, but deafening silence about the fact that two women are murdered by their partners every week, and that a child is vastly more likely to be killed or sexually abused by a parent or step-parent than by someone unknown. London's Metropolitan Police receive a report of domestic violence every six minutes of every day, and domestic violence alone accounts for one quarter of all violent crime (the police estimate that on average each call to them will be preceded by thirty or more assaults for which the ashamed or terrified victim seeks no help).[12] As far as children are concerned, the right of parents to mete out to their more fragile bodies the sort of violence which, were it to be directed against an adult would be considered a criminal assault, is still protected by law. Violence within families – from the stronger towards the weaker – is today still ignored and implicitly tolerated in ways that would be unheard of in other circumstances.

A famous study of suicide by Al Alvarez was called *The Savage God*[13] after the South American god Tezcatlipoca, who caused wars, bestowed favours and took prosperity and fortune away with capricious abandon. In life lived at the most primitive, retaliatory level, the jealous gods of the last generation seek to devour their children and will only be propitiated by sacrifice. So in another part of the forest, when Snow White begins to grow up and rival her mother's beauty, she is condemned to have her heart torn out of her body, her crime being the awakening of the mother queen's envious rage (*mirror, mirror on the wall...*). Unless Snow White can become a little less snow white – unless she can grow out of her mute childish obliviousness, unless she can name and confront the queen's envy and muster the resources and the allies that will help her to mature and survive its attacks – unless and until

---

[12] Figures from the Metropolitan Police, Adhikar Global Conference on Domestic Violence, London, October 2000.
[13] Penguin (1993).

then, she will be condemned to die, or as good as.

Our internal parents speak sometimes with jealous, controlling voices, no less powerful through operating at an unconscious level. They forbid us to aspire to more than they had themselves or to surpass them in our own achievements, and threaten us with punishment if we seek to live life by values different from their own. Finding ourselves in conflict with them, we are tempted to whimper and crumple, to give up, making an involuntary regression to a childlike state in which the jealous voices resume satisfied control: *honour thy father and thy mother*. Often we are more in thrall to our parental gods than we realize, children still of a Judaeo-Christian heritage in which meekness and obedience are idealized to the detriment and devaluation of more awkward (but potentially more helpful) qualities like courage, curiosity and initiative. Rather than confronting the voices that command our obedience, we grow up and substitute new ones – the company which employs us, the religion or current ideology to which we subscribe, the person we have married: she, he or they who must be obeyed.

The possibility of freedom from authoritarian voices – the possibility of living for oneself and according to one's own ethical values, rather than according to another's agenda – may bring about anxiety so great that it precipitates almost instantaneously a retreat into the certainty of 'knowing' according to the parental voice who says: *I will look after you if you have no other gods but me*. From such anxieties and insecurities, the internal parental voices of the workaholic, the obsessional or the anorexic rescue her by promising security and approval if only she works harder, controls more, desires less. The parental voice of the paranoid warns him never to trust anyone outside the family (and never to tell about what goes on inside it), while the parental voice of the depressive reminds her that she is worthless and useless, that her aggression and creativity are bad, that only her passive submission is good.

Plato too offers us an image of the cave as allegory of the human condition.[14] In Plato's cave, men live chained facing the

---

[14] Plato, *The Republic*, Penguin (1974).

wall throughout their lives; they can see the shadows cast by the light of reality upon the wall of the cave, but not reality itself. Such men, says Plato, would be afraid and resist if released to stand upright and to look directly at the light itself. This fear of the unknown, of independence, of reality itself – suggests Plato – keeps us trapped hopelessly in the cave of inhibited living. Unconsciously, it binds us to those internal voices which amplify through generations the echoes of our parents' and their parents' fears and resentments and turns them into self-fulfilling prophecies.

ESCAPE FROM THE CAVE

The story of the escape from the Cyclops' cave is the story of the individual's struggle to give birth to him or herself. The child is father to the man, and by mid life the task beckons for us to give birth to ourselves once more – it may take that long for us to develop sufficient internal awareness and resolve to become able to confront, in any sustained way, our punitive parental gods. But as the corpses left on the floor of the Cyclops' cave testify, separation can be bloody work. The confrontations with the hostile or life-denying parents which cannot be worked through within our own psyches may be acted out in relation to our current families, sometimes perpetuating cycles of abuse, pain and abandonment.

Our struggle to give birth to ourselves as individuals is also a struggle with death anxiety. For a child to be born, a pregnancy must terminate and an umbilical cord be cut – and as we move on to a new stage of life, a previous self must die and old loyalties be severed once more. Otto Rank conceived of the infant's birth as an experience of propulsion from a previously safe but now agonizingly constricting container into an unknown future, a terrifying new spaciousness.[15] The memory of being born – a trauma too overwhelming to be integrated into the baby's virtually non-existent ego or immature psychosomatic system –

---

[15] Rank, O., *The Trauma of Birth*, Dover (1993).

may persist unconsciously in the psyche–soma, and so we respond to later anxiety situations with the same stress responses of loss of breath, pounding of the heart, dizziness and disorientation as we experienced while being born. So the birth experience becomes the model for all our subsequent transitions, the archetype of our subsequent anxieties. *All* situations of anxiety, believed Rank, are separation anxieties, fearful responses to the threat of change which ultimately derive from the massive separation anxiety of birth; and all seek their resolution in the desire to return to the womb, whether through intoxication or the satisfaction of sexual desire, as an antidote to the burdens and responsibilities of separate living.

Birth sets in train a process of separation which has its own inexorable logic; separation anxieties cannot be avoided unless we try to buck our destiny and remain in the cave for ever – which brings its own problems. The Cyclops myth depicts how the cave which initially offers refuge and nurture becomes, when lingered in too long, a place of stifling horror: the Cyclops–parents begin to reverse the life-giving process and digest their own children. *I work all day to feed my family and look after them. There's nothing left for me ... I feel as if I'm being eaten alive and no-one notices.*

The feeling of being claustrophobically trapped and con-stricted with no way out may manifest as a panic attack, in which anxiety temporarily overwhelms the self's capacity to manage it, blurring and collapsing distinctions between body and mind. Panic attacks, a frequent symptom of the advent of mid-life crisis, may result from the fearful and disorientating suppression of an anger which would, under different circumstances, enable one to break free. The words 'anger', 'anxiety', 'angst' and 'angina' all come from the same Indo-Germanic root *angh*, meaning to constrict, a point noted by the Jungian analyst James Hollis.[16] Hollis suggests that we tend through our lives to repress large parts of our personalities until a point is reached when the cost becomes too great – which is why anger often erupts with such startling violence during the mid-life crisis:

---

[16] Hollis, J., *The Middle Passage*, Inner City Books (1993).

Virtually all socialisation represents a constriction of the natural impulses, hence a growing accumulation of anger is to be expected. But
where has the energy associated with those natural impulses gone?
Often it fuels our blind ambitions and drives us to narcotics to dull its
intensity, or leads us to abuse of self or others. If one has been taught
that anger is a sin or a moral failing, then one has been split off from
one's natural feeling of constriction. When acknowledged and channelled, anger can be an enormous stimulus for change. One simply refuses to live inauthentically thereafter ... the shadow encounter with
anger is troubling, to be sure, but achieving the freedom to feel one's
own reality is a necessary step towards healing the inner split.

Odysseus refused to let his anger be dulled or soothed away by
the narcotics of the lotus plant or the Cyclops' wine. Welling up
inside him, it gives him the power and energy to face up to the
oppressive Cyclops and to destroy its power over him, thus
achieving his triumphant (albeit surreptitious) exit from the
mouth of the cave. The exit from a constricting cavity into the
freedom of open space, together with the image of being washed
up naked on a shore, is one of the great organizing and repeating
images of the *Odyssey*. These birth images communicate at an
evolutionary level as well as a personal one, reminding us of the
inevitability of change and growth, of prehistoric cave-dwellers
emerging blinking into the light of consciousness, of newborn
babies swooshing out in a wave of liquid onto their mothers'
thighs, and of the first amphibians washed by random waves
onto dry land, millions of years ago. Our ancestors all, propelled
by forces beyond their control but also by their own instincts
towards new futures and new worlds.

On the subject of mid-life transition, Jung writes: 'whoever
protects himself against what is new and strange and regresses to
the past falls into the same neurotic condition as the man who
identifies himself with the new and runs away from the past ... in
principle both are doing the same thing: they are reinforcing
their narrow range of consciousness instead of shattering it in
the tension of opposites and building up a state of wider and
higher consciousness.'[17] In a world of constant flux, those who

---

[17] Jung, C. G., 'The stages of life' (1930–1) in *Modern Man in Search of a
Soul*, Routledge (1984).

survive and thrive are those who have the courage to move forward and to let go. Yet while the corpses left behind in the Cyclops' cave suggest that the cost of staying in the cave is stagnation and spiritual death, they also remind us that – until we are able to develop the state of higher and wider consciousness to which Jung refers – cutting and running entails problems all of its own.

ON BECOMING NOBODY

'Cyclops,' I said, 'you wish to know the name I bear. I'll tell it to you; and in return I should like to have the gift you promised me. My name is No-body. That is what I am called by my mother and father and by all my friends.'

The Cyclops answered me with a cruel jest. 'Of all his company I will eat Nobody last, and the rest before him. That shall be your gift.'

... [Then] out of the cave came Polyphemus' great voice ... 'O my friends, it's Nobody's treachery ... that is doing me to death.'

Picasso once said that every artist must kill his father. When he kills the tyrant father in the form of the Cyclops, Odysseus risks his own death. It is only the renunciation of his identity (in the form of his given name) which saves his life. Like all those who, following some mysterious impulsion of their own, go missing each day from the homes and families of modern Britain, leaving their identities – and their names – behind them, Odysseus becomes invisible and unaccountable.

Our first names are chosen by our parents, and our surnames belonged first to our fathers (or to our husbands' fathers) and to their fathers before them. From earliest years the calling of our name summons us into the presence of others, alerting us to respond to their enquiries and demands. Our names may be uniquely our own, but they can also symbolize our unthinking reaffirmation of our parents' own partialities and preferences and the ways in which these keep us in thrall to the conventions and obediences of the past. In extreme crisis, our names may be the anchor we hang on to – or the first ballast to be jettisoned.

It is said that mediaeval knights would die if they fell off their horses in battle – not from injury but because the weight of their armour was so heavy that it would immobilize them where they fell like giant inverted tortoises, helplessly waving their arms and legs until dispatched. Too much armour, too much baggage may hinder rather than help. When in danger, instead of armouring himself Odysseus decides – counterintuitively but brilliantly – to divest himself of all that was his. Slipping out of the cave in sheep's clothing, he gives birth to himself anew and becomes, temporarily, nobody. Like a newborn baby or like Picasso's artist, he is naked and nameless, defiant yet uncertain in a new world of his own creation.

Robert Bly wrote that it was only through becoming older that he discovered the beauty of renunciation.[18] But although the shadow of renunciation strangely haunts the edges of our consciousness in the form of our accelerating desertion and divorce statistics, it remains a difficult concept to come to terms with in a society as devoted as ours to acquisition and accumulation. Yet within most cultures, renunciation is an essential aspect of spiritual renewal. Rites of passage (such as christening, marriage or ordination) are often marked by the taking of a new name, and in their dreams and fantasies people reaching mid life often articulate the desire to become free and unencumbered, to shed possessions and obligations and step free of the ties that bind. To pass beyond the known over a mysterious threshold into an unnamed, unknown future is described by Joseph Campbell in *The Hero with a Thousand Faces*[19] as the transit into the sphere of rebirth. The passage over the threshold is inevitably a form of self-annihilation: 'no creature can attain a higher grade of nature without ceasing to exist'. It is only through undertaking this perilous journey into our own darkness, our personal spiritual labyrinth, says Campbell, that we will become able to dissolve, transcend and transmute the infantile images of our personal past.

---

[18] Bly, R., *The Sibling Society*, Hamish Hamilton (1996).
[19] Fontana (1993).

To identify, confront and ultimately to separate from controlling authoritarian inner voices is an imperative of internal growth. But as necessary as such acts of separation and destruction may be, they tend to leave us feeling rootless and aimless, stunned by the violence of our own determination, drifting towards breakdown unless the identity which has been rejected can be differently reclaimed. Odysseus cannot allow himself to creep away like a thief in the night. He must ultimately assume personal responsibility for what he has done, and so as he sails away he shouts back his name to the blinded and baffled giant: '*Cyclops ... your eye was put out by Odysseus, Sacker of Cities, the son of Laertes, who lives in Ithaca.*' The blinded Cyclops curses Odysseus and calls out to his father Poseidon, the god of the sea, to make sure that Odysseus shall never return to Ithaca: '*but if he is destined to reach his native land ... let him come late, in evil plight, with all his comrades dead, and when he is landed, by a foreign ship, let him find trouble in his home.*'

The blinding of Polyphemus brings Odysseus into conflict with the god of the sea himself, and the price he must pay is a high one – nine years of aimless wandering, shipwreck, loss and desolation. The confrontation with the internal parental tyrant – so often acted out at mid life within scenarios of marriage breakup, family estrangement or the otherwise unanticipated defiance of others' expectations – may leave us, like Odysseus, wandering in purgatory (literally, a place of purging), adrift, guilty and in conflict with aspects of our own unconscious. It may take time in exile to work these conflicts through.

A SECOND ADOLESCENCE

The soul at mid life yearns to cut loose and to drift. Yet this yearning comes upon us at a time in life when we may feel more bound, more committed than ever before, by responsibilities to others and also by our own need for security in the face of our private anxieties about getting older. The feelings, thoughts and wonderings that start to emerge tentatively from the unconscious at this time cannot necessarily be thought through, because of the extent to which they threaten everything previously held dear. Shying away from their implications, we become overtaken by strange moods and fancies – we lose our bearings, our temper, our car keys, our minds. We become moody, withdrawn and self-preoccupied. We flicker unreliably between belligerent rebelliousness, self-doubt and self-pity, and become prey to disturbing thoughts and dreams. The boundaries separating self from other begin to blur, and we seek out intense but unstable new relationships to stimulate the tentative stirrings within us. And it may occur to us that this unstable and mutating sense of identity – all at odds with the world and awkward in it – is in some ways surprisingly and mortifyingly similar to the experience of adolescence.

At mid life as at adolescence, *I don't know who I am any more.* Wrestling with our angels, we may begin to tip over into crisis or breakdown as our pre-existing sense of identity, and our sense of connectedness to our families and to the rhythms of our daily lives, starts to crumble – and with it, all ability to think things through. When we look back on such times at a later date, we may recognize their crucial and abiding significance. But at the time they are more likely to be confusing periods of great stress and internal disorientation, when the fear of falling under the sway of the primitive terror of losing identity – expressed so vividly in the great birth and transition myths as the fear of dismemberment or being devoured – becomes all too real.

At such times, daily life – weighed down with the effort to keep going – begins to feel exhausting and artificial while dreams, on the other hand, become disturbingly vivid. Dreams at mid life often express unconscious anxieties and conflicting loyalties played out in various themes: impossible tasks laid down by remote authorities, pursuit by faceless tyrants, scenes of theft, death, damage and laying waste, bewildering erotic encounters, departures and journeys, and the advent of unknown strangers into familiar situations. A 38-year-old woman dreams:

I am in a room full of clocks whose hands are going round too fast. There's an oven full of cakes that I know I should take out but I'm busy packing a suitcase. I don't know what to take and I'm afraid I'll forget the most important thing – but I don't know what it is. Outside there's a taxi waiting to take me to the airport. I'm afraid the plane will go without me.

And a man in his early forties dreams:

> I am holding up a leaking dam by my own efforts, banking it up with old furniture, rubble, anything I can see. I wander off alone along the side of a canal. I see children making sand castles in the mud along the bank and further on my wife, having a picnic with another man. She doesn't notice me. Then I am in a town; great floods of water come rushing down the streets and lanes. I realize the dam has burst. The water carries me along. I am naked.

The emergence of such dreams expresses the internal conflict and vacillation between holding on and letting go which characterize the movement into transition. The first dreamer is caught between her sense of urgency and momentum (the ticking clocks, the taxi waiting, the plane that may go without her) and her ties to the present (the cakes in the oven, the possessions she is sorting through without knowing what she needs to take with her). The cakes (buns) in the oven along with the ticking of the clocks indicate a desire to give birth, to a new self or perhaps to a real child – time is precious, and must not be wasted.

The second dreamer expresses the heavy personal cost to him of holding up his current life through banking up the dam with old furniture and rubble – domestic articles which are devalued and disparaged. Perhaps he would like to regress into childhood, making castles out of mud like the children he sees, with no mother to tell him off. At the same time he wonders how much he is really loved or would be missed if he gave into his longing to leave, for his wife seems to be with another man. She's having a picnic while he's suffering – but is it really the dreamer himself who is trying to deny his own adulterous desires, by stopping up the dam? He longs for violent change and to be swept away by a force outside himself – the logic of the dream means he doesn't have to take any personal responsibility for the damage caused by the bursting of the dam, sweeping water through the streets and him naked along with it.

The desire to divest oneself, to pass into this phase naked as at the first birth, is as powerful as it is dreaded. Murray Stein describes this state as liminality, after *limen*, Latin for 'threshold':

> A loss of this magnitude – psychologically, it is a loss of the heroic defence – draws the psyche into liminality which may be coloured most heavily by feelings of grief for a lost past. Liminality is created whenever the ego is unable any longer to identify fully with a former self-image... there is a sense of an amputated past and a vague future. Yet while this ego hangs there in suspension, still it remembers the ghost of a former self, whose home had been furnished with the presence of persons and objects now absent and had been placed in a psychological landscape now bare and uninhabitable without them.[20]

The internal struggle between the desire for freedom and the need for security is compounded by the way modern social conditions load us up with ever-accumulating responsibilities, while at the same time curiously conspiring to encourage a sense of drift and non-commitment. The family is frequently the context within which the mid-life crisis erupts, but families themselves are no longer the indestructible containers they once were. Today's changing family structures are located within a changing society, and our anxieties breed within a cultural dimension which consolidates and reinforces them. Western society at the turn of the millennium is going through a period of rapid and buoyant expansion. We are gaining unprecedented, exhilarating control over the natural world and its resources, but we greedily and carelessly deplete our environment, dismissing with indifference those forces which previously restrained us in fear. We live in a world of constant stimulation and change, which is nevertheless spiritually deadened; we have flashes of idealism, but find them, as much else, difficult to sustain. Our relationships with others are intense, but often diffuse and short-lived. We are sometimes promiscuous: why not? We search endlessly and restlessly, achieving more yet rarely satisfied, alternating periods of frantic activity with periods of passive torpor.

Self-centred not through moral depravity but because we see no reason to be otherwise, we think of ourselves as cynical – yet our gullibility and apathy make us perfect consumers, manipulated far more easily than we realize by economic and political

---

[20] Stein, M., *In Midlife: A Jungian Perspective*, Spring Publications (1991).

forces beyond our control. Adolescence as a concept may only have been invented a century ago, but it was an idea whose time had come: over the last century adolescence, rather than adulthood, is the state towards which we have been encouraged to aspire, and today the values of adolescence permeate far beyond the teen years. There are particular difficulties in working through the mid-life crisis within a society which often seems to foster the drift into eternal adolescence instead of offering a counterpoise to it.

In a world where everyone used to know their place, growing up used to be concerned with a reorientation away from the permissive maternal gods of childhood towards paternal authority, with all its constraints, privileges and rewards, and ultimately to an identification with this paternal authority. But today the gods of our fathers are collapsing – egalitarianism reigns, and the notion of progress through a preordained series of hierarchies has been turned on its head. Adolescence should be a time of transition: a bridge, between the infancy which kept us in helpless, ignorant submission to our maternal and paternal gods, and true maturity – not an end in itself. Globally, it seems we are moving through a time of transition, but while we have grown beyond our parents' jurisdiction, we have yet to create a new one. All dressed up, we have nowhere to go. And as Marx once observed, in the interregnum between two different political systems the strangest phenomena are likely to arise.

This generational collapse leaves in its wake a sense of familial confusion and disintegration, in which technology and consumerism enable us to dispense more and more with the need for intergenerational contact.[21] Shopping malls and Internet chatrooms replace the unique conflicts and passions of families and communities, while many of us live alone or with people to whom we feel only notionally or vaguely connected. Today's cultural icons are models and footballers who will be considered over the hill by the time they are thirty, though they – like the rest of us – may reprise that age for at least a while longer. For we all try, so hard, to stay young. When the achievement of maturity

---

[21] See Bly, R., *The Sibling Society*, Hamish Hamilton (1996).

offers no prestige to compensate for the inevitable losses of youth, we are left devising projects to recover our own lost youths – like Lester's planned seduction of the teenage Angela in *American Beauty*.

But in our hearts we may feel both fraudulent and defrauded – of the chance to act our age. Those of us now in our late thirties or forties may have freedoms and opportunities unimaginable to our own parents, but we are left uncertain of our prospects, our status and our entitlement, uncertain even about how to parent our own children who – deprived of an authority worth rebelling against – are left to shift as best they can. The dissolution of generational authority within a clearly structured society may have freed us from fearful submission and repression, but it leaves us also without any pricks to kick against, caught in an undignified scramble to maintain a false egalitarianism. This is the paradox we face at mid life: belittling and controlling internal parental voices must be confronted and neutralized if maturity is to be gained, yet our rejection of authority leaves the internal teenager holding sway, drifting in sulky, disobedient aimlessness.

Odysseus' initial departure with his gang of friends to rescue Helen of Troy was a flight from the demands of maturity. Like many men who leave home in an effort to avoid mid-life crisis, his absence leaves his wife Penelope alone and struggling to hold the family home together and to bring up their son Telemachus herself. Penelope stays in bed, cries a lot, has a difficult time with new boyfriends and becomes over-dependent upon her son, who has to grow up more quickly than he should. So far, so predictable. But Telemachus eventually resolves to set off on his own Aegean journey to search for his absent father, and it is his decision to do so which is the catalyst for the ensuing events of the *Odyssey* and their ultimate resolution.

Telemachus' resolve reminds us of the context of his father's wanderings – driven far from Ithaca, Odysseus nevertheless always keeps in his mind the sense of an Ithaca which will be worth returning to, as Penelope and Telemachus themselves maintain steadfastly in their minds their belief in a husband and father who will be worth rediscovering. Odysseus' wanderings take place within a countervailing set of social and spiritual values which assert the importance of a reconciliation and a homecoming which will ultimately be worth achieving, even though its form is not yet known. Without such a faith, there is a danger that the restless flight from maturity will become self-reinforcing, as much without direction as it is without end.

At mid life, frustrated by the failure of our living environment to respond to the inchoate and inarticulate impulses which stir within us, we turn elsewhere to explore them – to dreams and fantasies, towards multiple identifications within films, novels and myths, to songwriting and to poetry. Homer's images of a battered forty-year-old man trapped and awaiting death within a bloody cave while still hurling defiance at the giant who imprisons him, or pitching alone on a boat in a vast sea, have a simplicity and a bleak beauty which may resonate within the clutter and uncertainties of our own lives. The struggle to emerge from obliviousness through group identity to individual awareness and personal responsibility is the struggle that must be faced again by each one of us. Unless a new model of an adulthood worth aspiring to can be constructed, we run the danger of becoming stuck for ever in cynical and restless adolescent values – a hell of dope-smoking, iron-pumping, face-lifting anomie which becomes an end in itself rather than a transition. In *American Beauty*, Lester is transformed and liberated when he becomes able to relocate himself within his own generation, and to own his maturity. His original desire to magically restore his own youth through sexually exploiting the teenage Angela evaporates in the light of his newly discovered capacity for wonder and for tender, paternal concern. He discovers a new kind of beauty – which enables him to see and be seen for the first time.

We have explored how the developing mid-life crisis may run aground on the shores of denial or become mired in the problems created by alcohol and drug dependencies and stress-related illnesses, and we have traced its growing momentum through the conflicts which it kindles in the arenas of work, sexual relationships and the family. Underlying and fuelling these conflicts is the encounter with death and loss which lies at the core of the mid-life crisis – which must now be faced if a true resolution of the crisis is to become possible.

Part Four

CRISIS

8

Death

From 'Reflections on a Foreign Line of Verse' by George Seferis

TOO FAST TO LIVE, TOO YOUNG TO DIE

The death of John Kennedy Jr at the age of 37 in an air crash off the coast of Massachusetts in July 1999 carried for many people eerie echoes of the violent death of Diana, Princess of Wales, in a Paris underpass two summers earlier at the age of 36. These sudden deaths stunned the world, overwhelming millions of people who had never met either of them in a tidal wave of shock, grief and maybe guilt. Their deaths were accidents, arbitrary and capricious in their cruelty. Yet – in another sense – both may have been accidents which were waiting to happen, fates lurking in the borderlands of recklessness, ready to be tempted.

Circumstances of life had made Princess Diana and Kennedy Jr into *über*-celebrities in a celebrity-obsessed age, more real (as the outpourings of grief on their deaths suggested) to many of their fellow citizens than their own families. As little as we might know ourselves, we seemed to know them. The most intimate details of their lives became tidbits to tease and titillate a ravenous and unflagging media appetite which fed on their every word and deed, while at the same time their wealth and fame, their easy beauty and their charm, made them icons for the restlessly aspirational youth-worshipping identities of the nations of Britain and America who had given birth to them almost forty years before. Both Diana and Kennedy showed, at times, signs of being oppressed and disturbed by their status. Both, at times, exploited it. Yet though their obituaries spoke sentimentally of them having reached a time of new beginnings and having everything to live for, in the periods before their deaths it had occurred to some to wonder – as it might well have occurred to Diana and to Kennedy themselves – whether anything they were likely to achieve in the second halves of their lives could be more than a sad falling-off from the golden glamour of their youths.

Both John Kennedy and Diana Spencer had been thrust at tender ages, startled and exposed, into the harsh glare of a thousand flashbulbs and a fame which pursued them for the remainder of their abbreviated lives – in Diana's case literally, down the dark tunnel which led to her death. The teenage nursery school teacher fumbling awkwardly for her car keys, the pale child in his buttoned-up overcoat and shorts gravely saluting the coffin of his father a few days before his third birthday – these private scenes became public property, part of the archives of national identity. For neither Diana nor Kennedy could the preservation of anything resembling an authentic, private inner life have been easy. And both of them had their vulnerabilities; both had suffered in their childhoods an unusual degree of instability and loss.

'I've got what my mother's got. However bloody you're feeling you can put on the most amazing show of happiness. My mother is an expert in that. I've picked it up, kept the wolves from the door but what I couldn't cope with ... was people saying "it's her fault". I got that from everywhere, everywhere.'[1]

---

[1] Morton, A., *Diana, Her True Story – In Her Own Words*, Michael O'Mara Books (1997).

Diana's life had in fact been the subject of blame and friction from her birth. Her mother's failure to provide her father with a son and heir was a contributory factor in the break-up of their marriage when Diana was only six. She was sent to boarding school when she was nine, and in the holidays was shunted between her remarried mother and her depressed father who, according to Diana, would just sit alone in his study all day.

Surrounded by all the trappings of wealth and all the comfort that paid staff could provide, Diana grew up scared and lonely. The child who lay in bed at night listening to her little brother howling for his mother, too afraid of the dark herself to get out of bed to comfort him, and who painted the eyes of her cuddly hippo with luminous green paint in an attempt to reassure herself that someone was watching over her, developed into a teenager who was unusually alert, helpful and considerate, easily moved by others' suffering and quick to respond to their needs – qualities which evidently endeared her to her future husband.

Diana was nevertheless supremely ill-fitted to cope with the suffocating attention of the world's press on the announcement of her engagement to Prince Charles in 1981, when she was still only nineteen. By the time of her honeymoon she was suffering from bulimia, and she later spoke of a period of 'total darkness' between the births of her sons: 'We had a few trying to cut wrists, throwing things out of windows, breaking glass. I threw myself downstairs when I was four months pregnant with William trying to get my husband's attention, for him to listen to me.'

The marriage, inevitably, fell apart. But when Diana finally began a new relationship, it was with a man in many ways not unlike her ex-husband. Like Charles, Dodi (who was 41 in the fateful summer when he and Diana became lovers) concealed a tendency towards melancholy under a courteous exterior and could sometimes, it was said, be petulant. Like Charles, Dodi had a domineering father in whose shadow he had lived a life of drift and indecision. Failing to establish serious careers, both men were strongly attracted towards the pursuit of dangerous sports, perhaps as a way of proving their manhood and endowing their lives with meaning. Charles hunted, played polo and skied, and had only narrowly missed being killed by an avalanche while skiing at Klosters when he was 39, while Dodi also loved polo, as well as fast cars. In the end Dodi proved, for Diana, a fatal attraction – but it is hard to escape the conclusion that Diana herself bore at least some responsibility for the engineering of that last high-speed midnight game of chase through the streets of Paris.

The love of dangerous sports was a thread which also ran through the life of John Kennedy Jr, nicknamed by his friends the master of disaster.[2] Kennedy's life, too, was lived under the shadow of his father – a man whom he could barely remember but whose name he bore, whose achievements he could never hope to emulate and against whom he would always be compared. Kennedy's father was killed before his son was three. John's uncle Robert stepped into the gap and became a father to him, only to be murdered as well before John was eight. John later grew fond of his mother's second husband, Aristotle Onassis, but the marriage publicly fell apart after Onassis' son Alexander, John's step-brother, was killed in a flying accident in 1973 when John was thirteen. As an adult, Kennedy Jr did not settle easily into any career, becoming a reluctant lawyer. Eventually he gained some success with the political gossip magazine *George*, but by early 1999 the magazine's circulation was falling and the publishers were threatening to pull out. It was also rumoured that John's marriage was in trouble, plagued by infidelities and by his wife's dependence upon anti-depressants and cocaine.

'John wasn't afraid to face danger' said his friend, mountain guide Charles Townsend. 'In fact he loved the challenge. That was his great escape.' From childhood he had longed to fly but in his mother's lifetime deferred to her request that he should not learn, Jackie reportedly having said that there had been too many deaths in the family. Jackie herself died of cancer in May 1994, and in the spring of 1999 Kennedy was spotted having lost control when flying his Ultralight perilously close to high-tension power lines at Hyannis Point. Saved by a sudden updraught, he fractured his ankle on landing and was reported

---

[2] Andersen, C., *The Day John Died*, HarperCollins (2000).

to have shrugged when warned by police that he could have been killed. The ankle was barely healed a few months later when he set off with his wife and sister-in-law in his new Piper Saratoga II, on what was to be their final journey. Kennedy was an inexperienced pilot flying an unfamiliar plane. Although he took off after dusk, he was not instrument-trained and as he became disorientated in descending fog he neither radioed for help nor switched on the plane's automatic piloting device, which would have brought the plane in safely – presumably he was not aware of its existence. The Kennedys later bought off a wrongful death action brought by John's wife's family against his estate with compensation of £6.25 million.[3]

To some degree, we all live our lives caught between the rival claims of being and nothingness, between the urge to forge ahead and the longing to sink back into oblivion, between life and death itself. As the mid-life crisis looms, this precarious balance sometimes tips. We will never know whether it tipped for Diana or Kennedy, whether the drift towards death had gained a subtle power over them and drawn them into a reckless complicity in their own fates. Their deaths robbed us – and them – of the chance to discover whether either of them would ever really have been able to step out of the shadow of the inherited roles and the family expectations which had dominated their early adulthoods, and to find out whether they would have become able to confront the losses and transformations which mid life exacts of us, and to face maturity on their own terms.

Diana's very public mid-life crisis had seemed to be about sex, divorce, glamour and independence. But its end revealed to us abruptly and shockingly the underlying theme of mid life which percolates more quietly through quieter lives: the encounter with death. By mid life, as if by conspiracy, intimations of mortality arrive in all directions. They approach us regretfully in the passing of opportunities that won't come again, tenderly in the growth to independence of our children, ruefully in the mirror's changing reflection, wrenchingly in the decline into frailness and death of our parents, and most startlingly of all in

---

[3] *Daily Telegraph*, 26 February 2000.

the deaths of our own contemporaries. At the peak of our powers, having reached the crest of the hill, we glimpse the other side. For the first time we begin to measure our lives in terms of the time that may be left to us instead of the time elapsed since our births. And these accumulating losses – not least, the loss of belief in our own immortality – shake our sense of who we are at the deepest level. 'The Mid Life Crisis compels corniness and indignity upon you, but that's part of the torment', wrote Martin Amis in a memoir published as he reached the other side of fifty, ' . . . but later you see that there was a realignment taking place, something irresistible and universal, to do with your changing views about death (and you ought to have a crisis about that. It is crucial to have a crisis about that).'[4]

Cocooned within the protection afforded by marriages, families, companies and ideologies, resorting to busy and active lives of achievement, and developing self-assured and competent public personas, we often contrive successfully and for many years to protect ourselves from the logic of loss. But somewhere, at some time it catches up with us – and the more we have, the more we have to lose. And in as much as our behaviour patterns are defensive, they will be stretched to breaking point by the advent of the mid-life crisis and its accumulating losses – above all, perhaps, by the collapse of belief in our personal immortality. If, like Kennedy and Diana, we suffered earlier loss at a time when we were too young to be able to find ways of coming to terms with it, we may find ourselves now, as loss comes round again, feeling compelled to split it off and deny it once more, resorting once again to those strategies for the management of loss and death which were formed in our impressionable childhoods. Until we can do so no longer.

Michael VerMeulen, the aggressively successful editor of the London magazine *GQ*, was a man who by his own reckoning liked to work hard and play hard. 'I can't say that there's much I look forward to about being in my forties' he said in an interview with journalist Gail Sheehy. When Sheehy commented that there seemed a macho element in the way that men reaching mid life

---

[4]   Amis, M., *Experience*, Random House (2000).

would lead lives so unhealthy that they seemed to be daring a first heart attack, VerMeulen replied that maybe that was exactly what they wanted. 'It's quite possible they would prefer not to get up from that heart attack. Frankly, maybe these guys would just as soon go in a flash.' Five months later VerMeulen himself was dead of a cocaine overdose, at the age of 38.[5]

DEATH AND THE MID-LIFE CRISIS

The higher you climb the further there is to fall – the deaths of Diana, Kennedy and VerMeulen were as extraordinary and uncommon as their lives. Faltering in the face of the mid-life crisis and the encounter with death that lies at its centre as it percolates through our own lives, most of us are far more likely to shrink timidly back, drawing in upon ourselves as we reinforce our existing defence structures in preparation for the siege to come, than to orchestrate so final and dramatic an exit. But the very famous, the very indulged, or the very exposed, have more rope, and are more likely to end up hanging themselves. The closer we live to the edge, the more likely we are to take one careless backwards step too far.

Celebrity is the art form of our age; celebrities, like artists, reveal to us the lives we would live if we dared, in magnified and dramatized form. A study of the lives and deaths of 310 great creative artists – those who by nature and inclination might be most likely to take greater risks with their own lives and self-expression, and also to be most closely attuned to changes within their own psyches – reveals an unexpected jump in the death rate between the ages of 35 and 39. The closer one keeps to genius, discovered psychoanalyst Elliott Jaques, who carried out the study, the truer this holds: Mozart, Raphael, Chopin, Rimbaud, Purcell and Baudelaire all died in their late thirties.[6] For those who survive it, the mid-life crisis may still constitute a watershed, a time of personal reckoning. Some of those in

---

[5] Sheehy, G., *New Passages*, HarperCollins (1997).
[6] Jaques, E., 'Death and the mid life crisis', *International Journal of Psychoanalysis* 46.

Jaques' survey, such as Rossini and Ben Jonson, ceased any further creative output at mid life despite living for many years longer, while others, such as Gauguin, Goldsmith, Constable, Goya and Bach, only really began the work for which they are remembered after reaching mid life.

Even for those who work consistently through it, the experience of mid-life transition may be transformative: the Shakespeare who wrote *Romeo and Juliet* at 31 was a writer with very different preoccupations from the one who wrote *King Lear* only a few years later as he neared 40. Jaques suggests that the work of artists at mid life tends to change from the hot, spontaneous creativity of early adulthood towards a creativity which is more sustained and more slowly and deeply worked through. At the same time, the lyrical, intense and often idealistic creativity of early adulthood gives way to a view that is more tragic and yet, in the end, more serenely contemplative.

At mid life we have to face the fact that we ourselves are not immortal, and in the face of this awareness the ego-driven achievements of early adulthood may come to seem paltry and insignificant. At the same time, as we grow older it becomes harder to disown our destructiveness, hatred, envy, frailty and whatever else we don't very much like about ourselves, harder to keep on projecting them outside ourselves into others whom we can treat as enemies to be vanquished. Romeo and Juliet's violent desires have violent ends but the young lovers die with their idealistic love intact, thwarted only by a cruel twist of fate and by their warring families. The much older Lear is also betrayed by his own family, but for him the tearing apart of his family and his world triggers the tearing apart of his own psyche under the pressure of the contradictions raging within it. Lear's betrayal at the hands of others initiates a journey deep into his own soul where he must confront his own vanity, narcissism and blindness. Redeemed by the love to which he had previously been blind, he dies transfigured. After mid life either we must come to a final accommodation with the forces ranged against our narrow will-power, or die trying.

Why should the defences against fear and loss – which have previously served us so well – become less effective as we reach

196

mid life? The psychoanalyst Melanie Klein conceives of the young child's mind as a place no less racked than Lear's heath by warring dramas of love and hate, by the longing to relax into trust, and by the forces of envy and terror which rage against this longing. How can the child's immature psyche negotiate a way through the minefield of his or her own conflicts and anxieties becoming, in the end, able to recognize them as parts of him or herself and integrate them? Klein suggests that the core of the problem lies in the conflict between the intensity of the satisfied love that we feel when our desires are met and the frustrated hatred we feel when we are failed. Unable to cope with the conflict, we split our inner lives and project our conflicted feelings outwards.[7] Although in reality the person who meets my needs and makes me feel good may be the same one who frustrates my needs and makes me feel bad, in my mind I nevertheless separate them, idealizing the image of the one and demonizing the other. Then in my unconscious mind I end up not with one mother (towards whom I must learn to manage my own ambivalent and complex feelings) but two – a good mother who feeds me and a bad mother who denies me, on to whom I project all my own anger at my frustration and all my fears that I may not survive. The more unable we are to accept our own negative feelings, the more we create bad and increasingly persecutory internal figures, whom we then project into the forms of those who dare to cross us in the outside world. The more too we then need to create unrealistically idealized others to protect us from this persecution, and so the need to split and to project renews itself, creating a self-perpetuating cycle.

But there is a way forward. If, on balance, my experience as I begin to mature is a good and satisfying one which elicits mainly loving and trusting feelings, then my belief in the power of bad to destroy good diminishes and so does the need to split and project. Less fearful and less disturbed by my own destructive feelings, I can come to accept them. As my need to project destructive intentions on to others diminishes, I become more

---

[7] Klein, M., 'Notes on some schizoid mechanisms' (1946) in *Envy and Gratitude and Other Works 1946–63*, Virago (1988).

able to see – and to enjoy – reality and other people for the complex mixtures that they are, and I also become more able to tolerate the inevitable anxiety and threat to the self that accompany loss and suffering. For Klein, we oscillate between these two positions – the one tending towards oversimplifications, splitting, projection and self-justification, the other tending towards connectedness, integration and the ability to tolerate complexity, ambivalence and concern for others – all our lives.[8] At any time, increased levels of stress may overwhelm our capacity to cope and return us to our old ways of protecting ourselves by splitting and projection.

In early adulthood we are confronted by the instinctive need to rise to the challenges of the outside world. The imperative to direct attention inwards in the service of greater self-awareness and integration tends, in relative terms, to be less pressing. By and large, when faced with difficulties we are likely to continue to split the world into good and bad – idolizing some while hating others, seeing life in terms of a '*me and mine*' as opposed to '*them*' mentality, disowning our own negative feelings and attributing them to others. As we do so, we are buoyed up by our fantasies of personal immortality, which stem from the idealization of our intact and supposedly invulnerable selves. The development of competence and achievement of success on economic, sexual and social fronts in our twenties and thirties also obscures and allows us to defer the moment of reckoning. But once mid life is reached, old fears of abandonment, helplessness and disintegration stemming back as far as childhood are likely to recur with great intensity. At mid life, we stop growing up and start growing old. As we enter the prime of our lives and the fulfilment of our potential, we become at the same time helplessly aware that our time will be limited. The dawning awareness of mortality along with the failure of the ideals which have previously protected us indicate that we can no longer so effectively retreat into busy, extroverted activity as the panacea for all problems. The need to move towards a final and more

---

[8] Klein, M., 'A contribution to the psychogenesis of manic-depressive states' (1935) and 'Mourning and its relation to manic-depressive states' (1940), both in *Envy and Gratitude and Other Works 1946–63*, Virago (1988).

realistic accommodation of the conflicts between love and fear becomes more necessary and less postponable.

It is now that early conflicts revive. Again, we experience ourselves attacked by persecuting forces, both within and without ourselves. The orchestration of domestic disaster, emotional drama or the adrenaline-filled courting of physical danger are all ways of holding anxiety at bay – revving up to combat external threats, our minds empty themselves of the uncertainties and anxieties which would otherwise plague us. We can entertain the illusory but comforting belief that by mastering external threat we can take control of the fate which – we unconsciously fear – really controls us. Alternatively, we cut off thinking and purposeful action altogether, retreating into a life of rigidity and denial. Avoiding death as a fact, we experience it nevertheless in the deadness of depression, in phobias, hypochondriac anxieties, addictions and states of frozen nameless anxiety.

But if we are able to negotiate the crisis of mortality we become able to move forward towards an acceptance of death, and become able to maintain love and to find meaning even in the face of it. Our ability to do so may depend largely upon the extent to which we have been able to experience and internalize love as a resilient and reliable force in our lives, allowing bitterness at our own fatedness to give way to composure:

> Thus in mid-life we are able to encounter the onset of the tragedy of personal death with the sense of grief appropriate to it ... We can live with it without an overwhelming sense of persecution ... working through the infantile experience of loss and of grief gives an increase in confidence in one's capacity to love and mourn what has been lost and what is past, rather than to hate and feel persecuted by it. We can begin to mourn our own eventual death. Creativeness takes on new depths and shades of feeling ... at a much deeper level [we can develop] a detachment which allows confidence and hope to be established, security in the preservation and development of the ego, a capacity to tolerate one's shortcomings and destructiveness, and withal, the possibility of enjoyment of mature adult life and old age.[9]

---

[9] Jaques, E., 'Death and the mid life crisis', *International Journal of Psychoanalysis* 46.

But not before the journey through the valley of death has been undertaken.

A DEATH IN THE FAMILY

When I was a child of about eight, I remember lying in bed one night watching the clouds scudding past in the triangular gap between the edges of my bedroom curtains, and listening to the occasional slowing and swoosh of a car engine on the bend in the road outside our house. For a moment the red and black tumbling-dice pattern on the curtains would be lit from behind by moving headlights, only to be reclaimed by shadows. As I lay still, a thought passed across my mind: one day I would die, and nothing I ever did in my life could stop this happening. Even my parents' protection could not prevent it, for had they not been unable to prevent the death of my grandmother a few months before, of a stroke? They too, I suddenly realized, would die – and probably before me.

But at eight it was too much to hold. Daylight brought its usual blithe relief from night fears and I put away my secret thought – the thought that no-one else, not even the old, ever seemed to admit to entertaining. For I was part of the baby-booming golden generation of the affluent sixties, the post-War, pre-AIDS generation for whom progress would be infinite, all things would be possible and over whom death, it seemed, would have no dominion. We, unlike our ancestors, had not – unless we were profoundly unlucky – had to face the deaths of our elder brothers in war, the deaths of our little sisters from measles and diphtheria, the deaths of our mothers in childbirth or even the protracted deaths of our grandparents at the centre of the extended family. Medical advances connived with our complacent illusion that death could be postponed to an infinite degree and finally mastered, while the collapse of the extended family and the professionalization of care for the dying encouraged us to remove death further out of sight and out of mind. Religion lost the authority to remind us that in the midst of life we were in death – which was probably just as well, given that it had also lost its former power to console the grief of the bereaved and to relieve our mortal anxiety.

Instead of consolation, the flatness of denial. But there is nothing really new about the denial of death – except that we've got better at it. In the Hindu epic the *Mahabharata* the sage Yudhistara is asked what is the most wondrous thing in the entire world. He replies that the most wondrous thing is that all around us people can be dying, and we don't believe it can happen to us. 'At bottom no-one believes in his own death' echoed Freud on the outbreak of the First World War, noting that when someone else dies 'our habit is to stress the fortuitous element of the death – accident, disease, infection, advanced age; in this way we betray an effort to reduce death from a necessity to a chance event'.[10]

Yet still, our attitude to death remains profoundly ambivalent. Having banished it, we do not rest contented but hunt it out excitedly and voyeuristically – albeit at a safe remove. Unable to digest it, we still push it round the plate, toy with it and nibble at its edges – and death offers itself up to us obligingly and intriguingly, in the mangled cars at the sides of motorways, in bloody horror and gangster movies and in the tabloid tales of serial murderers and accounts of the lonely drug-ridden ends of the rich and famous, which sell more newspapers than sex, all seductively packaged to control our fear, to satisfy our *Schadenfreude* and to reassure us that it'll always be someone else. Coming as we do from a long line of murderers, says Freud, who had read his Darwin, we are unmoved by the death of strangers – in fact, such deaths often excite us. But Freud, writing as the Austrian army mobilized and his own sons were called up to serve at the front, pointed out that there is one way in which death will always be brought home to us with great impact, and that is through the death of those we love. And then, tasting it in the pain of our loss, we can no longer keep death at a distance. Our defences crumble; we collapse, we cannot be consoled. It is as if we lose a part of ourselves.[11]

A woman recently bereaved describes an old friend crossing

---

[10] Freud, S., 'Thoughts for the Times on War and Death' (1915), in *Penguin Freud Library* 12.

[11] *Ibid.*

the road to avoid her. Denying death, we learn to fear bereavement as if it were a contagious disease. Deprived of collective social structures in which individual mourning might be contained and validated and allowed to run its course, we muddle through as best we can. In the confusion, disorientation and isolation of modern bereavement it can be difficult to withstand the pressure to put the loss away, easy to allow oneself to be prematurely reclaimed by ordinary life. Yet the flight from mourning which is intended to reassert life can end up impoverishing it.

In the week which followed Diana's death, the lengthening queues outside Kensington Palace, and the towering piles of cellophane-wrapped carnation sprays, children's posies, photographs, candles and handwritten cards placed outside cathedrals, churches and town halls throughout the country testified – among other things – to the poverty of our modern mourning rituals, and the empty place that our inability to face death has left at the centre of our lives. Those who said the mass outpouring of grief was hysterical were probably right – not in the pejorative sense in which they meant it, but in the more exact sense that hysteria denotes a state where feelings become disconnected from the events from which they arose, and become attached to something else. Were the crowds who wept at Diana's death really weeping for this woman they had never known, or for their own dead mothers, for their buried yet unmourned daughters, wives and friends, for the failures and disappointments of their own lives? For a week or so at least, all these losses, it seemed, could finally be acknowledged and validated in a great swell of public catharsis.

'Is it not for us to confess', concluded Freud, 'that in our civilised attitude to death we are once more living psychologically beyond our means, and must reform and give truth its due?'[12] For half our lives or beyond, we protect ourselves from awareness of the inevitability of death. To begin with it is easy, but it becomes harder and harder to look the other way. Eventually, it is a full-time job. As we near mid life, through

---

[12] *Ibid.*

awareness of our body's ageing, through sickness, defeat and the loss of ideals, and most of all through the deaths of those we have loved, death begins to creep up on us, to call us by name. Having got home and leant on our front doors with a sigh of relief, we open our eyes to find death's been waiting there all along. And of all the losses which we have to come to terms with at this time, it is the death of parents which may be the most devastating and which has the most far-reachingly transformative effect upon our psyches.

The death of parents at mid life is a loss of a magnitude that may take us by surprise, a loss which both revives earlier unresolved losses and reminds us most forcibly of our own mortality. When they die, our parents suddenly cease to perform the function they have carried out throughout our lives, standing guard between ourselves and death, a source of stability in an uncertain world. When they die, we must now, unassisted, perform this function ourselves for the next generation. And the decline in their importance to us over recent years may only make the shock of our parents' deaths more acute, reviving as it does those memories in which they were the centre of our young lives.

'When did you last see *your* father?' wrote Blake Morrison in his memoir of his own father's death:

> I want to warn people: don't underestimate filial grief, don't think because you no longer live with your parents, have had a difficult relationship with them, are grown up – perhaps a parent yourself – don't think it will make it any easier when they die. I've become a death bore . . . I used to think the world divided between those who have children and those who don't; now I think it divides between those who've lost a parent and those whose parents are still alive. Once I made people tell me their labour stories. Now I want to hear their death stories . . .[13]

Morrison, who was 41 when his father died, describes feeling in the aftermath as if an iron plate had come down through his middle, locking him into a place of blackness. 'I had thought that to see my father dying might remove my fear of death, and

---

[13] Morrison, B., *And When Did You Last See Your Father?*, Granta (1993).

so it did. I hadn't reckoned on its making death seem preferable to life.'

IN THE LAND OF THE DEAD

'For I am every dead thing . . . and I am re-begot.
Of absence, darkness, death; things which are not
. . . [I] am the grave
Of all that's nothing.'[14]

The English psychoanalyst Wilfred Bion was, like Freud, deeply affected by the First World War, in which he served at the front. Bion returned at the end of the war to a world which had recognized the need to come to terms with the trauma of overwhelming loss and to find a way of remembering which would also enable the survivors to pick up the pieces and begin living again. His explorations of extreme states of anxiety and personality disintegration were prompted by his work with soldiers left shell-shocked at the war's end, their minds too disturbed by the death and destruction they had witnessed to be able to adjust to civilian life.

In infancy, believed Bion, we are all prey at times to states of extreme anxiety, a sort of nameless dread which has at its base a fear of disintegration and annihilation. This state overwhelms our rudimentary psychic systems. Unable to contain this state of dread within ourselves without being overcome, we attempt to communicate it to our first carers by projecting it into them – its powerful ability to convey and instil a sense of panic in the hearer is what makes a baby's wailing so unbearable. Bion suggests that if our parents and protectors are in their turn able to receive, to contain and to process this dread for us, we become able to receive it back from them as something very much less frightening – as an anxiety that can be thought about, managed and finally integrated within the self instead of a nameless dread

---

[14] Donne, J., 'A Nocturnall upon St Lucie's Day' in *Selected Poems*, Penguin (1972).

which cannot.[15] If this happens reliably and often enough, we learn to internalize this managing parent within ourselves and to process our own dread. Through our lives we will continue to call on those close to us to help us to process our emotions – this is why we tend to feel that a problem shared is a problem halved, and why our anxieties tend to settle and diminish when we are able to talk them through with a sympathetic other and feel heard and contained by their attentiveness.

Yet throughout our lives there will inevitably continue to be times when our anxieties will overwhelm our capacity to process them, resulting in disorientation and trauma. And in this sense, of all the losses we will suffer, the loss of those such as our parents and those others who in due course took their place, who protected us from our own anxieties and processed them for us when we could not, is the most difficult. The death of a parent unexpectedly catapults us back to those earliest feelings of dread from which, for many years, the same parent's presence protected us. Our parents' presence is part of the fabric of our childhood, and for many years their deaths seem as impossible as our own. Whatever their shortcomings in other departments, parents do just tend to keep on being there, guaranteeing the continuity of our existence through the continuity of their own, containing for us those memories of our own early lives that we ourselves cannot remember. It is inevitable that their deaths will shake our defences against awareness of our own mortality, exposing us to fresh terror at the same time as it robs us of the very parental protector who might – we unconsciously hope – have protected us from it.

'Do not go gentle into that good night ... Rage, rage against the dying of the light' wrote Dylan Thomas of his father's death, the lines taking their force not in relation to the dying parent himself but as the authentic howl of the fear and anguish of the terrified child who cannot bear his father to go, turning out the light and leaving him all alone to face the dark.[16] It is the same tone with which Shakespeare's Cleopatra berates the dying

[15] Bion, W., 'A theory of thinking' in *Second Thoughts*, Heinemann (1967).
[16] Thomas, D., 'Do not go gentle into that good night' in *Selected Poems*, Penguin (2000).

Antony ('Noblest of men, woo't die? Hast thou no care of me?'[17]), her grief marked by that unmistakable sense of disbelief and outrage which has at its core fear for her own survival once her former protector no longer stands between her and death, and the terror of a life made unmanageable and meaningless by his absence. In the end, Cleopatra elects to join Antony in death: such a loss may truly make death seem preferable to life, at least for a while.

And there are degrees of death. Unable either to mourn, and to become in due course reclaimed by the living, or to die ourselves, we may instead become haunted, drawn deep into an unconscious, death-like identification with those who have left us but whom we cannot let go.

David originally begins psychotherapy to help him come to terms with the end of his marriage: his wife of three years has recently begun an affair with a colleague at work and has left him. There are no children. It is clear at our first interview that David is depressed. He is underweight and his skin is waxy and pale. Devoid of any flicker of spontaneity, humour or emotion, he answers my questions like a tidy obedient child, and sits waiting for me to do something.

David says that his mother was diagnosed with cancer when he was in his early teens and over the next two decades underwent regular bouts of chemotherapy. She was often debilitated, often in pain but according to David rarely complained. In fact the cancer was rarely mentioned; the prospect of her death, never.

David started going out with his future wife when they were both in their twenties, but initially they both continued living in their parents' houses. Eventually – David having passed thirty and prospering in his job as a bank executive – they decided to marry. The wedding was planned and a house bought. But then his mother's cancer gained a more voracious grip. The date of the wedding was brought forward, but not by far enough. David's mother died three weeks before it but the wedding went ahead anyway, in a subdued form. David says that his mother always wanted everything just to carry on normally.

Mourning is a process of grieving and realignment which begins with denial and passes through the stages of anger, bargaining and depression towards final acceptance.[18] If we are unable to

---

[17] *Antony and Cleopatra*, Act IV, Scene 13.

[18] Kubler-Ross, E., *On Death and Dying*, Social Science Paperbacks (1987).

mourn we remain trapped in denial – denying the significance of death, of loss, and in the end of love and of life itself. Mourning allows us to disentangle ourselves from the dead and the pull to deadness, becoming in due course reclaimed by life with a sense of meaning enhanced rather than diminished by our experience. But this was an opportunity which circumstances and his own determination were colluding to deny David, for whom the world – like his love for his mother and his pain at her death – had become empty and devoid of all meaning.

'The funeral bak'd meats/Did coldly furnish forth the marriage tables.'[19]

For Hamlet, his mother's wedding, following less than two months after his father's funeral, was a source of bitter reproach. Hamlet – a man who literally becomes haunted by his dead father and is caught in a pull towards death which draws him and many others under its sway – inhabits a land, Elsinore, from which mourning and remembrance of the dead have been banished. Why, says Hamlet's new step-father Claudius, mourning the dead is a fault against heaven, against the dead and against nature. Let there be no more talk of the dead!

David, at his own wedding, like Hamlet at his mother's wedding, continued on in a world from which all talk of the dead has been banished – at his own dead mother's insistence. As he grew up, David's family had lived in a frozen state of denial policed by his mother's will-power in which David – possessing neither Hamlet's capacity for defiance nor his mordant, incisive wit – had become entirely trapped. Under the pressure of his need to deny the psychic significance of the death for which he had been waiting most of his life, David's psyche had split. In his conscious mind he had put the death away and was looking forward to his new marriage in his new house. But his unconscious mind remained deeply and morbidly entangled with the mother whom his wife could never replace.

This family taboo on acknowledging the emotional effect of David's mother's prolonged dying and death continued throughout the period of the funeral and the wedding preparations. Then David went on honeymoon and on his

---

[19] *Hamlet*, Act I, Scene 2.

return was quickly claimed by the demands of his job and a frantic programme of DIY on his new house. Always his mother's son, the ties that bound him to her kept him loyal to her way of managing her death: he never went with his father or sister to his mother's grave nor, if he could help it, back to the family home, where he would have had to acknowledge her absence. Avoiding grief or tears now as he had in his mother's lifetime, David retreated into a deadened silence, rejecting all his wife's attempts to talk to him about his mother's death and his own state of mind.

David's wife, having been continually rebuffed in her attempts to make emotional contact with him, began to spend more and more time away from home on unaccounted absences – she was, as he later discovered, beginning an affair. These absences filled David with terror, for they reminded him of his mother's unexplained absences in hospital as her illness had taken hold of her. The obedient child in him managed them in just the same way – by repressing his curiosity and his fear, never asking her where she had been, and carrying on as if nothing was happening. But underneath, David was being taken over by an overwhelming and paralysing feeling of panic that his wife, like his mother, would abandon him. As, in due course, she did.

David had grown up in the shadow of his mother's death, a death which had nevertheless remained unthinkable. No-one in David's family had been able to find a way of coming to terms with what was happening as his mother slowly died before their eyes. David's dread of her loss had not been defused but was returned to him magnified, compounded by everyone else's fear. What is more, as his mother's illness had gone on, David had unconsciously come to believe that he himself was keeping her alive, as if she were feeding on his own energy and his willpower. It was this belief that had kept him living at home until he was over thirty, sharing his mother's life with her as he shared her way of denying her death. If this was not so, why had his mother, who had defied death for so long, died just as he was planning to leave home? Had his abandonment of her killed her? Now, even though she was dead, as if by reparation he had to keep her alive inside him. More or less, he had let her take him over.

It is likely that David's mother (who had received the most advanced medical care possible in attempts to prevent her death, but no help whatsoever in coming to terms with the inevitability of it) had been deeply depressed for years. But the more she had become emotionally inaccessible to David, the more he had clung to her. So, a loving relationship – the loss of which could have been mourned – had been replaced by a numbing internal identification with a dying mother: *if I cannot be loved by my mother I will become her.*[20] And David himself had become more and more lifeless and depressed, helplessly resigned to the death of his marriage and the loss of the wife who had represented his only hope of reclamation by the living.

Like soldiers suffering from shell-shock or post-traumatic stress disorder, we compulsively rework in dream or flashback the traumas which our minds cannot yet integrate. When the impulse to remember and to mourn falters and fails under the pain of it, we become haunted by death and disaster, sometimes falling under the compulsion to recreate it by courting our own destruction in one form or another. Like Hamlet, we may find ourselves forging a strange and unholy alliance with the forces of darkness that we formerly kept at bay, expressed through self-sabotage or through the discovery of a hitherto unknown capacity for violence, ruthlessness or destruction. At least then, we can become the agents of our own destruction – as Hamlet himself becomes in spectacular fashion, contriving by the play's finale the deaths of nearly everyone in sight, including his own. Shakespeare wrote *Hamlet* in his own late thirties, about five years after the death of his only son Hamnet and soon after the death of his father in 1601, and implicit connections between the unfolding mayhem and a manic incapacity to tolerate mourning permeate the play. Despite his murmurings about studying at university, Hamlet himself is clearly indicated in the play to be a man in his thirties: *Hamlet*, from its hero's first discontented, alienated grumblings to its bloodstained finale, may be the definitive study of just how badly wrong a mid-life crisis can go.

David's destructiveness had been turned less spectacularly but no less devastatingly inwards upon his own psychic stage, where it had laid waste to the last vestiges of hope, faith and desire. It

---

[20] Modell, A. H., 'The dead mother syndrome and the reconstruction of trauma' in *The Dead Mother: The Work of André Green*, Kohon, G. (ed.), Routledge (2000).

was up to David, stuck in denial for so long, to find ways of giving his sorrow words, by making a stand on sorrow's behalf and following through his delayed mourning process in all its overlapping and labyrinthine stages. The loss of his marriage showed David what was at stake. Though he was not someone to whom introspection came easily, with the courage of the desperate he stayed doggedly with the process.

As the acknowledgement of his grief and anger became, over time, less frightening to him, his body became less tense and his mind less blank and defended, allowing the energy that had been frozen within him to begin to flow through him and become available in the present. Memories which had been wiped out because of their painfulness returned to him and slowly a sense of a past worth caring about – and a present worth fighting for – began to infuse his being. As his guilt for his imagined abandonment of his mother began to diminish, new loyalties began to make tentative claims upon him and new possibilities to assert themselves. A milestone was reached one Mother's Day when David went with his father to lay flowers on his mother's grave, and found himself weeping in his father's arms. It was impossible not to feel deeply moved by this and by the shy, sensitive and likeable man who began slowly – despite many false starts and backwards steps – to emerge from the zombie that he had once been.

David was helped by becoming able to go to his mother's grave with his father, to face and to mourn his loss. But the decline of religion in modern Britain has also meant the decline of mourning rituals which help the bereaved to come to terms with their loss and to give them – and others – guidelines of what is expected of them. Many people today will be protected from seeing the dead bodies of those they have loved despite the evidence that, however painful, this does help the mourning process. By contrast, rituals like the five-year mourning period undergone by women in rural Greece provide solitude in which it is possible to come to terms with the reality of loss:

Many Greek villagers subscribe to what can be called an indigenous theory of catharsis. They recognise that in spite of the desirability of immersing oneself fully in the emotions of pain, grief and sorrow, the ultimate goal of a woman in mourning is to rid herself of these emotions through their repeated expression. After five years, the mourning is over, the acceptance complete. The bones are exhumed and placed in the village ossuary. A new social reality is constructed which enables the bereaved to inhabit more fully a world in which the deceased plays no part . . . This process is brought about through a gradual reduction in the intensity of the emotions associated with death, through the formation of new social relationships with new significant others, and through the constant confrontation with the objective fact of death, climaxing in the exhumation of the bones of the deceased. The result of this process is as complete an acceptance of the final and irreversible nature of death as is possible.[21]

'*How is it unhappy man, that you have left the sunlight and come here to look upon dead men?*' Like David, Odysseus must journey through the Land of the Dead before he can be freed from its spell and finally be allowed to return home. Leaving his lover Circe, his course steered by a wind she has summoned up and acting upon her instructions, Odysseus reluctantly sails down through mist and fog into the depths of Hades, where he prays to the communities of the dead and makes sacrifice to them. Moaning, the souls of the dead close in on him. At first shocked and panicked by their approaching legions, Odysseus grows deeply moved by their longing for recognition and connection, and his eyes fill with tears when he meets his lost friends and comrades and gazes upon the face of Anticleia, his own dead mother.

Circe has warned Odysseus that once arrived in Hades, he must consult the blind prophet Teiresias who will tell him how to ensure his safe return home. '*My Lord Odysseus . . . You are in search of some easy way to reach your home. But the powers above are going to make your journey hard.*' Teiresias tells Odysseus that before his life can move forward again, he must make reparation for the wrongs he has done and must suffer further loss and disappointment in expiation for his own rash and violent acts, notably the blinding of the Cyclops. Even after he returns to Ithaca he must set out once again to go to a land where people have never seen the sea, to tell his story and to make sacrifice there to Poseidon, god of the sea. '*As for your own end, Death will come to you out of the sea, Death in his gentlest guise. When he takes you, you will be worn out after an easy old age and*

---

[21] Danforth, L. M., *The Death Rituals of Rural Greece*, Princeton (1992), quoted in Storr, A., *Solitude*, Flamingo (1990).

surrounded by a prosperous people.' Teiresias seems to be telling Odysseus that the task in front of him is the need to face limitation and death as a psychic fact – but not actually to die. As much as Odysseus' acts of aggression may have ensured his survival, they must nevertheless be paid for: Odysseus must make amends symbolically, through personal suffering, desolation and reparation. Life will for a while be full of pain – yet there will be a resolution, great fulfilment and when the time comes, a gentle and easy death.

The Cyclops whom Odysseus blinded was an image of the parental figure in its most harsh and inhuman form, an authority which had to be confronted for Odysseus to become truly adult. But now the defiant rage against the persecuting parental figure is replaced by a very different emotion – the compassion which Odysseus feels as he looks upon his mother's dead face and sees her helpless vulnerability and mortality, which is also his own. Odysseus' pain is the greater because his mother had been living when he had left Ithaca; he is shocked by her death and unprepared for it. Having – as we do – taken his mother's continuing survival for granted, the shock of realization is itself transformative. 'As the light darkens' writes Morrison, describing the scene at the end of his father's funeral:

> everyone prepares to leave, putting down paper plates and empty glasses, hunting for coats. We kiss or shake hands at the door: *See you again* I say but when will the next time be – my mother's funeral, their own funerals? You have a childhood and move away, and think vaguely that if you choose to come home again it will still be there, intact, as you left it. What was left of my childhood were these frail widows and widowers, stepping out into the snow, the coming night . . .[22]

The pain of the deaths of those we have loved never leaves us, but with time the harshness and terror of grief will soften. Finally, children no more, we look our own terrors in the face, seeing our parental figures no longer as authorities to be obeyed or defied; seeing, instead, that they suffer as we do, and will. This changing perspective forms the basis of mature compassion. Our own confusion and suffering in the face of their final, surprising

---

[22] Morrison, B., *And When Did You Last See Your Father?*, Granta (1993).

frailty may be our parents' final gift to us, the furnace within which the refinement and transformation of our selves is to be effected.

COMING TO TERMS WITH DEATH

Kisa Gotami was a young mother whose only child died of illness at the age of one. Almost mad from grief, she wandered from house to house clutching her dead child to her breast, refusing to let him be taken from her, begging for medicines with which to revive him, all to no avail. At last she came into the presence of the Buddha. Distraught as she was, the Buddha didn't give her a teaching but promised instead to revive the child if she could bring him a handful of mustard seeds from a house which had never suffered death. Kisa Gotami went off eagerly, going again from house to house. Every house had mustard seeds to offer her, but she found no family who had not suffered bereavement. 'The living are few but the dead are many' she was told. Death, she learns, comes to all. Finally she put the body of her child down in the forest and returned to the Buddha, at whose feet she sat quietly for a long time without speaking. 'Give me refuge' she said finally. The Buddha carried out the funeral rites for her dead child and ordained her, and in due course Kisa Gotami became a great spiritual leader in her own right.

By becoming able to face her own personal tragedy instead of denying it, Kisa Gotami becomes able to break through to a greater reality.[23] Having learnt that death is inherent in all life, she comes to understand that there is no permanence, and that to demand permanence as the basis for living is itself the source of suffering and delusion. She learns that the freedom from suffering for which she longs will come not from chasing after the security of a permanence which will – at best – always be provisional, but from learning to let go when this is what life demands of us. Having opened herself entirely to her own loss, she comes through the other side of it. The narrow perspective

---

[23] See Epstein, M., *Going to Pieces without Falling Apart: A Buddhist Perspective on Wholeness*, HarperCollins (1999).

which had brought her so much suffering and bitterness begins to dissolve into a more spacious and transcendent one.

Kisa Gotami was going from house to house seeking security, for someone to look after her and to take her fears and losses away. Her breakthrough is achieved through her bitter struggles with the worst of losses and her final acceptance. Seeing her own individual predicament as part of the inevitable human state, she ceases struggling against reality and learns to relax into it. Life itself can be terrifying, red in tooth and claw, destroying and creating in a never-ending cycle of careless profligacy in which individual life – so precious when it is our own – scarcely seems to matter. Like Kisa Gotami we struggle between these perspectives, and with the awareness that death is always with us.

Fear of death, transmitted through our genes, enhances our chances of survival, while the size of our human brain makes us uniquely able to understand death's reality. But it is a fine balancing act, for this awareness can also threaten to overwhelm us with paralysing anxiety or becomes a seductive temptation to succumb to the drift to easeful death. Why struggle? Why make an effort? We learn to defend ourselves against this fear – or temptation – by keeping death selectively out of awareness.[24] Like Kisa Gotami going compulsively from house to house in search of someone who will rescue her from herself, we invent personal projects – our obsessions with achievement, empire-building and the amassing of wealth, our narcissistic over-investment in our bodies, the urgency of our attempts to retain physical youthfulness – all in our efforts to outbid death.

The Buddha gently found a way of helping Kisa Gotami come to terms with death, in contrast with Christianity, which extends the hope that Christ will vanquish death and give us immortality.[25] Suffering and death are linked with sin, becoming a punishment for wrongdoing, a humiliation which we must try to avoid. But what's the alternative? In *Gulliver's Travels*, Swift describes a race of people, the Struldbrugs, who have become immortal. The Struldbrugs are peevish, covetous, morose and

---

[24] Becker, E., *The Denial of Death*, Simon and Schuster (1997).
[25] Symington, N., *Emotion and Spirit*, Karnac (1998).

214

vain, talkative yet lacking in natural affection, spontaneity or tenderness. Whenever they see a funeral they lament and repine that others are gone to a harbour of rest in which they themselves can never hope to arrive.[26]

Our striving as individuals to deny the inevitability of death may inform our greatest and most lasting achievements, our empires, our ideological systems and our accumulations of learning and wealth, but they also fuel our most defensive or destructive ways of behaving. The fear of death draws us to egocentric activities designed to exalt and reinforce the invulnerability and immortality of our individual selves – at the expense of others, on to whom we project our feelings of inferiority, fallibility, guilt and self-hatred. It is the disguise of panic, says Paul Tillich, that makes us live in ugliness.[27] Our over-valuation of control, together with the impossible compensatory demands we make of ourselves as a result, is a causal factor in depression. The aches and pains, the anxieties and depressions that lie waiting for us at mid life show the flimsiness of the meanings we erect against our fate, sand castles left along an evening beach before the tide comes in. At the same time, our insomnias and nightmares eloquently reveal our terror of letting go into the nothingness that tempts us: 'Oh God! I could be bounded in a nutshell, and count myself a king of infinite space, were it not that I have bad dreams' says Shakespeare's Hamlet.[28]

Left alone upon Ithaca, Penelope weaves her father-in-law's shroud each day but by night she unpicks it, thereby both accepting and denying the reality of death and abandonment. Turning a finite task into an endless one, Penelope fosters her own desire to believe in immortality and to make time stand still – but robs herself of the satisfaction of an ending and sinks ever deeper into a tearful paralysis, a state of suspended animation which is nevertheless, paradoxically, a necessary stage in her own mourning process. Making our happiness contingent upon our capacity to control events, we turn death into our mortal enemy. Repressing our knowledge that death will win in the end and our

---

[26] Swift, J., *Gulliver's Travels* (1726), Penguin (1994).
[27] Tillich, P., *The Courage to Be*, Yale University Press (1952).
[28] *Hamlet*, Act II, Scene 2.

helplessness in the face of loss, we slip into denial and depression.

'Not long ago I went on a summer walk through a smiling countryside in the company of a taciturn friend and of a young but already famous poet' wrote Freud in 1915, adding that this walk had taken place in the summer before the war broke out and robbed the world of its beauties.[29] This retrospective knowledge made the memory of the walk more poignant, but even at the time Freud could not help but observe the inability of his friends to surrender themselves to the beauty of the day. It seemed that their awareness of its inevitable transience robbed the experience of all pleasure and delight.

Why, wondered Freud out loud, should this be so? Why is our experience of beauty or happiness not sufficient in itself? The awareness of transience – the scarcity value of beauty or pleasure – should make us enjoy it more, not less. But his friends were unmoved by his musings. Freud realized that each of them in his own way was defending against an engagement with beauty which was fated to end in the pain of loss, one by falling into an aching depression, the other by denial of the truth – the states identified by the Buddha as aversion and delusion.[30] Unconsciously, Freud's friends were in a state of frozen mourning for what they had not yet lost – and their anticipation of what they would lose effectively stopped them enjoying what they had.

Freud concludes rather optimistically that this state must come to a natural end, and hopes that when the war is over the world will learn to appreciate the riches of civilization all the more for having discovered their fragility.[31] In the end, it is only by developing the capacity to experience life in an open way, one which sees transience – even our own – as something to savour and not to fight against, that we will begin to free ourselves from the suffering which comes not really from transience itself but from the unwinnable argument against reality which is defensive living.

---

[29] Freud, S., 'On Transience' (1915), *Penguin Freud Library* 14.
[30] Epstein, M., *Going to Pieces without Falling Apart: A Buddhist Perspective on Wholeness*, HarperCollins (1999).
[31] Freud, *op. cit.*

'For years I was full of panic' says Marguerite, a forty-five-year-old woman and the survivor of a bitterly contested divorce settlement. 'Every day, I seemed to be losing more of what I'd taken for granted. I struggled and raged and tried to regain control. My dentist told me that my teeth were starting to crumble because of how tightly I clenched and ground them in my sleep. But then in the end there came a point when I just got exhausted with fighting and began to learn to relax and breathe. I learnt not to hold on as I had been doing. I discovered what a frightened person I'd always been and I was brought to the depths of my fear – the fear that if I lost everything I wouldn't survive.

'But I did survive. And now having let go of so much, I seem to have come to a place where death doesn't frighten me so either. I never thought about death in my life before. Now I think about it every day, and it seems all right. Now I feel a softness and a tenderness within me where I used to be hard. Sometimes I lie awake in bed and listen to my sleeping lover breathe, just to hear that continuity, one breath after another and to feel the warmth of his body. Sometimes, it's a physical feeling, I feel the centre of my body opening to this feeling of love, and it just flows through me . . .'

We maintain our defences against death at increasing economic cost to ourselves as we grow older, and as the psychic awareness of death encroaches. Caught between the desire to give in to the drift towards death and the need to violently defend against it by creating false self structures and false refuges, we struggle as we reach mid life to find a new equilibrium. The awareness of death brings disillusionment – literally, the loss of the false illusions and defensiveness which sustained our early lives. Graced by maturity with a new sense of proportion and a new perspective upon our own lives, we can learn to abide and to relax in the face of transience without holding on, trusting to the vitality of the cosmos rather than to our own defensive will-power. And out of the discovery of this may come, strangely, the capacity to love with a new tenderness. Kierkegaard writes that he who is educated by dread is educated by possibility.[32]

A meditation practice taught by the Buddha traces the stages of death and of decomposition of the body, its purpose being to help us to come to accept impermanence at the deepest level of

<hr>

[32] Kierkegaard, S., *The Concept of Dread*, tr. Lowrie, W., Oxford University Press (1994).

our being. This is not a practice to be taken up lightly or without years of experience and skilled support – the Buddha himself was said to have misjudged the readiness of a group of monks to take on this practice and, returning later, found that they had all committed suicide. But if this meditation is practised within appropriately supportive conditions and developed gradually within a balanced and positive frame of mind, it is said to loosen our small-minded clinging to security and to create a new sense of confidence and internal freedom.[33] Socrates said that the courage to die is the test of the courage to be. He too advised us to practise dying each day, while Prospero, in his final farewell to his magic island and in some of the last lines attributed to Shakespeare himself, says that from now on his every third thought shall be of death.[34]

As our capacity to split, to deny and to retreat behind manic activity recedes, we may find cause to celebrate life's infinite and ingenious renewal of itself in the most unlikely ways: when transience is not merely an occasion for mourning, writes Adam Phillips, then we will truly have inherited the earth.[35] Becoming aware of our vulnerability to destruction as well as our destructiveness, we may finally become able to maintain, in the face of our mortality, a love transformed and fortified by our awareness. 'There is no death except of a totality' writes Winnicott.[36] 'Put the other way round, the wholeness of personal integration brings with it the *possibility* and indeed the *certainty* of death – and with the acceptance of death there can come a great relief, relief from fear of the alternatives, such as disintegration.' By learning to live fully, we may become able to accept death gently when it comes, as an act of completion of a full life, rather than the theft of an unlived one. Ripeness is all.

---

[33] Kamalashila, *Meditation: The Buddhist Way of Tranquillity and Insight*, Windhorse (1996).

[34] *The Tempest*, Act V, Scene 1.

[35] Phillips, A., *Darwin's Worms*, Faber and Faber (1999).

[36] Winnicott, D. W., 'Sum I AM' (talk given to the Association of Teachers of Mathematics, London 1968), quoted in Davis, M. and Wallbridge, D., *Boundary and Space: An Introduction to the Work of D. W. Winnicott*, Penguin (1983).

9

Depression

You may my glories and my state depose,
But not my griefs; still am I king of those.

From *Richard II* by William Shakespeare

A 1999 report from the World Health Organization suggested that the world ended the second millennium disabled by sadness and facing a growing epidemic of mental disorder.[1] Depression has become the primary cause of disability in the United States and the third in Europe, and is worldwide the leading cause of disability in adults up to the age of 44, claimed the report, and yet its impact upon our lives is largely ignored and neglected – mainly because of the stigma attached to it.

At any given time, around three per cent of the population is suffering from a severe depressive or anxiety breakdown, while one in ten of us is experiencing a milder yet still disabling form of depression. Between ten and fifteen per cent of us will have a major depressive breakdown at some point in our lives, and there is some evidence that the incidence of depression for both sexes seems to peak around or just after the mid-life period, before

---

[1]   Reported in the *Independent*, 12 May 1999.

dipping and peaking again in advanced old age.[2] And for all of us, depression rates are rising exponentially: there was a 50 per cent increase in the number of patients for whom GPs diagnosed anti-depressants in the four years from 1994 to 1998.[3] No doubt this is partly attributable to the relatively greater recent awareness and acceptance of depression and anxiety states (especially when they are redefined in a more functional and socially acceptable way as stress), but no-one can say for sure why the increase should be quite so great.

Yet the stigma attached to depression is still such that many of us will soldier on alone no matter how deadened, impaired or bleak our lives, behind a façade of coping. Sometimes even to the brink of suicidal alienation and despair, we try to maintain this façade towards others and even to ourselves. Much depression is concealed behind those physical maladies which are the closest many of us can let ourselves come to showing something is wrong and asking for help – and untreated depression does in any event tend to depress the immune system, and increases susceptibility to illnesses as diverse as cancer and heart disease.[4] Or we turn for help elsewhere: alcohol is itself a depressant, yet for many depressed or anxious people, their drinking or drugs may sometimes seem like their only unjudging friend in a cruel world. Addiction may in the end become a form of slow suicide and this, for the seriously depressed, may be part of its attraction.

But why do we get depressed? Although studies of identical and non-identical twins suggest that up to half of all predisposition towards depression may be genetic, it is most unlikely that anything like a gene for depression will ever be isolated. Our genes may create a predisposition, but for this to be triggered, other factors must come into play. Depression itself is a disorder of the emotional life in which relationships with others – or their

[2] *Key Health Statistics from General Practice* (1998), Office of National Statistics, London.
[3] *Ibid.*
[4] Booth, R. J. and Pennebaker J. W., 'Emotions and immunity' in Lewis, M. and Haviland-Jones, J. M. (eds), *Handbook of Emotions*, Guildford Press (2000).

failure – play a key role. Single-mindedly deploying energy in the pursuit of material gain, it is easy to miss the fact that wealth itself does not save us from depression – in fact depression, like alcoholism, seems to increase proportionately in countries which adopt a way of life based on consumer values. On the other hand, a sense of connectedness to others – a stable family life, secure employment or even religious belief – does seem to make depression less likely. Social factors correlated with depression are the breakdown of marriage and family life, increasing mobility and rootlessness, and the culture of competitiveness which sets us against each other and also leads us to nurse expectations of ourselves which may not be realistic, but which nevertheless become the punitive and shame-inducing standard against which we learn to measure ourselves.[5]

A crucial factor behind depression is consistently shown to be unresolved loss: the loss of love, of power, of an ideal – sometimes, the loss of hope itself. At a personal level, stressful life events such as divorce, bereavement, ill health or redundancy increase the likelihood of becoming depressed. Ageing itself, the loss of sexual attractiveness and fertility, the loss of children who have flown the nest or the final loss of children who were never born, the loss of role or status within the workplace – all these losses precipitate depression into the lives of people reaching mid life, and the fear of depressive breakdown lies at the centre of mid-life crisis. Faced with loss and change on all sides, our coping mechanisms threaten to crack under the strain. Yet with so much to lose, there may never be a harder time to let go – even a little.

Men reaching mid life seem, on the face of it, much less likely to become depressed than women (around 40 men out of 1000 in the 35–44 age group are prescribed anti-depressants by their GPs each year, compared with around 100 women)[6]. But alcoholism rates, for example, are the mirror opposite – much

---

[5] See the evidence amassed by Oliver James in *Britain on the Couch: Why We're Unhappier than We Were in the 1950s – Despite Being Richer*, Arrow (1998).

[6] *Key Health Statistics from General Practice* (1998), Office of National Statistics, London.

higher for men than for women. When the greater tendency of men to anaesthetize their moods by drinking or to submerge themselves obsessively in work is taken into account, along with men's much greater reluctance to come forward to get help, the gender gap narrows dramatically.

While women are more likely to try to defuse threat or trauma by developing cohesive group relationships, man *qua* hunter is, by contrast, hard-wired to need to prove himself to other men – not to advertise his vulnerability by seeking their help. Men tend to have higher levels of stress chemicals in their systems than women, and their adrenaline surges are sooner triggered, activating the fight/flight mechanism. At the same time a man's sense of his own masculinity may depend upon his ability to present himself as calm and unafraid in the face of attack, making him more likely to stonewall in response to difficulties he doesn't know how to deal with, and also more likely to process threat at a physiological level rather than at an emotional or verbal level. Hence, probably, men's greater propensity towards high blood pressure and circulatory and heart problems, and their relatively shorter life span.

After around forty or so, the muscle tone and energy of men who lead sedentary lives begins to wane, affecting their health, well-being and confidence. A man's body is no longer geared up to process without severe stress the constant surging of adrenaline which triggers the fight/flight mechanism – yet the need to show he can still cope may make him more likely to drop down dead with a heart attack than to admit he needs help. The fight/flight mechanism, functionally effective on the hunting ground, isn't so good at dealing with mid-life crisis, and withdrawal in the face of a threat to his emotional security or autonomy may begin a man's slide down towards the emotional deadness, unresponsiveness and nihilism of undiagnosed depression.

A man whose sense of well-being and self-esteem is based upon his sexual virility, his authority and his capacity to perform well in all arenas will be hard hit by the uncontrollable losses of mid life. His self-esteem may itself have been built upon an unspoken and unrecognized dependence upon others to maintain the emotional bonds which underpin his life. But his wife, recently freed from the ties of child-rearing, may now herself be focusing upon her career and be rarely at home, while his once bright-eyed affectionate children have become sarcastic, moody and indifferent adolescents and his own parents are elderly or dying. Feeling neglected, abandoned and at a loss, he is likely to respond by burying himself ever deeper in his work. Yet while a mid-life career may be peaking in terms of success and fulfilment, few careers today are without their insecurities, and the thought of what lies on the other side of the peak becomes more real every day. The loss of the identity, status or sense of purpose provided by work – through redundancy, unemployment, long-term sick leave, early retirement or a change in career – is a significant contributory factor in male depression.

The experience of loss mobilizes our defences against threat. The masculine fight/flight mechanism – the tendency to bluff and outface danger by resorting to action or, failing that, to retreat – means that while women are more likely to internalize, men are more likely to project. When women blame themselves, men will tend to blame others, and so fail to take on board the lessons that may be there to be learnt. Instead of having a breakdown himself, a man may be attracted towards a new relationship with a woman with emotional problems of her own, in which he can experience himself as a rescuer. But it is a precarious solution: the illicit thrills of many mid-life love affairs fend off the dread of encroaching depression.

The depression of a woman reaching mid life may be rooted in feelings of powerlessness and emotional exhaustion. Women in their late thirties and forties – especially those with children – are likely to be poorer than men and to suffer lower social status. Women also tend to bear the brunt of the emotional needs of their partners, children and ageing parents, while at work they tend to congregate in fields such as teaching, health care and the service industries and to have less directive and more consultative management styles. All of this makes heavy demands of women's abilities to process and manage others' emotions, and leads many women to feel, by the time they reach mid life, overextended and emotionally overdrawn – neglected, invisible, taken for granted, silently resentful. The prevalence of depression among the mothers of young children, especially where fathers are absent or uninvolved, provides an exception to the general rule that meaningful relationships with others protect against depression.

A woman reaching mid life may be anxious about the loss of her own sexual attractiveness and fertility, sometimes just as she is facing the break-up of a relationship to which she has devoted most of her adult life. She may be struggling to decide whether she wants a child while it is still possible (or alternatively to come to terms with the fact that she will not have one, be mourning the loss of the role of motherhood as her children grow up and away, or be anxious about her future career prospects in a youth culture and a man's world. The mood swings and physiological changes of the menopause must also at some point be faced – another loss. As Germaine Greer dryly remarked, the fact that a woman may live as long after her menopause as she did before it is bad news for those women who only feel alive as the lovers of men and the mothers of children.[7]

Greer sees the onset of menopause as potentially liberating women's capacity for leadership. But leadership does not come easily to Homer's Penelope, abandoned by her husband Odysseus to rule Ithaca and to keep his home and family together during his lengthy absence. Silently accepting her role, Penelope succumbs to depression and increasingly takes to her bed in tears. Penelope's house is overrun by unruly suitors – her energy is absorbed by her efforts to maintain a space for others to use and abuse while they, for their part, come and go at will, exploiting and draining her resources, as oblivious to her needs as the husband who left her many years before, who may – or may not – return. Bound by her continuing ties of loyalty, Penelope must work a careful balancing act, conciliating and appeasing her oppressors while keeping her true feelings and desires carefully concealed, politely doing her spinning each day and savagely ripping it out each night.

---

[7] Greer, G., *The Change*, Hamish Hamilton (1991).

Women's fear of hurting others, or provoking rejection or condemnation should they dare to show signs of independent thinking or desire, can be very strong. Men too may fear their own aggression – they have more reason than women to fear the harm their violence could do, and yet society does not extend the same tolerance to men's passivity that it does to women's. When any of us fail to assert ourselves over what we know in our hearts really matters, and when we collude with being ignored, overridden or treated without respect by others, we hasten our descent into depression.

Depression, said Adler,[8] is our refuge when we lose the courage to live. When we become depressed, aggression in all its forms becomes inhibited and feared: the American Amish who practise absolute pacifism and prohibit all aggressive and hostile behaviour have a threefold higher than average rate of depression.[9] The baby fiercely attacking the breast, the child arguing against received wisdom, the lover's penetration of the body of his beloved, the artist's assault upon her canvas or clay – all are forms of the necessary aggression which generates meaning but which in depression becomes disallowed and fraught with danger.

When we perceive the world as peopled with hostile others more powerful than ourselves, the display of self-assertive aggression becomes a dangerous luxury. The drooping shoulders, listless demeanour and monotonous voice of the depressed man or woman are in this sense a self-preserving functional response to a lowering of status, signalling to the powerful that here is no threat to be bothered with.[10] When we come to believe that relationships with others can only be preserved at the cost of self-abasement and the stifling of

---

[8]   Adler, A., *The Practice and Theory of Individual Psychology*, Kegan Paul (1924).
[9]   Wolpert, L., *Malignant Sadness: The Anatomy of Depression*, Faber and Faber (1999).
[10] Stevens, A. and Price, J., *Evolutionary Psychiatry: A New Beginning*, Routledge (1996).

personal initiative and aggression, we learn to develop a false self structure through which we relate to others, and which can eventually come to paralyse our whole being. This explanation of depression – as the inhibition of feared aggression in the face of loss of status – makes sense as far as it goes. Yet in itself it cannot help us to engage constructively with the suffering and despair which are at the heart of depression. To penetrate further, we need to look more closely at the experience of depression itself, and how it unfolds in individual lives.

TRYING TO DEFINE DEPRESSION

Doctors write millions of prescriptions each year to treat depression. Yet despite the medicalization of depression, it is an illness for which your doctor can offer you no blood test, brain scan or biopsy before making a diagnosis and writing a prescription. Your doctor is more likely to refer to DSM-IV, a widely used psychiatric diagnostic manual which says that you are depressed if over a two-week period you have experienced five or more of the following symptoms (including at least one of the first two):

- a continuing and recurrent depressed mood
- a markedly diminished interest or pleasure in most daily activities
- changes in eating habits (i.e. loss or increase in appetite and weight)
- changes in sleeping habits (i.e. insomnia or an excessive need for sleep)
- nervous agitation or retardation
- recurrent fatigue or loss of energy
- feelings of worthlessness or inappropriate feelings of guilt
- diminished inability to think, concentrate or make decisions
- recurrent thoughts of dying.

In addition, the symptoms must cause clinically significant distress or impairment in significant areas of functioning (a further proviso which you might have thought, in the circumstances, goes without saying), and they must not be symptoms that are better explained by bereavement.[11]

Even if we leave aside the circular nature of requiring a depressed mood to be present for depression to be diagnosed, most of these criteria are self-evidently subjective, and scientifically inexact. Their inclusive nature also means that many people suffering from anxiety disorders may be diagnosed as depressed (there may be a pragmatic reason for this – once doctors diagnose people with depression, they can offer them anti-depressants). Of course, states of depression and anxiety often do overlap, and it is also true that anti-depressants do help to alleviate the symptoms of depression, at least temporarily. But all of this takes us no closer to an understanding of what depression really is.

Another internationally recognized guide to classifying mental disorders (published by the World Health Organization) – also states authoritatively that depression is a disorder characterized by disproportionate depression.[12] The WHO's definition adds that this depression can usually be traced back to a distressing experience, and notes that there is often preoccupation with the psychic trauma that preceded the illness, such as the loss of a cherished someone or something. But what, we may wonder, is proportionate depression, and when does it become disproportionate? And at what point do normal grieving processes become pathological depression?

The difference between an unhappy mood and a full-scale depressive breakdown is essentially one of degree and duration rather than one of kind – the two states are on a continuum and despite the efforts of psychiatry and the pharmaceutical industry, it remains impossible to draw a line between ordinary unhappiness and clinical depression. The main difference may be that when we are miserable we seek to understand why and to deal

---

[11] *Diagnostic and Statistical Manual of Mental Disorders* (fourth edition), American Psychiatric Association (1992).

[12] *Mental Disorders: Glossary and Guide to their Classification in Accordance with the 9th Revision of the International Classification of Diseases*, World Health Organization, Geneva (1978).

with the problem – while the diagnosis of depression seems to absolve us of that responsibility.

It is not the fault of GPs, who bear the brunt of most initial calls for help from depressed people, that the six minutes or so allocated to each patient makes it more practicable to reach for the prescription pad than to embark upon taking a full case history of the losses, disappointments and unmet needs in the lives of each distressed patient. Nevertheless, the immodest assertion that depression is a disease which can be defined, diagnosed, treated and cured as if it were measles or pneumonia is misleading, and by raising false hopes may do more harm than good. It is a belief held in place by the economics of the health care industry, but also by the intensity of the shame and loneliness felt by many depressed people which may incline them to feel relieved rather than fobbed off when, instead of having their state of mind inquired into more deeply, they are given a bottle of pills. In the face of the pharmaceutical industry-funded rush to medicalize depression, exacerbated by the sheer numbers of people suffering from it and the stigma still attached to it, it is the understanding of the significance of the onset of depression in the life of any given individual that we are in danger of losing.

Depression is connected to changes in the brain's chemistry, specifically a depletion in the brain chemicals noradrenaline and serotonin, and an increase in levels of the stress hormone cortisone. It is for this reason that anti-depressants such as Prozac and Seroxat (which operate by inhibiting the re-absorption of serotonin by the brain's neurons) are sometimes – though not always – helpful in alleviating some of the symptoms of depression, in the short term at least. These chemical changes seem originally to be brought about by systemic stress: but what causes systemic stress? Our biochemistry is ultimately related to consciousness and emotional experience, which itself is connected to the choices we make in life and the values and beliefs which inform these choices. It may be as much an inversion of cause and effect to say that chemical depletions cause depression as it would be to say that crying causes sadness.

'Unwilling to accept its own gathering deterioration, the mind announces to its indwelling consciousness that it is the body with its perhaps correctable defects not the precious and irreplaceable mind – that is going haywire' wrote William Styron in *Darkness Visible*, a moving account of his own descent through depressive breakdown to the brink of suicide.[13] It was in the summer of 1985 when Styron was overtaken by the insomnia and persistent sense of malaise that would coalesce into a dark depression and engulf his life. By that time past mid life himself, he nevertheless came to believe that his depression had been waiting to happen for many years, hovering at the edges of his consciousness and kept at bay only by decades of heavy drinking a 'soothing, often sublime agent which had contributed greatly to my writing ... [but which was also] a means to calm the anxiety and incipient dread that I had hidden away for so long somewhere in the dungeons of my spirit'.

Styron first realized he was suffering from a serious depressive illness shortly before he went to Paris to receive the prestigious *Prix Mondial Cino del Duca*, an award made annually to an outstanding artist or scientist whose work reflects humanistic themes: the irony did not escape him. Neither his international reputation as a novelist nor his comfortable lifestyle and contented marriage were able to prevent him from collapsing deep into feelings of self-hatred and worthlessness as his depression worsened. As its grip upon his psyche tightened it began to erode his energy, sense of purpose and creativity, leaving him prey to confusion, failing memory, apathy to the point of paralysis, dislocation and panic.

Styron finally fell into a sort of trance – a storm of murk, as he memorably described it. His thoughts returned obsessively to death and to suicide: 'the pain of severe depression is quite unimaginable to those who have not suffered it', he wrote, 'and it kills in many instances because its anguish can no longer be borne'. For Styron this moment came one cold evening in early December. Having planned his suicide, he sat down to watch a final film. As he watched, his heart was unexpectedly and suddenly pierced by a soaring passage in the film from Brahms' *Alto Rhapsody*, a passage he later remembered having first heard

---

[13] Styron, W., *Darkness Visible*, Picador (1992).

performed by his mother, who had died when he was thirteen. He realized that he could not inflict this final destruction on himself or upon those he loved, and the next day, arranged to be admitted to psychiatric hospital. Here, slowly and painfully, he began over time to get well and to emerge once more into the light.

In time, Styron came to believe that his descent to near-suicide had come out of his attempt to come to terms with immense losses within his own life while at the same time trying to surmount them by denying their importance: 'My own avoidance of death may have been belated homage to my mother. I do know that in those last hours before I rescued myself, when I listened to the passage from the *Alto Rhapsody* – which I'd heard her sing – she had been very much on my mind.'

ATTACHMENT AND LOSS

'Loss in all of its manifestations is the touchstone of depression – in the progress of the disease and, most likely, in its origin' was Styron's final conclusion. 'At a later date I would gradually be persuaded that devastating loss in childhood figured as a probable genesis of my own disorder; meanwhile ... I felt loss at every hand.' As we all do, once we stop growing up and start growing older. Depression, born from experiences of loss and grief, gives birth in its turn to new losses. The feelings of worthlessness, self-doubt and internal paralysis which gain such a destructive grip in the course of a depressive episode lead to the loss of ordinary self-reliance and an incapacity to make self-determining choices. Instead there is a shaming fear of becoming a resented burden to others – or worse, the fear of being abandoned at one's hour of greatest need. There may be good historical reason to explain why the dawning awareness of emotional need often fills depressed people with feelings of shame and dread – their own earliest experience of dependency, the prototype of later relationships, may have been far from happy.

A host of laboratory experiments over the last fifty years have shown – presumably, to no-one's great surprise – that young monkeys or rats deliberately separated from their mothers exhibit signs of intense distress. But what has also been shown is that deprivations and disruptions in the mother – infant bond at this early stage have a lasting effect upon these unfortunate animals' mature neurobiological systems. Their curiosity and their adventurousness are, in adult life, also severely inhibited – as are their sociability and their capacity to form cohesive relationships.[14] In other words, they show the sort of behaviour which gets diagnosed as depression when it occurs in humans.

Likewise, continuing research into the workings of the human brain suggests that experiences from the past may be stored structurally within the brain (perhaps in the amygdala region which plays a central role in emotional responses and learning), where they are held out of awareness, yet nevertheless condition our emotional responses in ways we cannot consciously know or control.[15] Trauma, deprivation or abuse in early life seems to affect our own neurodevelopment just as it affects the monkeys – although our much greater cognitive ability also means that we are more able to modify these effects with later reparative experiences.[16] Early trauma may nevertheless remain isolated and hence unmodified within the mind for many years, lying latent until triggered by new stresses – when it causes the systemic stress which results in adult anxiety and depressive disorders.

As the psychiatric manuals acknowledge, it can be very difficult to distinguish between the symptoms of depression and bereavement – probably because the majority of those who are

---

[14] Harlow's classic studies were criticized as relating to conditions of extreme deprivation unlike those experienced even in the most dysfunctional families, but recent work by Rosenblum and Coplan, having created environments for the monkeys more similar to those of human families in difficulty, also showed that early events affect the neurodevelopment of systems central to the expression of adult anxiety disorders. See Rosenblum, L. *et al.*, 'Adverse early experiences affect noradrenergic and serotonergic functioning in adult primates' (1994), *Biological Psychiatry* 35.

[15] Damasio, A., *The Feeling of What Happens: Body, Emotion and the Making of Consciousness*, Heinemann (1999).

[16] Holmes, J., 'Attachment theory and psychoanalysis: a rapprochement' (2000), *British Journal of Psychotherapy* 17(2).

depressed actually *do* feel bereaved, by loss or deprivation in their early life that they cannot even remember, let alone come to terms with. Unhappy early experiences – of loss, disappointment or rejection – can, in the interests of survival, get covered up by the development of a false coping self, or a false self which cares for others while the carer's needs remain denied. But one day, a new loss or crisis will be the straw that breaks the camel's back. The façade cracks and pain and anxiety flood the nervous system which, unable to cope, founders and finally breaks down.

The relationship between early attachment disturbance and episodes of psychological distress in later life was the life's work of the psychiatrist and psychoanalyst John Bowlby.[17] Bowlby's studies – which the separations forced upon families by the war and the child-rearing practices of the post-war period gave him ample opportunity to pursue – inspired the development of a famous experiment known as the Strange Situation, an experiment which has been carried out over the years in many different cultural settings, with consistent results which validate Bowlby's findings. In the Strange Situation, a mother and her toddler are introduced into a new playroom and remain there for twenty minutes, after which time the experimenter asks the mother to leave the room and return in three minutes, the whole experience being videotaped.

When the tapes are studied, the toddlers fall into three main attachment patterns. The infants originally described by Bowlby as *securely attached* have mothers who are responsive and in tune with their needs. These children tend to be animated and to enjoy exploring and playing in their mothers' presence. When the mother leaves, her child becomes distressed, but on her return the toddler greets her, allows him or herself to be comforted, and returns to contented play. *Insecure-avoidant* children have much less emotionally responsive mothers. These children show much less distress when their mothers leave, and ignore them when they return. But their play is far more restricted and they tend to watch their mothers continually. The mothers of *insecure-ambivalent* children tend to be inconsistent,

---

[17] Bowlby, J., *Attachment and Loss*, Penguin (1985).

with their responses to their children dominated by their own moods. These children are distressed by separation and hard to comfort on their mothers' return. They seek contact but resist it by turning away, alternating between anger and clinging, and do not play or explore much. It has been shown in follow-up tests that the attachment style demonstrated by an infant is likely to remain remarkably consistent into adolescence and beyond.

If they are to survive in a sometimes hostile world, the young of all species need above all to preserve those bonds which guarantee their mothers' attention and protection. Securely attached children play and explore freely, apparently secure in their mothers' unconditional love, and grow up, it seems, to face the world with an attitude of basic trust. Their response to the departure of their mothers in the experiment becomes the model of their responses to the subsequent inevitable losses and failures of life. Loss is met with appropriate sadness and grief, but in due course comfort and consolation are found. In particular, the experience of loss does not lead towards internalizing beliefs about their own worthlessness, or towards feelings of help-lessness and paralysis.

Insecure-avoidant children, on the other hand, appear, on the face of it, relatively unaffected by loss. Unlike the securely attached children, they do not display overt anxiety when their mothers leave, nor do they seem to need comforting when they return – but the children's continual sideways glances at their mothers, and the inhibition of their curiosity and play, tell a different story. These insecure-avoidant children have discovered by the age of one that their mothers are made uncomfortable by emotional display and demands – their mothers make disapprov-ing noises, turn their faces away or leave their infants to cry alone in their push-chairs or cots. To avoid such rejecting responses, the child learns in due course to avoid his or her *own* emotions. Coming to identify with the mother's viewpoint, the child learns to feel shame at his or her own babyish longings for comfort or containment, and learns to repudiate them. If, in later life, feelings of anxiety or distress do overwhelm these defences, they are likely to evoke intense feelings of failure and shame.

Insecure-avoidant children often have strict parents whose love seems conditional upon the child achieving particular standards. Accordingly, the children are likely to grow up to value others' needs over their own, and to look to achievement to take away the emptiness they feel within – and to blame themselves when this strategy fails. They may find themselves attracted in adult life to relationships in which they struggle anxiously – and unsuccessfully – for approval from others. In both work and relationships they may demand of themselves impossibly high standards. Their tendency to blame themselves for failing to meet these standards fuels feelings of unworthiness and panic and renews the desperate struggle for others' approval. (There is some indication that insecure-avoidant attachment is more common in the countries of Northern Europe, where there is a strong work ethic and institutionalized intolerance of displays of grief and loss.)

Insecure-ambivalent children, by contrast, have parents who are unpredictable and self-absorbed – sometimes remote, sometimes intrusive, sometimes indulgent, sometimes rejecting. These children cling to their parents and show great anxiety when separated, yet cannot be easily comforted when their parents return. As they mature, they find it difficult to develop effective ways of signalling their needs to others, which makes them tend to conclude that they can expect little that is genuinely nurturing from relationships. Nevertheless, despite feeling lonely and unseen, they tend to cling to relationships as once they clung to their mothers, holding forlornly to the belief that if they can adapt themselves sufficiently to those they love, they will somehow gain the love they need for themselves. Struggling against their own aggression, they may end up in relationships in which they feel abused and angry, yet believe their relationships are too precarious to tolerate any emotional demands or any displays of aggression. There seems to be nothing to do except turn anger inwards against the self.

Colin's hair is lank; his shoulders droop and his face is pale and blank. A maths teacher in his early forties, he is on long-term sickness leave from work, suffering from stress and depression, and has been referred to a counsellor, Jenny, for help. Colin is married and has no children: he and his wife had fertility treatment but gave up two years ago, which Colin thinks may be for the best as he was unsure whether he really wanted children anyway. Colin was brought up by his mother and has two older sisters. His father left when he was three years old, and lost touch with the family.

Colin attributes his difficulties at work to his head of department, by whom he felt continually criticized and persecuted. He has also felt let down by his GP, who prescribed some anti-depressants which seem to be having little effect. From the beginning, Jenny does not find Colin an easy client, and she begins to anticipate the addition of her own name to his list of failed relationships with overbearing women. She casts about half-heartedly in her mind to think of another therapist to whom she can refer him.

The first session is filled with a vague yet vehement litany of complaints, but Jenny finds it hard to come to grips with anything Colin says. He speaks in generalizations which have an impenetrable, doomed quality to them, but when Jenny tries to glean more details, to explore anything at greater depth or even to point out the apparent contradictions in some of the things he tells her, Colin seems irritated rather than interested. He's also very sensitive to hearing her comments as implied criticisms – which is unfortunate, because the more Jenny sees of Colin, the more exasperated and critical she does indeed become.

Colin tells Jenny that he had a happy childhood. He had no memories of his father who had been a waste of space – what would have been the point in keeping in touch? It's unclear whose judgement this is. Colin says he had been glad to have his mother's attention all to himself, once his sisters had grown up. He has no memories of his mother playing with him or reading to him but that doesn't mean it didn't happen, he says – anyway, she was always very busy. He had been a difficult and naughty child, apparently, and prone to tantrums, for which he would be punished. At this point Colin starts shifting in his chair and rubbing his knuckles with the fingers of his other hand. He says that his mother had always done what was best for him. Sometimes she would let him come into bed with her when he had nightmares.

The departure of Colin's father, and the annihilation of his memory from the family, had deprived Colin of an adult male with whom he could identify and who might have helped Colin separate more from his mother and her view of things. A secure relationship with his father might also have given Colin a place in which his aggression could have been safely expressed and contained. But it was not to be. Too unsure of himself ever to confront his mother or to enter into conflict with her – he had, after all, already lost one parent and could not risk losing another – Colin grew up seeing women as aggressive and controlling.

Afraid to express his own aggression (except in the monotonous, over-rationalized unfolding of his criticisms) he projected it on to the women who became persecuting figures in his life. It transpired later that Colin would fantasize about sadomasochistic sexual situations which eroticized his anxieties and gave him some relief, but made him feel very ashamed afterwards and did not diminish his depression.

Underneath his cloak of passivity, Colin was terrified of his own aggression. His father's departure and his mother's cold severity in the face of his childish anger had left him with the abiding fear that to unleash his aggression would endanger his relationships with those he loved. Colin had grown up in a house of women: perhaps his mother had got rid of his father because he was too aggressive, too dominant? Perhaps (a thought relating to the domineering, inflexible side of his mother) she had eaten his father up and appropriated all his maleness to herself, becoming a terrifying phallic mother – a figure of absolute power from whom there was no refuge. By unconsciously inhibiting his own aggression, he had found a way of preserving his own place in the matriarchy. But it was at the cost of his creativity, aliveness and curiosity.

Colin's floundering counsellor wonders about the failure of the fertility treatment. Was it more significant than Colin admits, representing not only the loss of real children but the possibility of mending the damaged and useless father–child relationship in Colin's own psyche? His minimizing of its importance echoes his denial of the importance of the loss of his father. But every time Jenny tentatively suggests something along these lines, she ends up feeling both inept and persecuting.

Jenny begins to suspect that her own feelings of uselessness are connected to her having fallen into a collusive relationship with Colin, denying the significance of these two great losses for fear of being mocked and ridiculed if she makes the forbidden connections. Resisting her desire to refer him on to a male colleague, and bracing herself against his scathing incomprehension, in the following session Jenny returns much more firmly to the significance of these losses. She tells Colin she thinks that he has tried to deny the empty place in his heart left by his father's departure by making his mother replace his father and colluding with his mother's scornful dismissal of his father. 'But your mother could never be your father', she says, 'and in your heart you know it, and you've ended up feeling let down by every woman since. Now you think

I'm letting you down too. And you're right – if you won't feel your own pain and if you won't let me in like you won't let anyone in, then I will fail you too.'

Colin falls silent after this. After a while he says quietly that there is a children's playground near his house. At weekends he always drives or walks into town another way because he doesn't like seeing the fathers pushing their children on the swings and kicking footballs with them. As he finishes speaking he stares down at his shoes, blinking rapidly. For the first time, Jenny has a surge of feeling for him, and a flicker of hope that they may get somewhere together.

It is not easy to let ourselves hate those we also love and need. Colin could not hate his mother, and with regard to his father he did not dare let himself feel anything at all. Yet who else would we hate? Only those we have taken into our hearts really have the power to hurt us. Freud, struggling with the problem of the relationship between depression and mourning – trying to understand how depression grows like grieving out of loss, yet tends to get bogged down in feelings of worthlessness and self-hatred in the way that ordinary mourning does not – came to feel that the answer lay in this very ambivalence, in our forbidden hatred towards those we love. He tentatively formulated the process as follows. Because I love the other and do not want to lose her, I have taken her within myself. But because she has abandoned me or treated me badly, the other I have inside me is a bad, hating other who does not value me, and so I myself am bad, deserving of hatred.[18]

So in depression we end up treating ourselves as we once were treated and as we now believe we deserve to be treated, in an endless and self-reinforcing dialogue between our adult coping selves and our vulnerable infant selves. We internalize and eventually come to identify with the cold rejecting parent – or the demanding, needy, unreliable parent. And in a further, conclusive development we seek out relationships with others who will take on the reciprocal roles which we offer them, who will themselves treat us as we expect to be treated.

At the core of depression, then, is a state of severe sadness which has a doomed quality – a sense of inevitability, of history

---

[18] Freud, S., 'Mourning and Melancholia' (1917), in *Penguin Freud Library* 11.

repeating itself in a way the subject feels powerless to change. This sadness overwhelms the mind's capacity to process it, severely threatening feelings of entitlement to happiness. What seems to make depression different from ordinary sadness (and much harder to shift) is the depressed person's attempts to rationalize and explain their distress with negative, self-defeating and self-blaming patterns of thinking. But why can these negative patterns of thought not be tested out against reality? What seems to hold them in place is the intensity of shame which is such a powerful and characteristic feature in keeping the depressed person isolated in their suffering, and it is towards this important aspect of depression that we must now turn.

PAIN, SHAME AND BLAME

The biologist and broadcaster Lewis Wolpert began his own inquiry into the genesis of depression as a way of coming to terms with his own depressive breakdown.[19] Wolpert's investigations led him again and again to awareness of the connection between loss and depression, and he writes that unless we can understand mourning, we are most unlikely to understand depression. Wolpert's courage in outing his own depression is undeniable. Yet his book, which moves between a searching exploration of depression in general and an account of his personal experience, is a curious combination of disclosure and anti-disclosure.

No-one should be criticized for their unwillingness to make intimate or painful details of their private life public. Yet Wolpert chooses to talk about his own depression. When he does so, however, his tone shifts abruptly from reflectiveness to combativeness – something which the keen observer in him cannot help but notice. He remarks that he found himself unwilling even tentatively to entertain the possibility that his own depression might be linked to his personal experiences of loss, though he states that his wife thought it was significant that his depression emerged just as he was about to visit South Africa, where his father had been murdered many years previously. He himself

---

[19] Wolpert, L., *Malignant Sadness: The Anatomy of Depression*, Faber and Faber (1999).

preferred to attribute it to a drug he had been taking for a heart condition. 'From my own experience I can confirm that there is a considerable stigma still attached to depression' he says, continuing rather disarmingly: '... I must admit that I am not free of the stigma, for I prefer a biological explanation for my depression rather than a psychological one.'

But if depression is rooted in the pain of loss, why should this in itself be any more shameful than suffering a faulty heart rhythm or an adverse response to drugs? The answer must lie in our socially conditioned expectations of ourselves. Our cultural intolerance of introversion and of grieving itself makes us require mourning to be over and done with as quickly as decently possible. A child or adult struggling to come to terms with loss and grief who encounters anxiety, disapproval or defensiveness instead of understanding will learn to react to his or her own pain with shame and denial instead of being able to experience the relief of grieving.

Depression itself has been described as the shadow cast by the emotional deficiencies of our culture. We live in a world which idealizes competence and control and which encourages us to be compulsively extrovert and achievement-orientated. But these strategies can be defences against the narcissistic wounds caused by pain and loss – and the awareness we keep at bay of how much we really cannot control. As we get older these strategies inevitably become less effective, yet we determinedly press on at full speed and maximum effectiveness. Even when anxiety – or exhaustion – does overwhelm us and bring us to a standstill, we are most unlikely to respond to it with compassion for ourselves, or even attention. Underneath our rational façade there lurks a superstitious and archaic desire to construe psychological pain in terms of shame and blame, as if it were a punishment for wrongdoing or a moral failure.

'Childe Roland to the Dark Tower Came', a poem by Robert Browning, describes a journey through a nightmare landscape of ugly, broken objects, bleak vistas and betrayed ideals.[20] The

[20] Browning, R., 'Childe Roland to the Dark Tower Came' in *Men and Women* (1855).

vision of Roland, the poem's narrator, is coloured and distorted by his own depression: the scant grass looks like a leper's hair, the mud kneaded up with blood or churned by toads in a poisoned tank, and the frothing of a small brook seems spiteful, the trees bending over it as if in mute suicidal despair. As he travels, Roland comes across a blind, emaciated horse standing in a field, a picture of abject desolation. But Roland feels no pity or concern for the animal's suffering. 'I never saw a brute I hated so' he declares; 'He must be wicked to deserve such pain'.

Roland, struggling under the weight of anxiety and despair, is thinking as we do when we are very young or under severe stress. His thoughts turning constantly towards cruelty, failure and death, he projects his own state of mind into the world around him to explain the desolation he feels and sees. His response to the horse demonstrates the deep and archaic human belief that suffering must be a deserved punishment for wrongdoing, or for innate wickedness: the horse must be to blame for its own suffering. Traumatized children will go to great and poignant lengths to preserve idealized versions of their parents within their minds, and also to maintain their belief in the world as a logical and just place. The human brain is geared right from the beginning to link causes and effects and children will always find ways of justifying and explaining painful happenings, often – with the childish omnipotence that sees all causes as arising from the child's self – at their own expense. I am being hurt, thinks the child of a violent parent, so I must be bad. I am being hurt, thinks the child in hospital undergoing painful surgical procedures, so my parents must have abandoned me to this suffering because I am bad. Similarly the human race, in its infancy, created myths to explain the world and the suffering inherent in existence in terms of an all-powerful, just creator and sinful humans deserving of punishment. These myths became the religions which have informed our civilizations.

But belief that one's suffering is a punishment for badness is a terrible thought to grow up with, and one we are likely to repress – inhibiting our thought processes so that we can no longer make these connections. So, the depressed person gives up the search for understanding of the forces that have shaped his or her life, along with the hope that understanding may help to change his or her circumstances for the better. Too bad to deserve to get better, the depressed person turns his or her face to the wall, both figuratively and literally. While those who have been bereaved struggle painfully through the stages of grieving and finally emerge with new meaning reconstituted, in depression the loss is denied and this process cannot take place.

'My depression points to my not knowing how to lose' writes the French analyst Julia Kristeva. 'Any loss entails the loss of my being.'[21] Kristeva suggests that traumatic loss or insecurity in relation to our first major attachment figures keeps us turning back obsessionally, searching for that first reality which no alternative will ever be able to replace. In health, we reach forward towards the Symbol, which leads us into new worlds and can be infinitely replaced or modified, but in depression we turn backwards to search for the Thing, that archaic object for which we can accept no substitutes, and for whose loss we can never be consoled. Learning to symbolize enables us to experiment with finding replacements for our loss – so when we mourn we gradually become able to let go of the lost object and to be reclaimed by the world, and by new love and interest. But depression prevents us doing so. Mourning admits the other is starting to get away; depression refuses to acknowledge this, preferring to create a dead world all around, in which nothing can ever change.

Colin, like other depressed adults and like insecurely attached children, had lost interest in the world. His energy was turned inwards, his capacity for remembering and thinking impaired, and his capacity to love injured – not because of any inherent deficiencies, for Colin was an intelligent man, but because loving and thinking had become too painful and unrewarding to sustain. So, in depression we withdraw, our thinking slows down and language deserts us or seems pointless. Our voices flatten, our emotional range shrinks, and our curiosity about everything, including our own state of mind, dies. We pause, we sigh, we deflate. We lose interest, we fail to see the point. Like Colin, when pushed we generalize evasively, or idealize our childhoods

---

[21] Kristeva, J., *Black Sun*, Columbia University Press (1989).

in a blank, unconvincing way – sometimes as a defence against the pain and shame of real memory.

Colin's life had been overshadowed by a loss, the significance of which had been denied by everyone in his world. As an alert, questioning three-year-old, Colin had had no way of under-standing his father's departure except in terms of his own badness, as a child who was not worth staying for. The explanations which would over time have modified this belief were not forthcoming, perhaps because Colin's mother was defending herself against this loss by denying it had any meaning. So Colin learnt to be curious no longer – afraid of rejection and also afraid that his questioning might only lead to proof of the unpalatable reality of his own badness. Unable to come to terms with loss, he experienced instead a gap in his psyche, a sense of meaninglessness inexplicably connected for him with a dim sense of his own badness and worthlessness. If the loss of the other does not matter, there need be no pain. If their leaving had no meaning, there need be no shame. Yet the pain and shame do not go away – they become unconscious, where they cannot over time be modified by the development of new perspectives. Life becomes persecuting, full of obstacles and unreasonable demands – and yet Colin's tendency to blame others was only a projection of the way he blamed himself.

Depressed thought patterns have a way of stubbornly maintaining their self-defeating and self-punishing attitudes in the face of all alternative possibilities, and depressed people may accordingly sometimes seem manipulative and self-absorbed, as well as over-eager to blame others for their problems. This was why Jenny, Colin's counsellor, had at first found trying to help Colin such a deeply frustrating experience. The links which she tried to help him make to understand himself and to rediscover connections to the outside world were – initially at least – thrown back in her face. But from the unconscious perspective of the depressed person, such new opportunities are only a dangerous distraction from the compulsive need to keep placating the internal abandoning parent, and never to take one's eyes off them. Unfortunately, the depressed person's automatic rejection of the possibility of meaningful new relationship and under-standing from outside means that they will be thrown back more and more upon their own deprived, impoverished and self-accusing internal world. Eventually the feeling of being unlovable and worthless becomes encoded in the self, endlessly reinforced by those self-justifying patterns of thinking which reinforce the attachment to the rejecting internal object.

'My Father, why hast Thou abandoned me?' cries Jesus in his agony upon the cross. The terror of abandonment is at the heart of the Christian myth of the spiritual death and desolation which precedes the resurrection, as it is at the centre of the collapse of meaning which characterizes the depressive breakdown. The medical model of depression, eschewing as it does the possibility of depression having meaning, may seem to offer a way of diminishing the shame and blame felt by many depressed people. But it may have the opposite effect. Deprived of meaning, we desperately renew our unconscious search for it. Suffering threatens our ego control and the ego seeks desperately to restore its control by finding a meaning which relates back to its own wrongdoings. Depressed people do not stop blaming themselves because someone in a white coat tells them to – they already know their self-hatred is irrational *but it doesn't make any difference*. At a deeper level, they may just feel more abandoned in their suffering, stripped of the possibility that their suffering might have meaning, dignity or redemptive significance. And unless depression can be set within a larger context, the search for meaning will, for want of anywhere better to go, return again and again to the same repetitive, immobilizing feelings of self-hatred.

Perhaps, in the end, we suffer most because we are unwilling to suffer at all. We believe it is wrong, pointless and yet shameful to suffer pain: we should control or suppress it, and this is the aim of most psychiatric practice. Requiring ourselves to remain forever young, successful and narcissistically intact, our failure to rise above our flawed human nature is the ultimate cause of our shame. We have failed in our duty to be happy and successful – or at the very least to present ourselves that way, however awful we feel inside. Shame, I believe, plays a far greater part in cementing feelings of sadness and loss into the vicious circle of depression than is generally recognized – probably because we are all in the same boat, all hiding our own feelings of shame and our fear that we will be found out.

Shame is what we feel when we fail to live up to our ego ideal. The ego ideal is the name given by psychoanalysts to describe the self's conception of how it wants to see itself, formed through identification with parental views about what is expected of us if we are to deserve love and approval (Colin's ego ideal, for example, required him to be someone who did not miss his father or feel grief at his loss). Initially our ego ideals are based upon our parents' values, but as we mature they expand to include wider cultural values. While guilt comes from concern that we may hurt others, shame is anchored in the fear that others will think badly of us and reject us, and it is shame rather than guilt which thus informs many of the depressive's self-reproaches.

Shame is kept in place by evasiveness and denial, and it casts a long, obscuring shadow. Both Wolpert and Styron – intelligent, articulate and strong-minded men – describe becoming en-meshed in shame-driven pretence. Styron describes forcing himself to attend a dinner party, smiling and uttering small talk when he felt as if he should be on a life-support machine, while Wolpert's wife was so concerned about the effect she thought knowledge of his depression would have on his career that she initially told people he was recuperating from a minor heart attack. Both Styron and Wolpert locate their own decisions to enter hospital as the turning points in their illnesses and the start of the road to recovery, and this is no doubt due in part to the quietness, seclusion and support available in a sympathetic hospital environment. But just as important may have been the fact that their admission enabled both men to drop their last pretences and become able to admit both to themselves and to others the extent of their internal desolation – so freeing themselves from the controlling power of shame and allowing their depression to reach its catharsis, at which point internal healing processes could become mobilized.

Styron relates that Dr Gold, his psychiatrist, had advised him to avoid the hospital at all costs, owing to the stigma attached to hospitalization. As Styron fairly temperately remarks, this view seemed in retrospect misguided, given the suicidal depths of his anguish. Yet Dr Gold's remark comes out of a system of values to which most of us subscribe most of the time – in which even suicidal suffering and despair may seem preferable to letting the mask slip publicly and experiencing the shame of being seen as unhappy, not in control, or struggling.

Why should this fear of shame be so great that death itself can sometimes seem preferable? The answer may be buried within our Judaeo-Christian heritage. If the Supreme Being is not only all-good but also all-powerful, there really is nowhere to go to explain suffering except back to our own inherent badness – our original sin. Belief in God may be on the wane, but have we thrown out the baby only to keep the dirty bathwater? The depth of our shame about depression shows how much we still see our mental suffering as a punishment inflicted by an authoritarian god upon naughty children. For what crime? In myth, it usually turns out to be the crime of curiosity or independent thinking. Today we may have freed our curiosity to penetrate the mysteries of the external world, but we still do not find it so easy to turn our gaze inwards to question our internal authorities.

But what happens when an omnipotent deity is removed from the picture? In Buddhism, suffering is seen not as a sign of disgrace or moral failure but as an inevitable consequence of the conditioned human state – impermanent, mortal, prone to loss and fated to live painfully in the gap between the ideal and the real, between aspiration and reality. This perspective is neither punitive nor fatalistic – the inevitability of suffering does not absolve us of responsibility for the ways in which we relate to others, and in fact makes the development of active compassion towards others an imperative in the spiritual life. Most of the chains of conditionality which shape our lives may be beyond our control, but some of them are not. Curiosity and the desire to penetrate introspectively beneath our mental surfaces to deeper causes are qualities to be fostered – to help us develop the courage to change what we can, the patience to accept what we cannot and the wisdom to know the difference.

Shame itself, like praise, is a mental habit which keeps us blind and trapped in our egocentricity. When we stop blaming and start taking responsibility we learn to stop hiding like frightened children from ourselves and others out of our fear of disgrace, and to stop the endless mental rehearsing of blaming and

245

justification that holds it all in place – the moment described by W. H. Auden when the unhappy present begins to recite the past:

> Like a poetry lesson till sooner
> Or later it faltered at the line where
>
> Long ago the accusations had begun,
> And suddenly knew by whom it had been judged,
> How rich life had been, and how silly,
> And was life-forgiven and more humble,
>
> Able to approach the Future as a friend
> Without a wardrobe of excuses . . .[22]

While blaming and self-blaming keep us going round in circles, the assumption of responsibility allows us to begin to become less defensive and more open, and for sorrow and regret to work their way through and in due course be released. Only when we stop holding on to the past can we begin to see maturation as an interesting journey instead of as a punishment for a crime we never committed. But if suffering isn't to take us down the well-worn path of self-blaming, what can it still have to teach us?

CHARLOTTE'S BREAKDOWN:
A TALE OF THREE DREAMS

Charlotte is a forty-one-year-old GP, married with two young children. For years she has been a model of efficiency, too busy to think about how she's feeling, but now she can't ignore it any longer. She has lost a lot of weight and finds herself crying often, for no reason she can understand. She wakes at three in the morning and can't go back to sleep, though she's always tired. Her life has become a dull roster of work, work, work and she feels as if there's a dead weight on her chest, squeezing the life out of her. Charlotte's husband is away a lot, and when he is there they quarrel, or they just don't connect. Charlotte's voice is flat and expressionless. But then she says her husband has deserted her when she needed him most, and her voice quavers, her

---

[22] Auden, W. H., 'In Memory of Sigmund Freud' in *Selected Poems*, Faber and Faber (1979).

eyes fill with tears and she bows her head, shielding her face behind her cupped hand in a curiously childlike gesture.

Charlotte is the child of a vague, affable but distant father and a volatile, impatient mother who had little time for her family. Her mother drank heavily, and eventually died last year of an alcohol-related illness. Charlotte was always a high achiever. 'I learnt to get it right', she says, 'from day one'. Apart from an occasional peck on the cheek, Charlotte has no memory of being hugged or touched by anyone until her first boyfriend, when she was seventeen. As an adult, she washed her hands of her relationship with her mother, and mentally made her into a non-person. But when Charlotte's own children were born, she watched how her mother related to her grandchildren, seeing how quickly her efforts to be kind to them collapsed into irritation and impatience with their needs, how swiftly she disengaged herself when any of them tried to cuddle her or play with her, and how she would automatically walk out of the room in search of the gin bottle if any of them got upset or angry. Watching these scenes triggered many buried memories for Charlotte. As a child, Charlotte had managed the relationship with her mother by becoming infinitely adaptable and placatory, and adept at hiding her own feelings and had married a man who, like her mother, always needed to be the centre of attention.

Shortly after her mother's death, Charlotte has the following dream:

> I'm in a canteen. I am going to sit at a table by myself but a group of women call me over to their table and ask me if I would like to eat. There is a big catering trolley next to them full of stainless steel containers. As they take the lids off I see in each container simmering stews of entrails: a liver, intestines, a heart. I see that the heart is still beating and realize that these organs are my own. But the women are helping themselves and starting to eat. I am helpless, I can say nothing.

Going to the women's table to be fed, Charlotte discovers she's on the menu herself. But she sits and watches her own devouring with a polite smile. As usual, when she feels used by someone else, she takes refuge in silence. But the dream makes her feel frightened: as if she is disintegrating, as if she has no self left, as if she is actively participating in her own dismemberment.

Charlotte tries to talk to her husband about how she's feeling, but as she does so she feels his interest draining away. When she tries to confront him with what is happening in their relationship, he walks out of the room.

Just like her mother. Now when this happens, Charlotte is overwhelmed by the desolation she feels. Charlotte has grown up longing for deeper emotional contact yet terrified that if she ever reveals the deeper levels of her feelings people will think she is so bad that they will leave her. Being left, in Charlotte's mind, is a punishment for her badness, her emotionality, and it must never happen – but at the same time relationships themselves are becoming increasingly thankless for her. Then one day, Charlotte's husband comes home and tells her abruptly that he has been having an affair for some time, and has decided to leave. Having left so many times already, he now leaves for good, and leaves Charlotte alone with her hurting.

Throughout her earlier, milder depression, Charlotte had continued to function reasonably well at the surgery. But now the veneer cracks and she goes on extended sick leave. She lies in her bed for hours at a time, crying into the duvet or just staring mutely out of the window. She pulls herself together to be with the children but it is a great effort; she's liable to dissolve into tears at any time. She takes them to the library and has a panic attack while she's there: the books swim before her eyes, she can't breathe, her heart pounds and the walls begin to close in on her. She feels a desperate need to run away, but doesn't know where to go. That night she has another dream:

> I'm in a clearing in a forest and there's a dark pool of water. There are two bodies floating in the water face downwards, not touching. The air feels stagnant and heavy as if a storm cloud is gathering.

Charlotte's dream is redolent with despair and fear. The bodies which do not touch express the loneliness of the child who was never hugged or cuddled and also how she herself has preserved her loneliness in isolation, untouchable ever since. At the age of 41, the catastrophe that Charlotte's coping self had warded off for years by making herself important, valuable and necessary to others has finally caught up with her. Now she has, well and truly, been left. She has been found out – exposed, shamed, humiliated as the woman who was too bad for anyone to want to be with. Charlotte had never really experienced her most vulnerable and dependent needs being processed and mediated. Instead, she had learnt – as the children of alcoholics often do – to care for others as she would have liked to have been cared for herself, believing that if she looked after others enough she could bind herself to them and prevent them leaving. It is a common pattern for people who are drawn into the helping professions, and probably the reason why depression has been called the illness of valuable people. Around a third of newly qualified GPs have been found to be suffering like Charlotte from clinical depression, and female doctors seem particularly affected.[23]

Now finally there is no face to be kept up, nothing to hide, nothing left to protect. And nothing to distract her, nowhere to run to. For weeks and then months, Charlotte wakes up each morning with tears running down her face. She feels as if she's living in a back-to-front world on the other side of a shattered mirror through which, like a twisted crazy Alice, she has somehow been drawn. When she wakes in the morning she lies in her bed motionless, trying to gather herself from the absolute dissolution of sleep and dreading that first telling movement against the familiar surfaces and routines of her life, broken now into ugly jagged shards. A tentative movement against any of them may draw blood, reopening the wounds of the day before, the movement that would tell her: *I hurt*, reflecting the pain back to her from all directions in meaningless fragmented images of her own face and the faces she sees around her.

Nothing makes sense any more. It isn't that she wants to go back to how things were – she can see it had all started long before her husband's affair, and Charlotte begins to feel it wasn't even really about the failure of the marriage anyway. She can't see any way forward, but she certainly doesn't want to be where she is now. The worst part of it, without a doubt, is the confusion; the not knowing any more. It isn't how things were supposed to turn out.

For weeks, Charlotte lies in bed or wanders round like a sleepwalker, barely stirring until the children come back from school. The need to look after her children sometimes feels like an unbearable burden, yet remembering her own mother's lack of time for her, she does her best – with mixed success – to be there for them and to shield them from how she's feeling. And slowly, over the months it is her children who begin to return her to a joy in living. Walking in the woods with them to pick the first bluebells, she finds herself lifting up her face to enjoy the warmth of the shafts of sunlight between the trees. Lying cuddling her children watching videos under a pile of duvets, a game turns into a pillow fight and a wrestling match from which they all emerge red-faced, panting and laughing. At first these moments are fragile and fleeting, but they come more often. Charlotte still feels sad, insecure, shaken. But being alone gradually becomes less frightening, and the fear that she will disintegrate in the raging of her own grief and fear begins to abate. Charlotte begins to see more of her friends, to reach out to others in a gentler

[23] As opposed to six per cent of managers. Figures from Wolpert, L., *Malignant Sadness: The Anatomy of Depression*, Faber and Faber (1999).

and more tentative way than her old buoyant self would have done, and to talk about returning to work part-time. Around then, she has this third dream:

> I am going for a swim, but the swimming pool is full of black water like a swamp. I think there must be crocodiles in it. But then I see a child playing in the water, jumping and splashing. He takes my hand and pulls me in and I swim with him, deep down into the water which now seems light, full of ripples and sunlight. I seem to be playing there with him for a long time before I remember that I'm not supposed to be able to breathe under water. As soon as I realize this I start coughing and choking and I have to come up for air.

The crocodiles – who might shed crocodile tears of fake sympathy as they gobble her up – are an image of relentless greed which Charlotte connects back to the women in the earlier dream who eat up her internal organs. Intimacy is something Charlotte is still very frightened of – it means the dissolution of the usual defences which she uses to keep people at a distance, leaving her unprotected and at their mercy, fearful of becoming merged and swallowed up into them, as she had had to submit to being merged into her mother to preserve a relationship with her. And yet no crocodile actually appears in the dream – Charlotte is not sure now whether they really were there, or just in her own mind.

Although entering this dark pool seems like a dissolution, it is not sinister or oppressive like the pool in the earlier dream with the floating bodies. The pain and fear that Charlotte has confronted and survived over the last few months means that her psyche no longer has roped-off dark areas that she must avoid. She wants to relax and enter the water, for she cannot bear to be so lonely and exhausted any more, yet she still fears that to do so will expose her to the very terrors from which her distancing mechanisms had previously protected her. But as she draws back in trepidation, the boy – perhaps representing Charlotte's own playful and daring side, which she only allows to come out with her own children – reaches up from the dark pool and draws her in.

Dreams enable us to experiment with and explore those new self-states which our conscious identities are not quite ready to embrace. Like Jacob wrestling with his angel or Jung's struggles with the visions who haunted him in his own mid-life breakdown, the dream playing seems to represent Charlotte's struggles to embrace parts of her own self previously denied and alienated from her conscious identity. The new element seems a natural place to be in; it is only when her old identity tries to reclaim her – you're not supposed to be this sort of person! – that Charlotte begins to choke.

IN THE DARK WATER: DEPRESSION AND HEALING

William James, the philosopher brother of the novelist Henry, was himself a sufferer from serious depression, and he wrote of 'the salvation through self-despair, the dying to be truly born ... to get to it, a critical point must usually be passed, a corner turned within one. Something must give way, a native hardness must break down and liquefy ...'[24] Charlotte in her dream is pulled into dark water while Styron describes his breakdown as entering a storm of murk. These images evoke the *nigredo*, the alchemist's dark stinking bath in which outgrown forms dissolve in a process of invisible transformation. The ostensible quest of the mediaeval alchemists was to discover how to transform base metal into gold. But it has been speculated that their real interest lay in the study of psychospiritual transformation – a dangerous study for the times, which would have been blasphemous in the eyes of the church.[25] To avoid conflict with the ruling authorities, alchemy – like dreaming – had to find a way of disguising its true intent and carry on its work underground, through images, symbol and allegory.

In alchemy, the darkening of the element (like the storm gathering in Charlotte's second dream, or the gathering of the darkness of depression) is seen as a portent that something of significance is about to take place outside one's conscious control. In mediaeval woodcuts of the alchemic process, the male and female elements – the erstwhile king and queen, having lost their former trappings of power and control – sink together naked beneath the surface of the dark waters of the *nigredo*: 'it is

---

[24] James, W., *The Varieties of Religious Experience*, Penguin (1985).
[25] See Jung, C. G., 'Psychology and alchemy', *Collected Works* Vol. 12, Routledge (1993).

death for souls to become water.'[26] The dissolution into fluid symbolizes the descent into unconscious process – the breakdown of conscious habits of control, the collapse of outmoded ways of living and the exhaustion of the untrue fantasies with which we previously consoled ourselves, leaving nothing in their place as we sink into the dark matrix of depression.

'The corruption of one is the generation of the other ... No new life can arise, say the alchemists, without the death of the old ... nobody finding himself on the road to wholeness can escape that characteristic suspension which is the meaning of crucifixion.'[27] Sinking into the *nigredo* represents the death of the old, and a process of purification or catharsis; the waiting may be long and agonizing, and continues until all the old self's efforts at control and denial have been exhausted. Then there finally arises – often at the moment when all hope is given up – a new spirit, symbolizing the soul's renewal at the end of the dark night of despair. The alchemists represent this new spirit as a homunculus or a winged child, like the child of light with whom Charlotte plays in the pool in her final dream.

In myth as in alchemy, the encounter with death and despair represents a crucial turning point in the journey of the soul towards wholeness, a point which must be faced not at the end, but in the middle of life's journey – like Odysseus' descent into Hades, Dante's journey through Hell or the shipwrecks and drownings upon which many of Shakespeare's comedies of transformation turn. The counterpart of such myths are those mid-life dreams of floods, drowning, disintegration or dismemberment which embody both the terrifying nature of change and the hope inherent in it:

> Lady, three white leopards sat under a juniper tree
> In the cool of the day, having fed to satiety
> On my legs my heart my liver and that which had been contained
> In the hollow round of my skull. And God said
> Shall these bones live?[28]

---

[26] Jung C. G., *The Psychology of the Transference*, Ark (1983).

[27] *Ibid.*

[28] Eliot, T. S., 'Ash-Wednesday' in *Collected Poems 1909–1962*, Faber and Faber (1963).

Rites of passage and transformation through different cultures universally have three elements in common: withdrawal from society is followed by an ordeal involving the actual or symbolic infliction of pain, deprivation and severance. Only when this process is complete can there be rebirth. So, Christ's agonized experience of being forsaken upon the cross leads to his death but then to resurrection and new life, while the Buddha's encounter with the forces of evil and destruction as he sits under the Bodhi Tree at Bodh Gaya leads him finally to enlightenment. Like Christ, the Buddha is represented as being at mid life (in his mid-thirties) at the time of his spiritual transformation and apotheosis. Afterwards he returns to the world to live on – the same, but different – for another forty years. In our ends are our beginnings. When we are so accustomed, however, to think of depression in terms of pathology and failure, it takes a great shift to begin to think about it instead as a potential turning point in the journey through life.

WHAT THE CARDS TELL

Tarot cards, the oldest form of cards still in use, were introduced to Italy in the fourteenth century, probably by returning gypsies or crusaders, but their origins are shrouded in mystery. The Tarot, most notorious for its occult use in fortune-telling, can also be read as a representation of the soul's journey through life.[29]

The Major Arcana of the Tarot is made up of twenty-two cards in a chronological sequence, the early cards depicting the start of the journey and our formative relationships with parental authority figures – the Empress and Emperor, High Priest and Priestess. We move through the harnessing of erotic and aggressive energy in adolescence (the cards of the Lovers and the Chariot) to the assumption of the qualities of adulthood: Justice, Temperance and Strength. As the middle of the deck

---

[29] Sharman-Burke, J. and Greene, L., *The Mythic Tarot: A New Approach to the Tarot Cards*, Rider (1995).

approaches, the card of the Hermit appears, depicting the dawning awareness of the limitations of mortal life and the passage of youth into maturity: the card inaugurates a time of withdrawal, demanding humility and patience. The next card is the Wheel of Fortune, representing the unexpected blow of fate or a change in fortune, suggesting that a greater movement of destiny may be at work behind an apparently random event. The Wheel of Fortune introduces the sequence of cards representing the mid-life crisis itself: the Hanged Man, Death, the Devil and the Tower.

The Hanged Man is an image of sacrifice – like Christ taking up the cross or the Buddha refusing to move from under the tree until he gains enlightenment, it represents the willingness to renounce the past and move forward, through suffering, into an unknown future. It also represents the willingness to remain – at least for the time being – hanging in a state of suspense, while subject to the working of unconscious forces as yet not understood. The next card is Death. Only when we have detached ourselves from the cravings of the narrow egotistical self, with its clingings to the past, its attachments and its false reassurances, will we be confronted with the full intensity of the spiritual struggle, a dark terror of loneliness without consolation. Here we reach the experience of depressive breakdown, which can sometimes feel like the assault of an alien power which threatens to obliterate the self and put all that has been gained at risk.

The Death card represents irrevocable endings which must be acknowledged and mourned: it is followed by the Devil, representing the revival of the temptations of the ego and those cravings for carnal satisfaction and false reassurance which resurge to pull us backwards, even as we are beginning to let go. Then comes the seventeenth card, the Tower, which depicts the final collapse of discredited forms of authority, taking down with them our craven compliance, our pretences, our hollow values and all the myriad ways we have found to betray ourselves.

This sequence of cards represents the different forms in which loss, death and dissolution confront us as we reach mid life. Whether we are willing or unwilling, the sequence suggests, the tower will still one day fall. And once it does, we emerge from the darkness of the mid-life crisis. The following card, the Star, represents the emergence of hope. It is followed by the Moon and the Sun and the final synthesis, reconciliation and victory over darkness represented by the last two cards, Judgement and the World.

The moving into the unknown at mid life, which proceeds from the death or failure of previous ideals and values, is a place of emptiness which can feel dead, lonely and hopeless. But if it can be tolerated, the dark environment of depression may be the crucible of new growth. 'No creature ... can attain a higher grade of nature without ceasing to exist' writes Campbell. 'This is the process of dissolving, transcending or transmuting the infantile images of our personal past. In our dreams ... we may see reflected not only the whole picture of our present case, but also the clue to what we must do to be saved.'[30] Only by facing the loneliness that we have always avoided, in that infantile fear and clinging disguised by our adult competencies, can we discover how to transcend it.

Depression is kept in place by the shame which it instils in us – the feeling that we're not supposed to be like this – which erodes our self-esteem and makes us powerless to fight its dark, encroaching shadow. When sadness can be accepted as part of life, its pernicious ties to shame and self-hatred are severed. It can flow through us and we ourselves can be reclaimed once more into the stream of the living, at the same time recovering and integrating those lost parts of ourselves in which are locked our deepest and truest emotions and our most piercing intuitions.

As images of the movement through depression, the archaic images of alchemy and the Tarot are a long way from the categories of the psychiatric manuals. They offer us ways of seeing depression not in static terms but dynamically, as part of a process which unfolds within a greater context. The reframing of depression within a bigger picture, a bigger story, does not diminish the suffering and fear which it brings with it. But when we become able to find a way of holding sadness, grieving and

---

[30] Campbell, J., *The Hero with a Thousand Faces*, Fontana (1993).

the fear of loss of meaning and breakdown not as signs of personal failure or pathological aberration, but as painful, inevitable and perhaps essential stages of the growth to maturity, then the shame which is such a powerful factor in holding depression in place starts to dissolve. Placing depression within the context of a journey demystifies it of its motiveless malignancy and enables us to trace its beginnings and see it running its course – as it always does – to an end which will leave us different from how we were before. Depression in these terms may still be an illness: but it is an illness with a purpose.

BREAKING THE CYCLE

'Between nothing and grief I choose grief' said William Faulkner. The depressed person, by contrast, chooses nothing. In our panicked and self-defeating determination to pursue happiness at all times and at all costs, we can all too easily lose sight of the legitimate suffering which sponsors growth. Shielding ourselves from uncertainty and suffering, we learn to play safe and can end up living within parameters that are too narrow, declaring ourselves content to live with others' answers, however constricting they may be, rather than struggling uneasily but more creatively with our own wonderings. The depression which lies at the heart of the mid-life crisis is what we are left with when our attempts to soothe and numb and distract ourselves wear thin and finally lose their last vestiges of credibility.

Suffering is what happens when our soft bodies come up against the hard corners of life – when our needs, longings and aspirations collide against a wall of coldness, rejection and failure. Physical or mental suffering is ultimately just the body's or the mind's way of transmitting to consciousness that something has gone wrong and needs attention – the signal of pain needs to be urgent and insistent enough to arrest and break through our desire to ignore it and carry on as before. Yet relatively little in psychiatry or psychology has been written on the value or the meaning of suffering itself – only on how to avoid it or mask it.

256

'*You want the easy way*' Teiresias observes to Odysseus as he is drawn down against his will to face hell. '*But this will scarcely be possible.*' When we try to eliminate suffering or to invent distractions from it, we may be not only setting up inevitable failure for ourselves, creating spiralling feelings of internal deficiency and shame, but also robbing ourselves of a source of understanding and a catalyst for growth. 'Much of our suffering originates with our own discontent, emanating from the evaluations and attitudes that arise in protecting ourselves and separating ourselves out from the context of our own engagement' writes the Jungian analyst Polly Young-Eisendrath, who suggests that our obsession with trying to stay happy and in control, our efforts to explain more and more of our personal suffering through biology and genes, and our attempts to take flight from the boredom arising from the attempt to seal off our inner lives, can only lead us down blind alleyways.[31] Suffering itself, on the other hand, gives us an opportunity to engage in the sort of reflective self-examination that can give us real insight into the working of cause and effect in our lives, helping us to understand ourselves better and eventually to set ourselves free. If we ignore this opportunity we increasingly become prey to states of panic, resentment and hopeless desire, driven ever deeper into states of restless misery.

Suffering itself is an ethic, Young-Eisendrath goes on to suggest, which enables us to recognize a boundary between what we can and cannot control. When we accept our suffering:

> our thoughts, feelings, intentions and actions become ours, and we re-
> cognise the powers of being conscious, of making meaning. Knowing
> our own subjective freedom, we are able to surrender more fully to the
> effects of loss, ageing, illness and death which are the inevitable natural
> processes of life ... from the facts of our discontent, dependence, vul-
> nerability, and lack of omnipotence and omniscience, we learn what it
> means to be truly human. These 'negative' experiences open our
> hearts and allow us to connect to others through gratitude and com-
> passion.

---

[31] Young-Eisendrath, P., 'What suffering teaches' in Molino, A. (ed.), *The Couch and the Tree*, Constable (1999).

In these terms, trying to locate the causes of our suffering outside ourselves may be a grave error.

'Your pain is the breaking of the shell that encloses your understanding' writes Kahlil Gibran. 'Even as the stone of the fruit must break, that its heart may stand in the sun, so must you know pain ... Much of your pain is self-chosen. It is the bitter potion by which the physician within you heals your sick self. Therefore trust the physician, and drink his remedy in silence and tranquillity.'[32] At bottom, our greatest fear is not that we should suffer pain, but that our pain should be meaningless. Depression itself takes us into the depths of meaninglessness – but paradoxically only the following of this descent to its depths enables us, in due course, to reconstitute new meaning. While the immature ego will always seek to dodge suffering or to blame it on others, thereby repeating the cycle, with maturity there comes a greater capacity to tolerate suffering. Becoming able to sit with suffering for a while instead of running from it, learning how to examine and explore it, we allow ourselves to become open to the lesson it has to teach – a lesson which may have the capacity to redeem the past, restructure the present and refocus the future.

The feelings of discontent, disappointment and shame which manifest in depression are born out of the ego's failure to get what it wanted. The ethic of suffering brings us face to face with the failure of the ideals by which we have lived – that insistence on relating to others through patterns of unbridled control, dominance, individualism, competitiveness and exploitation which masks our unresolved infantile insecurities and complaints. In depression we face the limits of our control and see into the abyss beyond. The suffering experienced in depression may ultimately have a purging effect – Dante's *Purgatorio* was the place to which men and women were sent to suffer and to learn, their tasks being tied to their past sins: those who had lusted had to learn how to love, and material acquisitiveness had to be transformed into the yearning for wisdom. Adversity itself has the power to teach us to develop responsibility in the face of

---

[32] Gibran, K., *The Prophet*, Pan (1984).

misery, to lead us through awareness of our own suffering to compassion for ourselves and for others, and to forge personal meanings in the face of the collapse of outworn ideals: 'When we conceive of the self as wholly interdependent and impermanent, as a function rather than a thing, then we appreciate more deeply our true freedom in this world. It is the freedom of making new meanings, of opening ourselves especially to the conditions of our own limitations and exploring these into the roots of our suffering.'[33]

It is through our wounds that we learn to give birth to ourselves again. It is our body that always gives us away, at the moment when solid flesh melts and muscular control dissolves. We salivate when we are hungry, and sweat when we are afraid. Our genitals get wet when we are excited, we weep when we are sad and we bleed from our wounds – there is little we can do to control these flows from our body orifices, from these wounds which advertise our unwilling readiness to be moved and hurt by life. In myth, suffering must be willingly embraced before the wasteland can be made fertile and bloom once more. Jacob wounded in the thigh as he wrestles with his angel, and Jesus in his side as he bleeds on the cross, Chiron the healer and the Fisher King – all gain their spiritual authority not from their invulnerability but from their woundedness. Odysseus, Ulysses to the Romans, is named for his woundedness (from *oulos*, meaning 'wound', and *ischea*, meaning 'thigh') – the old wound on his thigh from the tusk of a boar will eventually help identify him as the true ruler of Ithaca and restore his kingdom to him. Freud placed the origin of the male oedipal complex in the boy's inadvertent glimpse of the female genitals, which he imagines to be a wound – but this wound which he dreads and fears will nevertheless become the erotic focus of his future desire, to which he will return again and again in fantasy and in the sex act itself, and is also the opening through which, in due course and with great pain, new life will be born.

Wounding and water. Water is everywhere in the *Odyssey*, in

---

[33] Young-Eisendrath, P., 'What suffering teaches' in Molino, A. (ed.), *The Couch and the Tree*, Constable (1999).

the sea which surrounds those small islands of human consciousness between which Odysseus' boat haplessly zigzags, in the great storms which wreak indifferent havoc on his careful plans, and in the tears which fall continually from the eyes of both Penelope and Odysseus, abandoned and dissolved in their grief and helplessness. Trapped on Calypso's isle for seven years, Odysseus passes his time weeping and staring out to sea, ruing his enforced sexual dependency on the woman who has enslaved him. Penelope, left alone upon Ithaca, weeps alone at night, trapped in her loneliness, shamed by her helplessness and her powerlessness. Their tears endow the *Odyssey* with emotional resonance and meaning. Weaving her father-in-law's shroud by day and unpicking it each night, Penelope refuses to be hurried in her mourning and will not respond to the calls of the suitors for her to re-enter the world until she is ready.

'If they survive the storm itself, its fury almost always fades and then disappears ... the affliction runs its course and one finds peace.'[34] When change does come, breaking the cycle of helplessness and depression for both Penelope and Odysseus, it seems to be through the advent of another – Athene, who appears to Odysseus and inspires him to build the boat and embark upon the journey to Ithaca, where he in turn will finally rescue Penelope from her despair. But does change come, finally, from outside or from within? Once the unconscious processes set in train by suffering have worked themselves through and catharsis has been achieved, we may discover that life was always there waiting to re-engage us. The fever of depression over, hope arises at first tentatively and then more strongly and we rediscover energy and connection. The appearance of Athene, the goddess of wisdom, symbolizes the recognition of split-off, hitherto unrecognized aspects of the self which now appear as a transformative possibility – like poets' muses, the *anima* figures which appeared to Jung in the fevered delusions of his mid-life crisis, or the figures who haunt our own mid-life dreams.

Much of this process happens at an unconscious level. The process of working through depression moves from self-

---

[34] Styron, W., *Darkness Visible*, Picador (1992).

examination through the re-experiencing of denied loss and pain and the release of self-blaming, towards final insight, reconstitution and reintegration. But for this to be possible, a time of withdrawal and safety – from the judging and critical voice of shame which attempts to restore the status quo, as much as from the actual demands of modern life – may be necessary, and it is to this need that we will turn in the next chapter.

Part Five

TRANSITION

10

Safe Space, Inner Space

Wavering between the profit and the loss
In this brief transit where the dreams cross
The dream crossed twilight between birth and dying
. . . This is the time of tension between dying and birth
The place of solitude where three dreams cross
Between blue rocks

From '*Ash-Wednesday*' by T. S. Eliot

Scenes of modern life:

Mark is a hairdresser. Sometimes he would like to be able to concentrate on his work in silence. But hour after hour he must entertain his clients – and keep talking. Anna has her hair cut by Mark. After a day at work besieged by faxes, phones and e-mails, her head throbbing, she longs to sink back in the hairdresser's chair and close her eyes in silence. But she feels obliged to chat animatedly to Mark.

An ordinary pub in a regional city centre: mid-week, mid-evening. Three wall-mounted televisions play end-to-end pop videos. A second completely different soundtrack throbs on the pub's sound system, competing with a loudspeaker carrying the landlord's voice bellowing out multiple choice questions, for it is Quiz Night! Along the further wall, ranks of fruit machines and electronic games buzz, burp and rattle. Outside the window, four lanes of cars, motorbikes, lorries and the occasional ambulance or police car, sirens blaring, race round the ring road. The few customers stare into their glasses, occasionally essaying a shout to attract each other's attention. All are drinking heavily.

Afraid to turn inwards, afraid of what we will find or fail to find, we demand to be taken out of and away from ourselves. We have lost the gift of silence, and of solitude.

THREAT AND THE CITY

To focus in on what is most important, life must be slowed down and simplified. But this seems hardly possible under the living conditions of the twenty-four-hour society, as our personal space is determinedly colonized by muzak, pagers, mobiles and e-mail, and environmental threat and noise pollution invade our lives from all directions. Goaded on by ever-accelerating social, work-related and financial expectations, we live subject to relentless demands on our time and attention which must be continually processed if we are to stay on top of our lives. Caught in a spiral of action–reaction, we seldom find time to process even our most meaningful experiences. We just hurry through them, and on to the next.

In our crowded, frantic, urban environment, too many of us are placed in permanent competition against each other for too few resources. Rats co-exist happily and productively within their social structures when they have plenty of space, but turn viciously on each other when crowded together in a cage. For humans, overcrowding tends to combine with – and to stimulate – the breakdown of social systems, and an increase in rates of crime and alcoholism. In crowded cities, strangers do not meet each other's eyes, or smile. The more we crowd in on each other, the less safe we feel and we protect ourselves accordingly – overcrowding, paradoxically, creates social isolation. And we overcrowd not only our space but also our time. Living in an unpredictable and increasingly violent and frantic world, we must perform competitively and unceasingly just to survive.

A focus group of New Yorkers in their mid-twenties were asked how safe they felt about sex, money, relationships, marriage, street violence and job security. The question elicited an urgent, unanimous response: 'None of the above. Unsafe at all levels. At all times.'[1] If those in their twenties feel threatened by the pace and insecurity of modern life, how much more will this be this the case as mid life approaches? The need for quiet and solitude tends to increase as we grow older – what the twenty-year-old mind experiences as stimulation, the forty-year-old mind is more likely to experience as stress. But we manage. We soldier on, armouring ourselves against the demands of the environment and against the demands of our bodies and spirits for peace and quiet. Living with threat, we end up defining success as the ability to manage threat successfully. Instead of living creatively, we learn to live reactively. The more complex our lives, the more there is to go wrong. The more pressured our lives, the less leeway there is for dealing creatively and reflectively with internal crisis when it does, as it must, occur. Instead, our minds struggle at such moments like drowning sailors, to organize the tidal waves of conflicting expectations and demands which threaten to engulf and fragment our vessels and force us to keep striving always to stay in control, always vigilant.

In the heart of our affluence there is poverty. Rich in material resources and in opportunities for choice, divergence and advancement, we have nevertheless become poor in relation to more fundamental human needs. The wealth and complexity of the world we live in does not guarantee us access to unpolluted food, water and air nor, often, to personal space that is reliably quiet and private and safe from invasion. Nor can we necessarily expect to have, as of right as we grow older, a secure and respected place within the larger community, regardless of personal achievement and wealth. Our shrinking families are more fragile and less reliable than the extended families of the past, while the collective social and employment patterns and the cultural and religious systems of belief which once underpinned them are collapsing in a cascade of insecurity which leaves no-one unscathed.

Life in a pressured and precarious environment demands that

---

[1] Quoted in Sheehy G., *New Passages*, HarperCollins (1997).

we stay alert and continually on guard. To relax into stillness or repose may feel unsafe and also – in terms of the Protestant work ethic that still colours our views – immoral. The Zen master D. T. Suzuki, in the course of a lecture he once gave in America, was asked a question about activity and passivity. 'Passivity, passivity', Suzuki replied, '*what's wrong with passivity?*'[2] Suzuki's answer challenges one of our most entrenched cultural assumptions. Living in a world in which success is measured in terms of our ability to dominate and control our environment, grabbing as many resources as we can from it in the scramble to stay on top, we idealize extroversion, busyness and control – the devil, we know, makes work for idle hands. For us to do *nothing* – to allow ourselves to be sometimes introverted, to willingly choose passivity over activity – seems dangerously redolent of failure, of self-indulgence. We disapprove. We come to equate passivity with the deadening hopelessness of depression, and fail to appreciate the value of a stillness that is open, alert and equable.

Suzuki's offhand remark suggests how much our moralistic overvaluation of constant busyness can create unnecessary stresses within our lives and load the dice against our own well-being. For when conditions support it, the ability to relax into a state of stillness can be a source of contentment and unshakable peace of mind, as well as the basis of self-transformation. 'If you want to find the meaning' says the Japanese poet Ryokan, 'stop chasing after so many things'.[3]

All too easily, we become addicted to stress, to threat. Our fear of falling apart – our fear of what might happen were we to let our hearts open and allow ourselves to dissolve and rest in the moment – keeps us compulsively busy, addicted to action, to sex, to consumption, to busyness itself and to the interminable chatter of our minds. Nevertheless, as we grow older the advent of the mid-life crisis signals the need to begin to turn attention inwards away from this scramble, towards tentatively stirring needs of a different order. This chapter is concerned with the

---

[2] Quoted in Eigen, M., *The Psychoanalytic Mystic*, Free Association Books (1998).

[3] Ryokan, *One Robe, One Bowl: The Zen Poetry of Ryokan*, tr. Stevens, J., Weatherill Inc. (1977).

importance of safe space as the necessary sponsor of internal growth, and with the need to begin to find ways of establishing it as the basis for personal renewal.

THE CAPACITY TO BE ALONE

Many of us only allow ourselves to be alone when driving, in transition between one demand and another – perhaps more than anything else it is this unrecognized, unheeded need for solitude that informs our love affair with the car. It is not, of course, that we fail to recognize the need to be alone and quiet sometimes: different voices tell similar stories. 'When I'm alone I can come back to myself.' 'Periods of aloneness help me recharge my batteries, keep my feet on the floor and help me to understand what's going on around me.' 'When I'm alone I find the answers to problems I've been struggling with just come to me. I can collect my thoughts.' 'Being by myself is about having my own space.'[4] But on the whole, however much we recognize these needs – and however stressed we get when they are not met – we do not prioritize them. However much we value undemanding solitude, we still go on organizing our environment to make sure we don't get enough of it. Clearly, our attitude to solitude is more ambivalent than we like to let on.

'The capacity of the individual to be alone [is] one of the most important signs of maturity in emotional development' writes Winnicott.[5] 'It is only when alone . . . that the infant can discover his own personal life.' By being alone, Winnicott is not talking about physical isolation – he writes, for example, of how we may most pleasurably experience ourselves as alone in the presence of another after making love and reaching orgasm. Being alone in this sense refers to a state free from external stimulus, impingement or demand. So, a child who can experience being alone without feeling abandoned becomes able to relax for a while without a focus or a need to react to others – a potential

---

[4] *Solitude*, BBC Radio 4, 5 December 2000.
[5] Winnicott, D. W., 'The capacity to be alone' (1958) in *The Maturational Processes and the Facilitating Environment*, Karnac (1990).

state which Winnicott considers to be vital in the progress towards true maturity. Then, 'in the course of time there arrives a sensation or an impulse. In this setting the sensation or impulse will feel real and be truly a personal experience ... a large number of such experiences form the basis for a life that has reality in it instead of futility.'

But what if we never learn to be alone? The pathological alternative is a false life built on reactions to external stimuli, in which there is compulsive excitement but no relaxation, no peace of mind and no real satisfaction. Unlike loneliness (which is forced upon us) or withdrawal (which is a fearful reaction to threat), the capacity to be alone – and to feel enriched and enhanced by the experience – is something which must be discovered over time. Initially it comes, suggests Winnicott, from the experience of being *alone in the presence of another* – that is, from the experience of being lovingly held within a relationship with a parent who can be reliably but non-intrusively present.

It is the child's trust in the caregiver's continuing presence, protecting the child's nascent consciousness from outside impingement, from overstimulation and from the anxiety generated by the fear of abandonment, which makes it possible for the child to begin to experience him or herself as alone. Then, the child can learn to disentangle his or her own impulses from those of the powerful others who shape his or her environment and start to explore and enjoy them. As a result there can be relaxation and what Winnicott describes as the capacity to become peacefully unintegrated. Unintegration, a temporary state of relaxation or reverie, is different from disintegration, an involuntary panicked feeling of being out of control. 'The opposite of integration would seem to be disintegration' writes Winnicott. 'This is only partly true. The opposite, initially, requires a word like unintegration. Relaxation ... means not feeling a *need* to integrate.'[6]

Our ability to become relaxed and unintegrated – to rest

---

[6] Winnicott, D. W., 'Ego integration in child development' in *The Maturational Processes and the Facilitating Environment*, Karnac (1990). Italics mine.

contented and secure in the temporary absence of external stimulation – depends, paradoxically, upon the extent to which we have become able to feel secure and loved within relationship, and upon the degree of personal security we have been able to establish inside ourselves. Unless we can learn to allow ourselves to be alone in this way we will compulsively (but often unsuccessfully) seek togetherness with others as a way of avoiding loneliness. The reality of being alone may still awaken in us the insecurely attached child's fear of abandonment – hence our ambivalence, however much we long for quiet time and know we need it.

For only when alone is our attention really free to go inwards: solitude is most likely to exert its ambivalent pull at times when new ideas are struggling to emerge from the psyche, such as when creative work is in process, and at times of transition and crisis, such as mid life. Reaching mid life, we begin to feel claustrophobically trapped and find ourselves longing, at whatever cost, to cut free – a feeling which signals the need to turn attention inwards towards negotiating internal change and a radical shift in core values. In childhood, attachments are central and essential to our lives, and early adulthood too tends to be structured in terms of our more or less urgent needs for competitive stimulation, sexual intimacy and pair bonding. The mid-life transition may be the first time that the pull towards aloneness makes itself felt. But once it has been felt, then – despite the flaring-up of mid-life love affairs and those intense but volatile relationships that foster and are fostered by changing needs within the psyche – there is often, over the long term, a decrease in the intensity of personal relationship and a lessening of emotional dependence and neediness. People who are or have become single learn to value the pleasures and autonomy of single living and to think twice, or thrice, before committing to the long haul of a new relationship.

We habitually, automatically, overvalue the importance of personal relationship as the panacea for all ills, suggests the psychiatrist Anthony Storr in his book *Solitude*: 'The burden of value with which we are at present loading interpersonal relationships is too heavy for those fragile craft to carry ... after major alterations in circumstances, fundamental reappraisal of the significance and meaning of existence may be needed. In a culture in which interpersonal relationships are generally considered to provide the answer to every form of distress, it is sometimes difficult to persuade well-meaning helpers that solitude can be as therapeutic as emotional support.'[7] The power of the mid-life pull towards solitude can be both unexpected and disorientating and may be a contributory factor in the break-up of many previously stable relationships, as we begin to realize the extent to which our relationships may have been used just to avoid loneliness – and how much we may have compromised and forfeited as a result. 'The best cure for loneliness is solitude' writes the poet Marianne Moore. Aloneness must be achieved, but loneliness is thrust upon us – yet, the capacity to be alone may mature, over time, out of loneliness. Rationalizing that the collapse of personal relation-ship has been caused by our own badness or worthlessness draws us into the lonely hopelessness of depression. And yet even from such an unpromising start, unwilling solitude may, in the long run, bring unexpected consolations.

Quiet, unpressured time alone enables us, gradually, to come to terms with loss, to mourn and to let go – to confront and to work through the insecurity caused by the loss of former ideals, the recognition of the reality of death and the encroachment of those ensuing feelings of loss and depression which lie at the core of the mid-life crisis. Once this worst has been faced up to, we may find – often to our surprise – that those needs for approval and protection which shaped so many of the choices of our childhood, adolescence and early adulthood and seemed an inalienable part of living, begin to fade away. As anxieties about abandonment diminish, the fear of loneliness begins to mellow into a more robust sense of internal freedom and the abatement of the compulsive need for others. Then in aloneness we find not loneliness but a blessed release from the need to suppress ourselves to avoid conflict or rejection, and from the need to pass our time in a state of adrenaline-fuelled, panicked reactivity to the demands of others.

[7] Storr, A., *Solitude*, Flamingo (1990).

'For me, the real healers were peace and seclusion' wrote William Styron of his own emergence from depression.[8] In peace and seclusion – however they arise – we can begin to access our deepest feelings, think our ideas through and change our attitudes. In the process we may discover or rediscover an internal sense of balanced cohesion, which helps us to become detached from outgrown roles and habits. Aloneness also enables us to discover or rediscover parts of the self previously projected onto others within relationships. So in the aftermath of the collapse of long-term relationships, men newly alone may begin to discover how much they had unconsciously relied upon their wives to process their feelings for them and to reinforce their self-esteem, and learn – by necessity – to encounter and explore their own emotional vulnerabilities. Women may feel the upsurge of the sense of autonomy and independence that comes from achieving status and security through personal effort and through making their own voices heard in the world. People who have always tended to over-adapt to others (and who find it difficult to break what may literally be the habit of a lifetime) may find that only in solitude can they allow themselves the internal freedom to get in touch with their deepest, most authentic feelings, and that only solitude can bring into being that precious space in which the self can become reconstituted.

Agnes' second marriage has just ended. She met her first husband at university, moved in with him when they graduated, and in due course left him for her second husband. Now in her early forties, Agnes had never in her life lived alone, and the first night she spent alone in the house after her second husband moved out gave her the creeps. Agnes took care not to break up with either of her husbands until she had a new partner lined up, yet now she finds herself holding back, curiously unwilling to move in with John, her new man. She has the following dream:

> There's a mountain I'm longing to climb, and John is ready, inviting me to climb with him. I have some new climbing boots and I put them on but they don't fit properly. I hesitate and try to force my feet into them

---

8   Styron, W., *Darkness Visible*, Picador (1992).

because I'm afraid otherwise John will go without me. But I realize that my feet are already badly blistered and the rubbing of the boots is likely to make them much worse. If I become lame and get stuck half-way up the mountain, I'll be in real trouble because there'll be nowhere to go and no-one to help me. So reluctantly I take the boots off and tell John I can't go with him at the moment. Then next to the mountain, I notice a small slope, at the top of which is a grocery shop. The shopkeeper is a woman with curly grey hair and a kind face whom I've never seen before. I go towards her and ask her if she has any blister plasters. The woman says she'll look after me until my blisters have healed and my new boots are worn in and I'm ready to climb. The sense of panic dissolves.

Agnes is become an anti-Cinderella. She'd like to slip her foot into her new Prince's glass climbing boot and surrender herself to him. But old unhealed wounds – the wounds of past relationships which irritated and constricted her – prevent her doing so. Agnes realizes that her new boots (like her new man) are likely to start rubbing in all the old familiar places and to break open and infect the blisters that are starting to form as part of the healing process, if she allows herself to be swept away, once more, by her need to become merged with someone else. Instead, Agnes resolves to take the new relationship slowly. She decides to try living alone for a while instead of moving straight in with her new partner as she had planned. She gets herself a flat and decorates it herself. In her new space, she begins to practise yoga and a few months later goes on a yoga and meditation retreat. Strangely, one of the meditation teachers on her retreat – a woman whom she'd never met before – bears more than a passing resemblance to the shop owner who offered her sanctuary in her dream.

Agnes realized that she needed time to learn to understand herself better, instead of once again getting swept away by the compulsions that were driving her. Stopping herself in mid action – in the act of lacing up her marching boots to begin yet another potentially fruitless journey – she broke a pattern and gave herself some time out instead. She found in private space and solitude the opportunity to stop and take stock, to avoid being swept along in an endless tide of reactivity.

Arthur Koestler, reflecting in a television programme on his experience of solitary confinement in a Spanish prison, spoke of the 'feeling of inner freedom, of being alone and confronted with ultimate realities instead of with your bank statement. Your bank statement and other trivialities are again a kind of confinement. Not in space but in spiritual space ... So you have got a dialogue with existence. A dialogue with life, a dialogue with death.'[9] Usually, says Koestler, we live on the trivial plane and only move to a deeper level when something exceptional happens – when we fall in love, when a parent dies, when we are very ill. But in the sort of solitude he endured, 'one had one's nose rubbed into it, for a protracted period'.

Stillness and solitude may make or break a person's spirit. 'There was no end and no beginning' wrote Nelson Mandela of the many periods of solitary confinement he suffered during nearly three decades of imprisonment:

> There is only one's own mind, which can begin to play tricks. Was that a dream or did it really happen? One begins to question everything. Did I make the right decision, was my sacrifice worth it? In solitary, there is no distraction from these haunting questions. But the human body has an enormous capacity for adjusting to trying circumstances ... strong convictions are the secret of surviving deprivation; your spirit can be full even when your stomach is empty.[10]

The strength of Mandela's sense of purpose enabled him not only to survive great isolation in the most adverse circumstances, but to make use of it for his own internal growth and the development of his personal and political philosophy. Quiet time for rumination and reflection enables us to pause and learn from experience instead of automatically repeating old habits. When the time for action does finally come, it can as a result be exponentially more effective.

When external circumstances change drastically, quiet periods in which life slows down and the demands of the outside world are kept to a minimum help us to step back and fundamentally reassess our lives, values and the direction we were headed. Having done so, we become able – in due course – to pick up the reins again and go forward with new energy: *reculer pour mieux sauter*. In retrospect, these periods of quietness and reflection – whether forced upon us or sought out more or less instinctively – may mark a watershed in our lives. In them, writes Germaine

---

[9] Koestler, A., *Kaleidoscope* (1981), quoted in Storr, A., *Solitude*, Flamingo (1990).

[10] Mandela, N., *Long Walk to Freedom*, Little, Brown & Co. (1994).

Greer, you begin to change 'into the self you were before you became the tool of your sexual and reproductive destiny ... you were strong then, and well, and happy, until adolescence turned you into something more problematical, and you shall be well and strong and happy again.'[11]

Such opportunities enable us to forge a new context for living, in which we can make our lives work for us instead of working for our lives, and in which the self can become at last the true owner of its own experience. And yet, however strong the yearning, letting go of old habits and certainties remains, nearly always, easier said than done.

LETTING GO

When I first started practising as a psychotherapist, I used to dread those moments – by no means infrequent – when, in the middle of a session with a patient, my mind would go completely blank and I would find that I had no idea what was going on, or what to say. After a while I came to realize that this sensation of blankness was often a sign that intense feelings were present which I was not yet able to grasp. Later still, I came to connect it with a sense that something new was struggling to emerge within the therapeutic relationship, something not yet fully formed and which could not, as yet, be described or named. Over time, I have become able to relax into such moments instead of pushing them away, and even to experience a pleasurable sense of anticipation in relation to them. I have discovered that the more I am personally able to free myself from my own need to organize, control and know the answers – to risk instead trusting the moment – the greater are the eventual gains within the therapeutic relationship. Becoming willing to let go of the old – temporarily to founder – creates space into which the new, tentatively, begins to emerge.

I came to realize that in the process of psychic change, any state of greater organization will be preceded by a period of

---

[11] Greer, G., *The Change*, Hamish Hamilton (1991).

disorganization – even, dauntingly, by a sense of losing grip, of chaos and unravelling, If we can allow ourselves to sit with these discouraging, disconcerting moments instead of fighting against them, those old habits, which have forced the self to develop within certain grooves in the service of an imposed or premature sense of cohesion, start to drop away. There is space then, over time, for new forms and impulses to coalesce, take shape and, eventually, to become endowed with meaning.

We can't make omelettes unless we dare to crack eggs, but when it is our own habits and attachments and our need to stay in control that are at issue, that sense of cracking up – or breaking down – can be intensely painful and frightening. Yet the times we push ourselves out into the unknown may also be the times we feel most real: only when the need for control is suspended can the self begin to unwind. Losing control many be our greatest fear, but all too often this fear is unfounded. Holding on too hard is what we do too much of, letting go what we need to learn. 'Most of us have developed our egos enough' writes Michael Epstein. 'What we suffer from is the accumulated tension of that development. We have trouble surrendering ourselves.'[12] Epstein suggests that we sometimes hold on so hard to our habits and attachments because of unconscious memories of having had to rely on ourselves prematurely – too often and too soon, at times when we were not yet able to take for granted our own capacity to organize and integrate our experiences.

A child, for example, may feel securely connected to her parents at first, but then feel dropped at the birth of a new baby. Once her helplessness and demands for attention delighted; now they only exasperate her tired mother – for approval now, she must show she can look after herself, sit unsupported in the high chair while her mother cuddles the new baby, and toddle on tired little feet beside a push-chair too soon relinquished to the new sibling. Too soon, she has become the one who must be responsible, must control herself, must know better. Or the mind of a parent may be numbed by post-natal depression,

---

[12] Epstein, M., *Going to Pieces without Falling Apart*, HarperCollins (1999).

agitated by an anxiety disorder, distracted by financial problems or disturbed by marital conflict or family crisis, unable – for whatever reason – to remain attuned to their child's needs. Implicitly, the parent's withdrawal signals to the attachment-seeking child that the world is unsafe, and protection cannot be expected.

The immature nervous system of a child who is not protected by a parent's intuitive understanding of what he or she can manage becomes flooded with confusing and overwhelming stimuli, sometimes including the parent's own distress or anxiety. Necessity being the mother of invention, children in such situations learn, precociously, that they themselves must hold their own world together and cannot afford to rely on others. Sometimes, as well, they must learn to manage and soothe their parents' moods and unhappinesses at the cost of their own needs. The protection of others – and the flight from the self – may become a lifelong role. But the precocious systems of management and control – those predictable habits and rituals which the child develops as a reaction to feeling unsafe, and which are designed to provide premature cohesion in the face of environmental failure – tend to have a rigid and joyless quality to them.

So many of us hold ourselves together – worrying, talking, consuming, doing – as an outgrown response to early failures of care, as a way of pre-empting the desolation of abandonment. The self ends up over-identified with the rigidly controlling ego; anything that challenges its primacy is experienced as a threat, and violently repudiated. 'When we are afraid to relax the mind's vigilance ... we start to founder. In this fear, we destroy our capacity to discover ourselves in a new way. We doom ourselves to a perpetual hardening of character, which we imagine is sanity but which comes to imprison us. Our shoulders get more and more tense.' One of the most important tasks of adulthood, Epstein concludes, is to discover, or rediscover, the ability to lose oneself.

When the environment fails us in later life, it is easy for this defensive, fixed sense of self to become even more rigid and fortified as a reaction to the disaster it was always secretly anticipating anyway. The alternative is to risk relaxing into the distress and going with the flow, trusting that life's subsequent hard-won gains of integration and organization will not let us down if we let go a little. But to do so may seem quite counter intuitive: it can be so difficult to stop and check an automatic response, to wait for a moment and suspend the desire to conceptualize, rationalize, control and package away every experience in terms of the already known – so difficult just to release tension and to allow the self to flow for a while within the stream of lived experience. Up against the edge of fear, it is so much easier to dodge the issue, to eradicate subjectivity in the service of obedience to internal ideologies and controlling voices. And then, all too easily, we end up repeating the past, over-defining ourselves solely in terms of our competence at executing preordained plans, in terms of function and efficiency rather than meaning. We become doing-machines instead of humans, bound within our compulsions and alienated from the experience of living within a self.

Our fear of changing – and, especially, of loss – makes us cling to the illusion of fixed identity, an illusion reinforced by massive accumulations of attachment, habit and prejudice. Yet in truth, our selves are always changing. The self as defined by the Oxford English Dictionary is no more (or less) than a permanent subject of successive and varying states of consciousness – our experience is continuous yet fragmented, and we are contingent beings caught in an experiential flux in a world that is itself never the same from second to second. The permanent self – such as it is – is not matter, but an organizing and integrating intelligence that does its work unconsciously. Hence the tendency of the self (the existence of which we take for granted when our mind is on other matters) to appear to evaporate as soon as we try to think about it. The self always eludes definition – it's what we live in, but cannot know.[13] In our quest for certainty and permanence as a bulwark against the fear of dissolution, we learn to displace our sense of self onto those attachments and habits which can be known, and to over-identify with them.

It is when those habits and attachments are questioned – as by

---

[13] Bollas, C., *Cracking Up*, Routledge (1995).

the advent of mid-life crisis – that we become afraid of falling apart, cracking up, breaking down. What is the nature of this fear? Fear of letting go, of the pain of loss, of becoming different, the fear that it's too late to change, the fear of sooner or later having an experience we can't predict or control. In this valley of the shadow of loss we become over-cautious and afraid to experiment. We rearrange new possibilities as foregone conclusions and endlessly repeat old procedures and self-fulfilling prophecies in an ultimately fruitless effort to assert the illusion of control and to protect ourselves against insecurity.

Yet catalogues of loss, notes Adam Phillips, may from another perspective be records of survival and ingenuity – for both Darwin and Freud, the catalogues of loss to which each in their own ways kept returning were, more often than not, opportunities for invention. 'Darwin and Freud … in their quite different ways are persuading us to become good losers; to be able, if need be, to dispel our attachment to people and ideas, and ultimately to ourselves.' For, says Phillips, the habits that sustain us can be deadly 'if we love our routines more than our futures – then we are fatally addicted to the past'.[14] Freud noted approvingly Darwin's habit, which Darwin recorded in his autobiography, that whenever he had a new thought or discovered a new fact that ran contrary to his previously established belief, he would make a special note of it, without fail and at once, 'for I had found by experience', wrote Darwin, 'that such facts and thoughts were far more apt to escape from the memory than favourable ones'.[15] Most of us, of course, are more likely to do exactly the opposite.

'The Old Ego dies hard' writes Samuel Beckett. 'Such as it was a minister of dullness, it was also an agent of security.'[16] Our addiction to the impervious, seductive perfection of youth and control set us up for humiliation and disappointment, as we insist on recasting the present and the future in the terms of the past,

---

[14] Phillips, A., *Darwin's Worms*, Faber and Faber (1999).

[15] Quoted in Freud, S., 'The Psychopathology of Everyday Life', in *Penguin Freud Library* 5.

[16] Quoted in Epstein, M., *Going to Pieces without Falling Apart*, Harper Collins (1999).

and fall with a semi-ironic reluctant awareness into the sort of middle age which is a defensive posture against loss and change, compulsively structured by overwork, affairs, drinking or whatever else serves to insulate and divert us from relaxing into the realities of our fluctuating experiences. And yet becoming familiar with the fluctuations of our inner worlds may in reality adapt us better to deal with the demands of the outer one. Those moments of distress or threat from which we run may, from another perspective, be the moments of our potential transformation or salvation – to which we scarcely dare yield.

Letting go of old beliefs and ideologies may leave us feeling cast adrift, fearful, grief-stricken. But suffering also softens us and loosens up our hearts. When we become able to break with the superstitious belief that pain is a punishment for failure or badness and instead just let our suffering happen, it becomes easier to resist the pull to manipulate others as a way of denying or avoiding insecurity. Once we start leaning into the curve instead of pulling against it, dissolving into the moment instead of fighting it, surrendering to reality instead of arguing with it, new possibilities of self-experiencing begin to emerge. 'The experience of certain feelings can seem particularly pregnant with the desire for resolution' writes the Buddhist nun Pema Chodron.

> Unless we can relax with these feelings, it's very hard to stay in the middle when we experience them. We want victory or defeat, praise or blame. For example, if somebody abandons us, we don't want to be with that raw discomfort. Instead we conjure up a familiar identity of ourselves as a hapless victim or . . . tell the person how messed up he or she is. We automatically want to cover over the pain in one way or another, identifying with victory or victimhood. Usually, we regard loneliness as an enemy. Heartache is not something we choose to invite in. It's restless and pregnant and hot with the desire to escape and find something or someone to keep us company. When we rest in the middle we begin to have a nonthreatening relationship with loneliness, a relaxing and cooling loneliness that completely turns our usual fearful patterns around.[17]

---

[17] Chodron, P., *When Things Fall Apart*, Shambhala Publications Inc. (1997).

The moment everything falls apart – the extended moment when everything is up in the air, before the dice fall again – is the moment when anything may be possible. Such is the lightness of being – such moments, freed from the baggage and the restraining orders of the past, may be disconcerting. Chodron writes of 'the courage to die, the courage to die continually ... only to the extent that we expose ourselves over and over to annihilation can that which is indestructible be found within us.'

The retreat from ageing and loss encourages us to entrench ourselves in habit, yet it is as we grow older that we most need to learn to cultivate a mind that can tolerate loss, change and being out of control without panic and disintegration. 'Do not look upon your body as yourself' said Sariputta, one of the Buddha's disciples, in a famous teaching. 'Your body can change and become otherwise but grief, lamentation, pain, dejection and despair do not have to arise.' Sariputta is teaching that it is possible to let the mind float free of identifications, even the most fundamental identifications with mind, body and consciousness itself. But often we pull away from this losing of the self even at the moments we most long for it, such as in states of sexual or mystical ecstasy – because to our conscious minds it may seem too much like disintegration or death itself.

The longing to float free of obligations and outgrown self-identifications fuels the mid-life crisis. But – paradoxically, agonizingly – it is often accompanied by a great terror of abandonment and loneliness. The losses of mid life and especially the dawning awareness of the inevitability of death have a tendency to find the chink, however well disguised, in our psychic armour, returning us back to our earliest needs for attachment and security and our fear of being abandoned. It's a paradoxical situation. For new impulses to stir within us – to become able to give birth once more to ourselves, at the start of a new phase of life – we may need to be alone. But to be alone we must first discover a space that is safe from fear.

TURNING INWARDS

In the intricate and complex life cycle of the butterfly, the segmented caterpillar emerges from the egg to feed and store food and to grow to full size, moulting its old skin several times as it does so. Then in due course – propelled not by any external event but by the exigencies of its internal developmental programme – the caterpillar loses interest in eating and simply wanders away from its food plant. As it prepares to enter the third stage of its life cycle and become a pupa, the insect's first task is to make itself safe, which it does by spinning a cocoon around itself or finding a secure hiding place. Some pupae attach themselves by their rear ends to leaves or other plants, while some spin their cocoons in grass. Many moth pupae, otherwise naked and unprotected, bury themselves in soil.

From the outside, the pupa is a smooth and mummy-like object which, apart from twitching or wriggling if disturbed, cannot move. But inside its cocoon the insect's developmental process continues uninterrupted towards its final apotheosis, as the organs of the caterpillar disintegrate and those of the adult butterfly form. Throughout this time the insect, undefended within its cocoon and with its focus entirely turned inwards, is at its most vulnerable – it relies entirely upon the efficacy of its hiding place or the durability of its cocoon for protection from external threat.

The outer shell of the pupa is made of a tough substance called chitin, and if this is disturbed the butterfly-to-be will be damaged. Upon this shell, the future features of the adult butterfly can sometimes be traced in shallow relief. As the time approaches for the butterfly's emergence, its outline becomes more pronounced, like the outline of a photograph emerging in a developing tray; in some species, even the colours of the future butterfly can be seen. Then, once the transformation is completed, the adult begins to struggle and eventually breaks out of its former casing. For the first hour or so its wings are limp, like small deflated balloons. But soon they harden, and flutter and spread for the first flight.[18]

The more radical the metamorphosis, the more complete the withdrawal and the more secure the protection required. And

---

[18] Hyde, G., *Butterflies*, Almark Publishing Co. (1974); Lyneborg, L., *Moths in Colour*, Blandford (1975); *Grolier Multimedia Encyclopedia* (1995).

the transformations demanded by mid-life transition – for brittle ego control to be relinquished in favour of a more flexible sense of self which can deintegrate and reintegrate according to internal rhythms, and for old values to be replaced by new ones – may be scarcely less great than the caterpillar's metamorphosis. Left alone upon Ithaca in circumstances of the greatest danger, assailed by intruders who rampage through her house and drain her resources while demanding her hand, her body and her life, Penelope too spins. Like the caterpillar, she spins every day, rhythmically weaving and unweaving, forming a protective barrier against the demands of her importunate suitors, a space that is as safe as she can make it, in which she can remain alone and undisturbed until the time of mourning and helplessness comes to its natural end, and the moment of change arrives and declares itself.

ON THE COUCH, IN A DREAM

'In almost all our psychoanalytic treatments', writes Winnicott, 'there come times when the ability to be alone is important to the patient ... this silence, far from being evidence of resistance, turns out to be an achievement on the part of the patient. Perhaps it is here that the patient has been able to be alone for the first time.'[19] The psychoanalytic technique has been described by Erik Erikson as a meditative process capable of yielding great healing insight for those who feel disturbed enough to need it, curious enough to want it, and healthy enough to take it – a combination which may, as he remarks, make the psychoanalysed feel like a certain kind of elite.[20] To the novice patient, however, the psychotherapy session may seem, at first, an alien and forbidding space which demands to be filled up as quickly and thoroughly as possible with well-rehearsed contents. But with time – if both therapist and patient are willing to take risks and to remain open to each other, and if the

---

[19] Winnicott, D. W., 'The capacity to be alone' (1958) in *The Motivational Processes and the Facilitating Environment*, Karnac (1990).

[20] Erikson, E. H., *The Life Cycle Completed*, W. W. Norton (1997).

therapist is able to contain and find ways of making sense of what the patient brings to the session – the quality of the relationship begins to relax and expand. In the spinning world, a still centre is discovered.

If the therapist neither judges nor retaliates, does not demand and is not seduced, but is able to remain reliably, empathically and thoughtfully present, then for the patient new self-experiences may begin to arise. Becoming able to be alone in the presence of the other itself sponsors the evolution of new ways of relating. 'The hallmark of the therapeutic session', writes the psychoanalyst Michael Eigen, 'is the discovery of intimacy in the face of unflinching aloneness'.[21] Within a containing relationship, the sense of shame or alarm stirred up by the revelation of hidden parts of the self begins to dissolve, and anxieties about being rejected or forsaken start to have less power to stifle and distort the self. Like the cocoon of the chrysalis, or the alchemic bath, the therapeutic relationship at its best provides a second skin, a sort of ego-support to the patient in profound transition.

Transition is a vulnerable and uncertain time when old patterns begin to die away, before new ways of being are confidently established. Our defences, however unhelpful and dysfunctional they may become, got established in the first place for a reason: to protect the young and vulnerable self against what it experienced as unbearable. When these established defences start to lose their power, the anxieties against which they formerly protected begin, inevitably, to re-emerge, sometimes creating a negative therapeutic reaction which threatens the collapse of the therapy. But anxiety is a response to being at the edge of the unknown, at the edge of change. It is a form of energy which – if it can be successfully mediated within the relationship – generates transformation. To discover ourselves in the presence of another we must be willing to lose ourselves, to risk dissolution.

Our identities are bound by our past and by past expectations, and much early work in therapy may be absorbed by the

---

[21] Eigen, M., *The Psychotic Core*, Jason Aronson (1993).

re-narration of those historic family dramas which have helped to form a person's sense of self and to construct the meanings by which they have made sense of the world. By focusing on the past, psychotherapy revives it. Yet paradoxically it is by reviving and then by repeatedly working through the formative experiences of the past – those pockets of unintegrated energy and distress buried within the unconscious psyche – that we loosen their structural power within our minds and learn to stop replaying and reliving them.[22] Psychotherapy is, in this sense, a process of letting go, a mourning process through which we retrieve and reawaken our attachments to the past, only to allow them, finally, to dissolve and fall away. Less encumbered, we become able to move more freely into our unknown futures.

This dissolution of conscious identity is something we also experience on a nightly basis, in our dreams. Our dreams deconstruct the world we knew and create in its place a world which is superficially similar to the old one, yet compellingly different. Initially puzzling or disturbing, the images and encounters of the dream reveal themselves (once the web of associations to them has been unravelled) as complex yet acute representations of our unconscious beliefs and ideas, and of the unconscious associations and connections which have formed them. Dreams reveal our unconscious efforts to construct new meanings through the dissolution of the old.

The extraordinary experience of dreaming is at the same time something so familiar that we take it for granted. Dreams may be a mechanism for reprocessing information important for survival. When we dream, it seems, we are testing out recent perceptions and ideas by comparing them against our pre-existing survival strategies (or, as psychoanalytic thinking would have it, against the core beliefs of the structural unconscious) which in the process themselves are re-evaluated and modified.[23]

---

[22] Freud, S., 'Remembering, Repeating and Working Through' (1914), in *Standard Edition* XII.

[23] From an evolutionary perspective, dreams and sleep itself seem like a colossal waste of time and energy: yet all mammals sleep and dream. The rapid eye movement sleep in which dreams occur evolved with mammals who, as their minds became more sophisticated, became more dependent

In dreaming, with our attention temporarily freed from external problems and turned inwards, we can start to think conflicting beliefs through and to work out a new orientation to them. 'I'll sleep on it' we say.

The belief that dreams reveal understandings normally concealed from our conscious minds is, of course, an ancient one. 'The evolutionary stratification of the psyche is more clearly discernible in the dream than in the conscious mind' wrote Jung. 'Through the assimilation of unconscious contents ... the patient can be led back to the natural law of his own being.'[24] Most of our difficulties, Jung believed, come from losing touch with ancient but forgotten sources of wisdom stored within us – the same reservoir which today's neurologists, using a different language, are suggesting that our dreams enable us to access.

Dreams are far more important than we realize for our continuing mental well-being; if deprived of dreaming we will lose concentration and memory and eventually die. People who say that they don't dream in fact do – they just don't remember their dreams, and perhaps don't really want to. While dreams will do their work whether we choose to attend to them or not, it seems likely that systematically recalling and reflecting upon them will accelerate the process of learning through experience, stimulating psychic growth and greater integration. Becoming better integrated and less conflicted itself enables us to make

---

upon memory and thinking. Were we to remember everything that has ever happened to us, it has been estimated that our brains would have to be so big that we'd need to carry them about in a wheelbarrow, but the size of a mammal's brain is necessarily limited by the relative size of its mother's pelvis at birth. Dreams, therefore, may be a way of sorting through the information we have stored in our most recent waking period and re-evaluating it in terms of survival strategies formed and tested in the past, working out what we need to keep and what we can safely jettison. Animals' dreams (which scientists have been able to focus on by incapacitating that part of the brain that inhibits movement during sleep, making animals get up and act out their dreams) seem to focus on survival issues (feeding, fighting, fleeing and fornication); ours, to a large extent, do as well. Yet we have also, it seems, adapted the dreaming function to facilitate personal learning and development. See Stevens, A. and Price, J., *Evolutionary Psychiatry*, Routledge (1996).

[24] Jung, C. G., *Collected Works*, Vol. 16, para. 351, Routledge (1967).

wiser and more intuitive choices, and it is perhaps this fact that gave dreams their widespread and enduring reputation for being able to predict the future.

Dreams help us to see the bigger picture, and return to our gaze those parts of it from which our conscious view has been averted. Particularly at times of transition, when the lie of the land is no longer familiar and old signposts have disappeared, dreams can point a new way forward. Charlotte, whose emergence from depression was described in the previous chapter, dreamt she went for a swim in a dark, swampy pool and was pulled under the water by a young boy, at which point the water became full of ripples of light. Engaging with her dream enabled her to make contact with the playful, exploratory part of herself which was struggling to emerge from a mind temporarily overwhelmed by dark foreboding and fear. Agnes' dream, in which she decided not to put her blistered feet into her boots and follow her new boyfriend up the mountain, offered her a space in which she could stop and reassess her automatic impulse. She began to feel less controlled by her erotic preoccupations and to discover for the first time the spiritual yearning behind them.

In dreams, wrote Yeats, begins responsibility.[25] Taking our dreams seriously enables us to open up a dialogue between our conscious and unconscious minds and to illuminate areas of internal life previously denied or suppressed. Dreams make intuitive leaps and connections at the point where our rationality stumbles and fails, in the baffling dissolution of the familiar. Dreams – if we dare remember them and take them seriously – educate us in possibilities. Like depth psychotherapy and spiritual experience, they open up new meanings through taking us into the sometimes frightening void of the unknown.

FINDING SANCTUARY

'At the very centre of psychotherapeutic experiences there is an

---

[25] Yeats, W. B., *Responsibilities* (1914), epigraph.

awesome hole … the hole is the very centre and heart of therapeutic change' writes Wilson Van Dusen. 'What are the holes? They are any sort of defect – blankness, loss of memory, failure of concentration or loss of meaning … in the obsessive-compulsive they represent the loss of order and control. In the depressive they are the black hole of time standing still … in every case they represent the unknown, the unnamed threat, the source of anxiety and the fear of disintegration.' If we can tolerate this void we can use it to find creative solutions to problems. But more often we struggle against it fearfully, and this fear is fostered by the pace of modern life which conspires to continually fill the void with objects and distractions.[26] A therapist who also fears the void will try to fill it up with advice and answers, but if its existence can be acknowledged, the fears that stop us entering it can be explored and dismantled. The void can then be entered and this may be a turning point in therapeutic change, for the void is really a place chaotic with possibilities.

Van Dusen likens this state to the psychological openness to grace cultivated by Christian mystics, and the No-Mind of Zen. Spiritual growth comes out of the void, and is fostered by those periods of solitude and contemplation which lie at the core of spiritual discipline and tradition. Jesus spent forty days wandering in the wilderness and testing out his resolve before returning to follow his calling, while Mohammed is said to have withdrawn each year during the month of Ramadan to the cave of Hera, and the Buddha, during the rainy season, into silent retreat. The saffron-clad *sanyassin* who signs away his worldly goods and lights his own funeral pyre before going forth as a wandering ascetic, and the Mediterranean woman shrouded in black who quietly tends the graves of her departed and prays before the candles she has lit for them upon the altar of her church, both embody a state of aloneness and a reorientation towards spiritual values, recognized within their own societies as appropriate to the time of life they have reached.

Spiritual insight may reveal a time of crisis to be a time of

---

[26] Van Dusen, W., 'Wu Wei, no-mind and the fertile void in psychotherapy' (1958), reprinted in Molino, A. (ed.), *The Couch and the Tree*, Constable (1999).

grace, and spiritual discipline extends the possibility of discovering true interiority within the search for ultimate meaning or the absolute. It is within this context that solitude becomes a spiritual practice. 'Hopefully, you're entering deeper and deeper into the depths of your own heart where the experience of the absolute can only be found,' said Father Michael Holleran, a Carthusian monk who lived in near-total solitude for twenty-two years within the containment of the Carthusians' Sussex community, 'and as you do that you enter into all sorts of levels of your being and your soul and your psychology which are frightening and exhilarating at the same time, waiting to be explored and unpacked and integrated and harmonised and understood. It's a great adventure.' Father Michael, having now left this seclusion for a new life in Manhattan, did not feel that solitude need be a permanent choice or vocation:

> Once you've interiorised the values that this original structure is meant to promote you don't need the scaffolding any more . . . I would recommend that everyone have some kind of hermit experience in their own life . . . the same kind of adventure of the human spirit which went on for me in solitude is continued in the adventure of the human spirit in Greenwich Village. It really is the same process and the same thing that's going on.[27]

The ancient monastic traditions of both Christianity and Buddhism are structured around the recognition that for spiritual life to be effective there must be at its centre a place of refuge protected from worldly demands. In contrast to the rapid decline in regular church attendance, the two years leading up to the turn of the millennium saw British monasteries reporting a fifty per cent increase in the number of people – typically, stressed professionals approaching mid life – going on retreat, drawn to the ancient monastic rhythms of devotion, meditation, study and communion with nature.[28] Making choices informed by the need for a greater measure of quietness and solitude in daily life enables the person reaching mid life to

---

[27] From *Solitude*, BBC Radio 4, 5 December 2000.
[28] *Independent*, 4 March 2000.

open the door upon a new spiritual landscape in which frenetic activity is replaced by simplicity and slowness, and restlessness and alienation begin to dissolve. Becoming centred in oneself allows the pleasures of internal creative and integrative processes to unfold. In meditation as in psychotherapy, the development of self-awareness is the first step towards higher integration.

But the discipline of meditation does not necessarily come easily when we are used to being constantly distracted from ourselves and allowing our mental energies to fragment, disperse and chase all over the place. Training the mind to meditate is like training a puppy. The puppy wanders about this way and that, keen to please but forgetful and easily distracted. Training takes patience. Noticing the mind straying, rather than becoming angry or self-critical or giving up in despair, the meditator calls it back to heel, over and over.

Sitting alone in meditation, I close my eyes and try to focus inwards, concentrating on counting my breathing, following a familiar mindfulness meditation technique. I hear the milkman downstairs at the front door. Did I leave him a note? My mind drifts to what I'm planning for supper tonight. 'Thinking' I say to myself, and I bring my mind back to my breathing. A few minutes later and I realize I've lost the count again. My mind was wondering about the lecture I'm to give that afternoon, and had drifted off to remembering a lesson with Mrs Straw, the headmistress of my junior school when I was eleven years old, putting up my hand without knowing the answer, afraid I'd be found out. 'Thinking again.'

Back to breathing, and I become aware that I'm breathing more heavily and rapidly. I'm now able to recognize this habit as coming from my anxieties about needing to please and to know the answers, and my fear of what will happen if I just sit still instead of continually jumping up to try to manage the world and people's reactions to me ... Now my breathing has slowed down again and I'm staying with it for longer periods between the eruption of distracting thoughts. A feeling of calmness and well-being is starting to spread through my body...

Meditation brings us up directly against our habits and compulsions. Sitting down to meditate for the first time, we may be astounded by how difficult it is to stay with experience for even the shortest lengths of time – even to the count of ten breaths – without reorganizing it into self-commands, conceptualizations, distractions. But as we persevere, we slowly learn to detach our minds from our habits and our immediate concerns, and become benign observers of our own thought processes. We learn to observe how our preconceptions control our perceptions, feeding our thoughts and fuelling our changing moods and body experiences, and how rapidly this process can have us at its mercy. We begin to become aware of our projections into others, of our restless cravings, our concealed dependence, our desire to control and the anxieties that lie behind it. The newly emerging observant self, watching the controlling chatter which reinforces the small and limited view of self, begins to become disidentified with it. Over time, these insights help us to begin to move from blaming towards responsibility, and to relocate ourselves at the centre of our own lives. Old self-concepts, self-identifications and self-deceptions begin to dissolve. The observing self becomes increasingly subtle and eventually is transcended, along with the experience of duality itself.[29]

The Buddha was once asked why anyone would want to follow his path of turning away from the pleasures that the world had to offer. It would be most difficult indeed, he replied, were it not that the pleasures to be discovered in meditating were in the end so much greater than the pleasures available elsewhere. Meditation teaches us how to be with ourselves in the deepest way possible. The drifting or reverie which happens in therapy and the lulling of habitual thought processes in meditation practice facilitate reflective and contemplative states. From such states we can begin to encourage the sense of awareness and kindness that will make our lives richer, more imaginative and more fulfilled, less helplessly dependent upon external stimulation and more creatively self-sufficient.[30]

TO CREATE, TO DIE, TO CREATE AGAIN

'The fear of dying is often at the root of the fight against change'

[29] Epstein, M., *Going to Pieces without Falling Apart*, HarperCollins (1999).
[30] Paramananda, *Change Your Mind: A Practical Guide to Buddhist Meditation*, Windhorse (1996).

writes the Jungian analyst Rosemary Gordon.[31] Fearing death, seeing it as a threat to the ego's precariously balanced identity, we refuse to move, to change, to grow. Yet to refuse to change is itself to enter the living death of stagnation. Creativity – in technical and scientific achievement and in the service of relationship and personal growth, as much as in artistic work itself – depends upon a fluid interaction between the conscious and the unconscious, the very interaction that a determined insistence on the supremacy of ego control distorts and stifles. Creativity itself lives within the flux of the moment, within the willingness to die continually and to create once more from the ruins.

Gordon identifies four stages in the creative process. In the initial preparatory stage, skills are developed and resources accumulated for the task in mind, and the psyche is orientated towards mastering external reality. Then comes incubation: like the alchemist's immersion in the dark crucible of the *nigredo* or Dante's stumbling in the forbidding and dreary woods of mid life, incubation is a time of unconscious drifting when one becomes immersed in chaos and uncertainty, assailed by anxiety and in danger of losing touch with the initial creative resolve:

> It is at that stage that doubt and pain and anxiety and despair rack and torture him who would create. Should he flinch, seek refuge or attempt a short-cut he will either return to that which has already been and so enter upon the process of repetition, stagnation, putrefaction or petrification. In that case what he then produces will turn out to be banal, stereotyped or slick. Or he will lose his roots altogether, inflate and like a balloon, drift off into the air. It is during this stage of incubation that a seed may take root – but if it does it happens unseen, in the depths of the unconscious psyche, in the dark.

This is the state described by Keats as the basis of all creative work, which he named Negative Capability, 'that is, when man is capable of being in uncertainties, mysteries, doubts, without any irritable reaching after fact and reason.'[32]

---

[31] Gordon, R., *Dying and Creating*, Library of Analytical Psychology (1978).
[32] Letter to George and Thomas Keats, 21 December 1817.

Eventually, the organizing capacity of the unconscious psyche is vindicated. From chaos and not-knowing, if they can be tolerated long enough, arises the third stage: inspiration, the moment when an answer comes, as it were, from out of the blue. The moment of inspiration can be so suddenly illuminating that it seems as if it must have come from elsewhere – so we speak of the visitation of the muse, or of Divine Grace, and so Hermes, the messenger of the gods, suddenly appears to Calypso and asks her to release Odysseus from his weary years of imprisonment to her. The third stage may be marked by feelings of release, exuberance or even ecstasy, but then in the fourth stage of verification the ego regains control and embarks upon the work of critical examination, in which the inspired idea can be tested out, organized and given relevant form. Freed at last, Odysseus sets to work to build a new boat with his own hands in which he can set sail for Ithaca. After the years of confusion and paralysis, the final resolution of the *Odyssey* is set in motion and begins to gather momentum.

These four stages are more fluid and may, in practice, merge into each other or even run in parallel. But it can be seen that in the first stage of preparation and the fourth stage of verification, conscious discriminatory and organizing processes predominate, requiring discipline and persistence. But in the second and third stages of incubation and inspiration, the conscious ego must be willing to surrender control to unconscious processes, to contain them and to wait – to be able to manage disappointment and the ever-present fear of failure while remaining in a state of trust and openness. A sufficiently flexible ego is not threatened by the unconscious but is able to contain, nurture and finally to find ways of articulating its rich fantasy life and its fluid and shifting identifications.

Creative work demands a ruthlessness and a willingness to follow the voice of inspiration when it arises, as well as the willingness to be receptive and patient, to sit with difficulties and conflicts until they begin to resolve themselves, and to work through experiences at deeper and deeper levels. If the creative impulse is trusted, it will in due course find its own appropriate form. The space of creativity has been called the third space – located between the inner and outer worlds, it is informed by both. Holding reality steadily within its personal vision, creative work transforms and transcends it.

In creative work we have the opportunity to discover and to recreate our selves over and over, to track continuity while encountering and exploring new identities, as Rembrandt did in the extraordinary series of self-portraits which he began in his early twenties and continued painting up until his death forty years later. 'Over Rembrandt's last two self-portraits, both dated 1669, the year of his death, there hangs an air of painful self-knowledge ... [He seems] to be divesting himself of worldly pretensions and illusions' writes his biographer Simon Schama. It had been thirty years since Rembrandt had painted himself posing as the archetypal Renaissance poet and courtier. 'Now these vanities had quite fallen away ... this is the truth and Rembrandt's face is lit only by the illumination of his unsparing frankness.'[33] Caught in the compelling gaze of these last portraits, it is hard to turn away. Illuminated by self-knowledge, Rembrandt's gaze knows nowhere it will not go. It looks out with unshakeable and unsparing honesty and with a candid and all-encompassing compassion.

The encounter with death and the power of destruction lies at the heart of creativity and Rembrandt, in these last portraits, looks it straight in the eye. Not to turn away afraid but to continue such exploration, demands a certain faith that the power of destruction and no-meaning can be contained within a higher resolution, within a realization of ultimate meaning. 'All creation', writes Hanna Segal, 'is really a recreation of a once-loved and once whole, but now ... ruined internal world and self. It is when the world within us is destroyed, when it is dead and loveless, when our loved ones are in fragments and we ourselves are in helpless despair – it is then that we must recreate our world anew, reassemble the pieces, infuse life into dead fragments, recreate life.'[34]

---

[33] Schama, S., *Rembrandt's Eyes*, Penguin (1999).
[34] Segal, H., *The Work of Hanna Segal: A Kleinian Approach to Clinical Practice*, Free Association Books (1986).

BACK TO THE GARDEN

In 1941, my mother cycled fourteen miles from the Women's Auxiliary Air Force headquarters where she was stationed into Coventry city centre, bouncing down roads gutted with potholes and strewn with rubble, through neighbourhoods unrecognizably flattened, past houses whose sides had been torn off by bombs, pictures and clocks still hanging on walls blackened by fire and opened to the wind and rain. My mother was peddling as fast as she could, so as to get to one of the few cinemas left standing in Coventry in time for the matinee performance of a new film, *Gone with the Wind*. She arrived just in time and – like millions of other women that year whose men were fighting overseas or were already dead, and who lived on a daily basis with rationing, bombing, constant upheaval and the ever-present threat of invasion and defeat by the Germans – thrilled to the sight of Scarlett returning to Tara just before the intermission, to fall on the ground and stuff soil and radishes into her starving mouth then stand, fist clenched before a Technicolor sunset, to declare that as God was her witness she would never be hungry again.

Scarlett has been sustained on her journey through the ravaged Georgian night, in the wake of the invading Yankee army, by her vision of a safe haven back home at Tara – only to walk through the door to find her mother dead, her father insane and the house ransacked. But after her first despair, Scarlett rallies her ingenuity and courage and embarks upon the work of restoring Tara to life. In doing so she recovers her own strength. And at the end of Margaret Mitchell's book, as Rhett famously exits not giving a damn, Scarlett's first thoughts are of returning once more to Tara:

> She had gone back to Tara once in fear and defeat and she had emerged from its sheltering arms strong and armed for victory . . . All she wanted was a breathing space in which to hurt, a quiet place to lick her wounds, a haven in which to plan her campaign. She thought of Tara, and it was as if a gentle, cool hand were stealing over her heart. She could see the white house gleaming welcome to her through the reddening autumn leaves, feel the quiet hush of the country twilight coming down over her like a benediction, feel the dews falling on the

acres of green bushes starred with fleecy white, see the raw colour of the red earth and the dismal dark beauty of the pines on the rolling hills.[35]

At times of threat and change, we are drawn instinctively to search for places of safety in which to heal and to become reconstituted: this need structures our unconscious fantasies and cultural myths at all levels. The Oscar for Best Film awarded by an America teetering on the brink of war to *Gone with the Wind* was won nearly sixty years later by *The English Patient*, another film whose emotional centre is a woman alone in a garden, beyond the walls of which a savage war – the same war which my mother had experienced at first hand – collapses into its own destruction. The Canadian nurse Hana coaxes tomato plants and lettuce seedlings out of the ravaged, shell-shocked earth of a ruined Tuscan villa and nurses Almasy, the English patient. Almasy is too damaged and burnt to survive the war but Hana's devotion creates a quiet place for him to die in his own time, and a place for new love to grow between herself and Kip, the Sikh sapper whose job it is to sweep the land for mines and make it safe again.

I'm riding my wooden tricycle down the garden path. Rhubarb leaves tower above me. The path goes on for ever...

I'm lying in a meadow looking at the sky. The angry voices back in the house echo in my mind but here I feel the firmness of the earth beneath my back and the warmth of the sun on my face and smell the meadow grass, and come back to myself. I am hidden from view, I am safe for ever...

Many people have very early memories of being by themselves in a garden. Early memories – like the creation myth itself – seem to naturally unfold in gardens, perhaps because gardens are a space beyond the domestic world our parents construct and control, beyond their prying eyes yet still enclosed within their protection. Often, gardens are the first places we explore by ourselves. Self-awareness arrives with the bite of an apple: here, perhaps for the first time, we learn to be alone. Our lives begin in gardens and often end in them, in the stillness of a memorial

---

[35] Mitchell, M., *Gone with the Wind*, Macmillan (1941).

garden or in a country churchyard as food for worms, feeding the earth's infinite capacity for self-renewal.

Nature is resilient, and endlessly forgiving. 'Nature', wrote Wordsworth in 'Tintern Abbey', 'never did betray the heart that loved her'. In 1798, the year that Wordsworth wrote these words, betrayal may have been much on his mind – his own betrayal of those who had depended upon him, as well as the betrayal by others of those ideals in which he had placed his trust. Though still in 1798 a relatively young man, Wordsworth had packed more into the previous five years than most people do in a lifetime. On a walking tour in France in his early twenties, he had been seduced by the romance of the French Revolution and had begun a relationship with a Frenchwoman, Annette Vallon, by whom he had a daughter, Caroline. But their differing religions, poverty and the outbreak of war between France and England had eventually forced Wordsworth to return to England alone. Tormented perhaps by his own faithlessness, by his loneliness, by his lack of recognition and direction and by his alienation from a country and a government whose ruling values he did not share, Wordsworth watched helplessly as the later excesses of the French Revolution shattered his ideals and turned his early admiration to revulsion and impotent despair.

Wordsworth seems, during this dark time, to have suffered a breakdown. But eventually he was able to get back on his feet and turn once more to poetry. On a visit to Shirehampton he crossed the Severn by ferry and walked with his sister Dorothy up the Wye Valley, retracing the steps he had taken five years before upon his return from France, when he had bounded over the mountains

> ... more like a man
> Flying from something that he dreads, than one
> Who sought the thing he loved.

Wordsworth's dark night of the soul had left him a sadder and wiser man. The aching joys and dizzy raptures of youth were no more, but in their loss, he wrote that he had found abundant recompense, for he had learnt to hear

The still, sad music of humanity,
Not harsh nor grating, though of ample power
To chasten and subdue. And I have felt
A presence that disturbs me with the joy
Of elevated thoughts; a sense sublime
Of something far more deeply interfused,
Whose dwelling is the light of setting suns,
And the round ocean, and the living air,
And the blue sky, and in the mind of man,
A motion and a spirit, that impels
All thinking things, all objects of all thought,
And rolls through all things...[36]

Wordsworth's great poem, both elegy and joyful affirmation, is the statement of a mind moving through despair towards regeneration and maturity while gathering from its past, in quiet present reflection, the energy it needs to move forward into its future. The tranquil restoration that Wordsworth feels beside the Wye's steep cliffs inform those feelings and beliefs that he now asserts and records with the moral confidence which will sustain him through a long and fruitful life:[37] the value of kindness, the need to cultivate a loving bond with all living beings and the willingness to surrender and to become at one with the deeper movement of nature.

---

[36] Wordsworth, W., 'Lines Composed a Few Miles above Tintern Abbey, on Revisiting the Banks of the Wye during a Tour' in Wordsworth, W. and Coleridge, S. T., *Lyrical Ballads*, Methuen (1971).

[37] Wordsworth was unusual, in that he went through the experience of disillusionment, despair and creative regeneration that is so typical of mid-life crisis at a particularly young age: he was only 28 when he wrote *Tintern Abbey*. Seven years later, in 1805, he published *The Prelude*, his great reflective poem on the unfolding of the human mind. It is generally agreed that there was subsequently a falling-off in the quality of his creative output, but the Victorians rated him highly and made him Poet Laureate in 1843. He lived on a further seven years to die in 1850 at the age of 80.

11

Meaning

Holding to nothing whatever

From the Buddhist *Heart Sutra*

The shouts of swearing and insult, the clash of weapons and the screams of the wounded have died away, and in the silence after the last battle Arthur, aching from his wounds, gazes along the bloodstained shoreline. A thick, chilly white mist had crept inland at the beginning of the battle, half-blinding the soldiers – they had slaughtered each other in an orgy of violence, fear and confusion, friend killing friend, the faces of old ghosts floating before their eyes as they fought. But now a northerly wind arises, and blows the mist away. Arthur, as he gazes, hears no cries and sees no movement except for the waves breaking among the lifeless faces at the water's edge, swaying limp hands, tumbling the helmets of the dead.

Tennyson's elaboration of the myth of King Arthur and Camelot tells how Arthur was betrayed by the adulterous liaison between his wife Guinevere and his friend Lancelot, and by the treachery of his own son Mordred, leading to the splitting and collapse of the chivalrous ideal of Camelot.[1] Arthur declared war upon his own people, and his forces drove Mordred's army westwards towards this final internecine confrontation at the edge of the sea. But now the fighting is over. All Arthur's men but one are dead, and Arthur himself has been fatally wounded as he killed Mordred in hand-to-hand combat. Staring at the silent scene, Arthur asks Bedevere – his first anointed and now last remaining knight – to lift him upon his shoulders. Stumbling under the king's weight through this landscape of chaos and destruction, Bedevere carries Arthur to a ruined chapel which lies between the sea and a lake, where he places him down gently.

Arthur knows he does not have long left to live. He tells Bedevere to take his sword, Excalibur, and to throw it with all his strength as far as he can into the lake. But having descended to the lakeside and raised the sword in obedience, Bedevere's mind falters and divides in doubt, and instead he hides the sword in the reeds at the water's edge. Then, returning to Arthur, he tells him that he has done as he asked. Arthur, faint and pale, curses him and sends him out again; again at the water's edge, lifting the sword from the reeds, Bedevere is dazzled by its glittering beauty and its exquisitely worked, bejewelled hilt. To lose the sword at this critical moment would mean the loss for ever of all proof Camelot had existed, and he reasons to himself that the king must be delirious and does not know what he is saying. Again he conceals the sword and goes back and lies to Arthur who, half-rising, threatens to kill him with his own hands unless this time he keeps his word. Bedevere runs from the chapel and leaps down the ridges to the waterside. Reaching among the bulrush beds, this time without thinking, he lifts the sword, turns and throws it. The sword cartwheels through the air, and as it reaches the surface of the lake a hand clothed in white satin reaches up from the water to catch it, brandishes it three times and draws it beneath.

Arthur receives the news breathing heavily and asks Bedevere to brace himself once more to take his weight and carry him

---

[1] In 'The Passing of Arthur' (1869) from *Idylls of the King* (Macmillan, 1982), which Tennyson based on Thomas Malory's fifteenth-century prose work *Le Morte d'Arthur*

down to the water before he dies, as his wound is growing cold. As they reach the water's edge, a dark funeral barge emerges out of the gloom, bearing three black-robed wailing queens who receive the body of the dying king. In anguish, Bedevere asks Arthur what will become of him. Slowly, between laboured breaths, Arthur tells him that the old order must change and give way to the new, and to trust that God fulfils himself in many ways. He tells Bedevere to comfort himself and not to underestimate the power of prayer, and bids him farewell. The barge casts off along the water to bear the dying king to Avalon; it is swallowed by the mist, and the wailing dies away. In the stillness of the winter dawn, Bedevere slowly and laboriously climbs back up the crag. Turning, he strains his eyes beneath his hand to catch a last glimpse of the disappearing barge as the new sun rises, bringing with it a new year.

Hamburg, 1915. A toddler develops a new habit of grabbing any small objects he can and throwing them under a bed or into dark corners – much to the annoyance of his family and their maidservant, who are constantly on their knees searching for items the boy has flung away. The child has a close and loving relationship with his mother Sophie who, unusually among middle-class families, looks after him herself. He also has a special toy, a bobbin with a string attached to it. When Sophie goes out he does not protest or cling to her, but instead invents a new game, holding the reel by the end of its string and throwing it over the edge of his curtained cot so that it disappears. This throwing is accompanied by the same loud, long-drawn-out '*o-o-o-o*' of interest and satisfaction that accompanied the throwing of the other objects. Then the bobbin is reeled back, its reappearance hailed joyfully – '*da*' 'there'.

The boy's grandfather, Sigmund Freud, is in Hamburg for a few weeks to visit Sophie, his favourite daughter, and to see his first grandson. He agrees with Sophie that the child's *o-o-o-o* sound seems to be an attempt at the word *fort* ('gone' in English). *Fort – da* was thus 'the complete game – disappearance and return'.[2] At

---

[2] Freud, S., 'Beyond the Pleasure Principle' (1920), *Penguin Freud Library* 11.

one level, Freud can explain the game in terms of the boy's attempt, through repetition in play, to gain mastery of an unpleasant event (his mother leaving him) over which he had in reality no control. But Freud also notices something more – the boy stages the *fort* or throwing part of the game far more often than the *da*, or return part, although he certainly takes more pleasure in the return than in the disappearance.

Five years later, Freud is writing his paper *Beyond the Pleasure Principle* and struggling in his own mind both to formulate his new ideas about life and death and to come to terms with recent bereavements of his own – including the sudden death of Sophie herself from pneumonia at the age of twenty-six. As he writes, his thoughts turn to the game he had witnessed in her house. Why, wonders Freud, had his grandson preferred the throwing part of the game to the reunion? It was perhaps related, he speculates, 'to the child's great cultural achievement ... the renunciation of instinctual satisfaction which he had made in allowing his mother to go away without protesting'. In the space created by her absence – a space in which this securely attached child had not suffered the terror of abandonment – the child had been able to discover his own creative impulse and allow himself to be consoled by it. Freud, foundering now in his own grief, is drawn towards noticing how higher levels of integration and creativity seem to emerge from the void created by loss. For Freud's grandson struggling with the departure of his mother – as for Bedevere struggling with the death of his king and the collapse of the ideals by which he has lived – letting go is an experiment with loss, an investment in an unknown future.

Facing the suffering that comes in the wake of change and loss, we have two options. In our minds, we can cling desperately to what is slipping out of our lives – but harbouring these damaged, dying or rejecting others within us may lead to worse depression. Or, taking courage, we can let go – as Bedevere does when he overcomes his doubts and throws Excalibur into the void, as Freud's grandson does with his bobbin, and as Odysseus does when he launches himself, yet again, into the unknown of another sea voyage.

MID LIFE: THE CRISIS OF MEANING

To gain something new, we must be willing to create a space by letting go of what we have previously possessed, and mid-life crisis calls us – often in surprising ways – to do just this. But letting go is a doubtful pleasure at best, and may seem to the frightened ego like death itself. It is made more difficult still within a culture which endorses only those material values – attracting sexual partners, raising children, establishing a secure financial footing and proving ourselves through work – which by mid life are beginning to feel cramping and confining. If we let go of them, what else is there to live by? Our economic systems encourage us to see ourselves as amoral competitive agents, each for himself, and we have learnt to accept an evolutionary view of ourselves as organisms hijacked by the selfish gene, prepro-grammed to compete relentlessly for environmental resources and to reproduce ourselves in a value-free universe, endlessly consolidating our own status at others' expense, at whatever cost.[3]

But mid life brings with if the end of reproductive life. After it, the biological imperative to propagate the species has scant use for us, and ideologies that see humanity solely in terms of our productive and reproductive functions have little to say about the purpose and meaning of the second half of life, or about what – as we age – we should consider a life worth living and values worth living by. If life has no purpose beyond the fulfilment of material and reproductive aims, why are we the only species who have developed a programmed end to our fertility – often, today, continuing to live as long after the end of our fertility as we did before? Far more people now live into old age than ever before, as scientific and health care advances push average mortality rates back further and further – making the issue of the purpose and value of the many decades of active life remaining after mid life a more pressing question for increasing numbers of us.

Living into one's seventies, eighties or even nineties is not, in

---

[3]   Dawkins, R., *The Selfish Gene*, Oxford University Press (1976).

fact, a recent phenomenon. Though *average* life expectancy at birth is now higher than ever and steadily increasing, *absolute* life expectancy (the full span of human life if disease or accident do not intervene to curtail it) has remained relatively constant for the last three millennia, at about 120 years. In the past, average life expectancy at birth was distorted (as it is still is in most third-world countries) by high rates of mortality in infancy and a further statistical bulge in the twenties and thirties due to female deaths in childbirth and male deaths in war. Childhood and early adulthood were dangerous businesses, but those who succeeded in navigating them – with the robust immune systems, strong constitutions and well-honed survival skills implied by this achievement – could reasonably anticipate living on almost as long as we can today: in 1841, the year that records began, life expectancy at birth was 40 years for men and 42 years for women (compared to 74 and 79 years respectively today). But men and women who had already reached 45 could, in 1841, expect to live until 68 and 69 respectively (76 and 81 respectively today).[4] In other words, the difference between life expectancy at birth in the past compared to today is enormous – over 30 years – but by age 45, not very much at all. Dante wrote the *Divine Comedy* towards the end of his life, but located the spiritual crisis and journey which it describes as having happened to him in his mid-to-late thirties, which – just as we would now – he refers to as his mid life.

In evolutionary terms, why has our great longevity been selected for? Is there, in fact, an in-built developmental programme for the second half of life – a potential which, if we are not to fall back into a sense of despair and redundancy, we must learn to identify and find ways of realizing? Elephant herds prosper best when they are led by an elderly matriarch who passes on her survival skills and the encyclopaedic memory-based knowledge of her environment to the younger adults around her. In primitive human societies, older humans – freed from the rigours of childbearing, the daily grind of labour and the perils of

---

4 Figures from the Office for National Statistics, supplied by the Government Actuary's department.

hunting and making war – become agents for transmission to the young of their survival skills, and also of those cultural and spiritual values which have come to distinguish humans uniquely from all other species. 'A human being would certainly not grow to be seventy or eighty years old if this longevity had no meaning for the species to which he belonged' wrote Jung in the years after the resolution of his own extensive mid-life crisis.[5] 'The afternoon of human life must also have a significance of its own and cannot be merely a pitiful appendage to life's morning.' He locates the significance of the first half of life as lying in nature, not culture. 'In youth, we value achievement, usefulness and so on – but these ideals cannot guide us in the development of that wider consciousness to which we give the name of culture; and we may be wrong to think they will be of much use at all to us as we pass beyond forty ... Culture lies beyond the purpose of nature. Could by any chance the guardianship of cultural and religious heritage be the meaning and purpose of the second half of life?'

Jung is suggesting that the values of youth will betray us if we continue to follow them blindly as we grow older; that a life with direction is better, richer and healthier than one that is directionless; and that from mid life onwards, concern with transcendent values is likely to become a central preoccupation in our lives, however it may be disguised. In another paper written around the same time, he says he has come to the conclusion that the problems of all the patients he had treated in the second half of life related, in the last resort, to their need to discover a religious attitude.[6] But what is a religious attitude? Jung places the search for internal wholeness and integration at the heart of it – yet if there is nothing more, this search runs the danger of becoming self-referential and sterile, while the notion of submission to any ideology, religious or otherwise, will ring warning bells in many ears – especially when we are vague (as we so often are) about the values that such submission might imply. The blankness which we feel about what a life not focused solely

---

[5] Jung, C. G., 'The stages of life' (1930–1) in *Modern Man in Search of a Soul*, Routledge (1984).

[6] Jung, C. G., 'Psychotherapists or the clergy', *Collected Works*, Vol. 11, Routledge (1970).

around earning and child-rearing might have to offer us – and others – as we grow older is a problem which has gone hand in hand with the failure of religion itself as a force in the world in which we live.

THE FAILURE OF RELIGION

How did religion first become established within human society? Through prehistoric times, the steady increase in the size of our brains enabled us to invent and begin to use tools and to become better at manipulating external reality, setting us upon the path towards civilization. But this enlarging mental capacity also gave us something else that no animal had ever had before – a dawning awareness of the inevitability of death. This in its turn brought about an existential anxiety which could all too easily degenerate into depression, nihilism and a crippling sense of futility. Expanding human consciousness caused this problem: but it was also equal to finding at least a partial solution to it, in the first stirrings of human religious sensibility. Cultural and religious rituals began to evolve, mediating the fear of mortality by setting it within an overarching context which both reiterated the value of human life and dignified death. The first burials by humans of their dead – probably about 100,000 years ago – was as significant a leap forward in human consciousness as the discovery of fire or the first use of tools.

What is the difference, asks Symington, between a society that tosses a body to one side to rot or be devoured by scavengers, and one which pays respect to the dead body through religious ceremonial?[7] Burial, he suggests, signifies that the individual who has died is recognized as an 'I' by those who survive him or her, and continues to live on in their minds. 'This realisation articulates thought; it is the object of the thought. The transition from feeling to thought occurs at this point' – and with it the birth of the *representational* or symbolic self, and the mythology of a soul that survives death. Over time, burial of the

---

[7] Symington, N., *Emotion and Spirit*, Karnac (1998).

dead, the work of mourning and the preservation of human meaning in the face of death – through transmission to succeeding generations in ritual and symbolic form – came to define an essential role for those elders who had survived into the second half of life.

The dawning of consciousness also brought with it a greater understanding of cause and effect, and of human intentionality – *I can think something and make it happen*. But this awareness, too, brought fear. As they became aware of the power of intention, early peoples projected their own mental states into the gods they worshipped. They began to see cosmic or divine intentionality at work in every event, from the death of a mother in childbirth to the loss of the harvest through late rains, while the mentalities of the gods they attempted to please and placate mirrored their own, being quarrelsome, retaliatory and heavily conditioned by tribal loyalties. These are the gods who haunt the fringes of the *Odyssey* as unconsciously projected aspects of its human protagonists – mischievous and jealous spirits who must be continually appeased and propitiated by placatory rituals and sacrifices, whose constant meddling ensures that the humans never have to take full responsibility for their own intentions. In Judaeo-Christian lore these gods evolve into an authoritarian father god, unquestioning submission to whose arbitrary will – as interpreted by his priests – becomes the greatest of all possible goods.

The tribe who worshipped a god or spirit in a sense saw themselves as owning it – and so as being entitled to receive its special favours in preference, say, to their rivals on the other side of the river. In an unconscious reflection of family structure, this dependence upon the parent-god leads to explosions of sibling rivalry, with each tribe jealously demanding recognition, through their own practices and rituals, of their status as the only true believers. In tribal or ethnic religion, gods are adored with the passion of self-interest as idealized extensions of oneself or one's own group, while aggression and hatred are split off and directed towards outsiders. Religious ideologies first evolved not to mitigate this dynamic but to justify it – proving, to the believer's own satisfaction, that outsiders are as deeply wrong as one knows oneself to be right. The devaluation or persecution of the outsider becomes not only justifiable but divinely sanctioned.

Religious belief initially took hold in agrarian and mainly static societies, fuelled by helplessness and fear in the face of the forces of nature beyond human control. Then, in 800–200 BC, human consciousness went through another great upheaval. The Buddha in India, Isaiah and the Hebrew prophets in the Middle East, Confucius and Lao Tzu in China, and the Iranian sage Zoroaster, as well as the Greek civilization which gave birth to Homer, Pythagoras, Socrates and Plato, all belong to this period, called the Axial Age because of its pivotal importance in human development.[8] As societies metamorphosed from agrarian to trading economies and surpluses enabled a new educated elite to become established in the developing centres of civilization, new religious and philosophical attitudes started to emerge which reflected the growing importance of the individual and of individual consciousness. Sacred truth began to be seen as something that must be actively sought rather than passively received, and people became emboldened to question and to reflect upon their own experiences: 'The new religions sought inner depth rather than magical control. The sages were no longer content with external conformity but were aware of the profound psychic inwardness that precedes action. Crucial was the desire to bring unconscious forces and dimly perceived truths into the light of day.'[9]

The revolutionary awareness of the possibilities of individual freedom, thought and choice were central to the Axial Age. But its great thinkers also pointed out the dangers of individualism – of unrestrained competitiveness and greed, and of the anxiety and cruelty which internal insecurities could generate. In their different ways they warned against unbridled egotism and stressed the importance of ethical development as a function of personal freedom. In their thinking, the primitive need to propitiate a cruel parent-god began to evolve into faith in one's felt potential to mature and to actualize the best within oneself.

---

[8] Jaspers, K., *The Origin and Goal of History*, tr. Bullock, M., Routledge (1953).

[9] Armstrong, K., *Buddha*, Weidenfeld and Nicolson (2000).

This more mature religious thinking was less credulous of superstition and magic, emphasizing the possibility of self-transcendence through one's own efforts. It began to be recognized that it was possible to purify emotions by systematically detaching them from baser instincts, and from the egotistical grasping and attachments that lead to self-deception. The importance of learning to know – and to master – oneself was emphasized, along with the value of developing an ethical, compassionate attitude capable ultimately of transcending the limitations of dualistic ways of thinking. The paranoid anxiety and projective mechanisms of primitive religion – the need to make others wrong so that one can be right – begin to give way to an awareness of one's kinship with other beings, concern for their suffering and, ultimately, a loosening and dissolution of the ego boundaries themselves.

In mature religion, the emphasis changes from fear of punishment (*'for I the Lord thy God am a jealous God, visiting the iniquity of the fathers upon the children unto the third and fourth generation of them that hate me'*[10]) to a faith in the transformative power of love. The expectation of being scrutinized and judged by an external divine authority turns to an emphasis on self-scrutiny, personal responsibility and the higher integration of internal processes. With Socrates saying that it is better to suffer wrong than to do wrong, we have for the first time the notion that the quality of one's inner life may matter more than anything.[11] Despite the loneliness and internal struggles which such a path may entail, concern with the quality of emotional life brings its own rewards. While hatred and divisiveness lead to internal impoverishment and the exploitation of others to loneliness and fear of retaliation, generosity and love lead to psychic enrichment: 'Hate is not conquered by hate: hate is conquered by love. This is a law eternal . . . the man who does good is happy in [this world and the next].'[12]

Moral and spiritual leaders such as Jesus, Socrates and the Buddha did not seek to found new religions but to transform

---

[10] Exodus, 20:5
[11] Plato, *Gorgias*, Complete Works, Hackett (1997).
[12] *Dhammapada*, tr. Mascaro, J., Penguin (1973).

existing tradition, through teaching the development of consciousness. But their hard questions did not always go down well. They made people uncomfortable, threatening their attachments and the ways they preferred to see themselves – two out of these three eventually ended up meeting their deaths at the hands of those they had sought to enlighten. In general, it is hard to escape the conclusion that most religions – despite the efforts of their great reformers – have harboured a regressive tendency to revert back to the tribal mentality of primitive religion, mired in fear, appeasement rituals and superstition. Monotheistic Western religion has always struggled (not particularly successfully) to emerge from its own beginnings – the dominance of tribal mentality over the stirrings of individual awareness, and the infantilization of the self through submission to a divine other who will, in return for unquestioning obedience, protect and save his chosen people – while conveniently relieving them of the burden of growing up.

Today, many people find little direct spiritual experience in conventional religion. More often it seems like a spent social force, vaguely well-meaning yet fatally linked to traditional conservative values based on deference to paternal authority. But it continues nevertheless to influence our value systems, in the belief, for example, that we as humans have a right – surely god-given – to exploit and harm animals of other species and the ecosystem of our fragile planet itself without constraint; and in our over-valuation of compliance (now transferred from a religious to an economic God) and our habit of structuring our lives in terms of rewards for obedient behaviour – the drink at the end of the working day, the holiday at the end of the working year, the cottage at the end of the working life – instead of living as if we were responsible, each day we live, for our own fulfilment.

Modern psychology, following on from Freud,[13] has developed a sophisticated and credible understanding of the extent to which religions have unconsciously tended to correspond with

---

[13] Freud, S., 'Totem and Taboo' (1913) and 'Moses and Monotheism' (1939), in *Penguin Freud Library* 13.

the fantasies of infantile life, and in doing so has devastatingly robbed them of their authority. At the same time, scientific understanding has made us feel more in charge of our destinies than ever before, and has exposed as myth those creation stories which were the foundations of the concrete beliefs of mono-theistic faiths. Nevertheless, the dawning awareness of mortality and the reorientation of our internal energies away from reproductive and material concerns mean that as we reach mid life the need to find spiritual meaning may exert as strong a pull upon our minds as it did upon our forebears – albeit a pull that is more perplexing and problematic. It may be that this need for spiritual meaning is innate – and that it drives the human developmental programme after mid life as much as the need to mate, to procreate and to establish status through work drive it beforehand. Religion may have failed us, but like jilted lovers who can't take no for an answer, many of us still search for it, sometimes idly, sometimes compulsively – after sex and health, religion is the most popular topic of Internet searches.

In some parts of the world, fundamentalism has taken hold as a way of filling the void left by the collapse of traditional belief. Characterized by the view that humankind is inherently sinful and will only be saved by a concrete belief in the literal truth of the holy writings. Fundamentalism in any religion is a reactive force which holds out the offer of salvation from the uncertainties, anxieties and conflicts inherent in the human maturational process, by taking a defensive posture against mental empathy and imagination.[14] It offers absolute certainties, which it achieves through the denial of scientific truth and through the use of those splitting and projective mechanisms which must be endlessly renewed by finding new enemies to condemn or convert.

Fundamentalism requires belief at the expense of reason and imagination; at the other end of the spectrum is that dabbling in new age spirituality which demands no particular belief at all, so commending itself to the terminally uncommitted. Here the

---

[14] Brooke, R., 'Emissaries from the underworld: psychotherapy's challenge to Christian fundamentalism' in Young-Eisendrath, P. and Miller, M. E. (eds), *The Psychology of Mature Spirituality*, Routledge (2000).

consumer is queen, as she wheels her trolley round the towering pick-and-mix displays of Zen aesthetics, feelgood Christianity, astrology, shamans, tree worship, reincarnation, clairvoyance, scented candles and Feng Shui interior design. Here – adeptly dodging whatever displeases her senses, liberated from inconvenient adherence to any ethical framework and from any tedious process of self-examination – she is free to live from moment to moment with a whimsical vagueness about the real demands and challenges of spiritual growth.

But finding new products and experiences to consume is not the same as finding a context within which to live. And without one, life – as we reach and pass forty – is likely to become more difficult, with our individual time-limited existences becoming overburdened by our need for them to carry more significance than we know (in our hearts) that they can. Without a spiritual context to mediate it, the fear of death – and beyond that, of meaninglessness – threatens to become overwhelming. We can only repress it, taking refuge in decreasingly successful rituals of competitiveness, wealth accumulation and drug and drink dependency until the only refuge left is the numbness of depression. Living as we do within a culture that provides us with no language in which to express our existential and spiritual aspirations and no framework within which to explore and fulfil them, how is it possible – without turning back from the hard-won gains of mature discernment, and infantilizing ourselves once more – to find a spiritual meaning that will be worth committing to?

For life's core meaning to be reconstructed, the willingness not to know already – and the panicked feelings that go with it – must be tolerated. Then, the question of spiritual growth can be approached. To sponsor this inner growth, two things are necessary. The first, with which the last chapter was concerned, is the need for periods of solitude and contemplation. The second is the need to find a language with which to begin to explore and to tease out a spiritual context capable of containing our individual lives. When the words and stories we have used to describe who we are and what is important to us start to lose their conviction, we start groping to find new ways of talking about ourselves. At mid life, the most mundane worries that draw people to begin searching and questioning – the persistent headaches, the partner who doesn't understand, the compulsive working, the empty feeling inside – may all be manifestations of a dawning existential concern for which we can find no language. Making sense of one's place in the world is an existential issue which demands to find ways of establishing and articulating itself in the wider interpersonal dimension, through language and through the forms of self-exploration and self-expression to which language gives birth. Thoughts cannot become thinkable until there is a language available in which they can be articulated:[15] until then the impulses behind them lurk in the unconscious, giving rise to obsessional symptoms, irritable moods, incomprehensible dreams and problems of indigestion.

We have lost the ability to speak, and to hear, a religious language – lost the possibility of exploration and communication within a shared linguistic structure with sufficient power, authority and beauty to mediate and amplify our deepest existential strivings and to return them to us understood and valued. So, mid-life crisis now draws us towards affairs, where once it drew us towards monasteries: the failure of religious belief has left us with no language other than the language of sexual relationship to use as a way of giving shape to and validating internal feelings. At least falling in love enables us to insert ourselves into a pre-existing – albeit tiresomely clichéd – syntax of romantic phrases, songs, poems, moods and so on. If I only allow myself to take my inner life seriously when I fall in love, then it stands to reason that if I do want to start to take myself more seriously – to explore and to reflect upon my inner life and the state of my soul – I'll have to fall in love. So sexual love ends up having to carry the weight of all the inner needs which other cultures define and mediate in more existential or spiritual terms. Not surprisingly, it often collapses under the strain.

This over-idealization and overburdening of sexual relationship – which leads so many people into such deep unhappiness – stems from our alienation from the traditions of the past. Are

---

[15] Freud, S., 'The Unconscious' (1915), in *Penguin Freud Library* 11.

we, wonders Martin Buber, really so rich that we can dispense with tradition?[16] Perhaps the problem is not so much with the religious myths of the past themselves as with how we hold them. Myths present us with archetypal models, paradigms for the development of the human spirit. But conventional religion has encouraged us to objectify these myths and in doing so, to distance ourselves from them. It is easier to invent gods in our own image and fall down and worship them from a personally unthreatening distance – or to loftily dismiss them as fairy stories – than to engage and identify with the nature of the existential struggles that the great religious myths portray. Yet myth, writes Campbell:

> is the secret opening through which the inexhaustible energies of the cosmos pour into human cultural manifestation . . . it has always been the prime function of mythology and rite to supply the symbols that carry the human spirit forward, in counteraction to those other constant human fantasies that tend to tie it back. In fact, it may well be that the very high incidence of neuroticism among ourselves follows from the decline among us of such effective spiritual aid.[17]

Narrative gives logic and structure to the raw material of our lives, making them manageable and then meaningful. From the first glimmerings of consciousness, it is for plot, for story, that we hunger, for the chance to impose meaning on chaos, to engage in imagination as the protagonists – rather than the victims – of our own lives. And in the end, our mental health and happiness may depend upon the quality of the stories we tell ourselves about ourselves, and whether these stories are brutal, chaotic, banal or illuminated by transcendental understanding. The stories of Jesus, the Buddha, Odysseus and Penelope, or Oedipus, do not provide easy answers to the existential problems with which we struggle at mid life. But imaginatively engaging with them at a deep level may enable us to find a language in which we can begin to identify and to articulate our own existential struggles and longings.

---

[16] Buber, M., *I and Thou*, tr. Kaufmann, W., Touchstone (1996).
[17] Campbell, J., *The Hero with a Thousand Faces*, Fontana (1993).

Religion itself was defined by Erich Fromm as any group-shared system of thought and action which gives the individual a frame of orientation to the world and an object of devotion. There is, as he observes, no culture of the past, and could probably be no culture in the future, which does not have religion in this sense.[18] In this most inclusive sense, our religions are the systems of thought we use to make sense of the world and to create order and value out of its raw material. The objects of our religious devotion may be trees or ancestral gods, money, family or the body beautiful, while our value systems may be pragmatic and materialist, based around a narrowly defined self-interest, or else authoritarian and punitive, or chaotic and random. Our religions may be static or dynamic, self-justifying or self-transformative. As we reach mid life, the issue is whether the religion to which we have subscribed still serves our changing needs. The greatest – and in the end, the most helpful – myths and religions are informed by their own compelling internal logic, profound narratives of doubt, disillusionment and trial, of self-transcendence and ultimate redemption.

As we reach mid life, the need to find spiritual comfort and spiritual meaning – to find a personally transcendental narrative by which to live – is expressed in the quickening of a sense of awe and reverence in the presence of art and the beauty of nature; in a deeper concern with the quality of emotional life; in a more profound awareness of our connectedness with others; and in an increasing apprehension that all actions have consequences and that – if we live long enough – we will reap what we sow. The passing of time brings the longing to forgive and to find forgiveness, to pursue reconciliation rather than letting life be wasted in an endless cycle of competition, hate and retaliation; and to find a larger context in which to come to terms with transience, with loss, with the meaning of life and, ultimately, with one's own mortality.

The longing that dare not speak its name, which assails us so powerfully at mid life, is the longing to find a spiritual context that will be capable of dissolving our anxieties, integrating our

---

[18] Fromm, E., *Psychoanalysis and Religion*, Yale University Press (1978).

energies, transcending our egotism and endowing our lives with meaning – without, at the same time, insulting our intelligence. If we can find no form for the expression of these inchoate, unarticulated longings, they may falter and collapse under their own weight. Then, falling into existential anxiety, we turn away from our own deepest needs with anger or cynicism and give up the search, reverting back to the worn habits of first adulthood or shrinking in on ourselves in depression. But if we are able instead to stay with this anxiety we may become able, eventually, to break through to a new understanding.

A FAITH TO LIVE BY

'The courage to be', writes Paul Tillich, 'is rooted in the God who appears when God has disappeared in the anxiety of doubt.'[19] Tillich, a German-American Harvard theologian, took a dim view of the various religious revivals of twentieth-century America, which he saw as desperate and mainly futile attempts to regain past certainties. We have learnt to work so hard and play so hard, says Tillich, not because we are more industrious or more playful than our ancestors, but because we are so much more afraid of what will happen when we stop.

For Tillich, the anxiety of doubt is a state of affairs to be embraced. The new 'comes only in the moment when the old becomes visible as old and tragic and dying, and when no way out is seen. We live in such a moment; such a moment is our situation.' Faith is what we discover in the midst of suffering – love in the face of hate, good in the face of evil, courage in the face of despair. Tillich's God is a cosmic force above the God of patriarchal theism, present yet hidden in every divine or human encounter. His courage is a willingness to participate in that which transcends the self, an affirmation of being that does not avoid or deny non-being but includes it. Within this willingness, self-love and love of others are interdependent – just as selfishness and abuse of others are interdependent.

---

[19] Tillich, P., *The Courage to Be*, Yale University Press (2000).

The Buddha spent his early years living in a palace under his father's protection. He was drawn towards the spiritual life when one day he saw – as if for the first time – an old man, then an invalid, and finally a corpse being carried on a stretcher to the burning ground. Realizing at that moment that no amount of luxury and protection could prevent these fates befalling him as well, he went forth to seek a way of living that was capable of containing the reality of suffering, ageing and loss, while at the same time transcending it.[20] More usually, we try to avoid suffering: whatever faith we have is threatened, or shattered, by it. Yet doubt, for Tillich, is the condition of all real spiritual life: the crisis of doubt and the anxiety that follows it turns us either towards despair – the despair of depression which avoids non-being because it avoids being also – or towards the courage to live.

We have had to learn to live in a world which has largely lost its faith in progress as an automatic good, within a universe which no longer revolves around us and which has no known limits and no obvious meaning. As we grow older we start to think more about such things; an existential anxiety creeps over us. We try to stifle it with the use of drugs, sex, overwork and so on – by becoming self-absorbed or self-alienated, an object in a world of objects, a means in the service of means. But this anxiety can never entirely be dispelled. If we cannot come to terms with it, we fall into depression. Alternatively – looking it right in the face – we can choose to live, to participate.

'In man, nothing is "merely biological" as nothing is "merely spiritual"' says Tillich. 'Every cell of his body participates in his freedom and spirituality.' If we turn our backs on our spirituality, we lose that part of ourselves in which vitality and intentionality unite: in life, the power of being actualizes, and increasingly requires us to learn to recognize our shadow sides, to transform them through recognition, and to find ways of integrating ourselves at increasingly higher levels. Finally, self-actualization rests upon the openness to grace which one cannot

---

[20] Asvaghosa, *The Buddhacarita*, ed. E. H. Johnston, Oriental Books Reprint Corp. (1972); quoted in Sangharakshita, *A Guide to the Buddhist Path*, Windhorse (1995).

command any more than one can be commanded into it, but which becomes possible through the development of the transcendent function within the self. The more power of creating beyond itself a being has, the more vitality it has; the more self-relatedness we have, the more we can participate, and through participation we change things, and ourselves. Out of the working through of conflicts within the self comes a new third level which elevates and contains the former opposites – Hegel's thesis and antithesis, which, brought together, create synthesis.

Religion in its true sense is higher synthesis, says Tillich: 'the state of being grasped by the power of being itself ... the relation of man to the ground of his being'. This religious sense may not be recognized when we give ourselves wholeheartedly to those relationships and projects that take us out of and beyond ourselves, but it is, nevertheless, never completely absent. By affirming our being we participate in the affirmation of being itself, which is neither subjectively nor objectively present – neither a cause separate from its effects nor an object separate from us as subjects. Grace, finally, is the acceptance of the unacceptable, our redemption by the power of love – or God – in which we participate but which ultimately transcends us.

Tillich's 'courage to be' shares with mysticism the yearning to be released from the constricting boundaries of the small egotistical self through union with the transcendental. But it is a mysticism which is not mystified, a faith for our times which advocates not ascetic withdrawal but participation, not evangelical certainty but a reflective doubt that must be constantly explored and engaged with. The faith that can contain negativity is contentless, absolute and undefinable. It is an ability to remain present in the face of despair, and is illuminated by the awareness that there is no non-being without being, and no meaninglessness without meaning: 'Without the No he has to overcome ... the divine Yes would be meaningless.'

Matthew's home life has, over the last few years, become increasingly unhappy. Matthew and his wife have three children aged nine, seven and five, and on the surface at least, Matthew has reached just where he wanted to be by the age of forty. But he feels lost, lonely, depressed. He has become withdrawn and is often sarcastic and irritable with his wife and children.

One Saturday evening Matthew calls at the house of a recently divorced friend of his wife, to pick up his children who have been spending the day with hers. Waiting for the children to finish playing, he falls into conversation with this woman. They talk inconsequentially: he makes a joke and she laughs. Their eyes meet in appraisal, and Matthew recognizes a glint in hers which breaks through his moodiness and sense of alienation. With a frisson of sexual excitement that makes him feel alive again, he accepts another glass of wine and – discovering he has no desire to go back home just yet – tells his children they can play for a while longer. Matthew enjoys the liberation of desire, the long forgotten sense of being noticed and enjoyed for himself, as a man. He realizes he is capable of entering an entanglement that could go much further, and that it is a path that may lead to nothing but damage and frustration.

Matthew backs off and enters psychotherapy, where he talks at length about his attraction to his wife's friend, his sense of emptiness and his inner turmoil. But when his therapist begins to ask more searching questions about his relationship with his wife, Matthew breaks the therapy off abruptly. He does not feel able to look at the depths of disappointment and disillusionment which he feels in relation to his marriage; he reasons to himself that if psychotherapy is going to threaten his shaky marriage still further instead of helping him shore it up, he's better off without it. But things get no better at home. Matthew sinks into a depression and arranges extended sick leave from work. Unable to bear the company of his family around him, he borrows a friend's small weekend cottage at the edge of the Yorkshire Wolds and takes himself off there for a month with only a pile of books, a journal, some walking boots and his dog for company.

Among the books Matthew takes with him is an introduction to meditation, and in his new isolation he decides to try sitting down to meditate each morning. At first, as he sits, his mind slips naturally down well-worn routes, cataloguing his grievances against his wife and elaborating detailed sexual fantasies. But Matthew perseveres, and develops a new daily routine to help him focus. Each day he does some stretching exercises when he gets up, and after a cup of tea and some toast goes for a long walk in the woods with his dog. Then he sits down to meditate, sitting quietly by himself on a stool with his eyes closed, following the instructions in his book and paying attention to his breathing.

As Matthew begins to settle into this quiet and solitary life, his old preoccupations become less urgent, his mind drifts more gently and his experiences on the meditation stool begin to change rather disconcertingly. Matthew begins to experience shivering sensations in all his limbs, especially the tops of his inner thighs. He starts to get stomach cramps which can build rapidly from the mild to the agonizing in a crescendo of pain – frequently ending his daily meditation prematurely in an undignified rush to the bathroom with violent diarrhoea. The strange thing is, though, that the rest of the time – while he's digging his friend's garden, chopping wood for the fire, reading or out walking – he feels quite well. In fact, he feels better than he has done for a long time.

Then one day when he's walking in the woods with his dog, two pheasants suddenly fly up from the ground with a great flapping of wings, almost in Matthew's face. After he calms down and collects himself, Matthew realizes that his body's response to the shock – a rapidly beating heart, shortness of breath, a lurching stomach, weakness in his legs and a rush of adrenaline – echoes the sensations he has been having each day in meditation. He realizes that what his body has been feeling is the physical dimension of the one emotion he never lets his mind feel, and to which he could not previously have put a name – fear.

When the stomach cramps start again during his meditation session the next day, Matthew resolves to try and breathe into them, and to stay with them instead of rushing to evacuate them. It isn't easy; but over time, as he perseveres, the physical cramping and trembling begin to diminish. In their place, Matthew begins to experience the emotional dimension of the fears he had been holding at bay for so long. At first, he thinks his fear is about his marriage breaking up: fear of failure, fear of letting everyone down, fear of social disapproval, fear his children will turn against him, fear of poverty, fear of becoming an outcast, fear of the loss of everything that holds his life together, fear of having no-one there to look after him if he becomes ill or as he grows older. This last fear leads Matthew to begin to think for the first time about his own mortality, which will demand that one day – whether he likes it or not – he will have to let go of everything.

Unwelcome memories of his early childhood begin to flash before his eyes. Matthew remembers what a fearful child he used to be, clinging to his mother's skirts, shrinking from her impatient voice. He remembers his terror about being left by her on his first day at school. But school had been a turning point. It had changed him and helped him to develop the confident and friendly personality that had served him – quite well on the whole, he thought – through his adolescence and adulthood.

Until now. Matthew feels consumed with fear and uncertainty. The daily routine of life in the cottage starts to disintegrate. The simplest decisions seem beyond him – he can hardly drag himself out of bed in the mornings. Strong emotions and moods overwhelm him as if from nowhere and leave him crying and trembling. Even his dog seems troubled. Sometimes he fears he may be losing his mind, but he feels within him a deep determination to continue with his meditating – mainly, he ponders ruefully, because he doesn't know what else to do.

Yet after a few more days, Matthew starts to realize he has become less afraid of his own fear and has begun to relax into it. His body becomes less tense, his consciousness less constricted, his awareness more expanded. His wife – whom he had almost forgotten – comes back into his mind. He remembers the girl he had first known, whose eyes would light up when she saw him across a crowded room; he thinks about how nowadays their eyes avoid each other, as if afraid of what they might see. He wonders what his absence has been like for her, and whether his children are missing him – the first time this thought has struck him. Reflectively now and without anger, he wonders about his wife's tiredness and lack of interest in him. He knows she had not found motherhood easy; her efforts to be a loving and available mother to their own children had made her exhausted and depressed – while Matthew, not knowing what to do and resenting how the children had deprived him of her attention, had ignored her struggles and buried himself in his work. Tracing the problems with his wife back to the birth of their children, Matthew realizes how powerfully the birth of his children had awakened his own attachment needs, only to frustrate them. Going further, he traces his frustration and anger towards his wife back to his own childhood, clinging to a mother who never had time for him. He thinks then about his mother herself, who had found it so difficult to relax and to play, and tries to recollect what he knows about her own childhood in the 1930s. His grandmother's husband had died when Matthew's mother was five months old, and his grandmother had had to go out to work during the Depression and support her five children through her own efforts. She too was someone for whom nothing had come easily.

Here Matthew's trail grows cold. But as he sits and thinks on into the day, until the dim October light begins to fade outside the small cottage window, Matthew has a vision of his parents and his parents' parents, an endless chain linking him back into the mists of prehistory. He imagines each one wanting to do better for their own children than they had been done by, each struggling with their own needs against their fears and resentments to build a better future, sometimes failing, sometimes succeeding – a great procession of human effort that had brought him to this moment in the present, sitting in the cottage, reflecting on it all, feeling at one with it all, letting his heart open with a sense of gratitude and of peace as evening falls. Matthew's frustration and bitterness melt away and he sees the faces of his wife and children before his eyes and feels for them, at one with the endless reaches of struggling humanity, reaching on through his own children as far into the unknown future as it reaches into the unknown past. As it gets dark he gets up quietly and goes out following a rough track that leads him up through a plantation of pine trees to a small ridge. It's a clear night: he lies on his back and looks for a long time at the sky, which is full of stars.

The next morning, as Matthew sits down to meditate, he begins to have a sense – at first in momentary, elusive flashes and then for longer and more sustained periods of time – that he is not alone in the room. It's as if he is surrounded and contained by a gentle, loving presence – perhaps it has been there all along, but he has never felt it before. This experience causes his heart to soften and open still further. Through the day, feelings of anxiety and doubt return sporadically, but at other times he connects again with this presence, and finds himself unselfconsciously weeping like a child, his heart filling up with a sense of awe and of love to which he can give no name.

The only god worth keeping, writes Martin Buber, is a god who cannot be kept. The god who cannot be kept – like the presence that Matthew discovered at the end of his tunnel of frustration, fear and loneliness – is a god who cannot be named, a god who cannot be spoken of but only spoken to, a presence that comes into being in the willingness to drop all defences and to relate fully in the moment.[21] The process of detachment which Matthew had entered into in his isolated Yorkshire cottage took him through the collapse of all his previous certainties and into a new internal landscape, illuminated with a sense of peace and awe and imbued by a loving awareness of the connectedness of all beings.

Matthew did not think of himself as having been engaged in a spiritual quest – he had just wanted to get a grip on himself and to make sense of what was going on inside him. Yet in a sense, anyone who is trying to understand themselves better is engaged in a form of spiritual activity which is likely to sponsor new levels of growth.[22] In 1577, at the age of 35, the Spanish monk Juan de Yepes – later canonized as St John of the Cross – suffered a period of solitary confinement in a Spanish dungeon. Here, a process of determined and dogged self-examination became the

---

[21] Buber, M., *I and Thou*, Simon and Schuster (1996).
[22] Symington, N., *Emotion and Spirit*, Karnac (1998).

beginning of a spiritual journey which took him far down into what he was later to describe as the dark night of the soul. In a later commentary, John wrote of how, as he drew further into the process he had begun, his previous certainties collapsed, his senses became dulled and his reason faltered and failed. It was as if the power of his ego was being gradually dismantled – agonizingly purged of defences, disabused of self-importance and gradually prepared for union with the divine. Purified and humbled, he found his soul drawing nearer towards loving contemplation of the divine, a contemplation which he found to be 'nothing else but a secret, peaceful and loving infusion of God which, if admitted, will set the soul on fire with the spirit of love'.[23]

The more one goes into it, the harder it becomes to make a clear distinction between psychological and spiritual processes – at best, we can only place them on a continuum.[24] Psychologists and psychoanalysts – generally more at home when studying states of pathology, neurosis and disintegration – have fought shy of exploring those self-states of higher integration and transcendent experience once seen as the preserve of religion. But at the most fundamental level, the habit of close and regular attention to the inner life has the power to begin to liberate the self from the pitfalls of a life limited and constricted by aims that are solely and unreflectingly material. The act of understanding – of coming into awareness – is itself revolutionary, transforming the very contents it has set out to investigate. As mental contents are, over time, subjected to consciousness they become freed from the compulsion to repeat and become subject to moral choice. If we recognize evil, said Socrates, we become unable to do it. Those spiritual and psychotherapeutic programmes which promote growth do so by directing psychic action to the task of seeking out and dissolving those distortions of understanding

---

[23] St John of the Cross, *The Dark Night of the Soul*, Chapter X, HarperCollins (1995). See also Labouvie-Viet, G., 'Affect complexity and the transcendent' in Young-Eisendrath, P. and Miller, M. E. (eds), *The Psychology of Mature Spirituality*, Routledge (2000).

[24] Maslow, A. H., 'A theory of human motivation' (1943) in *Psychological Review* 50. See Chapter 3.

and the lack of compassion for others into which our ego's drive for survival continually leads us.

How we treat others determines our own moral and emotional state, which itself determines whether we are at peace with ourselves – or not. Grounded in the capacity for thinking and discernment, fired by the courageous impulse towards personal evolution, mature spiritual belief is not static but dynamic, and is characterized by a sense of freedom from internal tyranny. It includes within it a faith in the human capacity for making reparation, for regeneration and renewal at all stages of our continuous development, right into old age. The mid-life crisis advertises the fact that the defences and habits of first adulthood have been outgrown; the willingness to let go, to rest undefended in the moment, opens us to new self-experiences and to spiritual growth. At its most fundamental, the choice we have at mid life is the choice between an orientation towards self-centredness or towards self-transcendence: it is in this deepest sense that the mid-life crisis which pans out in the archetypal currents at work under the surface of our urban and suburban lives, is a religious, spiritual or existential crisis which can lead towards self-redemption and regeneration.

The relationship, writes Buber, is the place where we first become human, the form that reaches out to be filled.[25] In infancy, relationship is a state of merger from which we must learn to separate; as we grow, relationship starts to be about the many ways in which we find we can use others to satisfy our desires and allay our fears. Only gradually do we arrive at an understanding of our individual differences and our shared humanity, and develop an intersubjective capacity for empathy and concern. Awareness of our connectedness brings compassion for both ourselves and others; serenity and happiness are found in the move towards higher and higher levels of integration. Once the mind's need for autonomy and the heart's need for attachment are no longer at war with each other, energy previously needed to defend ourselves against ourselves and

---

[25] Buber, M., *I and Thou*, Simon and Schuster (1996).

others becomes free for living, promoting ever-increasing levels of health and competency.

People who have been able to develop the capacity to love beyond their own personal attachments and needs become unafraid, effective in the world, and at peace both within relationship and within themselves. This developmental achievement of mature adulthood is described by Erikson as generativity, which for Erikson implies a concern to provide for the growth and the flourishing of others, not just for one's own children but in the creation of a world fit for all children to inherit, a concern for humanity and a concern for our fragile planet itself which reaches beyond the boundaries of the narrow self.[26] 'Twenty years ago I used to contemplate emptiness' writes the Dalai Lama. 'Although I still admire the idea of cessation, these days I have a stronger admiration and aspiration for the compassion and tolerance which comes with the awakening mind.'[27]

Love itself is a basic force in nature, a developmental force leading towards connection and growth. Through our willingness to reach out imaginatively towards others, we transcend ourselves and become one with this force. As we do so, the context within which we live our own lives expands. Love has been described as the willingness to extend oneself in the service of one's own or another's spiritual growth:[28] the act of loving is an act of self-transcendence – a choice, not an emotion, a leap outside the prison of conformity and the narrow boundaries of the ego into the unknown, a process of spiritual evolution which is capable of growing from strength to strength even as our bodies are beginning to decline. This is the evolutionary view described by Teilhard de Chardin, who sees matter continually evolving into consciousness and the whole universe continually moving towards a point – the Omega point – at which all matter, life and consciousness converge and find meaning. This is not a state of dissolution: the more we become united with others, the

---

[26] Erikson, E. H., *The Life Cycle Completed*, W. W. Norton (1997).

[27] The Dalai Lama, *Awakening the Mind, Lightening the Heart*, HarperCollins (1995).

[28] Peck, M. S., *The Road Less Travelled*, Hutchinson (1986).

more we become ourselves, each in the other and in the principle that unites all others together.[29] While nature in its material aspects tends towards entropy, decay and disintegration, love itself is a force which transcends the body's decay, leading to higher and higher levels of understanding and complexity.[30] In our complex world, there is always more to understand, and the commitment to understanding itself requires us to put personal defences and agendas to one side and pay attention. Coming to understand itself is an act of love, of unification.

We cure through love, wrote Freud to Jung in 1906.[31] Through the death of Sophie, the rise of the Nazis and the onset of the cancer that would eventually kill him, Freud continued right until his final writings, just before his death in London in 1939 at the age of 83, to ponder the psychic struggle between the forces of life, love and integration on the one hand and death, disconnection and disintegration on the other: 'the aim of [the love drive] is to establish even greater unities and to preserve them thus – in short, to bind together; the aim of [the death drive] is, on the contrary, to undo connections and so to destroy things'.[32] Dante's journey takes him through the horrors of the nine circles of the hell created by alienation and destructiveness, and through the rigours of purgatory where he finds people who are suffering, each with tasks to perform in reparation for their own past failings, and who do so willingly, having learnt that their efforts enable them to leave their suffering behind and to move towards the light. Finally reaching the end of his long journey, Dante himself enters paradise, and the final stanza of the *Divine Comedy* glows with a serene and unshakeable confidence:

> But now my desire and will, like a wheel that spins with even motion,
> Were revolved by the Love that moves the sun and other stars.

---

[29] Teilhard de Chardin, P., *The Phenomenon of Man*, tr. Wall, B., Collins (1965).
[30] Lear, J., *Love and Its Place in Nature*, Yale University Press (1998).
[31] Letter, 6 December 1906, *The Freud/Jung Letters*, Penguin (1991).
[32] Freud, S., 'An Outline of Psychoanalysis' (1940), *Penguin Freud Library* 15.

Part Six

REGENERATION

12

Coming Home

Odysseus' legendary homeland, Ithaki (Ithaca) is described thus in Homer: 'There are no tracks, no grasslands ... it is a rocky, severe island, unsuited for horses but not so wretched, despite its small size. It is good for goats.' In some ways, not much has changed; the island's landscape, much of it almost vertical, precludes any significant development ... Ithaki's beaches are almost entirely pebble, with some sand deposits and sandy seabeds.

From *The Rough Guide to the Ionian Islands*[1]

Odysseus' seven long years languishing on Calypso's island are over. Released from her spell by the intervention of the gods, he builds a boat and embarks yet again for Ithaca. But the sea god Poseidon, still nursing enmity towards Odysseus for blinding his son the Cyclops, is not so easily thwarted. Just when all – at last – seems to be plain sailing, his rage darkens the sky and sends from the north a great storm which snaps Odysseus' mast and splinters his ship like matchwood. Odysseus is flung deep down into the sea but, gasping and spitting, manages to regain the surface. Stripping himself of his waterlogged clothing, he lashes himself to one of the ship's beams and for two days he rides the great waves, facing death with every breath.

---

[1]   Penguin (2000).

Then on the third day, dawn rises to reveal a calm sea and a wooded island. Weak, speechless and naked, his body bruised and swollen from the pummelling it has taken, Odysseus drags himself ashore and stumbles up the beach to a copse, where he falls into an exhausted sleep. He is awoken some time later by the arrival of Nausicaa, the beautiful daughter of King Alcinous of the Phaeacians, who has come to a nearby creek with her maidens to attend to the palace laundry. Breaking off a leafy bough to preserve his modesty, Odysseus makes himself known. At the palace he is received kindly, and eventually reveals his identity and tells his story. King Alcinous promises Odysseus he will arrange his safe return to Ithaca, and a ship is loaded with gifts and treasures. Once on board, however – despite his eagerness to return home – Odysseus lies down on the bed obligingly provided by the Phaeacians, and falls into a deep and dreamless sleep.

When he awakes, he finds himself lying on a sandy beach in a sheltered bay by the mouth of a cave, still covered by his bedclothes and completely alone. It is misty; leaping to his feet, he scans the horizon and recognizes nothing. His treasures have been carefully stacked in a pile by a great olive tree that stands nearby; weeping bitterly, he curses the Phaeacians for leaving him in such an outlandish spot. It is not until Athene, disguised as a shepherd, appears to him and disperses the mist that he at last understands that he has come home. Falling to his knees, he kisses the soil of Ithaca.

Storing his treasures carefully in the cave, Odysseus goes to seek shelter with Eumaeus, a swineherd who lives in a homestead some distance from the court. Eumaeus does not recognize Odysseus but nevertheless receives him kindly, offers him shelter and introduces him to his friend, a cowherd, who like Eumaeus has stayed loyal to Odysseus over the nineteen years of his absence. Odysseus' son Telemachus then appears, summoned by Athene, and Odysseus reveals himself. Telemachus tells Odysseus that the suitors are running riot in the palace. Penelope has remained faithful but is worn down by the suitors' demands and – now her son has grown up and she is no longer responsible for protecting him – she is getting ready, reluctantly, to choose a new husband. Together, father and son plot the overthrow of the suitors and the reclamation of Ithaca.

Odysseus disguises himself as a beggar and goes to the palace where he is recognized only by his old dog Argus, now abandoned and full of vermin. Argus wags his tail and drops his ears when he sees Odysseus, but is too weak to approach him; the shock is too much, and he dies. Odysseus, hiding his tears, goes into the palace. There – in his own banqueting hall – he endures the taunts and humiliations of the suitors quietly and without retaliating, as Athene has decreed he must if he is to reclaim his kingdom. Penelope, meanwhile, cornered by the suitors, has decided to set them a test. She goes to a locked storeroom in a remote corner of the palace and, standing on tiptoe, reaches up to the highest shelf and drags out her husband's great bow, untouched for nineteen years. Sitting with the case on her knees, she is overcome by weeping but pulls herself together and, returning to the suitors, tells them she will marry the one who can best string and shoot it. None can do so, but then the beggar asks if he can try. In the meantime, Telemachus and the two loyal servants have quietly hidden the suitors' weapons, armed themselves and sent Penelope and her women off to another part of the palace. Once Odysseus has the bow in his hands, he turns it upon the suitors and a bloodbath ensues, from which not one of them escapes alive.

Penelope receives the news of the battle with a leaping heart tempered, somewhat, by scepticism. She walks down to the hall looking calm and composed, but riven inside by uncertainty. Not knowing what to do, she takes a seat on the opposite side of the fire from the man who claims to be her husband, who is sitting with his own eyes downcast, and for a long time says nothing at all. Telemachus chides her, but Odysseus sends him off with a smile and teases his wife, saying he'd better have a single bed made up for himself. Penelope tells the maid to bring out the big bed they shared together from the bedroom – but Odysseus interrupts to say that this would be impossible, and reminds her how he had carved the bed himself from a great olive tree growing up inside the room. The bed is a part of the room itself, and could not be moved from it. This is information that only Odysseus himself could have known: Penelope's knees tremble as she recognizes the fidelity of his description, her heart melts and relaxes, and she falls into his arms.

Before they go to spend the night together, Odysseus realizes that he must let his wife know about the promise he made to Teiresias in the Land of the Dead. He tells her that he must leave again to make a final journey, taking an oar and travelling until he reaches a people who know nothing of the sea, where he must plant his oar in the ground and make offering to Poseidon. Only then will he be free to return to Ithaca to enjoy an easy and prosperous old age and, finally, death in its gentlest form. Penelope receives this news calmly and pragmatically, commenting that if he is to have a happy old age then he can always be sure of escaping from his troubles.

The next day Odysseus rises from his bed and goes to visit his elderly father Laertes, who lives in a farmhouse in the depths of the country. Laertes, whom Odysseus finds digging his vineyard in his filthy old gardening clothes, does not recognize his son until Odysseus reminds him of how, as a little boy, he would follow him around this same vineyard, and how Laertes named the trees to him, taught him about the rows of vines selected to ripen at different times and gave him fruit trees of his own to tend. A tender reconciliation between father and son follows, but it is interrupted by the realization that the families of the suitors are plotting revenge and planning to march upon the farmhouse. Odysseus prepares to fight, but the impending battle is halted by Athene. At the sound of her voice, both sides drop their weapons and the suitors' families retreat. With a happy heart, Odysseus obeys Athene's command to end the feuding and to establish peace between the contending forces, and so the *Odyssey* comes to an end.

MOVING BEYOND MID LIFE

The drama of first adulthood that is the *Iliad* ended abruptly upon the windswept battle plain of Troy, on a note of shock and grief for the death of Hector and the collapse of the heroic ideal of youth. The *Odyssey* by contrast draws to its close in a garden, upon on a note of recognition and regeneration. The hero, tested and proved by the suffering he has endured but with his sense of love and belonging intact, reaches maturity and comes home to himself.

The regaining of Ithaca is Odysseus' final ordeal, when the qualities of maturity he has learnt the hard way are put to their final test. He shows himself able to act alone and to keep his own counsel, and does not waste energy in vain posturing, but he also recognizes when it is time to trust others, and sees who is worthy of trust. He can be affectionate and playful. He is patient and gives himself as much time as he needs to think things through, but recognizes when the time has come to act swiftly, with courage and decisiveness in the service of his ultimate values. Almost ten years before, Odysseus had entered the cave of the Cyclops, seeking – as the suitors do now – to plunder resources he had not earned, without any concern beyond his own immediate gratification. It was the violence and selfishness of his actions then that brought about the death of his companions and his years of wandering and alienation. But now the tables are turned – now Odysseus has to rid his own house of the delinquent elements that are despoiling it. With their greed, their irresponsibility, their restless impulsivity, their vainglorious boasting and the casual pleasure they take in humiliating the weak to bolster their own self-importance, the suitors symbolize those aspects of immaturity which the mature self learns to identify and encounter within itself, and to vanquish.

It has been estimated that by the year 2020 those aged between 50 and 75 will be the largest population group in the UK; many of us can expect the time left to us after we reach mid life to be longer than the whole of our childhood, adolescence and first adulthood combined. The generation reaching mid life at the turn of the millennium are the baby boomers who, as Spock babies and children in the 1950s and 1960s, teenagers in the 1970s, yuppies in the 1980s and parents in the 1990s, swept everything before them, transforming cultural attitudes in their wake as they moved through the stages of life. As this generation reaches mid life and passes beyond it, will the narrative that begins to unfold on the other side of it be one of decline, or one of anticipation and fulfilment?

'At fifty', wrote George Orwell, 'everyone has the face he

deserves.'[2] We become, as we age, more truly ourselves and it is our attitudes about ageing that above all else will determine the quality of our third age, for our beliefs about reality affect our attitudes and behaviour and thereby construct the world in which we live. We have our stereotypes about ageing – that the elderly are narrow-minded, parochial, parsimonious, dutiful, resigned or complacent, rigidly bound to their gender identities, over-deferential towards authority, self-denying and emotionally repressed. But many of the attitudes we unconsciously identify with ageing are characteristic not of ageing itself but of those whom *we* have known as old – the generations senior to ourselves who reached adulthood in the early to mid twentieth century, whose formative views were shaped by the privations of two world wars, and who kept the mindsets of their youth as they kept its fashions and hairdos as they grew older. Our prejudices and stereotypes about ageing may have little to tell us about the process of ageing itself.

We can age passively and unreflectively by walking backwards with our eyes on what we have already left, or actively with a continuing commitment to our own personal development and that of those around us. 'The life cycle', says Erikson, 'does more than extend itself into the next generation. It curves back in the life of the individual, allowing ... a reexperiencing of earlier stages in a new form.'[3] What does the story of Odysseus' homecoming have to tell us about the key to a successful resolution of the mid-life crisis and about building the foundations that will see us, too, through to a peaceful and prosperous second half of life?

Reconciliation of Masculine and Feminine Parts of the Self

Odysseus' years of wandering are over, and so are Penelope's years of weeping depression. They have learnt much from their trials. To keep her position as Queen of Ithaca, protect her son

---

[2]   Orwell, G., last words in his notebook, 17 April 1949, in *Collected Essays, Journalism and Letters* (1968), Vol. 4.

[3]   Erikson, E. H., *The Life Cycle Completed*, W. W. Norton (1997).

and fend off the suitors, has demanded of Penelope great resources of courage, wit and ingenuity while Odysseus – stripped of his power and kingship and living for so long at the mercy of forces beyond his control – has had to nurture within himself patience, intuition and the capacity to contain and process his own emotional states. In their aloneness, each has had to find within themselves the qualities they previously sought out within others, becoming in the process more whole; and now the man and the woman themselves come together as Odysseus reclaims his lands and is recognized by Penelope.

The resolution of the *Odyssey* turns upon the act of recognition – Odysseus' sudden recognition of Ithaca and then Penelope's recognition of Odysseus, finally reuniting the separated couple. Recognition of what was formerly beyond conscious awareness makes possible its integration within an expanded sense of self, as Penelope's reunion with Odysseus symbolizes and confirms the mid-life reconciliation of previously polarized and alienated masculine and feminine energies within a single psyche. Having become integrated within themselves, Odysseus and Penelope as individuals become able to love each other without clinging or control; having come together they can separate once more, and so Penelope receives Odysseus' announcement of his new journey without protest and with good humour, and Odysseus expresses his confidence in Penelope's ability to rule Ithaca wisely in his absence.

To identify with one gender to the exclusion of the other is, of course, a fundamental aspect of human life. But the psychological sense of gender which organizes adolescence and early adulthood is more influenced by hormones, and hence more subject to fluctuation, than we may realize. Changes in our hormone levels as we move through the life cycle profoundly affect our values, motivation, self-image and the way we relate to others. At the extremes of life – in little children and very old people – the genders appear all but indistinguishable, while gender polarity is greatest in the late twenties and thirties, as we mate and bear and rear our children. At this time the male body is flooded with androgens, especially testosterone, which are linked to assertive sexual activity, status-related aggression, territoriality, tenacity, transient bonding, sensation-seeking and predatory behaviour – a list which, as Gail Sheehy wryly remarks, more or less sums up what women tend to complain about in men.[4] Maleness and those values traditionally associated with masculinity – assertiveness, competitiveness, single-mindedness and so on – are in a sense the success story of early adulthood, a time when men tend to have higher status, more free time, more disposable income and to suffer less from depression than women. But after mid life the picture changes: 'Still the king, the master of all things?' King Oedipus is warned as, shocked and blinded, he automatically tries to go on exercising his old autocratic ways: 'none of your power follows you through life'.[5]

As men move into their forties and fifties, earlier preoccupations with earning power and status tend to become overshadowed by worries about stress levels, health and well-being and by a growing concern with the quality of personal relationship. In the process, values traditionally associated with femininity, such as the prioritizing of personal relationship and intimacy, the development of a sense of interiority in which emotions can be processed, and the need for balance, reflectiveness and self-awareness, begin – for those men whose sense of self is resilient and flexible enough to take them on board – to come into the ascendancy. Men – and women – who thrive in the second half of life tend to be those who are able to develop and to value these aspects of their psyches; the importance of staying in touch – one way or another – with the feminine is underlined by the fact that, according to one American study, men between the ages of 45 and 64 who are married live, on average, ten years longer than men who are not.[6]

Women are now free to embrace the self-assertive qualities previously associated with masculinity. Like many men, women who do so may find themselves, as they reach mid life, in increasing conflict between their orientation towards achievement and their growing desire, as they begin to mature and to slow down, to allow themselves to relax into a more spacious and

---

[4] Sheehy, G., *New Passages*, HarperCollins (1997).
[5] Sophocles, *Oedipus Rex*, I. 1675–7, Penguin (1984).
[6] Anger A., *For Men, Better Wed than Dead*, New York Times Syndicate (1990). See also Bernard, J., *The Future of Marriage*, Penguin (1976).

expansive internal landscape and a richer repertoire of emotional responsiveness. Other women may already have structured a sense of balance into their lives, perhaps combining a successful career with an emotionally centred home life, while others still struggle as they reach mid life to free themselves from the role of homemaker and mother, as they become less adaptive to the demands of their families and less willing to live their lives vicariously as the helpmate and support of others. The ratio of testosterone to oestrogen in a post-menopausal woman may be up to twenty times higher than when she was menstruating, prompting a resurgence of the adventurousness, assertiveness and robust self-expression which girls sometimes lose at puberty.[7]

For both men and women at mid life, the masculine and feminine qualities inherent in the self, unbalanced and distorted by the vicissitudes of the previous decades, begin to seek each other out to find a new equilibrium. When we think about embarking upon a mid-life love affair, it may be that we are seeking a new sexual involvement with another person. Alternatively, and more ambiguously, we may – like Jung visited by his *anima*,[8] Dante seeking Beatrice[9] or Coleridge's woman wailing for her demon lover[10] – unconsciously be looking for something more like a new and expanded experience of self, in which, with the shock of the new, we can reconnect with and explore contrasexual aspects of our own erotic psyches. The mid-life love affair – tender, tentative, full of yearning – has a way of blurring the distinctions between self and other, and the reversals of mid life often have a confusing and disorientating effect upon sexual identity (in the patriarchal world of ancient Greece, suddenly it is the women who are ruling the islands while the men are all at sea). Odysseus' confused dalliances with Circe and Calypso, and Penelope's with her suitors, show the changing self learning to play with and to explore its new erotic potential. At the same time, such affairs are rehearsals for the

---

[7] Sheehy, G., *New Passages*, HarperCollins (1997).
[8] Jung C. G., *Memories, Dreams, Reflections*, Fontana (1993).
[9] Dante, *Divine Comedy, III: Paradiso*.
[10] Coleridge, S. T., 'Kubla Khan' in *Poetical Works*, Oxford University Press (1974).

renewed forms of sexual relating that become possible as we complete mid-life transition and begin to settle down into ourselves.

A less polarized gender identity allows more room for sexual playfulness, as we become liberated from the tyranny of needing to perform and to impress, and as aspects of the self previously denied and projected into others – especially sexual partners – can be owned and embraced. Once men depend less on women to process their emotions for them, and women depend less on men to help them separate from their mothers and to give their lives direction and meaning, we can begin to enjoy each other more as individuals. If negotiation of the mid-life crisis has brought greater self-understanding and integration, the need to control and manipulate others into gratifying our unconscious, unresolved infantile needs begins to dissolve.

Once we are less at the mercy of the repressed aspects of our unconscious minds, we also learn to see reality more clearly – and to value the ability to do so over the mind's ability to project and distort in the service of its own fantasies. When Odysseus is told he has landed on Ithaca, and later when Penelope is told of Odysseus' return, each feels a flash of exultation – but neither acts immediately upon their impulse. Each has lived long enough not to underestimate the treacherous ability of the mind to believe what suits it, and so they cautiously test out the reality of the situation before acting. Once expectations diminish, so does the need to force life to fit our fantasies instead of experiencing it as it really is. Then, relationships become freed to be enjoyed – perhaps for the first time – for what they are instead of what they are not. And as our sense of gender identity becomes less threatened by the other sex and our weight of expectation diminishes, we become able to see *them* – again, perhaps for the first time – for who they really are. 'That was why I liked him' says Molly Bloom, James Joyce's Penelope, of her husband: 'I saw he understood or felt what a woman was.'[11]

The reconciliation of psychic masculinity and femininity is revealed in that capacity for effective, directed action which seeks

---

[11] Joyce, J., *Ulysses*, Random House (1961).

to express responsibility for the self rather than to find means of avoiding it. Once the self is no longer divided by conflict and denial, an energy arises which is a powerful force, being more self-aware, calmer, more resilient and more focused than the reactive energy of first adulthood. This resurgence of energy may explain why so many people find that their fifties are a time of much greater inner contentment and fulfilment than the angst-ridden late thirties and early forties. The internal reunion of the active or masculine force with the containing or feminine force – the *hierosgamos*, or royal marriage, of the alchemists – sponsors the rebirth of the self and the regeneration of hope in the future. In the *Odyssey* it is symbolized by the great olive tree which grows up and is contained within Odysseus and Penelope's bedchamber, fashioned by Odysseus into the marriage bed in which the future is conceived and born.

We live, for the most part, in a world in which dualistic and combative ways of thinking structure the ways in which we educate ourselves, pursue justice, organize politically and conduct our emotional lives. Opposition and conflicts are provisionally useful, and teach us to think – people who fear conflict tend, like the Lotus-eaters, to be unable to change or to grow up. But conflict is only useful up to a point. Ultimately – and increasingly as we grow older – it becomes wearisome. As we become less repressed and more tolerant of ourselves, we become less rigidly identified with one side or another in any given problem, less prone to be blinded by the passions and bitterness of sectarianism, more able to see that in taking sides we eliminate half of reality and trap ourselves in a prison of our own making, and more able, finally, to say that nothing is alien to us, for we are a part of humankind. At this point, paradox and contradiction no longer have the power to frighten or to irritate but can be embraced and enjoyed within an ever-evolving, self-transcending consciousness. A great mind, said Coleridge, is androgynous.[12]

---

[12] Coleridge, S. T., *Table Talk*, 1 September 1832, quoted in Woolf, V., *A Room of One's Own*, Penguin (2000).

Loving Connectedness to Others

'The great secret of morals is love', wrote Shelley, 'or a going out of our own nature, and an identification of ourselves with the beautiful which exists in thought, action, or person, not our own. A man, to be greatly good, must imagine intensely and comprehensively; he must put himself in the place of another and of many others; the pains and pleasures of his species must become his own.'[13] It is his loving sense of connectedness to Ithaca that sustains Odysseus through his wanderings and finally brings him home, and love that impels Penelope to maintain an Ithaca to which it will be worth returning.

This love is organic and interconnected, like the tree rooted in the earth – Odysseus' first act after he realizes he is home is to kiss the soil of Ithaca. The bed that cannot be brought out of the bedroom because it is a rooted tree symbolizes the indivisibility of love, and it is this tree which helps Penelope identify Odysseus, just as Odysseus' father Laertes recognizes Odysseus through the shared memory of the trees they tended together, each planted to bear fruit at a different time, connecting their family tree to the movement of the seasons. This love is not the love of sexual passion, but is experienced by both Odysseus and Penelope as an ethical obligation, a mutually acknowledged bond which unites the homecoming Odysseus with his country, his subjects, his child, his wife and his father. 'Love', says Aristophanes in Plato's *Symposium*, 'is simply the desire and pursuit of the whole.' The natural courtesy, consideration and hospitality shown by Telemachus and Penelope, and also by the two lowly farm labourers who befriend Odysseus when he returns disguised as a penniless beggar, are contrasted in the final books of the *Odyssey* with the greed and rudeness of the suitors, whose malicious, disruptive and contemptuous behaviour eventually brings about their own downfall.

'Love is the responsibility of an I for a You' writes Martin Buber: it is the immediate unmediated apprehension of

---

[13] Shelley, P. B., *A Defence of Poetry* in *Poems and Prose*, Everyman (1995).

another's being.[14] Love sees clearly and sees the whole – hatred, in contrast, is blind, for we only ever hate a part. Often, we find ourselves relating to another as an It rather than a You, an object to be used to satisfy our needs rather than another being who deserves recognition. Only the spell of separation needs to be broken, says Buber – and for that, we must give up that false drive for self-affirmation which makes us turn our relations into our possessions. Love carries within it a recognition of the responsibilities involved in the ties that connect us to others, including especially those most dependent upon us – such as the elderly, the young or the disadvantaged – and understands that to love is not only better than to demand to be loved, but in the end more creative and enjoyable.

We are most likely to experience love in this way first of all towards our own children, if we have them. But as we become more psychologically integrated and more spiritually mature our capacity to love spreads beyond our immediate family and friends in ever-widening circles to embrace, ultimately, humanity itself. It expresses itself in the wisdom of forgiveness – as the closing words of the *Odyssey*, stating that it is time for the feuds to end, make clear. As we find we have fewer positions to defend, we become more willing to let go of old grievances and reach out to estranged or alienated parents, children, former lovers and all whom we have wronged or been wronged by. Forgiveness, which redeems us from self-perpetuating cycles of hatred and revenge, is a generous and wise impulse which has the power to dissolve guilt and to heal the wounds of shame and self-hatred. Envy, competitiveness and insecurity all prevent us loving and valuing others but as these abate we become increasingly able to take pleasure in others' achievements, to desire their well-being and flourishing as well as our own. So, we affirm our capacity for loving connectedness regardless of the circumstances.

Generativity is described by Erikson as the crowning achievement of mature adulthood.[15] Generativity – a word with

---

[14] Buber, M., *I and Thou*, tr. Kaufmann, W., Touchstone (1996).
[15] Erikson, E. H., *The Life Cycle Completed*, W. W. Norton (1997).

overtones of creativity, generosity and a concern for succeeding generations – is a form of post-narcissistic love, and Erikson distinguishes it from the 'love' we feel when we are younger, which may be only an expression of attachment needs, or a form of sexual idealization; it is a feeling that may start to grow in the wake of suffering or breakdown, when our egotism collapses and the pain that we suffer gives us new sensitivity to the pain of others. The Buddha recommended developing detachment through meditation, not to make us cold and impervious but because – on the contrary – only detachment can transform our early attachment-seeking love, which is a form of craving and can be controlling and manipulative, into genuine compassion. The capacity for loving kindness or compassion – the Christian *caritas* (charity), which is patient and kind, does not envy, and is not self-seeking or easily angered,[16] or the Buddhist *metta* – is the experience described by Buber that brings us into direct confrontation with each other's humanity and, ultimately, divinity. 'Feelings dwell in man, but man dwells in his love ... Love does not cling ... love is a cosmic force.' This impulse expresses itself naturally and organically in action, enabling us to act, help, heal, educate, raise and redeem.[17]

Unless we achieve generativity, says Erikson, we will fall in our later years into stagnation – the consequence of failing to negotiate the challenges of the mid-life crisis and to resolve our early narcissistic needs leaves us trapped in self-absorption and neediness, and prey to feeling increasingly unhappy and neglected as we grow older. Erikson describes generativity in terms of a threefold responsibility of care: to be careful (to exercise appropriate restraint), to care for (to love and cherish others) and to take care of (to extend consideration and protection when it is needed). For Jung, the generative impulse seems to have followed organically from the resolution of his own mid-life crisis: 'When I look back upon it all today and consider what happened to me during [this] period', he wrote towards the end of his life, '... it seemed as though a message

---

[16] Corinthians I, 13:1–4.
[17] Buber, M., *I and Thou*, tr. Kaufmann, W., Touchstone (1996).

had come to me with overwhelming force ... It was then that I ceased to belong to myself alone, ceased to have the right to do so. From then on, my life belonged to the generality.'[18]

The same is true for Odysseus, who regains Ithaca only to leave once again, to keep the promise he made in the Land of the Dead to travel to a distant land to tell his story to those who live there. Odysseus' journey back to Ithaca was made under the compulsion of his yearning for home; his new journey away from Ithaca will be undertaken voluntarily, from an internal ethical imperative, not for personal gain but for the well-being of others as yet unmet. He will travel this time not as a man of action intent on outwitting others but in a more reflective and creative mode, to fire the hearts and imaginations of others with the story of his journey. Odysseus always has his eyes on the future: even in the *Iliad*, while others are identified as the sons of their fathers (as in 'Achilles, son of Peleus') he alone is described as the father of his son, Telemachus – an appellation which singles him out as a man with his energies focused more on creating new futures than pleasing a dead past. Now, in his mysterious promise to Teiresias to take his story to new lands where people have not seen the sea – symbolically, those who are out of touch with their unconscious imagination – Odysseus becomes identified with Homer himself, the poet whose insights and experiences will be passed on to new generations to touch the hearts and minds of those as yet unborn, in unknown lands and times.

What sort of obituaries do we hope for? As the Buddha lay dying, Ananda, his closest friend and companion for over twenty years, went to a nearby hut where, leaning against the doorpost, he wept bitterly. In his grief, Ananda did not recall the Buddha as the founder of a world religion or for his penetrating insights into the nature of mind. 'The master is about to pass away from me', he said, 'he who is so kind.'[19] It was the kindness that mattered. As we move into the second half of adulthood our choices in the external world are narrowed: in some respects –

---

[18] Jung, C. G., *Memories, Dreams, Reflections*, Fontana (1983).
[19] *The Long Discourses of the Buddha (Digha-Nikaya)*, sutta 16.

for good or ill – the die is cast. But this narrowing of possibilities in the external world may be well compensated for by a broadening out of sympathy and imagination, in a profound sense of connectedness to others and the willingness to relate to them in ways that sponsor their own growth. In the end we may, after all, find immortality, through the place we gain in the minds and hearts of others, through the torches we light and pass on to future generations.

Coming Home to the Self

Towards the end of the First World War, Jung, by then in his mid-forties, began to emerge from the darkness of his own mid-life crisis. While in France on military service, he kept a notebook beside him, and found himself sketching, each morning, a small circular mandala. *Mandala* is a Sanskrit word meaning 'circle', and circle drawings have been found in ancient rock carvings all over the world, often illustrating the sun, moon and stars, and eventually coming to depict and represent sacred space. Mandalas have been used by Christian mystics such as Hildegard of Bingen and Jakob Böhme, and dazzling examples of them can be seen in the great rose windows of Gothic cathedrals. Tibetan mandalas, also known as thangkas, are used as devotional aids, serving as maps of inner reality that, as visual aids to meditation, guide and support the psychological development of those wishing to advance in spiritual awareness.[20]

For Tibetan Buddhists, working with the mandala is a way of working upon the dissolution of the ego's belief in its separateness, and so moving towards enlightenment – the mandala, a symbol of integration, can also be seen as a symbol of the psyche's coming home to itself. For Jung, mandala-drawing was crucial in his recovery from the chaos of mid-life breakdown. 'Only gradually did I discover what the mandala really is ... the self, the wholeness of the personality which if all goes well is harmonious, but which cannot tolerate self-

[20] See Fincher, S. E., *Creating Mandalas*, Shambhala (1991).

deceptions.'[21] Jung's freehand mandala-drawing became a way of working on his psychic development, abandoning the idea of the primacy of the ego and allowing the unconscious to enter into dialogue with the conscious mind, both exploration and celebration of personal wholeness.

Moving beyond mid life draws us naturally towards those pursuits – such as painting and meditation – which can be undertaken in quiet and solitude and in which we can experience a coming home to ourselves, sometimes after years of self-neglect. The abatement of early attachment needs and the ebbing of the urgency of sexual desire enable us to begin to be curious about our own mental processes and to enjoy the free play of thought and imagination. We develop a sense of interiority, of inner spaciousness, discovering our minds in their interplay between conscious and unconscious as interesting and surprising places, in the inhabiting of which we become rich enough to dispense with exaggerated external stimulations and cravings for attention.

A room of one's own, wrote Virginia Woolf, in which to shelter from the claims and tyrannies of one's family – preferably one with a lock on the door – is an essential condition of creative work, which demands that we remain true to ourselves and not alter our values in deference to the opinions of others.[22] Woolf's book, based on a series of lectures given to a group of women undergraduates at Cambridge when she was 46, and written with deep personal feeling, seems as much a mid-life manifesto as it is a feminist rallying call. What do we mean, Woolf ponders, by the unity of the mind? Often we hold parts of ourselves back, but to create we need to acknowledge our own internal masculinity and femininity: 'it is when this fusion takes place that the mind is fully fertilized and uses all its facilities ... the androgynous mind ... is naturally creative, incandescent, and undivided'. To reach this state of creative fertility we must first experience ourselves fully at home within our own minds, able to draw upon all parts of them freely. 'I find myself saying briefly and prosaically',

---

[21] Jung, C. G., *Memories, Dreams, Reflections*, Fontana (1983).
[22] Woolf, V., *A Room of One's Own*, Penguin (2000).

concludes Woolf, 'that it is much more important to be oneself than anything else.'

There is a saying that if you want to be happy for a year, fall in love, to be happy for ten, get married, but to be happy for a lifetime, plant a garden – for in gardening we ground ourselves in the earth and learn to create and enjoy our own landscapes, external corollaries of that process of developing fertility and harmony within our minds that Anthony Storr sees operating in the final work of great creative artists.[23]

In the words of Ecclesiastes,[24] set to music by Brahms in his four last songs composed the year before he died: 'Wherefore I perceive that there is nothing better, than that a man should rejoice in his own works; for that is his portion: for who shall bring him to see what shall be after him?' Then again, in Beethoven's last works 'nothing is conceded to the listener … instead the composer communes with himself or contemplates his vision of reality thinking (as it were) aloud and concerned only with the pure essence of his own thoughts.'[25]

Unlike the suitors – who have come to stay in a place that is not their home, grasping greedily and enviously after what is not their own – Odysseus' relationship to Ithaca is a relationship not with what he is not, but with what he is. Coming home to Ithaca, he comes home to himself. 'We must exist right here, right now! This is the key point' writes the Zen master Shunryu Suzuki. 'You must have your own body and mind. Everything should exist in the right place, in the right way. Then there is no problem.'[26] Like Odysseus, like Spielberg's ET, we all want to come home, long to rest content within our own minds. Discovering that the most important – and the most interesting – battles in life are those that are fought and won within the self, we learn to value the freedom that comes from realizing that there is, in the end, no-one else at all who must be pleased or impressed. 'Spiritual growth', writes the Buddhist teacher Jack

[23] Storr, A., *Solitude*, Flamingo (1990).
[24] Ecclesiastes, 3:22.
[25] Cooper, M., *Beethoven: The Last Decade*, quoted in Storr, A., *Solitude*, Flamingo (1990).
[26] Suzuki, S., *Zen Mind, Beginner's Mind*, Weatherhill (1996).

Kornfield, 'is not about form but a resting in the heart ... everything must be included ... spirituality has shifted from going to India or Tibet or Machu Picchu, to coming home'.[27] Learning we no longer need to use life to prove points, defend positions, pursue agendas or chase after what we don't have, we can finally begin to enjoy life for itself:

> Home is where one starts from ...
> We shall not cease from exploration
> And the end of all our exploring
> Will be to arrive where we started
> And know the place for the first time.[28]

Willingness to Be in Process

Odysseus comes home – not to rest on his laurels, but to plan a new departure. In Tennyson's poem 'Ulysses' we meet Odysseus years later, elderly now but still the same indomitable wanderer:

> For always roaming with a hungry heart ...
> I am a part of all that I have met;
> Yet all experience is an arch wherethro'
> Gleams that untravell'd world, whose margin fades
> For ever and for ever when I move ...[29]

How dull it is to pause, to make an end, says Tennyson's Odysseus. One of the liberations of reaching and passing mid life is to become, in Christopher Bollas' phrase, mercifully free of the idea of completeness or perfection.[30] Released from the oppression of ideals, from the defensive posture of omnipotence that needs to control everything in sight, we begin to experience life not as a series of tasks to fulfil but as a constant process of becoming, in which the point is always arrived at in each

27 Kornfield, J., *A Path with Heart*, Rider (1990).
28 Eliot, T. S., 'East Coker' and 'Little Gidding' in *Four Quartets* in *Collected Poems 1909–1962*, Faber and Faber (1963).
29 Tennyson, Alfred Lord, *Works*, Macmillan (1892).
30 Bollas, C., 'The destiny drive' in *Forces of Destiny*, Free Association Books (1989).

moment, and in which the willingness to live fully in the present is also a psychic investment in an unknown future. The creative process never ends, because it is self-generating: Maslow, listing the motivations and gratifications of self-actualizing people, describes them as people who tend to be attracted to mystery, unsolved problems, the unknown and the challenging, rather than being frightened by them. They also tend to love the process of *doing* their work and to do it for its own sake rather than for any extrinsic reason such as money or status.[31] The process of becoming oneself is not, paradoxically, a fixed goal but that which is always in the process of becoming, dissolving and reforming – the alchemists' *solve et coagula* – in the eternal tension of opposites.

This is not, of course, how we have been taught to live. The orientation towards goal achievement and the demanding pace of modern life has made us very good at producing and consuming, but not so good at making relationships work, maintaining health and well-being, or even really enjoying ourselves. Our obsession with achievement makes us feel alienated from our own lives – stressed, hostile, controlling, always planning ahead, unable to rest in the moment. Yet goal orientation as a way of life has such unchallenged supremacy in our minds that its alternative – as we get older and begin to have neither the means nor the desire to produce and achieve as compulsively as we did before – is, sadly, for many people not a reorientation towards a different way of living but a sense of obsolescence and redundancy.

But it need not be so. Okinawa is an archipelago of islands in southern Japan where people not only live longer than they do anywhere else in the world but remain remarkably free from those chronic diseases of ageing – menopause-related problems, osteoporosis, heart disease, strokes, cancer, dementia, depression and so on – which we tend to think of as inevitable. Okinawans tend to enjoy extraordinarily rude health up until their eighties and even nineties, usually until just a few months before they die.

[31] Maslow, A. H., 'A theory of metamotivation' in *The Farther Reaches of Human Nature*, Penguin (1993).

Their success is not due to socio-economic factors (Okinawa has been invaded by foreign powers since 1609, a third of the population was killed during World War II and Okinawans have the lowest socio-economic status in Japan), nor is it genetic; when Okinawans move away and adopt different lifestyles they soon succumb to the same problems as the rest of us.

The Okinawan lifestyle has been the subject of a twenty-five-year scientific study to discover the secret of the Okinawans' success in the second half of life.[32] Partly it seems due to the Okinawan diet, which is rich in vegetables, legumes, whole-grains, soya and fish. Although they eat more in bulk than we do, their low levels of fat consumption mean that the Okinawans' calorie intake is considerably less than our own; they take longer to prepare food, eat more slowly and ceremoniously, and tend to stop eating before they are full. Okinawans also seem less likely than Westerners to use the intake of food, caffeine, alcohol, cigarettes or drugs to meet displaced emotional needs, which are met instead by high levels of social support, both informally and in more structured ways. Many people belong to *moais*, or support groups, which meet regularly to offer each other practical and emotional help in times of need, to offer guidance and to share life experiences. Such groups provide an underpinning sense of continuity and stability for their members – the researchers discovered one group of eighty-eight-year-olds who had been meeting regularly in the same *moai* since primary school, for over eighty years.

Okinawans also exercise regularly, but do not see exercise as something to be hurried through as quickly as possible to get thin or healthy. Instead, they participate in activities such as Tai Chi, traditional dance, gardening and walking which they enjoy for themselves, and which also reverberate for them with emotional and spiritual significance. Okinawans have a completely different attitude to time and an approach to punctuality so casual that it initially disorientated their Canadian researchers, and tend generally in their approach to life to be adaptable, easy-

---

[32] Willcox, B., Willcox, C. and Suzuki, M., *The Okinawa Way*, Penguin (2001).

going, playful, optimistic and emotionally stable. They also tend to have profound spiritual convictions, with the eldest members of the family responsible for preserving spiritual connections with ancestors, and to incorporate regular quiet time into their days for prayer and meditation.

Meditation, as the researchers observe, 'helps slow us down – inside and out. It helps set our rhythms to Okinawa time.' A ten-year study to test the effect of meditation upon human ageing in North America similarly showed that the three markers of ageing chosen – eyesight, hearing and blood pressure – could all be improved with long-term meditation; those who had been meditating for five years or more measured, on average, five years younger than others, while those meditating longer scored twelve years younger.[33] Further large-scale surveys have showed that meditators use medical services almost 50 per cent less than non-meditators and have 80 per cent lower rates of heart disease and 50 per cent lower rates of cancer. If any drug had been shown to have such remarkable results (and without any negative side effects) it would be hailed as a wonder drug and universally clamoured after. But Western health care invests in products, not processes.

Instead it is up to us individually to take responsibility for the effect that the health of our minds and spirits has on the health of our bodies. Meditation and other practices which help us live in the present teach us that the richness of life is here to be enjoyed in the present, not at some notional point in the future. Giving ourselves time to enjoy the scenery and to stop and examine what we find along the way, we become more relaxed, more playful, more curious – like Odysseus himself, enriched by the journey. Ithaca, we are told over and over again in the *Odyssey*, is a poor and barren island with nothing much going on there – a description anyone who has visited it recently will be able to confirm, although it is also a rugged and beautiful place. Its importance as a mythic or spiritual destination lies, in the

---

[33] Wallace, R. K., Dillbeck, M., Jacobe, E. and Harrington, B., 'The effects of Transcendental Meditation . . . on the aging process' (1982), *International Journal of Neuroscience* 16.

words of Cavafy in the epigraph to this book, in the marvellous journey itself.

A Sense of Making Sense

In the end, our lives are what we make them, and what we make of them. Ithaca ... *if you are, myth you are* ... is the thought that never leaves Odysseus, the mantra he uses to keep his mind safe through all his dangers and adventures: keep Ithaca always in your mind, says Cavafy. Ithaca, in the end, represents that internal centre of constancy – constancy to our own authenticity and also to those values and ideals beyond the self that we believe, at the deepest level, are worthy of preserving – which finally constitutes our sense of core integrity.

In Chapter 2, the mid-life crisis was described in terms of four dynamics: the desire to let go, the upsurge of erotic energy, the encounter with death, and the need to find a new way of accounting for oneself – of making sense. At all stages of our lives, but especially when coming through periods of transition and also as we get older, we need to find ways of looking back and making sense of our lives. In retrospect, the struggles of the past may become illuminated by an understanding that those struggles themselves helped to forge, enabling us to forgive transgressions and failures while taking responsibility for the choices we made. Affirming the path that has brought us to where we are now, we become able to recognize the continuity that has informed it and the internal consistency of its trajectory.

The psychoanalyst Heinz Kohut, reflecting in an interview upon the changes in his life which had taken him from being a little boy in the Austrian Alps to the presidency of the American Psychoanalytic Association at the age of sixty 'in a place whose name I hardly knew when I was that young', spoke of his own personal sense of his life's continuity, his awareness that, although he might not remember much about his six-year-old self any more, the child still lived within him. We must become our own historians, said Kohut, to establish the continuity of our individual selves. He described receiving, among the many accolades that greeted his sixtieth birthday, an unsigned telegram from his elderly mother: 'To me', she had written, 'it seems like yesterday'. 'You get the point?' asked Kohut. 'That was all she sent. I will never forget that. It was one of the best things she ever did.'[34]

'Do you remember when ...' is a game we all like to play, especially, perhaps, when we are quite young or quite old. Odysseus establishes his identity with his wife by reminding her how he had made their bed, and with his father by reminiscing about the garden they tended together. Shared remembering is a joyful experience because it connects us to each other, affirming our enduring identities, our shared pasts and our continuity as beings, while simultaneously acknowledging separateness and the passage of time. The narrative of our lives, which evolves over time through thought and reflection – if it is truthful enough and profound enough – helps us to understand what the great challenges of our lives have been, the forms in which they continue to manifest, and how we can continue to live and work with them now in the service of our self-actualization.

So, a life may begin to seem something like a symphony, in which the overture gives way to the main theme, which is recapitulated with increasing depth, complexity and power as it moves towards its final resolution. As we find ways to make sense of the life we have lived and to organize value out of our experiences, our engagement with these themes inevitably percolates through to how we relate to others and how we live our lives now, in the present moment. So the work of remembering and understanding redeems the past, transforms the present and liberates the future: it is the work of the making of our souls. This is the achievement of integrity, the final task described by Erikson in his charting of the stages of life, a state of internal authenticity, finally assured of order and meaning.

This sense of personal integrity and transcendental meaning will, for some, be naturally articulated as a spiritual impulse and manifest as religious belief. Freed from the shackles of authoritarianism and superstition, religious commitment may

---

[34] Kohut, H., 'On the continuity of the self' in *Self-Psychology and the Humanities*, Norton (1985).

encourage the growth of the whole person, enabling and sponsoring our becoming all that we are capable of being. 'Man can only do justice to his relationship with God', writes Buber, 'by actualising God in the world in accordance with his ability.'[35] As we move on through mid life, some of us may be surprised and pleased to discover (or rediscover) a spiritual home in one of the great world religions, finding stimulation in its overarching intellectual coherence, and consolation and peace of mind in communion with the profound spiritual experience enshrined within its hallowed traditions. But a sense of spiritual meaning is not the exclusive property of the overtly religious:

> They say that Ulysses, sated with marvels
> Wept tears of love at the sight of his Ithaca
> Green and humble. Art is that Ithaca
> Of green eternity, not of marvels.[36]

Odysseus' homecoming is, in the end, not a miracle at all but a secular affair, and no less meaningful for that.

The Willingness to Let Go

In the end, we must learn to let go. *The Tempest*, like the *Odyssey*, is a narrative of redemption through recognition after years of suffering and exile in which – through shipwreck and disaster – what had been lost at sea is mysteriously, but differently, restored.[37] Prospero and Odysseus, exiled kings both, must each relinquish their self-importance and their desire for revenge and learn to rely upon the justice of the sea, a justice that is bigger than themselves, which unfolds through the willingness to surrender and to trust – and to be continually surprised by – the

---

[35] Buber, M., *I and Thou*, tr. Kaufmann, W., Touchstone (1996).

[36] From Jorge Luis Borges' 'Ars Poetica' in *Selected Poems 1923–67*.

[37] And both are set on islands. Interestingly, the island of Scherie, the green and welcoming country of King Alcinous from which Odysseus sets forth on the last leg of his journey back to Ithaca, has sometimes been identified as Corfu (which lies to the north of Ithaca in the Ionian sea), which has also been claimed as the island upon which Shakespeare set *The Tempest*. See, for example, Durrell, L., *Prospero's Cell*, Faber and Faber (1997).

process of living itself. Odysseus regains Ithaca through his own efforts, yet the intervention of the mysterious Phaeacians, who return him in his sleep to Ithaca – leaving him wrapped up on the beach in his bedcovers, as if to show that the whole thing was no more than a strange dream – and Athene, who appears to guide him in his moments of deepest confusion, are reminders that his life is also overseen by benign forces which in the end prove greater than the force towards impulsive destruction represented by Poseidon. Prospero too, at the end of *The Tempest*, voluntarily relinquishes his omnipotence as he puts his trust in benign and forgiving forces beyond his own will:

> Now my charms are all o'erthrown,
> And what strenth I have's mine own
> Which is most faint . . .

Having become unafraid of dying, he states his intention to retire to Milan, where he will learn to meditate upon death, and where every third thought shall be of his grave[38]

To return home, Odysseus had to be willing to lose everything over and over again:

> a condition of complete surrender
> costing not less than everything.[39]

Every cell of our bodies dies and is renewed every seven years, yet not until we have really worked through the encounter with death that lies at the heart of the mid-life crisis can we understand the real implications of impermanence. The willingness to let go when the time comes also implies the resilience to face that which is, without bitterness, blaming or passive depression: the resolution of the mid-life crisis requires us to relinquish our omnipotence and our self-idealization, to enjoy what life has to offer and in the end to accept death gracefully.

Charlotte was the GP with two young children whose collapse following the break-up of her marriage was described in Chapter 9. In the wake of her breakdown, Charlotte had come to question deeply the values of her previous life. The dream she had during her breakdown – of the young boy

---

[38] *The Tempest*, Epilogue.
[39] Eliot, T. S., *Four Quartets* op. cit.

who reached up and pulled her deep into the murky pool that became trans-fused with ripples of sunlight – had affected her very much. In its aftermath, wanting to find out more about the part of herself which the young boy in the dream seemed to personify, she began a course of art therapy, and as her interest in painting grew she began to paint seriously. Over the next few years, she had several inconclusive affairs with different men, but found she had come to enjoy living by herself with her children. Then, at a New Year's Eve party given by the owners of a gallery where she had shown some of her work, she met Adam, a shambling, gentle painter in his mid-fifties who had recently been widowed.

Charlotte and Adam began a relationship and as their respective children be-gan to grow up and leave home, they bought an old house in the country with a large overgrown garden. Now in her mid-fifties, Charlotte seems content with her quiet life there, and at peace within herself:

> The years of what in retrospect I suppose I'd have to call my mid-life crisis were ... well, a lot of it is just a blur. Thankfully, really ... I lost so much and in a way my heart still aches for all that, and for the hurt I caused too, especially to my children. But there was a narrowness, a harshness – a hidden desperation – in the old me. I was on a collision course. I lost a lot, but from the ruins of it all, new things have grown in my life which are infinitely more precious. I can't say in a simple way that it was worth it, but maybe there wasn't any other way. Given who I was then I probably did have to go through it all to become who I am today ...

'Despite so many ordeals', says Sophocles' Oedipus as he draws towards the end of his life, 'my advanced age and the nobility of my soul make me conclude that all is well'.[40] The six aspects of mature adulthood discussed above – the reconciliation of the masculine and feminine aspects of the psyche; a loving sense of connectedness to others, feeling at home within the self, being willing to live in process; a sense of making sense, and finally, the willingness to let go – are six aspects of the same state of mind. To allow ourselves to reach out towards and to inhabit this state of mind is a revolutionary act, capable of bringing happiness in this world within our grasp as we move onwards through our forties and fifties and beyond.

---

[40] Sophocles, *Oedipus at Colonus*, tr. Blundell, M. W., quoted in Sheehy, G., *New Passages*, HarperCollins (1997).

Appendix:

The Menopause

The menopause is, strictly speaking, the moment when a woman stops ovulating. and her periods end. For most women this will happen on average around the age of 51. More broadly, the menopause is the name given to the changes brought about in the female body by fluctuating and declining hormone levels as menstruation becomes erratic and ceases. This process, also called the climacteric, generally begins around the age of 47 or 48 and lasts for about 3 years, although it may start earlier and may continue for up to 5 years or even longer.

Many symptoms are commonly associated with the menopause: hot flushes, dryness and irritability of the vagina, headaches, muscle pain, loss of libido, anxiety and irascibility, insomnia and fatigue, weight gain, palpitations, poor concentration and memory loss. Of these, only hot flushes and vaginal dryness (the latter usually occurring towards the end of the climacteric) have been conclusively connected to the drop in oestrogen levels brought about by the menopause itself, although it is quite possible that other symptoms, such as headaches, swollen ankles, palpitations, changes in skin and hair, and mood swings, are also connected to declining oestrogen levels and the adjustments the body must make to these.

But given that the menopause is a natural part of ageing, it is difficult – and probably fruitless – to try to disentangle many of the supposed symptoms of the menopause from changes to do with ageing itself. For example, metabolic changes related to ageing, especially when combined with taking less exercise, drinking more or comfort eating, may be responsible for weight gain (although changes in hormonal levels may affect weight distribution, making menopausal women more likely to put on weight around the abdomen rather than, as previously, around the bust or hips). Insomnia may be caused by nocturnal hot flushes disrupting sleep patterns; but as we saw in Chapter 9, insomnia and tiredness are also symptoms of depression, as are changes in eating habits, poor concentration, bad memory, anxiety and irritability.

Hormone Replacement Therapy (HRT) has been prescribed by doctors since the 1940s to help alleviate the symptoms of menopause. HRT replaces and stabilizes the hormone levels that begin to fluctuate and drop at the climacteric, notably oestrogen and progesterone, by mimicking the levels at which these hormones were previously produced in the monthly cycle. Early HRTs were made from the urine of pregnant mares but most are now derived from plant sources. HRT may now be made from natural or synthetic sources and is available as tablets, patches, implants or gels.

For some women, the offering of HRT as a matter of course implies that a natural event is being medicalized and treated as a problem. On the negative side, HRT has been linked to breast cancer and its use may not be indicated if other risk factors are present (for example, a family history of early breast cancer). In the past it was also linked with womb (endometrial) cancer, although the addition of progestogen, thereby creating artificial periods which remove the lining of the womb and any potentially pre-cancerous cells, seems to have dispelled this problem. Some women do not like the forced return to monthly periods, and some also report side effects from using HRT such as bloatedness, breast tenderness, nausea, vomiting and weight gain.

On the positive side, HRT can give relief from menopausal symptoms such as night flushes, painful intercourse and even depression. It also protects against the increased risks of osteoporosis associated with post-menopausal oestrogen deficiency and possibly also against heart disease and strokes (although preliminary evidence from the largest placebo-controlled intervention study ever carried out on HRT suggests that HRT may, on the contrary, increase the risk of heart disease). It also may reduce the risk of contracting Alzheimer's disease. It has been claimed by its supporters that HRT reduces deaths among its users by 40 per cent – a dramatic increase in life expectancy, if true.

The clinical picture is complex – but clearly, the use of any powerful hormone drug will always carry risks which, for some women, will outweigh their undoubted benefits. There are no guarantees, and the final decision between a woman and her doctor should be based on individual risk factors as well as personal preference. HRT is not a magic bullet, nor an elixir of youth which dispels all the problems associated with ageing. In any event, it also makes sense to protect the body by exercising regularly, by stopping smoking, by eating a diet rich in vegetables, wholegrains, pulses and fatty fish, and by cultivating peace of mind and a serene outlook – the sort of lifestyle that makes the menopause far less problematic for Okinawan women and which, for many of them, makes the question of whether or not to take HRT a non-issue.

Lying beneath a problematic menopause there may be anxieties about ageing and mortality, fears about the loss of sexual attractiveness and identity, as well as unresolved traumas or attachment disorders going back to childhood, and issues of self-esteem generally – in other words, an unresolved and un-worked-through mid-life crisis. If the crisis remains unrecognized it may combine with menopausal symptoms, locking the sufferer into an alarming spiral in which stress creates more physical symptoms, which create more fears about loss and going out of control, creating more stress, and so on.

Women who are most able to surf the waves of the menopause – and who, whether or not they resort to HRT, experience the least troublesome side-effects from the climacteric – tend to be those who are most relaxed about the process of changing and getting older. Such women tend to be optimistic about the prospects opening up to them as they move through this change in their lives and all it symbolizes, and develop inner resources to cope with it – including a network of supportive relationships in which they are respected and listened to. The more we are able to face the mid-life crisis as it unfolds, to use it to evaluate our physical, psychological and spiritual health and to move in the direction we need to go, the more the passage of the menopause can become something to be celebrated, not fought.

THE MALE MENOPAUSE

The existence of a biologically based male menopause, or andropause, is rather more controversial. There is no change comparable with the cessation of menstruation in women and all that stems from it, and male reproductive capacity does not shut down after mid life, as it does for women. Nevertheless, the level of bioavailable testosterone (the male hormone directly responsible for energy, sex drive and erectile capacity) radically declines in men from around the age of 45 by about 1.7 per cent a year, reducing the male sexual drive and also sometimes exposing men to increased risk of osteoporosis and heart attack. Should men therefore consider HRT? Studies from America, Germany and Eastern Europe have reported improved levels of energy and libido in men given testosterone replacement therapy, yet concerns have also been expressed about increased rates of prostate cancer.

Hormone levels do drop as men age, and clearly this has an effect on both the body and the psyche. While many doctors remain deeply sceptical about the andropause, others see it as a valid medical condition. A questionnaire designed by an American professor at the St Louis Medical Center in Virginia claimed to be able to diagnose whether a man was andropausal from the following symptoms: a decrease in sex drive; reduced erectile capacity; a decrease in energy, strength and endurance; loss of height; deteriorated work performance; decreased enjoyment in life; sadness or irritability; and tiredness. Other symptoms may include night sweats, broken sleep, trouble concentrating, memory lapses and mood swings. But – clearly – many of the symptoms on this familiar list are the ordinary effects of ageing, while the presence of others may indicate undiagnosed depression.

In some ways, the controversy over whether the male menopause exists is a contrived one. Male anxiety about decreasing sexual performance seems central to its diagnosis, underpinned by a mechanistic, performance-orientated view of human sexuality. Specific ageing-related problems may well be alleviated or cured by modern medicine but it is debatable whether encouraging men to see ageing itself as a syndrome which is treatable and fixable by medical intervention – instead of in the context of wider physical, psychological and existential changes that will, one way or another, eventually have to be accommodated – is, in the long run, doing no-one any favours. For men, as for women, the changes of mid life cannot be denied and must, in the end, be negotiated.

REFERENCES

Carruthers, M., *Maximizing Manhood: Beating the Male Menopause*, Thorsons (1998).
Family Encyclopedia of Medicine and Health, Robinson Publishing (1999).
Greer, G., *The Change*, Hamish Hamilton (1991).
Understanding the Menopause and HRT, British Medical Association (2000).
Willcox, B., Willcox, C. and Suzuki, M., *The Okinawa Way*, Penguin (2001).

Index

Entries in bold indicate principal treatment of a subject

Index

Index

367